CW00820841

Stand-Up Preaching

Stand-Up Preaching

Homiletical Insights from Contemporary Comedians

JACOB D. MYERS

CASCADE *Books* · Eugene, Oregon

STAND-UP PREACHING
Homiletical Insights from Contemporary Comedians

Copyright © 2022 Jacob D. Myers. All rights reserved. Except for brief quotations in critical publications or reviews, no part of this book may be reproduced in any manner without prior written permission from the publisher. Write: Permissions, Wipf and Stock Publishers, 199 W. 8th Ave., Suite 3, Eugene, OR 97401.

Cascade Books
An Imprint of Wipf and Stock Publishers
199 W. 8th Ave., Suite 3
Eugene, OR 97401

www.wipfandstock.com

PAPERBACK ISBN: 978-1-6667-0280-4
HARDCOVER ISBN: 978-1-6667-0281-1
EBOOK ISBN: 978-1-6667-0282-8

Cataloguing-in-Publication data:

Names: Myers, Jacob D., author.

Title: Stand-Up preaching : homiletical insights from contemporary comedians / Jacob D. Myers.

Description: Eugene, OR: Cascade Books, 2022 | Includes bibliographical references and index.

Identifiers: ISBN 978-1-6667-0280-4 (paperback) | ISBN 978-1-6667-0281-1 (hardcover) | ISBN 978-1-6667-0282-8 (ebook)

Subjects: LCSH: Wit and humor—Religious aspects—Christianity. | Preaching. | Comic, The—Religious aspects.

Classification: BV4647.J68 M90 2022 (paperback) | BV4647 (ebook)

VERSION NUMBER 100622

For
Melissa Browning
A stand-up preacher, teacher, and friend

Contents

Foreword by Frank A. Thomas
Acknowledgments | xi

Introduction: Who's Laughing Now? | 1
Stand-Up Spotlight
Dick Gregory between Jokes and Justice | 14

1 Seriously Funny: Preaching between Comiletics and Humorletics | 21
Stand-Up Spotlight
Daniel Sloss between Punchlines and Provocation | 42

2 Homiletical Humor: Why Preaching Is No Laughing Matter | 50
Stand-Up Spotlight
Hari Kondabolu between Humor and Harm | 73

3 Language Games: Standing Up with Words and Forms | 81
Stand-Up Spotlight
Dave Chappelle between Comedy and Critique | 102

4 Narrating Experience: You Can't Make This Stuff Up | 110
Stand-Up Spotlight
Hannah Gadsby between Deconstruction and Dehumanization | 131

5 Staging Identity: On Persona and Authenticity | 138
Stand-Up Spotlight
Wanda Sykes between Invective and Irony | 156

6 Bodies Matter: On Voice and Gesture | 164
Stand-Up Spotlight
Hasan Minhaj between Identification and Alienation | 184

7 Just Joking: Preaching the Political and the Profane | 192
   Stand-Up Spotlight
   John Oliver between Seriousness and Stupidity | 214

Conclusion: To Tell the Truth | 223

Works Cited | 229
Subject and Name Index | 255

Foreword

Frank A. Thomas

Since the 1960s, it appears that every twenty years or so, the academic preaching community produces a scholar who takes seriously/humorously the relationship between preaching and the comical. Without mentioning previous published titles (as Myers does), Jacob D. Myers makes an outstanding, valuable, and critically worthy twenty-first-century contribution to the homiletical field and task by the study of stand-up comedy and preaching. With a sweep of analysis that is impressive from the stand-up of Dick Gregory, Daniel Sloss, Hari Kondabolou, Dave Chappelle, Hannah Gadsby, Wanda Sykes, John Oliver, and Hasan Minhaj, this book is an intellectual, spiritual, and cultural tour de force—all the while grounding insights into the theological and rhetorical aspects of preaching, relevant not only to the scholarly community, but to pastors who simply want to preach "prophetic sermons with pastoral sensitivity."

Myers locates and names the wonder and wistful view that many preachers have of stand-up comedians. As I read Myers, I reconsidered Frederick Buechner's statement in the brute honesty of his book, *Telling the Truth: The Gospel as Tragedy, Comedy, and Fairy Tale*:

> The weight of these sad times we must obey, and must obey just because they are sad times, sad and bewildering times for people who try to hold on to the gospel and witness to it when somehow in so many ways the weight of our sadness all but crushes the life out of it.[1]

Buechner does not seek to ignore, deflect, or medicate the sadness, nor cover it with the cotton candy of a cheap and syrupy grace and hope or sink into despair such that we live defeated and hopeless lives. He encourages

---

1. Buechner, *Telling the Truth*, 15.

preachers to obey the sadness of the time, and rather than preach what ought to be said about the gospel, or what would appear to be in the interest of the gospel, as "we ourselves have felt about it," a true, honest, and balanced experience of the gospel. For Buechner, our task is to preach the gospel as tragedy, comedy, and fairy tale. For me, this evokes Myers's sense of the comedic in preaching. As a matter of fact, he labels his conclusion, "To Tell the Truth."

My sense is that preachers and homileticians are all too familiar with the sadness that Buechner describes. I believe the true weight of the sadness drives us to the comedic. On the surface, preachers envy comedians because they, for the most part, have the ability to make people feel good. We want that in our sermons—we want to preach the gospel in such a way that resolves the sadness and makes people feel good. But Buechner and Myers will not let us get away with it. Life is too complicated for making people feel good with simple answers. Myers challenges us to the comedic:

> Engaging the world of stand-up comedy, this book aims to help preachers think critically and creatively about the comical and the humorous. . . . These . . . discursive modalities overlap, but they are not the same. . . . Contemporary stand-up comedy necessarily contains humor. Comics are up there to make us laugh . . . Some comics also engage what I am labeling *the comical* . . . the comical signifies an element at work in some comedy that employs humor to make us think in new ways. It aims at *metanoia*. The comical is political in the broadest sense of the word . . . the comical engages the power dynamics operative in societies between individuals, groups, and institutions, often (though not exclusively) in a humorous way.

Why I believe that Myers's book is so important is that it might be that the comical engages the sadness with more integrity than our serious theology. In these days of an outrageous pandemic and ever-widening polarizations, to just name a few challenges, it is the comedic that might engage the truth more honestly, as we come to explore how, as one scholar has suggested, "laughter is hope's last weapon."

Maybe that is why every twenty years or so, when the sadness almost chokes the life out of the serious homiletical gospel, a prophet arises in the wilderness, a lone voice saying to give laughter and the comedic an opportunity that preaching might once again become "foolishness."

Acknowledgments

There are so many folks to thank for their support and encouragement through the writing of this book. First and always, I wish to thank my incredible wife, Abby. Not only did she endure my many paltry recitations of stand-up comedy, she also read the entire book and provided invaluable insights. I'm also thankful for my amazing kid Taylor, for the silliness and joy they bring to my life.

I also want to thank Matthew Wimer, Rodney Clapp, and Cascade Books. Thank you for believing in this project and nurturing it to completion.

I could not have written this book without the support of my Columbia Theological Seminary colleagues. I am grateful for the CTS Board of Trustees, President Leanne Van Dyk, and Dean Love Sechrest for providing me an academic workload conducive to the life of the mind. I appreciate the support of my colleagues in practical theology, and especially my partner in crime, Anna Carter Florence. I am also thankful for the wise counsel of my friends Brandon Maxwell and Raj Nadella. I received much support from my students, particularly Abby Post, who assisted me in the early stages of my research, and Ashley Lewis, whose copyediting skills saved me from many embarrassments. Those that remain are, of course, my own.

Once again, I am indebted to the amazing staff of the John Bulow Campbell Library for the community of scholarly inquiry they support and sustain. I am grateful for the work and encouragement of Kelly Campbell and Erica Durham. A special word of thanks is owed to Mary Martha Riviere. Theological libraries do not carry many comedy books or journals in their collection. I owe a great debt to Mary Martha for her timely processing of my many interlibrary loan requests.

This book is dedicated to my beloved friend and colleague in ministry, the Reverend Dr. Melissa D. Browning. Though just two years my elder, she was a mentor to me as a fledgling undergraduate religious studies student at Gardner-Webb University. Through her gentle nudges and critical questions, she loved me out of my fundamentalism, helping me to become the scholar and teacher I am today. Melissa was a light that burned so brightly for far too little time. I miss her every day. She blessed everyone she taught and those with whom she worked. Her infectious laugh, her constant optimism, and her relentless pursuit of justice for the disenfranchised, the incarcerated, and the neglected have taught me what it means to be a stand-up person. Rest in peace, my dear friend.

Introduction

Who's Laughing Now?

*The laughter that breaks up and interrupts is a more encompassing form
of laughter; it suggests an orientation for faithful ministry that is deeply
rooted not only in the gospel, but also in its ritual appropriation through the
centuries.*[1]

—CHARLES CAMPBELL

*But every attempt at humor and every laugh has the potential for violence
that one must accept responsibility for. The question is how to make humor
an ethical interruption.*[2]

—STEVEN BENKO

I have a hypothesis: stand-up comedy both enthralls and terrifies preachers. There are several reasons for this. We preachers watch a Netflix or
HBO comedy special, and we can't help but note the similarities between
the performative aspects of stand-up comedy and those of preaching. In
both art forms, for the most part, we witness a lone person on a stage speaking to an audience that is more or less open to what the speaker has to say.
Most comics and preachers share a spatio-techno similarity in that they are
elevated above their audience and their voices are amplified to nurture a
more intimate, conversational atmosphere. Some give and take is expected
in both contexts—either as shouts of acclamation, nods of assent, or raucous

1. Campbell, "Ministry with a Laugh," 198.
2. Benko, "Otherwise Than Laughter," 82.

belly laughs—situating preaching and stand-up between a monologue and a dialogue. And despite the wildly divergent ethos of a comedy club from that of a church, both social settings enforce a standard of decorum. Even if hecklers are more prevalent in comedy clubs than in churches (thanks be to God!), measures are in place to limit *excessive* heckling. They're called bouncers.

But these surface similarities are not what really enthralls us. What captures our attention most—and dare I say, our envy—is the *effect* of stand-up comedy. Stand-up comedians seem to hold their relatively diverse audiences in the palm of their hands. Comics speak, and their words elicit an immediate bodily reaction. A brief aside is in order here.

While it is true that much humor elicits laughter, there is an element of hocus-pocus to contemporary stand-up that we preachers ought to factor into our evaluative calculus. The magic of these televised comedy specials is in the fancy movement between the comic's punch lines and the audience's response. We are reminded often through jump cuts that the audience is having a good time.[3] Starting with HBO's *The Original Kings of Comedy* and its spin-offs (*The Queens of Comedy, The Original Latin Kings of Comedy*), televised stand-up specials are highly edited. Because we do not have access to the original performance, we are not free to judge the merits and demerits of jokes and bits due to frequent cutaways to the audience. We hear the comic deliver a punch line, and then we see the audience laughing hysterically. We are then coerced into believing that if we find a joke lacking, the problem is with us. The producers communicate to us, in essence, "Everyone here thought this joke was funny. If you aren't laughing, the problem is with you." All of this adds to the prestige we preachers attribute to stand-up comics.

Then we step into the pulpit on Sunday morning and stare into the bleary eyes of congregants who do not seem to be enjoying themselves nearly as much as the stand-up audience we witnessed the night before. We may wish to possess the gifts of the comic, to draw our listeners in rhetorically until they are on the edge of their seats and then, through a sudden twist of expectations, send them roiling with laughter. Oh, what power these comics wield! Oh, to be able to employ our words to elicit an autonomic bodily response!

But then we remember that we are preachers, not entertainers. Despite our many points of divergence and disagreement, homileticians find a rare

---

3. See Kingford, "How to Film Stand Up." Some comics, such as Chelsea Peretti, Fred Armisen, and Maria Bamford, record their "live" specials in a way that parodies or subverts the traditional recorded stand-up. See Gillota, "Beyond Liveness," for an insightful examination of this recent trend.

point of unanimity here. Teresa Fry Brown says it best when she challenges homiletical tactics that aim merely to entertain. Fry Brown castigates those who employ their bodily movements and voices as "Pavlovian behavior modification bells for church calisthenics." Preaching, for Professor Fry Brown, is about proclamation. "The preaching moment is God centered, not preacher centered," she argues. "It is really not about us. We serve merely as conduits for [the] transmission of God's Word."[4]

If the temptation to elicit laughter through entertainment were not enough, there's another reason preachers are enamored with stand-up comedy. The medium of stand-up comedy rises or falls on the perceived authenticity of the comic. Comics work hard to present a version of themselves that appears so natural, so uncontrived, so ineluctable. Authenticity is more complicated for preachers. We do not have the luxury of adopting a homiletical persona that strays too far from our everyday selves. The great British alternative comic Stewart Lee tempers our feelings about the comic's performed authenticity. In fact, he comes to the very possibility of comic authenticity with some dubiousness. He marvels, for instance, at the reception Eddie Izzard has received for his "supposed improvisational skills, when in fact his real skill was to make his prepared ideas to look as if they were utterly spontaneous."[5] What we are witnessing here is the subtle science of preventing our form from intruding upon its content. Good structure always seems inevitable. If the structure were different, we would have an entirely different substance. As H. Grady Davis writes, "The right form derives from the substance of the message itself, is inseparable from the content, becomes one with the content, and gives a feeling of finality to the sermon."[6] Mutatis mutandis, the formal performance of authenticity does its job best when we forget we are watching a performance at all.

What, we may wonder, might lead preachers to study the work of stand-up comics if their discursive contexts, intentions, and effects are so different from ours? And, I hasten to add, much of their content offers little to inspire our homiletical imagination. These substantial differences notwithstanding, might there be a payoff for engaging stand-up for preaching? I think there is, and I see contemporary stand-up so illuminating for preaching on two fronts: 1) Speech that invites participation amid cultural difference and 2) speech that challenges ideologies and structures of inequity without completely alienating audience members. The first point aligns

4. Fry Brown, "Action Potential of Preaching," 54, 56.

5. Lee, *How I Escaped My Certain Fate*, 65. On the performance of improvisation in the pulpit see the illuminating analyses of Gardner Taylor's preaching in Alcántara, *Crossover Preaching*, 91–138.

6. Davis, *Design for Preaching*, 9.

with increased attention to preaching contexts that are increasingly diverse. The second point supervenes at the intersection of what homileticians label the pastoral and the priestly.[7]

PREACHER GOT JOKES?

Everyone wants to be funny. Never have I met someone who has disavowed humor in toto. In fact, having a sense of humor—at least a *sense*—is something we all claim. Even if we don't consider ourselves funny on the order of professional comedians like Richard Pryor, Robin Williams, Wanda Sykes, or Dave Chappelle, we all like to have fun and to *be* funny. We like to laugh with friends and to make them laugh. We enjoy a good time, which requires, I would argue, some ability to take a joke—both in the subjective and objective sense.

In *Rock This!* Chris Rock addresses the overlap and tension between funny people and stand-up comedians. He writes, "Everybody knows somebody who's funny at the water cooler or around the dinner table. Unfortunately, lots of those people also think they can easily do stand-up. And people believe them. Somehow, in this crazy culture, 'funny guy' and 'professional comedian' have ended up meaning the same thing."[8] I find this point sobering. I think of myself as having a great sense of humor. I like to laugh and even manage to land a decent joke now and again, but I by no means think I have what it takes to become a stand-up comic. The good news is that I have a day job that I find immensely rewarding. I hope you do too. But we need not think of this as a zero-sum game; preachers can employ their sense of humor in the pulpit without having to don the mantle of a professional comedian—and if we are tempted to do so, we would do well to reread Dr. Fry Brown's admonition against preaching as entertainment.

Engaging the world of stand-up comedy, this book aims to help preachers think critically and creatively about the comical and the humorous, which I discuss at length in chapter 1. These often synonymous discursive modalities overlap, but they are not the same. While they cannot be fully separated, conflating them adds confusion. Contemporary stand-up comedy necessarily contains humor. Comics are up there to make us laugh. Period. If a comedian fails to make us laugh *at all*, they have failed. Some comics also engage what I am labeling *the comical*, and these are the comics most interesting to me. In brief, the comical signifies an element at work in some comedy that employs humor to make us think in new ways. It aims

---

7. I will discuss these points in detail in chapters 5 and 7.

8. Rock, *Rock This!*, 41.

at *metanoia*. The comical is political in the broadest sense of the word. It finds resonance with second-wave feminism's claim that "the personal is political." Transcending mere party politics or generic observations that effect little (e.g., "white people act like this"; "lesbians act like that"), the comical engages the power dynamics operative in societies between individuals, groups, and institutions, often (though not exclusively) in a humorous way.[9]

We see the comical operative in the comedy of one of the harbingers of contemporary stand-up: George Carlin. Carlin recognized that stand-up comedy can be an effective way to engage an audience's mind. He writes, "*Laughter is not the only proof of success. . . .* Not laughs, but some ripple of agreement, a collective 'Oh Yeah!' Pleasure in sheer ideas."[10] Stand-up employs humor to strip bare its subject matter and its audience. Carlin explains that "laughter is a moment when we are completely ourselves," and this setting provides a moment "when you can slip in a good idea."[11] It might seem strange at first glance that a Christian homiletician would enlist the support of a comic such as Carlin, a man who spent his career trouncing Christianity. But theological congruency is not the sole marker of value. As Iain Ellis observes in his book *Humorists vs. Religion,* Carlin

> brings the kind of moral certitude, missionary zeal, and barnstorming delivery one is more likely to find in a preacher than a stand-up comic. As with [Lenny] Bruce, language matters, and Carlin teases religion by teasing the rhetoric by which it operates and manipulates. His deconstructions of the symbols, rituals, and practices of religious institutions are as artful as those of any French post-structuralist—only funnier![12]

And lest we get too proprietary, let's not forget that none other than Karl Barth argued that the atheists Ludwig Feuerbach and Friedrich Nietzsche ought to be standard reading for Christian ministers, going so far as to declare them "the wisest of the wise of this world."[13]

Both the comical and the humorous may cause laughter, but only the comical aims toward the kind of sociopolitical critique common to Scripture, theology, and preaching. I contend that only the comical is worthy of proclamation. More on this later. To facilitate such engagement, we shall

---

9. Part of the work of this book is to help us break away from a series of either/or binaries that are common to much humor research, *viz.,* the humorous vs. the serious, the political vs. the apolitical, laughter vs. outrage, etc.

10. Carlin, *Last Words,* 247.

11. Carlin, "Napalm, Silly Putty, and Human Nature," 192.

12. Ellis, *Humorists vs. Religion,* 9.

13. Barth, *Church Dogmatics,* III/2, 242, 280.

consider together the work of contemporary stand-up comedians from a variety of traditions and representing a range of racial, ethnic, gender, and sexual identity expressions. We'll look at what contemporary stand-up can teach preachers in our efforts to challenge racist, sexist, and heterosexist ideological assumptions and social structures.

As with any practical theology worthy of the name, this book situates itself at the nexus of theory and praxis. Thus we shall move back and forth between real-world exemplars of comedy and the philosophical, sociological, and psychological theories their stand-up exemplifies—and sometimes subverts. All the while we will be considering together the theological and homiletical implications of insights emerging from humor scholars and stand-up comedians.

SERIOUS QUESTIONS FOR SERIOUS PREACHERS

Even as we are living in a supposed "golden age of comedy,"[14] preachers have been slow to employ comedy in their preaching. To be fair, the connection between stand-up and preaching is not immediately obvious. For much of church history, the standard sermonic situation has been that of a serious person proclaiming serious words in a serious way. Think of Jonathan Edwards declaiming the lot of sinners in the hands of an angry God. It was Edwards, after all, who forbade humor and laughter on Sundays.[15] But his was far from a minority report. John Wesley went so far as to attribute laughter in prayer to satanic influence.[16]

Our twenty-first-century homiletical contexts are much more open to humor than earlier generations.[17] But that does not obviate the risks inherent in approaching the comical from the pulpit. As John McClure puts it, "The undercurrent of joy that accompanies the proclamation of good news is naturally accompanied by laughter. This does not mean that the preacher becomes a joke teller."[18] While it's difficult to imagine laughter without jokes, McClure is right to waffle on the use of humor in the pulpit, and I confess that this is why I write this book with some hesitancy. While I believe stand-up comedians have much to teach preachers, I'm worried

14. Izadi, "New Rock Stars."

15. McClymond and McDermott, *Theology of Jonathan Edwards*, 64.

16. McClymond, ed., *Encyclopedia of Religious Revivals in America*, 48–51.

17. As one scholar puts it, albeit critically, "Many preachers now seem to think that they cannot begin to preach without 'softening up' their hearers with a little bit of stand-up comedy." Murray, "Serious Preaching in a Comedy Culture," 328.

18. McClure, *Preaching Words*, 52. See also Buchanan, "Punch line."

about the risks preachers assume in attempting to emulate stand-up in the pulpit. So, before we go any further, here are some serious questions for you to consider at the outset.

Have you weighed the risks of homiletical humor against your preaching context?

Even as there is a greater openness to homiletical humor today, attempting to employ humor from the pulpit presents risks that fluctuate according to one's preaching context. Congregations and parishes are far more likely to include members of varying racial, ethnic, and sexual orientations than earlier generations. While this can be a blessing for a church, it also presents a challenge for the contextualization of humor. Like other forms of creative expression, humor plays off preexisting norms, including *appropriate* violations of those norms.[19] In other words, we must hold the norm in tension with its violation. But like any violation, humor carries inherent risks.

A joke or story that leaves congregants rolling in the aisles in one context might prove highly offensive in another. While this difficulty transcends the white/Black racial binary in America, attending to the cultural dynamics between Black and mixed-race audiences exemplifies the problem I'm trying to underscore. As the celebrated folklorist Daryl Cumber Dance highlights in her edited anthology of African American women's humor, "the same items that can cause raucous laughter among an all-Black audience would be very painful to a Black person in a mixed audience, who would likely respond with awkward silence and resentful anger."[20] In addition, people of color have long used comic misdirection and coded language to ridicule cultural norms that could not be confronted publicly without reprisal, so thinking about the identity of the speaker is not enough. The audience itself must also factor into our humorletical calculus.

The issue of audience demographics has become even more challenging in the wake of the ease of disseminating comedy through cable and streaming platforms and on social media. A relatively recent example highlights this dilemma. In his 1996 HBO special *Bring the Pain*, Chris Rock addressed a "civil war going on in Black America" between Blacks and "n*ggas."[21] While Rock's bit received raucous applause from his mostly Black audience, the widespread dissemination of that bit led him to understand the

19. For a fascinating investigation into the relationship between creativity and humor see Luria, Baer, and Kaufman's edited volume *Creativity and Humor*.

20. Dance, ed., *Honey, Hush!*, 428.

21. Rock, *Bring the Pain*.

implications of his routine vis-à-vis stereotypical constructions of Blackness in a white supremacist culture. On the one hand, Rock received backlash from certain segments of the African American community, who were quick to label Rock a "Black conservative." On the other hand, Rock found his white audience members at subsequent shows a little too enthusiastic about that particular bit. He addressed this latter concern unequivocally in his 1997 comedy album *Roll with the New* and in his best-selling book *Rock This!*, where he insists against the use of the n-word by white people.[22]

Stand-up comic and late-night talk show host W. Kamau Bell underscores a similar contextual difficulty preachers face when attempting humor from the pulpit. In reflecting upon the successes and failures of his late-night talk show on FX entitled *Totally Biased with W. Kamau Bell*, Bell names a difference between performing stand-up and hosting a news program. With stand-up, the comic is free to adjust, improve, or scrap jokes that fail to hit the right notes. "In late-night," Bell writes, "you better get it right the first time. Because you will hear about it the next day if you don't."[23] As with late-night hosts, the preacher doesn't get a do-over when a joke fails (or fails to offend—whatever the case may be). People have this annoying capacity to remember what we say from the pulpit, and once we've said it, it's out there in the world forever.

Are you willing to show your congregation who you really are?

The way we joke reveals much about our truest selves. The joke provides a window into the soul of the joker.[24] Sigmund Freud argued that jokes provide as much insight into our unconscious desires as do our dreams.[25] Freud

22. See Rock, "I Love This Show," in *Roll with the New*. In *Rock This!* he writes, "Any black person can say 'n*gger' and get away with it. It's true. It's like calling your kid an idiot. Only *you* can call your kid that. Someone else calls your kid an idiot, there's a fight" (20). NB: I take Rock's charge seriously in this book. As a white scholar, I follow scholarly convention to employ an asterisk when citing direct quotations from the work of African Americans who use the n-word in their stand-up or writings.

23. Bell, *Awkward Thoughts of W. Kamau Bell*, 284.

24. A number of recent psychological studies have uncovered the hidden connections between one's sense of humor and their ideological core. See Kennison and Messer, "Humor as Social Risk-Taking"; Filani, "On Joking Contexts"; Saroglou and Anciaux, "Liking Sick Humor"; Saucier et al., "'What Do You Call a Black Guy Who Flies a Plane?'"; Sunday and Filani, "Playing with Culture"; Caudill and Woodzicka, "Funny Business,"; Gutiérrez et al., "'It's Funny if the Group Says So'"; and Sierra, "Linguistic and Ethnic Media Stereotypes in Everyday Talk."

25. Freud, *Jokes and Their Relation to the Unconscious*, 46. In *The Interpretation*

taught us that humor and its concomitant laughter require a loosening of the superego, allowing the id to express itself beyond the constraints of the rational mind and its many rules and repressions. Are you willing to present your unconscious desires to your congregants or parishioners? Don't be too quick to respond. Ponder this for a moment.

It will come as no surprise to learn that stand-up comedians are not normal. As journalist Bruce Dessau observes in his book *Beyond a Joke: Inside the Dark Minds of Stand-up Comedians,* "comedians . . . are not just funny onstage, they are often also funny in the head."[26] It is impossible to imagine someone wanting to stand on a stage and risk humiliation in hopes of getting a few laughs. Stand-up comics are not normal people, but neither are preachers. As my Columbia Seminary colleague Anna Carter Florence constantly reminds our students, preachers are *weird.* She argues that to preach, you can't be in your right mind. You have to be a little out of it.[27] In her book *Preaching as Testimony,* Carter Florence puts this point even more strongly:

> Preachers are not always in touch with the eccentric element at the heart of our calling; these days the pressure is to look professional, to blend. . . . We are so used to *not* standing out in a crowd that I wonder sometimes if we might benefit from a good dose of eccentricity, of actually looking as nuts as our calling truly is. Attending can get us back in touch with sheer craziness, the set-apartness of preaching that we might otherwise only access in moments of loneliness and soul-searching.[28]

So even if preachers and stand-up comedians share a certain eccentricity, it would be an overstatement to equate the oddness of one with the other. At the same time, preachers who attempt humor in the pulpit risk shining a light on areas of our selfhood that might hinder our pastoral capacities.

Are you willing to be misunderstood?

We are living in a strange period in comedic history. Not since the trials and travails of Lenny Bruce are comics being held so accountable for their

of Dreams, Freud had already drawn attention to the similarity between dreams and jokes: "If my dreams seem amusing, that is not on my account, but on account of the peculiar psychological conditions under which dreams are constructed; and the fact is intimately connected with the theory of jokes and the comic" (405n).

26. Dessau, *Beyond a Joke*, viii.
27. Carter Florence, "Preacher as One 'Out of Your Mind,'" 151.
28. Carter Florence, *Preaching as Testimony*, 137.

words.[29] The comedy stage has long been a space where the rules of polite discourse are held in abeyance, where one may say things that are taboo or offensive. To quote Carlin again: "I think it's the duty of the comedian to find out where the line is drawn and cross it deliberately."[30] Even as audiences expect comics to cross the proverbial line, they are now holding comics accountable for the *effect* of their words to an increasing degree.

Here I am less interested in the hackneyed cry for comics to be able to say whatever they wish with impunity.[31] Much humor requires a "butt," a target, an "other" about whom we may laugh. Accordingly, racist, sexist, ableist, and heterosexist jokes have been a part of comedy for ages; but I don't think I need to argue against the use of such humor from the pulpit for two reasons. First, the strongest argument against the Christian's use of humor pertains to the kind used to denigrate others.[32] Second, there are many comics who manage to say a lot of things that are really, really funny without doing harm to marginalized populations (e.g., Hannah Gadsby, Nish Kumar, Hari Kondabolu, W. Kamau Bell, Sara Pascoe, Mark Watson, Sophie Duker, Daniel Sloss, and Mae Martin). It sometimes takes a bit of extra work; you must be aware of your own privilege and you should educate yourself to avoid using damaging language, but even with the greatest of caution this by no means suggests that you won't inadvertently make someone the butt of a joke, or that people will misconstrue who you are actually targeting.[33]

To an increasing degree, stand-up comedians are being #canceled for comedy that even comes close to offense. In his comedy special *41st Best Stand-up Ever*, Stewart Lee states that he is anxious about the possibility that his jokes could be misinterpreted as endorsements of racism or xenophobia. He worries that his jokes could do real-world harm to certain people, even when his intention is to subvert systems of racism and xenophobia through the comical.[34] Worry over whether his comedy was being misunderstood was one of the primary reasons Dave Chappell walked away from his wildly successful eponymous sketch comedy show on Comedy Central in 2005. Amy Schumer, Louis C.K., and Margaret Cho are often accused of racism or sexism for comedy that seeks to subvert those very systems and structures.[35]

---

29. See Collins and Skover, *Trials of Lenny Bruce*.

30. Quoted in Farmer, "Medusa," 563.

31. For a helpful framing of this debate, see Krefting, "Savage New Media."

32. See Morreall, "Rejection of Humor in Western Thought," 243–66. We'll look at this in chapter 2.

33. This has been an issue for Sarah Silverman. See Shouse and Oppliger, "Sarah is Magic."

34. Lee, *41st Best Stand-up Ever*.

35. See Chun, "Ideologies of Legitimate Mockery"; Middleton, "Rather Crude

Progressive comic W. Kamau Bell shares a poignant moment in his comedy career when a friend challenged a subtle sexism accompanying his efforts to combat racism. Bell reflects on how easy it is to make certain people groups the unintended butt of your jokes. He writes, "Some jokes are like a shotgun blast, where a bunch of pellets come out and hit whoever's in the area." After being called out for doing this, Bell redoubled his efforts to be "very target focused" in his comedy.[36]

Employing comedy in your preaching presents greater risks for the preacher than other modes of discourse. Common tools in the comic's tool belt are irony, sarcasm, parody, satire, and hyperbole, and much comedy depends on the audience to discern these rhetorical strategies. When such forms of speech play off the tension between denotation and connotation or between literality and figurality, the speaker risks being misunderstood.

Are you willing to do more work?

"All the comedian has to do is talk to people and make them laugh," writes comedy coach Logan Murray.[37] He is right about the comedian's presumed *raison d'être*, even if he is rather cavalier about the simplicity of this task. For preachers, the end goal of our energies is not laughter. Preaching aims at more than entertainment.[38] When we preach, we seek to empower, to convict, to console, to encourage, to teach—and any number of other functions. If our sermons spur laughter, it is almost always in service of some higher purpose. If our primary calling is to proclaim the good news, adding pressure to make people laugh strains an already difficult practice. What this means for stand-up preachers is that we must do the hard work of transposing what we might say directly into a humorous and/or comical key. Here comedic preaching shares a similar level of investment from the preacher with narrative or poetic preaching through its emphasis on indirect discourse and inductive logic. The benefits are likewise similar. As Michael Brothers points out, "aesthetic distance" between the speaker and the hearers facilitates not only reception of the preacher's message but also the room and space for transformation.[39] But such aesthetic distance doesn't just happen. The preacher must create it.

Feminism"; and Champion and Kunze, eds., *Taking a Stand*.

36. Bell, *Awkward Thoughts of W. Kamau Bell*, 173.

37. Murray, *Be a Great Stand-Up*, Kindle loc. 188.

38. Long, *Witness of Preaching*, 12; Fry Brown, "Prophetic Truth-Telling," 132.

39. Brothers, *Distance in Preaching*, ch. 3. Building on Fred Craddock's homiletic of indirect communication, Brothers lists humor and irony as "distancing devices . . . that

Another reason employing comedy in your preaching calls for more work pertains to the weekly rhythms of preaching. Stand-up comedians build to a set. The stand-up specials we see on HBO, Netflix, or Comedy Central were field tested and honed for months and sometimes years with live audiences. While contemporary stand-up comics give the impression that everything they say is extemporaneous, the performance we see on TV belies countless hours of reworking material and perfecting the timing of its delivery. With a sermon, you don't get a do-over if your jokes fall flat or offends your congregants or parishioners. And working preachers need new material every week. While it is helpful to be thinking about sermons more than six days out from when we will preach, we simply do not have time to perfect our performance to the same degree as stand-up comics. In his foreword to Mel Watkins's illuminating book *African American Humor: The Best Black Comedy from Slavery to Today*, comedy trailblazer Dick Gregory reminds us of one important reason why the preacher's job is somewhat harder than the comedian's: "They have the same audience every Sunday, so they can't use the same material over and over again."[40] It's hard enough to come up with something new to say week after week. What preacher has the time to make this new material funny as well?

Jerry Seinfeld and Chris Rock have a running debate concerning the comic versus the act. Seinfeld insists that people come out to see the comic, and he is unafraid to employ the same act for different audiences. Rock disagrees. He associates himself with the Carlin/Pryor school of comedy. These were comics who constantly changed their act to fit the ever-shifting tone and tenor of the culture. Rock does not like to recycle old material because the changing world has changed *him*, and he does not want to do stand-up from a place that lacks authenticity for himself.[41] Rock says that his words "have to be an event. It has to be a big deal."[42] We preachers would have to side with Rock on the need to constantly adapt the content of our message to the changing culture out of and into which we preach.[43]

---

allow hearers to step back, take stock, get their bearings, and breathe" (74–75).

40. Gregory, "Foreword," xii.

41. See the debate on this between Rock and Seinfeld in the HBO Documentary *Talking Funny*.

42. Rock interview in Apatow, *Sick in the Head*, 63.

43. For help with this, I highly recommend Lisa Thompson's *Preaching the Headlines*.

Are you willing to lose your job?

Let's be real. If you offend someone at a comedy club, they might boo you or storm out in a huff; they might even slap you; but they can't fire you.[44] At church they can. We train with live rounds. I am aware of the militaristic imagery upon which this metaphor relies, but I think it provides a sobering connection between the world of the preacher and that of the stand-up comic. Preachers speak on matters of life and death. When a comic fails to elicit laughter, they are said to have *bombed* or *died*. When a show goes well, the comic is said to have *killed*. Stand-up comic Amanda Seales notes her objective as that of defying racial barriers and stereotypes using comedy as her "artillery," and to do so "while always keeping social justice in [her] scope."[45]

Comedy scholar Sophie Quick notes how important the atmosphere of the comedy club is to the audience's reception of a comic's point of view. She writes, "Stand-up combines genuine challenge with a relaxed approach to the concern for truth and a relaxation of everyday standards of decency."[46] This "delightfully irresponsible" combination encourages listeners to suspend their propensity to take offense. The ecclesial atmosphere bears a similar ethos, one in which listeners expect to be challenged, to broaden the scope of debate constrained by fixed viewpoints. But if comics are rewarded for being irresponsible or irreverent, this is not the case for most preachers. As I frequently remind my preaching students, when you are preaching, you are always also pastoring. If we come across as flippant or denigrating, we might find ourselves in a rush to update our resumes (not to mention the harm our words could cause others). Especially in our contemporary cultural contexts in North America in which many congregations are "purple," engaging sensitive topics can have dire repercussions.[47] This is not to say that pandering to those with power is the answer; rather, I just want to make it clear how much easier it is for them to fire you for attempting humor than if you stick with "serious" discourse in the pulpit.

Okay, you've been warned. If you keep reading, the joke's on you.

---

44. This is not to say that stand-up comics do not face economic and psychological—and sometimes physical—harm following their acts. See Hogan, "Ethics of 'Rape Jokes,'" and Fulford, "Complete and Utter Loss of Time."

45. Seales, *Small Doses*, 85.

46. Quick, *Why Stand-Up Matters*, 207.

47. See Schade, *Preaching in the Purple Zone*, and Thomas, *Surviving a Dangerous Sermon*.

Stand-Up Spotlight
Dick Gregory
between Jokes and Justice

*If there's any God at all, and there is, and that God
doesn't do something to punish America, then that God
owes Sodom and Gomorrah a serious apology.*[1]

—DICK GREGORY

Stand-up comedians reflect society, but they also lead it a bit. They are simultaneously products and producers of culture. So much of our ideological
infrastructure—as individuals and as a society at large—resides beyond our
conscious awareness. While many comics seek laughter above all, stand-up
comics such as Dick Gregory are able to hold the humorous and the comical
in productive tension, eliciting laughter as well as fresh insights and perspectives. While humor may not dismantle entrenched systems of racism,
as Jonathan P. Rossing argues, humor may prove emancipatory in drawing
to the forefront perspectives and knowledge that challenge dominant ways
of seeing and knowing.[2]

Dick Gregory is the paradigmatic comic for this study because he
found a way to be political without being divisive—at least on the comedy
stage.[3] The contemporary American pulpit is a similarly contentious space
due to our polarized sociopolitical climate. As homiletician Leah Schade
has recently argued, preachers who find ways to preach in the "purple zone"

---

1. Gregory, *Defining Moments in Black History*, 132.
2. Rossing, "Emancipatory Racial Humor," 615.
3. I am well aware that my racial, gender, and sexual privilege colors my values here.

are engaging in a deeply prophetic activity.[4] Stand-up comedy is similarly dialogical, and a successful comic's repertoire must present attitudes and performances that construct commonality in the context of difference. Dick Gregory paved a path to doing this.

A STAND-UP GUY

Born in St. Louis in 1932, Gregory was raised in the Jim Crow South. After spending two years in the Army, Gregory moved to Chicago with hopes of becoming a stand-up comedian. He was among a coterie of Black comedians that included Nipsey Russell and Bill Cosby, all of whom broke with the minstrel tradition of Black comedy. Unlike Russell's double act, vaudeville styled comedy, and Cosby's observational comedy, Gregory leaned into his racial identity and directly engaged American culture to face up to the systemic oppression and marginalization of African Americans. Also unlike his fellow Black comics, Gregory was the first successful crossover comic, performing stand-up in predominantly white comedy clubs.[5]

Gregory was known for his biting satire that addressed the systemic marginalization and oppression of African Americans. But being the first Black comic to perform stand-up in predominantly white clubs presented an extra layer of complexity to his comedy. What made Gregory a favorite among white and Black comedy lovers was his ability to take aim at sociopolitical injustices without alienating either constituency. He displayed the gift of "signifying," which Frank Thomas identifies as a rhetorical form that hints at multiple meanings. Drawing on the scholarship of Mitchell-Kernan, Thomas emphasizes the sophistication of this art form: "It takes some skill to construct a message with multi-level meanings, and sometimes it takes equal expertise to unravel the puzzle presented in all of its many implications."[6]

4. Schade, *Preaching in the Purple Zone*, 86.

5. He was not the first Black comic to attempt this. Minstrel personas such as Jim Dandy and Stepin' Fetchit were successful Black performers. Timmie Rogers was the first Black comic to perform comedy beyond minstrelsy. He donned a suit and tie and commented on current affairs in the fashion of white comics such as Mort Saul, but his contract was quickly terminated.

6. Thomas, *Introduction to the Practice of African American Preaching*, 81–82. On Gregory's use of signifying, see Watkins, *On the Real Side*, 396. In his illuminating book *Furiously Funny*, Terrence Tucker highlights the rhetorical link between African American literature and Black stand-up. Tucker focuses in particular on the transference of African American vernacular traditions into previously European forms. "In literature, Black oral tradition manifests itself through the needed flexibility of language that demonstrates an understanding and internalizing of American values and ideals

Comedy is "friendly relations," Gregory argues; it forges a space for reasoned arguments while sustaining relationships between contentious cultural constituencies.[7] Here's an example. "Segregation is not all bad," jokes Gregory. "Have you ever heard of a collision where the people in the back of the bus got hurt?" Another joke goes like this: "Last time I was down South, I walked into this restaurant, and this white waitress came up to me and said, 'We don't serve colored people here.' I said, 'That's all right, I don't eat colored people. Bring me a whole fried chicken.'"[8] Such jokes tread the line between critical resistance and outright aggression.

When we label so-and-so a "stand-up person," we are speaking colloquially about that person's character. But being a stand-up person constitutes more than moral uprightness. A stand-up person is courageous and loyal in a combative way. In standing up for what is right, we take on a degree of risk. In our neoliberal democratic contexts, rarely are we persecuted for our personal beliefs. But when we refuse to be quiet, to keep these convictions to ourselves, we enter a realm of danger described most aptly by Frank Thomas. In his book *How to Preach a Dangerous Sermon*, Thomas lifts up voices such as those of Martin Luther King Jr. and Robert F. Kennedy, men who exhibit a "moral imagination" and who were willing to risk their lives to speak up for the marginalized and oppressed. Thomas opens his book with a word of caution:

> It is dangerous in this white-supremacist America to move the sphere of one's moral concern out of the circumference of one's group, and include the outcast, stranger, marginalized, and hated. It may or may not get you killed, but it certainly will get you persecuted; fired; harassed; labeled "enemy," "traitor," and such, especially if you chose to preach dangerous sermons.[9]

Though Thomas doesn't comment on Gregory in his book, I feel confident in including him as one who exhibits a "moral imagination."

Gregory is paradigmatic for stand-up preaching for another reason. He carried a spiritual sensibility with him into the spotlight. Whether he was speaking to audiences in comedy clubs or to his fellow protestors in the civil rights movement, Gregory brought a sense of moral urgency to his discourse. Where he differs from preachers—apart from his biblical exegesis—is his humorous mode of engagement, which enticed audiences to

---

while also providing a form of resistance understood by other African Americans." Tucker, *Furiously Funny*, 97.

7. Gregory, *n*gger*, 132.

8. Barnes, "Dick Gregory, Trailblazer of Stand-Up Comedy."

9. Thomas, *How to Preach a Dangerous Sermon*, xx.

embrace a playful suspicion of religious authorities and texts.[10] This suspicion would allow them to grapple with the oppressive presence of religion in the long history of Western colonialism, in the US context of slavery, and in the violence and segregation of Jim Crow America. Following this religious suspicion, however, Gregory's consistent goal was to implement just social teachings stemming from progressive readings of the Hebrew Bible and the teachings of Jesus in the Gospels.[11]

A PROPHET WITHOUT CONTEMPT

Homiletician Luke Powery argues for a kind of spiritual preaching steeped in the preacher's blood, sweat, and tears because proclamation is costly and lives are at stake. He writes, "Because of the weightiness of the gospel and this age of death, there are no excuses for disinterested preaching."[12] Powery's assertion holds equally well for Gregory. James R. McGraw edited and wrote the foreword to Gregory's 1968 *The Shadow that Scares Me*, which the white Methodist minister described as "a book of impious sermons" that stood "in the best tradition of evangelistic preaching."[13] Unlike other Black performers such as Nat King Cole and Sam Cooke, who believed their greatest contribution to the civil rights movement was their success on the stage, Gregory felt that his stand-up routines and the satire they exuded could only go so far. He believed that his actions off the comic stage validated what he said on the comedy stage.[14] As Gloria Richardson, a SNCC leader and frequent collaborator with Gregory, said, "Everybody respected him because he was always putting his body on the line."[15]

Gregory's comedy found a way to be prophetic without provoking condemnation, a difficult position that Cathleen Kaveny labels "prophecy without contempt."[16] Such discourse charts a middle course between ideological rigidity and flexibility. A favorite tactic of Gregory's was to find points of resonance from which to gently challenge racism in America. For instance, Gregory has a joke about Willie Mays. He states that he loves baseball because it's the only sport in America where a Black man can shake a

10. See Gregory, *Bible Tales*, for examples.

11. Booker, "'Deplorable Exegesis,'" 188–89.

12. Powery, *Dem Dry Bones*, 70.

13. McGraw, "Meet the Turkey General," 15.

14. Gregory, *Callus on My Soul*, 83.

15. Richardson interview in Raymond, *Stars for Freedom*, 152.

16. Kaveny, *Prophecy without Contempt*.

stick at a white man without starting a riot.[17] This joke illustrates a mode of comedy where the setup encourages investment from his audience and the punch line capitalizes on that investment with prophetic potency. In white 1960s America, baseball was unrivaled in its claim as America's favorite pastime. By asserting that he loves baseball, he finds a place of common ground between himself and his white audience members. The unexpected twist of the punch line pivots from something white Americans celebrate to something many of his audience members (they are paying to watch a Black man perform stand-up) would prefer to ignore. His *reason* for liking baseball is at once playful and critical. It capitalizes on the dissonance between contexts where a Black man (the batter) is supposed to shake a stick/bat at a white man (the pitcher) with impunity and one in which such action signals the threat of impending violence. The expected context denotes play; the surprising content connotes seriousness.

Describing how he learned to tailor his comedy for white audiences, Gregory writes: "I've got to go up there as an individual first, a Negro second. I've got to be a colored funny man, not a funny colored man." To this he adds, "I've got to make jokes about myself, before I can make jokes about them and their society—that way, they can't hate me."[18] Such humor connected with an audience that remained racially segregated. As one white reporter observed, "If there is one key to Mr. Gregory's success, it is probably his ability to examine the foibles of both the black and white races without a trace of rancor or pretention and without any stooping or loss of dignity."[19] Comedy historian Gerald Nachman adds nuance to this interpretation. "Some critics said that white audiences laughed to neutralize their guilt, but something else was at work: Gregory was helping to defuse black-white anger by getting whites to laugh at his racial jokes."[20]

TAKEAWAYS FOR STAND-UP PREACHING

Gregory's brand of comedy in the 1960s and 1970s offers much for homiletical attention. As Rossing observes, "Gregory was not a comedian-turned-activist but an activist who embodied humorous styles and attitudes in

17. Gregory at the Hungry I club in San Francisco, www.huntleyarchives.com, video 1097974. In a similar routine, Gregory suggests that football is the perfect sport for African Americans because "it's the only sport in the world [where] a Black man can chase a white man and 40,000 people stand up and cheer." Gregory, *Mo' Funny*.

18. Gregory, *n*gger*, 132.

19. Gelb, "Comic Withers Prejudice Cliches."

20. Nachman, *Seriously Funny*, 494.

every facet of his performance."[21] But even as he opens preaching to fresh insights for critical, comical resistance, Gregory reminds us that sermons can only take us so far. He did not regard stand-up as direct action, but an escape from the action.

We must learn from this prophetic funnyman the need to put our bodies on the line in pursuit of justice. Later in life, especially in his writing, Gregory was less concerned with embedding his critiques of racism in humor. For example, he writes,

> I am so sick and tired of seeing a black person shot in the back, shot dead, followed by people saying, "Not all cops are bad." You know how many lawyers get disbarred every year? But you never hear, "Not all lawyers are bad." You know how many doctors lose their medical licenses? But you never hear anybody talking about, "Not all doctors are bad." Police departments are filthy. If I pay a lawyer, I don't expect him to sue me. If I go to a doctor, he's not supposed to give me a disease. But we pay taxes so cops will protect us, and they shoot us instead—and the response is, "Not all cops are bad"? And still we think we're part of America.[22]

Reflecting on a series of demonstrations organized by the SNCC in Greenwood, Mississippi, Gregory pulls no punches in challenging the church establishment. He writes of being "abandoned" by the Negro preachers. "Our church was failing us in this battle for civil rights. It was the preachers' fault that whenever we made a gain we said: 'Thank the United States Supreme Court,' instead of saying 'Thank God.'"[23] Staring down his fellow African American leaders—school teachers and principals, but especially preachers—Gregory volunteers to lead the people in the demonstrations the next day.[24]

At day's end, it is Gregory's political savvy and his political activism that guides stand-up preaching. He was patient and pragmatic, which Barbara Lundblad identifies as a central component of transformational preaching.[25] The key for us is to not grow so patient that we fail to be prophetic. Mel Watkins observes a similar insight in Gregory's comedy:

21. Rossing, "Dick Gregory and Activist Style," 70.
22. Gregory, *Defining Moments in Black History*, 133.
23. Gregory, *n*gger*, 180.
24. Gregory, *No More Lies*, 350.
25. Lundblad, *Transforming the Stone*, 121: "Transformational preaching takes place over time. There may be a rare life-changing sermon, but more often it is a lifetime of sermons inviting the listener into God's alternative vision that leads to transformation."

Gregory had devised a stand-up persona that cast him as a patient, self-assured ironist, capable of dispensing witticisms about racial relationships with cool detachment. His monologues mirrored the bitingly satiric perceptions of the most alienated segment of Black America but, because they were delivered deftly and without rancor, were not perceived as obloquy. Sophisticated, aloof, and seemingly observing from a viewpoint of amused neutrality, he was able to introduce into integrated settings a racial satire that, while more aggressive than that of his predecessors, was clearly more palatable to white Americans.[26]

Leonora Tubbs Tisdale argues that for preachers to speak for God calls us to speak on the "cutting edge of what is just and what is unjust in the local communities in which we find ourselves; to bring God's Word to bear on key events and at crisis moments in the life of the church, nation, and world; and to have a bias in our preaching toward the liberation of God and the upending of powers and principalities, thus bringing in a reign marked by peace and equality and justice for all."[27] The challenge of doing this, as Tubbs Tisdale observes, is to remain on the "cutting edge" while simultaneously resisting the temptation to (metaphorically) cut anyone. For preachers who struggle to negotiate the callings to be prophetic and pastoral/priestly, Gregory offers us fresh perspectives. He models a way to balance critique and *communitas*, which is the goal of stand-up preaching.

26. Watkins, *On the Real Side*, 498.
27. Tubbs Tisdale, *Prophetic Preaching*, 6.

1

Seriously Funny
Preaching between Comiletics and Humorletics

Human existence at its best, both individually and collectively, is a running interplay between seriousness and laughter, sense and nonsense, sacred concerns and comic interludes.[1]

—CONRAD HYERS

Let me remark, by the way, that there is no better starting point for thought than laughter; speaking more precisely, spasms of the diaphragm generally offer better chances for thought than spasms of the soul.[2]

—WALTER BENJAMIN

There are few forms of discourse that seem to reinforce the serious/funny binary in Western thought than preaching and stand-up comedy. We see this bifurcation reinforced in the field of homiletics. For instance, in addressing the homiletical reticence to think about preaching as a kind of performance, Jana Childers and Clayton Schmit write, "It goes without saying that [homiletics] is a field where stand-up comedians and hams coexist

1. Hyers, *Spirituality of Comedy*, 1.
2. Benjamin, *Understanding Brecht*, 101.

with prophets and martyrs."[3] Childers and Schmit seem to perpetuate a duality here between preaching that is comical and preaching that is oriented toward justice. This perspective is far from unique. As we will see, there are very few homileticians who see the two as symbiotic.

Stand-up preaching rejects the binary between the comical and the prophetic. Part of the work of this book will be to participate in the deconstruction of this binary. We'll examine forms of stand-up that exude seriousness without sacrificing humor. And we'll think together about how these forms of stand-up can help preachers hold the seriousness of our calling in creative tension with a certain comical sensibility. Such work will call us to resist what Charles Campbell and Johan Cilliers label a "closed homiletical seriousness."[4] As contemporary preachers, we would do well to learn from their call to learn from the wisdom of fools and to abide in such a state of liminality apropos to we who are between the times. If we broaden our homiletical and theological horizons to include ways of knowing, being, and behaving that refuse to capitulate to the status quo, there's no better place to focus our attention than the comedy stage.

But even as we come to recognize the false dichotomy dividing seriousness and funniness, preaching must move beyond mere assertions of its foolishness. It's not enough to claim with the Apostle Paul that preaching is folly and be done with it (1 Cor 1:17–25). Such declarations leave the wisdom/foolishness binary intact, albeit inverted. As value judgments, both wisdom and foolishness and seriousness and funniness require contextual frames to make them meaningful. If you've ever tried to translate a joke across cultures, you know what I mean.

There can be neither wisdom nor folly apart from epistemological contexts that determine and delimit what each of these terms means in relation to the other. By the same logic, there can be neither funniness nor seriousness apart from affective contexts.[5] Michel Foucault names this situation well in mapping epistemological shifts whereby the wisdom of fools was abandoned at the so-called dawn of reason. In this liminal moment, "Madness was denounced and defended, and proclaimed to be nearer to happiness and truth than reason itself."[6] It is the "madman," Foucault argues, who employs foolishness to outwit the wisdom of the wise. Might we

---

3. Childers and Schmit, eds., *Performance in Preaching*, 14.

4. Campbell and Cilliers, *Preaching Fools*, 68.

5. Here I draw upon the important work of Sarah Ahmed, *Promise of Happiness,* and John Protevi, *Political Affect,* on the intersubjective and political dimensions of affect, which eludes any narrow focus on bound subjects exercising independent agency over their ways of thinking and behaving.

6. Foucault, *History of Madness*, 13.

imagine today's "funnyman" employing humor to subvert the seriousness of the serious?

An illustration might prove helpful here. American Express ran a commercial in the late nineties that bears witness to the cultural situatedness of humor along with the affective implications of this situatedness. The commercial opens with none other than Jerry Seinfeld, at the height of popularity for his eponymous sitcom, performing stand-up in England. We enter his comedy set just as he drops a punch line about the seventh inning stretch. This is, of course, a reference to *America's* national pastime. No one laughs. Undeterred in his efforts to connect with his audience, Jerry proceeds to hang out with Brits in pubs, to chat them up at the meat monger's, and to take in their jargon on the cricket pitch. The commercial ends with Seinfeld back on the comedy stage, and this time his punch line is so colloquially British I can't even make out what he says. But what he says matters less than the connection that has been made, which is proven when the audience responds with uproarious laughter.

Especially in cultural contexts in which the cross of Christ has lost all traces of foolishness, where it has become *the* wisdom of Christendom, we would do well to reconsider what we really mean when we speak of preachers as fools. Unfortunately, we will find little help in the work of preachers themselves because the preaching of preachers is always already marked by a certain wisdom—i.e., homiletics—that determines what is proper, what is appropriate. I argue that stand-up comics offer preachers a vision for reimagining the proper means and ends of preaching itself, precisely by being *im*proper. Especially in the work of those comics who employ humor to discuss matters of utmost seriousness (e.g., xenophobia, white supremacy, heterosexism, colonialism, misogyny, income inequality, androcentrism), we preachers may discern a comical vision oriented toward *metanoia*, which carries practical implications for sermon development and delivery.

I wish to emphasize here at the beginning of this book that this is not about helping you write and deliver funnier sermons.[7] Given the cultural rootedness of humor, any attempt at this on my part would have to presuppose the most generic preaching context. Besides, in my experience, the best humor emerges serendipitously and auspiciously. While it is true that the brightest of us can plan for humor, the rest of us whose name is not Jerry Seinfeld are better served by nurturing a disposition toward the incongruous and practicing a certain playfulness with the biblical text and our congregational contexts—not, I repeat, because we do not take biblical

---

7. If that's what you seek, I highly recommend you check out *Preaching Punchlines*, by Susan Sparks. It's a delightful and illuminating read.

interpretation or pastoral concerns seriously. And let's be real. If you were already a "funny preacher," why would you bother reading a book written by a homiletician? We homileticians are not known for our sense of humor, so I will not fault you if you are slow to associate humor with homiletics. In turn, I ask you not to fault me for not packing this book with jokes and witty asides. It's not that I'm not funny; rather, it's that I'm not trying to be funny.

There is a well-known framework to orient us toward humorous or comical sermons beyond the use of hackneyed ba-dum-bum jokes. As narrative preaching had established itself in North America as the homiletical method à la mode, Eugene Lowry pushed us to think of narrative preaching beyond the use of stories in our sermons. In *The Homiletical Plot*, Lowry stressed that sermons are fundamentally *events-in-time*. Evans Crawford made a similar point when he encouraged preachers to think of sermonic time "not as something passed but as something plotted."[8] Sermons are more than a collection of disparate parts. There exists in every good sermon a unifying and generative structure that moves the sermon from its opening to its conclusion. Lowry makes a compelling case for preachers to reimagine what a sermon *is*. He asks, "Why not conceive *every* sermon as *narrative—* whether or not a parable or other story is involved?"[9] *The Homiletical Plot* is no more concerned with plopping stories into sermons than *Stand-Up Preaching* aims for preachers to pepper their sermons with more one-liners, whimsical anecdotes, or observational witticisms.

A sermon *is* plot-like inasmuch as it arises out of a sensed discrepancy (i.e., the "homiletical bind") and proceeds by seeking resolution for the very discrepancy that prompted the sermon in the first place. As an event-in-time, a sermon moves from crisis to catharsis, from itch to scratch. In Lowry's words, "The particularized problem, discrepancy, or bind provides the problem of every sermon. It constitutes the central ambiguity the sermon seeks to resolve. The analysis of that discrepancy determines the shape of the sermon, including the form of the good news proclaimed."[10] This is why preaching is, at base, a *narrative* art form. A similar insight emerges when we nudge the metaphysics of preaching in the same direction as Lowry.

What if a sermon *is* comical, whether it contains a joke or not? What if preaching *is* humorous even if no one laughs? Such a metaphysics of preaching would lead preachers in the direction of a *comiletical* framework for challenging the epistemological, affective, and political status quo. Such a metaphysics of preaching would press us to cultivate a *humorletical*

---

8. Crawford, *Hum*, 31.

9. Lowry, *Homiletical Plot*, 13.

10. Lowry, *Homiletical Plot*, 40–41.

disposition sufficient to the radical in-breaking of God when we were least expecting her to show up. With these portmanteaus, I'm not being cheeky—well, I'm not *only* being cheeky. Sometimes we need new words to signify new ways of thinking.

I am not suggesting we should engage comedy because it is true. We should engage comedy for its capacity to help us discover the truth. Despite its popularity, I'm less interested in engaging humor because it is good than I am in its potential to help us approach the good. In short, I'm inviting us to reconsider our metaphysics of preaching. A homiletic open to learning from the humorous and the comical forces us to ask ourselves again for the first time about the why, the what, the how, and the who of Christian preaching.[11]

THE METAPHYSICS OF HOMILETICAL HUMOR

Metaphysics investigates the nature of being. Plato got us started in this direction in the West by inquiring into the essence of things, to being *as such*. Aristotle followed the same path in a different direction, moving from empirical observation to the first causes of things, i.e., that which does not change. If preaching "is" serious, and if humor "is" defined in opposition to seriousness (though I challenge this bifurcation), then humor has no place in the Christian pulpit. Period.

A strong anti-humor contingent focuses on the serious task of preaching itself. The great Charles Spurgeon, for instance, was a stentorian advocate for the seriousness of preaching. He said, "If someone asked, 'What in a Christian minister is the most essential quality for securing success in winning souls for Christ?' I should reply, 'Earnestness'; and if I were asked a second or a third time, I would not vary the answer, for personal observation drives me to the conclusion that, as a rule, real success is proportionate to the preacher's earnestness."[12] Spurgeon's admonition calls for two addenda. First, not all would agree that soul-winning is the proper end of preaching or its ultimate measure of success or failure. Nor would we all agree that

11. Note the nominalizations, which are central to my argument in this book. With *the humorous* and *the comical* I'm leading us to think beyond humor and comedy per se. To begin, the humorous and the comical disrupt the semantic ambiguity concatenated in much scholarly discourse on humor and comedy.

12. Spurgeon, *Lectures to My Students*, 275. But Spurgeon also advises his preaching students to "be so thoroughly solemn that all your faculties are aroused and consecrated, and then a dash of humour will only add intenser gravity to the discourse, even as a flash of lighting makes midnight darkness all the more impressive" (189).

preachers are ultimately responsible for conversion.[13] The second adden-
dum is that, like Karl Barth, Spurgeon's preaching practice did not always
line up with his homiletical declamations. Spurgeon frequently employed
humorous anecdotes and illustrations in both his own preaching and his
homiletical instruction, declaring that it is "less a crime to cause a momentary laughter than a half-hour's profound slumber."[14] This discrepancy
notwithstanding, there is a comforting consistency between Spurgeon's
theology of preaching and his argument for preachers to take this task seriously. If the eternal fate of parishioners hangs in the balance, how could a
preacher not approach the pulpit as if preaching were a matter of life and
death?

We see a quite different homiletical *raison d'être* in the work of David
Buttrick. Buttrick is a helpful exemplar because his scholarship is so self-
consciously theological. Of central importance for Buttrick were the gaps
between the first-century gospel context and that of a twenty-first-century
congregation.[15] Buttrick was also a method guy. He writes, "The task of our
age is not only to speak the gospel but also to find and form new ways of
preaching for an emerging new human consciousness." For Buttrick, homiletic method is much more than a "how-to program for desperate preachers." It is a "strategy for the presentation of the gospel in a strange, turbulent
new age."[16] Given our contemporary epistemological situation in the West,
Buttrick refused to bifurcate homiletical theology and homiletical practice.
The two are inextricable.

In his *Homiletic: Moves and Structures,* Buttrick acknowledges the use-
fulness of employing humor in the pulpit, but he places much more stress
on its dangers. He is especially wary of sarcasm, which he regards as a form
of hostility that is "essentially murderous" and "clearly alien to the gospel."[17]
He urges caution in the use of humor because its rhetorical benefits can

13. Cf. Willimon, *Proclamation and Theology,* 2: "Our job as preachers is to stand up
and speak the truth as God gives it to us; congregational response is God's business." He
continues, "We must recover a sense of preaching as something that God does—a theological matter before it is an anthropological matter—preaching is the business of God
before it is our business." The takeaway for me is that if preaching ultimately depends
upon God for its success or failure, it matters little whether a preacher is altogether
earnest in her preaching.

14. Spurgeon, Preface to *The New Park Street Pulpit,* vol. 1. See also Strickland,
"Spurgeon's Humor in the Teaching of Preaching," 21–29. Spurgeon the preacher was
no joke teller, writes his biographer, but he "had a gift of humor, and at times it came
into play as he preached." Dalimore, *C. H. Spurgeon,* 76.

15. Buttrick, *Preaching Jesus Christ,* esp. 17–22.

16. Buttrick, *Captive Voice,* 80.

17. Buttrick, *Homiletic,* 146.

skew the gospel message. Buttrick continues, "All in all, our two rules stand: (1) Congregations should laugh only when you want them to laugh, and have *good reason* for their bemusement; and (2) If you are a naturally funny person, your problem is control; if you are not a naturally funny person, do not try!"[18] Let's unpack this. Buttrick makes several arguments here. The first coincides with an understanding of the gospel, which appears antithetical to the hostility baked in to some forms of humor. He urges preachers not to let the appeal of being funny interfere with their charge to preach the gospel above all else.[19] Buttrick also makes a pair of rhetorical arguments that pertain to the strategic use of humor to elicit laughter and for the congruence between a preacher's homiletical rhetoric and their personality. We'll look at each of these more closely in the next chapter.

A final illustration. In their magisterial monograph *Preaching Fools: The Gospel as a Rhetoric of Folly*, Charles Campbell and Johan Cilliers link preaching's foolishness with the folly of the cross (1 Cor 1:17–25). Accordingly, they lift up a fundamental aspect of humor, namely, its capacity to disrupt the status quo and to unsettle certitude. "Gospel foolishness so disrupts our systems and securities that it calls both preacher and church to in-between, liminal places where fools make their home and where theology is unsettled and identity is in flux."[20] Gospel foolishness, in other words, fosters a particular epistemology that may only assert itself over and against the dominant and domineering epistemologies of the empire. Campbell and Cilliers suggest that the peripheral and liminal character of fools actually enables preaching fools to perceive differently from those who are less marginal to society. The holy fool is a "delighter, deliverer, disturber, all in one."[21] At the heart of Campbell and Cilliers's work are particular understandings of power, the gospel, and the paradoxical power of preaching the gospel. Here we may discern a clear line of sight between their metaphysics of preaching, their theology, the preacher's identity, and the preacher's rhetoric. Preaching exists to unsettle us.[22] The very liminality of the gospel message structures a particularly unsettled and unsettling homiletic. Like Buttrick, Campbell and Cilliers describe the context of preaching in terms of flux and liminality: "In both society and the church, such a circling of the wagons represents

18. Buttrick, *Homiletic*, 146–47.

19. Gospel for Buttrick is a discursive genre all to itself, wherein the radical character of gratuitous love disclosed in Christ is neither one of social accommodation nor inevitable fate. Thus, Buttrick argues that Christian faith is neither tragic nor comic. The character of Christ transforms the genre of the human story. *Homiletic*, 15.

20. Campbell and Cilliers, *Preaching Fools*, 2.

21. Campbell and Cilliers, *Preaching Fools*, 3, 81.

22. Campbell and Cilliers, *Preaching Fools*, xii.

a grave temptation in liminal times. . . . In such situations, the preaching fool, like the cartoonist, is called to step in as the instigator and sustainer of liminality."[23] Accordingly, the preacher (as fool) employs (foolish) rhetoric to proclaim the (foolish) gospel to a world and church so utterly convinced of its wisdom.

Every homiletic is metaphysical. Every homiletic builds praxis (method) upon a theoretical foundation (theology). This is why we cannot separate homiletical theory from preaching praxis. The two are inextricable. This is also the reason homileticians are so eager to secure preaching's source, ends, heart, essence, and so forth. Such metaphysical commitments give us our praxeological bearings. As we proceed to learn from stand-up comics and humor studies scholars, we will need to remain vigilant to the metaphysical commitments harbored therein.

PREACHING FROM "HA-HA" TO "A-HA"

In this book, I want to demystify stand-up comedy and to engage this allied discipline for homiletical insight. The whole reason I decided to write *Stand-Up Preaching* is to offer preachers a critical awareness of how comics do what they do and to consider how their methods might serve our homiletical goals. In addition, I believe that the work of stand-up comedians can help us think more deeply about homiletical theory. This means that the content of stand-up is less important than the forms and theories that undergird them. This is good news for preachers—I mean, let's face it, few congregants would tolerate the number of expletives or discussions of sex that are the *sine qua non* of much contemporary stand-up.[24]

But let's not get ahead of ourselves. Before we can look at exemplars of stand-up as such, we have to wrap our heads around what stand-up is, and, more specifically, how it relates to humor on the one hand and comedy on the other. Lawrence Mintz defines stand-up as "an encounter between a single, standing performer behaving comically and/or saying funny things directly to an audience, unsupported by very much in the way of costume, prop, setting, or dramatic device."[25] Ian Brodie emphasizes stand-up's generic

23. Campbell and Cilliers, *Preaching Fools*, 63.

24. This is not to suggest a division between thought and form. As H. Grady Davis puts it, "An unformed thought, a thought not yet turned to a shape, is only a vague impression, sensed but not grasped, an airy nothing, until given a local habitation and a name. . . . The image must have a name, a word, a sound that stands for it. By this process it is given a recognizable form." Davis, *Design for Preaching*, 2.

25. Mintz, "Stand-up Comedy as Social and Cultural Mediation," 71. Mintz adds, "Yet stand-up comedy's roots are . . . entwined with rites, rituals, and dramatic

markers that set it apart from other forms of discourse. He calls it simply "verbal play . . . [that] utilizes humor."[26] With these two definitions of stand-up a number of elements manifest, which calls for insight from allied disciplines—especially performance, rhetorical, literary, cultural, political, and communication studies.

Contemporary stand-up amalgamates two ancient forms of discourse: humor and comedy. A challenge for us is that scholars continue to debate the meaning of each of these terms even as they use them to analyze the work of stand-up comics. Nearly every scholar who proffers a theory of humor begins with an admission of the futility of such a task. E. B. White once averred, "Humor can be dissected, as a frog, but the thing dies in the process and the innards are discouraging to any but the pure scientific mind."[27] Jewish philosopher Ted Cohen says flat out that there can be no such theory of humor to account for its many varieties and contexts.[28] Holding these admonitions in mind, we still need to provide a general sketch of what we mean by the designation *humor*.

For starters, humor has always been associated with the body. In early Western physiological theory, humors referred to bodily fluids that determined a person's temperament. The four cardinal humors were blood, phlegm, choler, and melancholy. The variant mixtures of these humors in different persons determined their "complexions," or "temperaments" (their physical and mental qualities), and their dispositions. This etymological link persists in the English word *humid*, which signifies that which contains or is effected by water or vapor. Humor remains closely linked with the body's various moistures, and particularly those originating from what Russian literary scholar Mikhail Bakhtin termed the "material bodily lower stratum."[29] This is why so much humor revolves around our reproductive and excretory systems. Humor loves to remind us that despite our lofty and urbane ambitions, humans still copulate, menstruate, ejaculate, and defecate. Our animality is far from overcome in our humanity. To think otherwise is laughable.

Comedy, or the comical, has proven just as elusive to pin down as humor. The great early twentieth-century French philosopher Henri Bergson noted that ever since Aristotle, comedy has had the effrontery to elude every

---

experiences that are richer, more complex than this simple definition can embrace."

26. Brodie, "Stand-up Comedy as a Genre of Intimacy," 154.

27. White, *Subtreasury of American Humor*, xvii.

28. Cohen, *Jokes*, 10.

29. Bakhtin, *Rabelais and His World*, 23–24.

definition, calling it a "pert challenge flung at philosophic speculation."[30] Sigmund Freud expressed a similar sentiment, arguing that the problem of defining the comical has proven "so complicated and all the efforts of the philosophers at solving them have been so unsuccessful that we cannot hold out any prospect that we shall be able to master them in a sudden onslaught."[31] This admission, of course, did not stop him from attempting such an onslaught. Nor should it dissuade us.

Like humor, comedy also comes to us from ancient Greece. In Greek, a *kōmōidia* was an amusing spectacle. The noun probably originated from the word *kōmōidos*, an actor or singer in the revels. The compound noun links the *kōmos* (revel, carousal, merrymaking, festival) with an *aoidos* (singer, poet). Painting with broad strokes, if humor focuses mainly on our bodily existence, comedy focuses on our social existence. Comedy links the individual with the community. It is performative and political. As with any revelry, comedy requires a crowd.

It is easy to see how contemporary stand-up draws upon humor and comedy. Stand-up comics make us laugh and they make us think. They focus on our bodily vicissitudes and social faux pas.[32] They present an individual comic's point of view while establishing an intimate environment for the audience to join them. While we don't want to put too much emphasis on a word's etymology to determine its future signifying capacities, I find this distinction helpful to see the great appeal of humor and comedy in Western thought, along with the tensions it engenders for dualistic thinking. Even as we isolate *comodus/humus*, the distinction remains pedagogical. Such division dissolves in the performance and reception of stand-up. I hope the benefits of this analytical distinction outweigh its practical deficits as we connect stand-up with preaching, which has its own history of bifurcating the mind from the body and the individual from the community.

In contemporary scholarship, humor and comedy are often muddled. The words are sometimes treated as synonyms and other times they are treated as antonyms. A similar confusion emerges from where scholars locate humor or comedy. Some situate humor with the intention of the comic.[33] Others situate humor with the effect of a joke, bit, or gag on a particular audience.[34] Others still focus on the words themselves as the

---

30. Bergson, *Laughter*, 9.

31. Freud, *Jokes and Their Relation to the Unconscious*, 181.

32. Ali Wong is a master at this. See Wong, *Baby Cobra* and *Hard Knock Wife*.

33. Gimbrell, *Isn't That Clever*, 5, and Krefting, *All Joking Aside*, 9.

34. Latta, *Basic Humor Process*, 8; Carroll, *Humour*, 4, and Thomas, *Working to Laugh*, 5–7.

ultimate factor in humor[35] or on the relationship between a joke and the sociopolitical context in which it is told.[36] In her masterful account of comedy as a rhetorical and literary genre, Jan Walsh Hokenson reframes the locus of comedy in an entirely different way. She argues, "The 'idea of comedy' is not the writers' conception of their art form but that of their critics and theorists, those who have reflected on comic texts and performances in an attempt to isolate the lineaments of comedy as art."[37] In other words, comedy resides in the analytical framework of the comedy theorist.

Just as we cannot separate the private from the political, we cannot separate the humorous from the comical. Even as both humor and comedy are too ambiguous phenomena (or clusters of phenomena) to be defined in an unambiguous way, we nevertheless need some sort of working definition to be able to know what we are talking about. In this book I define comedy as a discursive form that employs humor to prompt an audience to see the world in fresh ways. I define humor as a rhetorical structure that uses language, vocal inflections, and gestures to prompt laughter. There are various types of humor, which include verbal puns, jokes, funny stories, and so on, just as there are various types of comedy (e.g., slapstick, romantic comedy, political satire). Both humor and comedy can serve a range of intentional objectives. They can reinforce or challenge the status quo. They can foster connections or alienation. They can belittle or build up. I shall do my best to hold these tensions in view as we proceed.

Comiletics: All Joking Aside

What most excites my homiletical imagination, and what holds the greatest potential for informing what I am labeling *stand-up preaching*, is the kind of comedy that moves from "ha-ha" to "a-ha." Or, more accurately, because I want to resist the bifurcation of the humorous and the comical, I focus on stand-up comedy that unites the "ha-ha" with an "a-ha." In the 2016 documentary *Dying Laughing*, Chris Rock sets his own brand of comedy against that of comedians who only want laughs in response to their jokes. Rock says, "I like laugh, *boo!* Laugh, *gasp.* Laugh, 'Get outta here'/disbelief. I like to mix emotion with laughter."[38] I don't think Rock is setting laughter in

---

35. Raskin, *Semantic Mechanisms of Humor,* xiii, and McGowan, *Only a Joke Can Save Us,* 20.

36. Critchley, *On Humour,* 9–11, and Eagleton, *Humour,* 14.

37. Hokenson, *Idea of Comedy,* 20.

38. Rock, *Dying Laughing.*

opposition to emotion but expanding the emotional register by which we judge the successfulness of stand-up.

Stand-up, as Rock's career has proven, can do more than elicit laughter. It can foster the conditions of possibility for seeing the world differently. While humor *may* bolster our ideological foundations, some comics can lead us to reflect upon—and even question—our ideologies.[39] We witness such a conception of comedy in Trevor Griffiths's long-standing play *Comedians*, in which an elderly stand-up comic, Eddie, tries to inspire budding comics to aspire to more than racist, sexist humor. A true joke, Eddie explains, "a comedian's joke," must pursue a change of heart and mind (i.e., *metanoia*). Eddie declares,

> A real comedian—that's a daring man. He *dares* to see what his listeners shy away from, fear to express. And what he sees is a sort of truth about people, about their situation, about what hurts or terrifies them, about what's hard, above all, about what they *want*. A joke releases the tension, says the unsayable, any joke pretty well. But a true joke, a comedian's joke, has to do more than release tension. It has to *liberate* the will and the desire, it has to *change* the situation.[40]

Transposing this into homiletical parlance, we might say that a true sermon—a preacher's sermon—will do more than delight or teach. A true sermon will prompt *transformation*.[41]

The comical is a more precise way to designate what both comedy scholars and homileticians name through adjectival modifications to humor itself. Rebecca Krefting, for instance, differentiates humor from *charged humor*. Humor for Krefting emerges out of and reinforces cultural identities and communities. By contrast, charged humor subverts staunchly held stereotypes by disarming listeners into refiguring how they imagine other communities of belonging. Charged humor is a tool to foment social change.[42] This is a brand of comedy that employs humor to subvert systems and ideologies that subordinate certain groups of people so that other

---

39. The subjunctive mood is key here. As Nicholas Holm has recently argued, the comic need not be necessarily critical via-à-vis the status quo. See Holm, *Humour as Politics*: "[H]umour is frequently tied to the expectations of liberal democratic society, taken up as a measure of social tolerance and self-critique, and declared an indispensable attribute of the reasonable subject of liberal society" (27–28).

40. Griffiths, *Comedians*, 20.

41. Augustine, *De Doctrina Christiana*, 4.12. Augustine lifts this straight from Cicero, *De oratore*, 69. See Baldwin, "Saint Augustine on Preaching," for commentary on this connection.

42. Krefting, *All Joking Aside*, 23.

groups of people remain ascendant. Though Krefting does not speak in such terms, charged humor is a form of prophetic indictment. But rather than speaking abstractly about economic and political injustices, charged humor speaks concretely about the incongruity the comic perceives. The punch lines of such humor elicit both laughter and critique. Sometimes it exploits racial, ethnic, or sexual stereotypes in order to subvert them.[43] This is a style of stand-up that originated with Lenny Bruce and Jackie "Moms" Mabley. It was perfected by Richard Pryor. It has found contemporary development in the comedy of Margaret Cho, Wanda Sykes, Hannah Gadsby, and Hasan Minhaj.

Cynthia and Julie Willett argue for *progressive humor*, which functions to render boundaries of social identity less binary (us vs. them) and more porous. Progressive humor combats the dominant culture through "immanent critique," which traffics in the effects of our social identities and interrogates a society's hypocrisy, arrogance, and ignorance.[44] Willett and Willett illustrate such progressive humor in *The Axis of Evil Comedy Tour*. Organized by Dean Obeidallah in the wake of the anti-Arab impulse following 9/11, the tour featured Arab American comedians who employ humor to diffuse tensions and foster a "contagious solidarity."

Charles Campbell writes of *risky humor*. Risky humor attends to the logical consequences of the powers and principalities of this world to "unmask them for what they are, bust their pretentious bubbles, and free worshipers from their tyranny." Campbell stresses that risky humor aims at more than "somber, self-important sermons dealing with such matters as capitalism or individualism . . ."[45] In preaching with risky humor, preachers lampoon the absurdity of the powers' claims to create space for the redemptive power of the Word.

I don't disagree with any of this. But rather than modifying what we mean by humor, I find greater value in employing *the comical* to name the deeply sociopolitical impulse operative within charged, progressive, or risky humor. By redirecting humor in the ways Krefting, the Willetts, and Campbell do, it seems to suggest that humor in and of itself is not charged, progressive, or risky. The assumption here aligns with an understanding that humor is inherently conservative.[46] This presents us with challenges when

---

43. See Watkins, *On the Real Side,* and Limon, *Stand-up Comedy in Theory.*

44. Willett and Willett, "Going to Bed White and Waking Up Arab," 98.

45. Campbell, *Word Before the Powers*, 119.

46. Bergson, *Laughter*, 198.

we encounter other theorists who emphasize humor's purportedly innate rebelliousness.[47]

Native American stand-up comic Bobby Wilson of the comedy troupe the 1491s has this to say about comedy: "What upsets people most is comedy that speaks truth in between the lines. And with those [people], if you think the world is, like, perfect and you think that it's going great for everyone, comedy's probably not for you, because a lot of the best stuff is pointing out all of the stupid shit."[48] Here Wilson identifies stereotypes and microaggressions as particularly helpful for comical subversion. Lauren Berlant and Sianne Ngai also use comedy to designate the communal aspects of humor. "Comedy helps us test or figure out what it means to say 'us.' Always crossing lines, it helps us figure out what lines we desire or can bear."[49]

To comprehend the comical is to risk overlooking the structure of *incomprehensibility* endemic to it. Theologians and philosophers who have reflected upon the comical—either for or against it—have tended to subordinate it to the demands of philosophical reason. In an insightful examination of the comedy of philosophy, Lisa Trahair argues that comedy emerges from a relationship between reason and unreason.[50] Such comedy employs more than mere humor. If *Stand-Up Preaching* is more concerned with the comical than the humorous, it is merely an attempt to counter the tendency in homiletics to emphasize the humorous over the comical. This book is a work of homiletics. Homiletics inquires into the nature and practice of Christian preaching. When we orient homiletical inquiry to the comical, we have *comiletics*.

Humorletics: Laughing with God

We've focused thus far on the comical. This emphasis runs against the grain of homiletical scholarship, which has emphasized the humorous over the comical. But this inversion in no way regards the humorous as unworthy of homiletical attention. Humor springs from a clash of incongruous aspects— a sudden shift of perspective, an unexpected slippage of meaning, an arresting dissonance or discrepancy, a momentary defamiliarizing of the familiar.

---

47. Terrence Tucker views humor as a way to express rage without resorting to actual violence: "Comic rage works to prevent [Chris] Rock's rage from being expressed through actual violence." Tucker, *Furiously Funny*, 245.

48. Wilson interview in Kongerslev, "'Good Comedy Can Upset People,'" 345.

49. Berlant and Ngai, "Comedy Has Issues," 235–36.

50. Trahair, *Comedy of Philosophy*, 30.

There are two major reasons why humor deserves sustained homiletical attention. We might label these spatially as the vertical and the horizontal dimensions. Humor opens us to a perspective beyond our finitude. Humor, as Brian Edgar rightly argues, is an essential part of the Christian vision, and the laughter it produces is fundamental for a healthy spiritual life.[51] Reinhold Niebuhr went even further, advancing a theological vision of humor as a prelude to faith and of laughter as the beginning of prayer.[52] In his *Meditations of the Heart,* Howard Thurman has this to say about humor:

> Humor may not be laughter, it may not even be a smile; it is primarily a point of view, an attitude toward experience—a tangent. It requires a certain quality of objectivity—the inspired ability to step aside and see one's self go by. . . . True humor is a weapon, but it is used creatively when it is held firmly in the hands of a man who uses it against himself and his own antics. All the gods of depression, gloom and melancholy must shriek with alarm when there rings down the corridor the merry music of the humorous spirit. It means that fear is in rout, that there is deep understanding of the process of life and an expansive faith which advises the spirits that, because life is its own restraint, life can be trusted.[53]

By Thurman's account, humor is a worldview, an attitude open to awe and wonder. Here he is close to Ludwig Wittgenstein, who saw humor as less a mood than a worldview.[54]

The horizontal dimension of humor is just as important for preachers. Here the focus is upon the community inaugurated by humor. When we laugh with others, we are simultaneously grounded in our unique, bodily existence and opened to the hearts, minds, and bodies of those who laugh with us. Ted Cohen has written about this in terms of intimacy. When we recognize others laughing along with us, we know we are not alone. Laughter is a moment when our defenses are down. When others laugh with us, they are likewise vulnerable. Humor leads us close to what the New Testament labels *koinonia.*

Intimacy has two components. The first is epistemological. Laughing with others bears witness to a shared set of beliefs, dispositions, prejudices, preferences, and so on—in short, a shared outlook on the world. The second

51. Edgar, *Laughter and the Grace of God*, 3. See also Morreall, *Humor Works*, ch. 4.
52. Niebuhr, *Discerning the Signs of the Times,* 111.
53. Thurman, *Meditations of the Heart,* 73.
54. Wittgenstein, *Culture and Value,* 78.

component is affective. Laughing with others signifies a shared feeling, a shared response to the same stimulus. Cohen writes,

> When we laugh at the same thing, that is a very special occasion. It is already noteworthy that we laugh at all, at anything, and that we laugh all alone. That we do it *together* is the satisfaction of a deep human longing, the realization of a desperate hope. It is the hope that we are enough like one another to sense one another, to be able to live together.[55]

Nicholas Holm also stresses the horizontal capacities of humor. He argues that humor is an aesthetic mode that calls upon the audience to entertain at least two conflicting frames simultaneously. When these frames come into conflict with one another, the audience is presented with a situation they can interpret as funny. This is the textual operation we recognize as humor. Holm goes on to state that the subsequent perception of funniness relies upon three textual aspects: the content of the frames themselves, the formal relation of their connection, and the separation between them.[56] If we are unable to perceive a connection, then the incongruity will appear too weird. If we are unable to perceive a separation, then the joke is not funny; it just is. If the interpreter objects to either frame of reference—if she has strong aesthetic, ethical, or political reactions to them—then odds are she won't find the humor to be funny. But this does too make the juxtaposition unhumorous. We might also reject the proposed relation between the two frames of reference on the grounds that it may be too extreme or profane.

Despite this chorus of witnesses in support of humor, there remains some ambivalence about what exactly we mean when we speak of humor. Philosopher of comedy John Morreall argues that humor not only fosters virtues, but "is best seen as itself a virtue."[57] Morreall has written much to celebrate the power of humor to work as stress suppressants that can boost the immune system and enable us to cope with difficult situations.[58] Konrad Lorenz regards humor as both a bond and a weapon.[59] The same joke may foster friendship (in the sense that fellowship is forged through antagonism) or it may inflict harm on another person or people group.

Unsurprisingly, some homileticians share an ambivalence toward sermonic humor. Jennifer Copeland, for instance, asks preachers to examine

---

55. Cohen, *Jokes*, 29.

56. Holm, *Humour as Politics*, 191–92.

57. Morreall, *Comedy, Tragedy, and Religion*, 154.

58. Morreall, "Humour and the Conduct of Politics," 73; Morreall, *Humor Works*, ch. 4; Morreall, "Humor and Emotion," 297–304.

59. Lorenz, *On Aggression*, 284.

the nature of their communication. In so doing, she juxtaposes words that are serious or frivolous. The latter, she argues, could dilute the integrity of sermonic content: "humor does not promote trust."[60] Reflecting on Augustine's tripartite *terminus ad quem* for preaching—namely, to teach, to delight, and to persuade—Paul Scott Wilson writes, "Historically the delight part of Augustine's teach, persuade, and delight trio has fit least comfortably with the church. Preaching in history was generally too serious a task for much encouragement of imagination, humor, or delight. Delight was dismissed as mere entertainment, pandering to the public tastes, and could be seen to conflict with the sober and urgent need for repentance and salvation."[61] With the neologism *humorletics* I'm hoping to turn our attention toward delight. Such work stands to strengthen ties between homiletics and our bodily, spiritual, and communal capacities for humor.

CONCLUSION: STAND-UP PREACHING

My thinking in this chapter finds support in the work of Iain Ellis at the intersection of humor and religion. Ellis writes,

> Besides their fundamental differences in beliefs and perspectives, the arts of stand-up and preaching share striking similarities. Both concentrate power, control, and purpose on a stage within a singular being whose task it is to convince and win over audiences; both rely upon techniques of timing, voice, inflection, and body language in order to connect and communicate; both seek to inspire joy and release, using both mental and emotional appeal simultaneously; both are teachers whose "sermons" must be carefully constructed and paced in order to rouse spirits and earn validation.[62]

Beyond these surface similarities between stand-up and preaching, humorous discourse offers other opportunities for preachers. Andy Mendhurst argues that comedy is a shortcut to community. He writes, "One of my main contentions is that any analytical consideration of how ideologies of belonging are forged and sustained through cultural forms needs to give comedy a prominent place, since laughing together is one of the most swift, charged

---

60. Copeland, *Feminine Registers*, 87.

61. Wilson, "Homiletical Theology of Promise," 79.

62. Ellis, *Humorists vs. Religion*, 61.

and effective routes to a feeling of belonging together."[63] Stand-up preaching celebrates humor's capacity to forge community out of otherness.

Stand-up preaching will also broaden the scope of the comical and the
humorous beyond mere laughter. The comic may or may not be funny. The
comic bears witness to incongruities in such a way that those incongruities
are deconstructed. Many stand-up comics employ a mixture of the comical
and the humorous in their routines, shifting seamlessly between ridiculous
bits and serious bits. Some comics are so skilled and sneaky that the serious
manifests out of the humorous. We see this clearly in the comedy of Richard Pryor. For instance, in his classic 1976 comedy album, Pryor confronts
the sociopolitical disparities African Americans experience vis-à-vis white
supremacy.[64] Amid national pride about America's bicentennial Pryor recognizes what the celebration is really about: "We are celebrating 200 years
of white folks kicking ass."[65] As Glenda Carpio observes, "Pryor highlights
his country's founding contradictions: its profession of democratic values
despite its history of racial oppression."[66] Terrence Tucker comes to a similar
assessment: "Looking at a very different America from the one caught up in
two-hundredth-anniversary celebrations, *Bicentennial N*gger* sees a country still struggling to live up to its most basic democratic principles."[67] The
weight of systemic injustice topples the scales America has lifted up as a sign
that it is about "justice for all." Pryor helps us laugh to keep from crying.
Danielle Fuentes Morgan observes that such efforts at comedic laughter do
several things at once. It opens up the power of Black selfhood by pushing
back against the status quo and it revels in the inherent absurdity of race and
racialization to subvert it.[68]

Preachers today face a dilemma in the pulpit. Especially in North
American preaching contexts (though there are parallels in other preaching
contexts[69]), we struggle to marshal the cultural intelligence to speak across
intersectional planes of difference. As Ronald Allen and O. Wesley Allen

---

63. Mendhurst, *National Joke*, 21.

64. In *Pryor Convictions*, he calls this "my fourth and most political album" (148).

65. Pryor, *Bicentennial N*gger*.

66. Carpio, *Laughing Fit to Kill*, 72.

67. Tucker, *Furiously Funny*, 231.

68. Fuentes Morgan, *Laughing to Keep from Dying*, 2. Some scholars question the
political efficacy of such tactics, which I discuss in chapter 7. See McClennen and
Maisel, *Is Satire Saving Our Nation?*

69. Deeg, "Disruption, Initiation, and Staging," 7: "If I were to name the greatest
problem in preaching in the present day (at least in my German context) I would bring
it down to one term: *conventionality*. I could also call it boredom or far too great pre-
dictability." See also Cilliers, "Prophetic Preaching in South Africa."

Jr. put it, "Any approach to the Christian faith that assumes the church can isolate itself from the multilingual interaction and multivalent interpretation that is constant in the twenty-first century is anachronistic and naïve."[70] Scholars are pressing preachers to be more culturally intelligent and adaptive to shifting demographic trends.[71] Even as multicultural worship contexts are becoming more the norm than the exception, these shifting demographic trends make the preacher's dual prophetic-priestly callings more important than ever.[72] Preachers in such contexts may struggle with how to "speak truth to power" without completely alienating their congregants and parishioners. Kenyatta Gilbert writes, "Any polarizing resolution that privileges the priestly over the prophetic, predictably, fails to account for the ways in which Christian praxis, at every level, must hold the priestly and prophetic roles as indispensable to one another."[73] Similar arguments for balancing the prophetic and priestly callings in preaching are commonplace in the homiletical literature.[74]

In his book *The Revolution Will Be Hilarious,* Adam Krause aligns the paths of tolerance and comedy, insisting that a "comedic mindset" can help develop a more free and democratic society. Krause argues that a comedic mindset can help us move from self-centered to multicentered worldviews, can increase our understanding and tolerance for one another, and can teach us to develop the widest possible range of non-harmful behaviors. "Comedy can increase our sensitivity to the plights and pains of unfamiliar people, make it even more difficult to marginalize and persecute other human beings, and allow us all to work together more effectively. A little more 'foolishness' could make us all a lot wiser."[75] Alison Dagnes puts this argument even stronger. She argues that the philosophy of conservatism is incompatible with political humor because it aims to uphold the status quo. Liberalism, especially in the form of political satire, aims to disrupt the status quo. She is quick to add that this doesn't necessarily mean there is bias afoot. Her observation is that this orientation to the status quo means there is going to be more left-leaning material than right. She writes, "The very

70. Allen and Allen, *Sermon without End*, xii.

71. Alcántara, *Crossover Preaching*; Kim, *Preaching with Cultural Intelligence*; Kim-Cragg, *Postcolonial Preaching*, esp. 87–104.

72. Kim, *Christian Preaching and Worship in Multicultural Contexts,* argues that because prophetic preaching aims to liberate both the oppressed and oppressors, ". . . all preaching is to be prophetic, particularly in our multicultural context" (34).

73. Gilbert, *Journey and Promise of African American Preaching*, 61.

74. See Tubbs Tisdale, *Prophetic Preaching*; Voelz, *Preaching to Teach*; McMickle, *Where Have All the Prophets Gone?*

75. Krause, *Revolution Will Be Hilarious*, 59.

nature of satire mandates challenges to the power structure, targets across the board, and an ability to take a nuanced or relativist examination of an issue in order to make the joke, and this falls squarely into the tool belt of liberalism."[76]

This is not to suggest that stand-up preaching will only work in progressive congregational or parish contexts or that progressivism couldn't stand to be knocked down a peg from its elitism and presumptuousness. What it does mean is that preachers will have to examine how the humorous and the comical will play in our respective ecclesial contexts. Krause and Dagnes signify a political orientation at the heart of the comical. Such discourse gives rise to thought—and, perhaps, action—in humorous ways. It bears witness to a worldview, which finds a homiletical corollary in the work of Fred Craddock.

> Humor, properly joined to the matter of the sermon, feels at home and is thus free to frolic, laugh, and celebrate the grace of God. Humor is, after all, inevitable in truly good preaching because all the right ingredients are present: concrete and specific references, no one laughs at the general and abstract; concern for the significant and sacred, why else are things funnier in classrooms and sanctuaries, at weddings and funerals; and a sense of freedom, only God is God, liberating us from postures and pretenses. Humor is, then, a genuine response to grace . . .[77]

Craddock speaks to a worldview that might fit equally well in congregational contexts across the political spectrum.

I have argued in this chapter that homiletical arguments for and against humor emerge from metaphysics of preaching. Beyond the use of witty allusions and metaphors, an undiscovered comic side to preaching is also found in the work of preaching itself. Take Martin Luther King Jr., for example. His preaching was an extension of his personality, and his personality was attuned to humor. As Lewis Baldwin explains, "While he was always serious-minded and focused when he ascended the pulpit, he never lost that genuine, deep sense of humor for which he was so well-known, and he used it to elevate the power of preaching as the spoken word and the performed art."[78] King possessed that rare ability to simultaneously entertain,

---

76. Dagnes, *Conservative Walks Into a Bar*, 6.

77. Craddock, *Preaching*, 219–20. He adds, "All this, of course, makes no sense to the humorless calculator who carefully inserts a joke here and there to break up the monotony of a sermon which in its intense effort to be totally serious, generates smiles and muffled laughter" (220).

78. Baldwin, *Behind the Public Veil*, 271.

enlighten, and move people to tears. Lewis adds that King always began his sermons and speeches with "jovial informality, and he routinely warmed up his audiences by turning to measured humor, joking with them, sharing humorous anecdotes, and making them laugh, thus putting them at ease with him and preparing them for his message."[79] King's intention was to not only induce laughter, but to create a climate conducive to congregational participation in the preaching event. Humor was hardwired into Dr. King's homiletical DNA. It was a sort of personality filter for proclamation even as it also served his rhetorical aims.

Beyond the homiletical significance of his humor, King also understood humor to play a vital role in the struggle for justice. As his friends and fellow civil rights leaders Harry Belafonte, Andrew Young, and Ralph David Abernathy put it, "even in the movement's darkest days, we still had room for humor"; "Martin was great at turning fear into laughter"; and "That kind of humor relaxed us in the midst of the tension and the frustration of the movement."[80] Richard Lischer notes how, in a sermon preached at Alfred Street Baptist Church in 1963, King employed humor to allay fears about the upcoming protests. King related the use of firehoses by police against Black protesters to Baptists' penchant for full-immersion baptism, and, about the police dogs, he joked, "And dogs—well, I'll tell you, when I was growing up I was dog-bitten for *nothing*, so I don't mind being bitten by a dog for standing up for freedom." Lischer assesses the situation thusly, "The humor does not appear to have gotten out of hand or become an end in itself. In a Christian context, laughter in the face of danger . . . represents trust in God's authority over earthly rulers."[81] King, a preacher whom none would describe as lacking conviction or seriousness, taps into an undiscovered comic side to preaching, and even if it served his rhetorical ends, it ultimately emerged from a deep theological conviction fueled by hope and spurred by justice.

79. Baldwin, *Behind the Public Veil*, 271.

80. Belafonte, *My Song*, 247; Young, *Easy Burden*, 194–95; Abernathy, *And the Walls Came Tumbling Down*, 471. This was also a tactic employed to great effect by Dick Gregory, using comedy to set demonstrators at ease. See Gregory, *n*gger: An Autobiography*, 215–16.

81. Lischer, *Preacher King*, 259.

Stand-Up Spotlight

Daniel Sloss
between Punch Lines and
Provocation

You are fully, 100 percent allowed to be offended by any one of the jokes in the show. That is your right. All I ask is that, if you're offended by one joke, could you just have the common fucking decency to be offended by the rest of them?[1]

—DANIEL SLOSS

Some issues are too politically volatile to address directly. When people have already made up their minds on an issue, the temptation is great to batten down our ideological hatches. Some contemporary comics offer us paths to approach controversial issues obliquely. This does two things. First, it keeps the dialogical levees open as long as possible, preserving the continued flow of discourse. Second, it lays the groundwork for helping listeners to see things in nuanced ways. Between Twitter's character count, clickbait on online news outlets, and pithy but puny aphorisms from politicians and pundits, we could use more nuance these days.

One contemporary stand-up comic who offers insight into preaching that is obliquely prophetic is Daniel Sloss. Sloss is a twenty-something Scottish comic. His comedy juxtaposes dark and juvenile material with topics that are politically and culturally contentious. Sloss positions himself as both the source and target of most of his jokes. His comic persona is that of a hypermasculine, heavy drinking bloke who says, thinks, and does things

1. Sloss, *Jigsaw*.

that are beneath the dignity of his more or less woke audience. To put Sloss into perspective with classical comedy theory, he presents himself as a buffoon and in so doing exemplifies what Plato and Aristotle found so problematic with comedy. He presents himself as worse than the average citizen, and therefore unworthy of emulation. Plato supported only those forms of imitating life (*mimesis*) that encourage virtue in its observers. Aristotle, likewise, denounced vulgar and buffoonish comedy as it detracts from the *via media* that marks a well-lived life.[2]

Even as Sloss presents himself as an idiot and a clown, this persona is a ruse. He is not an idiot, and the part of Sloss's comedy that is so worthy of homiletical attention pertains to how he structures his stand-up to address matters of grave sociopolitical significance amid his buffoonery. Stand-up preaching, as I've suggested, attempts a delicate balancing act that forces us to embody a dual identity in the pulpit, at once pastoral and prophetic. Humor helps us strike this balance. As Teresa Fry Brown writes, "The presence of the preacher in the life events of the parishioners eases the acceptance of a compelling Word as well as the humor life affords."[3] Though she is talking about preachers here, her homiletical wisdom aligns with a similar balancing act we may discern in Sloss's stand-up. By presenting himself as a run-of-the-mill bloke, Sloss forges connections with his audience that he can leverage later in his sets for prophetic indictment.

DARKLY DECONSTRUCTING BITS

Contemporary stand-up is comprised of bits. Bits may take multiple forms, including jokes, amusing anecdotes, observational asides, and rants. String a bunch of bits together and you have a set. As moves are to sermons, bits are to sets. Sloss masterfully arranges his bits to modulate the affective atmosphere around him. The reason for this is pragmatic. We require some emotional and mental breathing room when confronting dark topics. We need space for psychological release. A general rule of thumb is that the more intense the topic, the more levity ought to be leavened into it. Take abortion, for instance. In his 2018 stand-up special *Dark*, Sloss discusses his aunt's stance against abortion. Sloss notes the irony that his aunt is so opposed to abortion in principle when she has herself had five abortions. Following a trickle of half-hearted laughter, Sloss addresses the audience directly. "Some of you are clearly letting the subject matter of that joke get

2. Plato, *Republic*, 816d3–817a1; Aristotle, *Nicomachean Ethics*, 4.8.1127b34–1128a7.

3. Fry Brown, "Action Potential of Preaching," 55.

in the way of how expertly written it was . . . and that's not fair to comedy."[4] These meta-comedic asides are frequent in Sloss's stand-up. They emerge throughout his sets as minor indictments, as critical commentary on the crowd's mood, or as goofy asides.

A major part of both *Jigsaw* and *Dark* is a comedic and philosophical reflection on the notion of "dark comedy." This is comedy that seemingly breaks the pact between comedian and audience to keep the subject matter light and playful. The first few bits in *Dark* juxtapose his parents' intelligence with his (purported) stupidity. His mother has a PhD in microbiology and chemistry and his father is a computer scientist with ten patents to his name. In Sloss's mind they were perfect, liberal parents, and a central feature of this extended bit is the ever-expanding gap he declaims between his absurd antics and his parents' rationality. He plays off the trope that for him to be a successful comedian, he has to have a troubled past. He depicts his parents as nothing but compassionate and affirming. This setup allows him to segue into a series of stupid sex stories, which culminate in his dubious idea to apply mouthwash to his penis. He ends this bit by saying, "It's better than the alternative: a penis-flavored penis." The joke earns him some sympathy chuckles, which leads Sloss once again to go meta:

> I can see some of you want a better punch line there. Uhhh, there's not one. And that's because it's a true story. See, some of the best comedians in the world will tell you these amazing "true stories," and at the end of these "true stories" there's a perfect punch line. It's a mixture of a callback and a pun. Perfectly ties the whole joke together. Do you know how they came up with those punch lines? They fucking lied! And I would never do that to you. I think comedy comes from truth. [Sloss pauses for effect.] I could do that, I could have said, "And that's why the ladies call me Dental Sloss."[5]

This juxtaposition between the pressure for comedic punch lines and the pressure to speak the truth carries Sloss's thesis about the essence of "dark" comedy. Here I believe Sloss manifests a form of critical, comical resistance that can inform preaching.

Terry Eagleton writes in *The Function of Criticism* that one of the most vital tasks of the justice-minded public intellectual is "the resolute popularization of complex ideas, conducted within a shared medium which forbids patronage and condescension."[6] Humor can be a tool for accessibility. But

---

4. Sloss, *Dark.*
5. Sloss, *Dark.*
6. Eagleton, *Function of Criticism,* 113.

at the same time, it serves as a kind of *Verfremdungseffekt,* to use the term coined by the German playwright Bertolt Brecht. The *Verfremdungseffekt* of humor makes a particular aspect of the world less familiar and thus "de-naturalizes" it, making it possible to think of it in another way, thereby paving the way for the possibility of social change. Brecht wrote that the artist's objective is to appear strange, even shocking. The performer achieves this by looking strangely at himself, his work, and his world.[7] Sloss achieves this in his comedy, and in so doing, lays the groundwork for critical thought by "de-naturalizing" his experience. This positions him as the butt of his jokes but also as a case study that challenges the norm.

Later in *Dark*, Sloss segues to the topic of disability. He manages to joke *about* disability without joking *at* disabled persons. His younger sister was born with severe cerebral palsy. As he describes his sister, Sloss interrupts himself to make an aside about disability as fodder for comedy. Some people, he argues, are opposed to jokes about disability. Sloss reckons that their discomfort with joking about disability is their lack of exposure to disabled persons. He counters, "Disability can be hysterical. You just have to make sure that you're on the right side of the laughter. If you're laughing at the disabled person, congratulations, you're a pile of shit. But if you're laughing with them, what a joy. But to say disability is never funny, to me, that is dehumanizing."[8] He asserts that the reason his audience is opposed to comedy about disability is because it makes them uncomfortable and they don't know how to deal with this discomfort. His indictment draws the entire set into relief. "Instead of dealing with it [discomfort] rationally, you've nominated yourself to be offended on behalf of people who you think are weaker than you, so you decided to stand up for them. And nobody asked you to do that."[9]

Throughout the next series of jokes involving his disabled sister, Sloss interrupts the flow of his narrative to draw attention to the discomfort in his audience. He repeatedly asks us to interrogate why we are offended and who or what is actually the butt of his joke. The climax of the show revolves around the details of his sister's death at seven years old. The show has been building and building to where the audience expects the tension to be released in a final moment of catharsis. Sloss doesn't do that. He builds from joke to joke to joke to death. And the death of his disabled sister, at that. The silence is palpable. This leads Sloss into a final moment of meta-discourse

7. Brecht, *Brecht on Theatre*, cited in Sigurdson, "Emancipation as a Matter of Style," 240.

8. Sloss, *Dark*.

9. Sloss, *Dark*.

about comedy. He confesses that he manufactured the structure of the whole story so that the punch line would synchronize with the revelation of his sister's death. Of course, he could have told the story differently. He could have softened the impact of this dark moment, but then he would have missed the opportunity to teach something important, and he would have robbed his audience of a moment of possible insight.

TO TEACH, DELIGHT, AND PERSUADE

Augustine, following from his Roman rhetorical forebears, argued that these are the three chief ends of rhetoric: to teach, delight, and persuade. The mastery comes in deciding how to structure one's words to achieve the intended effect.[10] Sloss is a genius when it comes to the rhetorical flow of his stand-up. For instance, in his award-winning HBO special X Sloss struggles to extricate himself from an epistemological quagmire wherein he must reconcile his current progressive positions on matters such as human sexuality and gender equality with his lingering homophobia and misogyny.[11] There's an incongruity that emerges from Sloss denying that he has toxic masculinity and the pejorative ways he sometimes thinks about men and women. He names this tension directly. He presents himself early in the set as one who is clueless about how his views about men and women structure unhealthy relationships and keep him from being the kind of man he wants to be. He confesses that he's bad with emotions, and he attributes this to a culture that encourages boys/men to suppress their negative emotions and avoid positive emotions (e.g., telling a male friend he loves him).

He's trying to "fix the shit" in his brain. He finds himself having opinions that pop into his brain that he doesn't even agree with. He confesses that he's not a bad person but that he hasn't consciously updated all the opinions in his head. His brain plays "the classics," opinions that he developed when he was fifteen and has not managed to supplant. For instance, he shares a story about meeting a female professional footballer at a pub. When he meets her he absurdly believes he could play football (a.k.a., soccer) better than her. He knows this is ridiculous because he hasn't played football since he was fifteen. He names the "echos of a less educated me" or the "residue of ignorance" that persist in the back of his brain. To illustrate this, he imagines his brain is like a huge warehouse, a "ramshackle clusterfuck of different horrible opinions." The caretaker of this facility is a man named Nigel who wears a monocle. Nigel becomes the physical embodiment of the

10. Augustine, *De Doctrina Christiana*, 4.12.

11. Sloss, *X*.

psychic tension Sloss names between his outmoded opinions and what he professes to be his current views on a number of topics. The tension here is between his purportedly progressive, tolerant views on subjects such as human sexuality and gender relations and the androcentric and heterosexist opinions he struggles to overcome.

The payoff for this long, meandering reflection on the tension he perceives in himself is difficult to summarize. Essentially, he moves from this epistemological conundrum to the real-world implications arising from his sustained ignorance. The punch line of X is anything but funny. We don't realize it until after it's already happened, but his seamless movement from punch line to punch line turns out to be a provocation of the audience members' resistance to taking action against sexualized violence. His indictment is every bit leveled on himself alongside his listeners when he describes the circumstances that led one of his male friends to rape one of his female friends. Such provocation throws the whole show into relief. What seemed to be lingering speed bumps on Sloss's journey to wokeness turns out to have far direr consequences for those who do not share his cultural privilege.

TAKEAWAYS FOR STAND-UP PREACHING

If Sigmund Freud is right about the psychosocial function of jokes—namely, that laughter arises from our bodies as a physical marker of psychic release—then comedy cannot only make us feel better but can also make us aware of the structures that make a joke funny in the first place.[12] We live within the bounds of our respective cultures, all the while desiring to step beyond those bounds with impunity. Properly constructed and executed punch lines deliver us from the tyranny of our epistemological and affective structures. For Sloss, punch lines are a means of provocation, and that is why I find his stand-up so instructive for stand-up preaching.

A central aspect of Sloss's comedy is its elegant structure. We find a homiletical parallel in the work of Frank Thomas. In his book *They Like to Never Quit Praisin' God*, Thomas stresses the need for preachers to design their sermons to celebratory effect. Thomas encourages preachers to regulate the sermon's emotional process.[13] Here the focus is on the telos of a sermon. If sermons ought to lead listeners from the vicissitudes of life to an experience of the good news, the preacher must remain vigilant to how congregants are receiving what the preacher is saying. While Sloss's telos in his comedy specials is less about celebration than provocation, his attention

12. Freud, *Jokes and Their Relation to the Unconscious*, 254.
13. Thomas, *They Like to Never Quit Praisin' God*, 49.

to structure and flow could inform preaching that must balance addressing sensitive and/or divisive topics while fostering participation from the
audience.

Sophie Gilbert names another important takeaway from Sloss's comedy. She recognizes that Sloss's provocative stand-up forces the audience to
figure out what's a real transgression and what's a fake one.[14] Because Sloss
blends the two so seamlessly in his stand-up, it is not until after the punch
line that the listener is able to discern what has been the target of deconstruction. To illustrate, in the opening bit of *Jigsaw* Sloss admits to having
"evil thoughts" and proceeds to describe the joy he feels when he imagines
a young boy tripping and falling on his face.[15] Although his audience might
not share his perspective, they still laugh at the absurdity (or rather, impro-
priety) of the pleasure he describes. Sloss then tries to redeem himself in
his audience's eyes and says that "evil thoughts don't make you evil; acting
on them does." This stance could be well translated as a perception of dark
humor, which, for many, seems to be a significant characteristic of stand-up
comedy. Rhetorically this forces the audience into an impossible situation:
casting judgement on Sloss's shenanigans while also laughing at/with him.

O. Wesley Allen Jr. offers similar wisdom to preachers. He argues that
it is insufficient for preachers to merely speak of idolatry. We must show
idolatry in action. The reason for doing so is pragmatic. As Sloss observes,

> The reason [people make dark jokes] is they are trying to bring
> a level of humanity—laughter—back to a moment that seems to
> lack it: tragedy. They're trying to make you, the individual, laugh
> in your moment of sadness so just for the briefest of seconds,
> you have a minor moment of respite where you forget how shit
> things are and you get to have a giggle with yourself. But what
> that does manifest itself as is . . . they say fucked-up things.[16]

Like Sloss, Allen urges preachers to ease congregants into examining their
ideological commitments. To do this, he suggests beginning with "small
idolatrous foibles at which people can laugh a little . . ."[17] This approach is
risky. In risking offense, the preacher/comic bears the audience's judgment.
But this approach is also rewarding. Only through making himself the target of judgment is Sloss able to sustain the distance necessary to regard our
idolatries and ideologies in a critical light.

---

14. Gilbert, "Daniel Sloss Shows How Comedians Should Talk About Assault."

15. Sloss, *Jigsaw.*

16. Sloss, *Jigsaw.*

17. Allen, *Preaching and the Human Condition,* 39.

A final takeaway for preachers pertains to Sloss's efforts to challenge unconscious perspectives that conspire against the flourishing of others. Sloss's stand-up resonates with the insights of Paul Scott Wilson: "Deconstruction has a creative side in opening up possibilities not formerly seen, and in reducing the power of fixed systems that need change."[18] As we have seen thus far in this book, stand-up can employ humor to force us to think in new ways. There is a deconstructive bent to Sloss's comedy that can offer preachers a model for creative and generative deconstruction. Such creativity, I believe, can open us to the Spirit's work among us.

18. Wilson, *Preaching as Poetry*, 64.

2

Homiletical Humor

Why Preaching Is No Laughing Matter

What a deadly religion if it has no humor—what a dreary life where that precious venture has not emerged. Thank God for humor![1]

—HOWARD THURMAN

Men have been laughed out of faults which a sermon could not reform.[2]

—FRANCIS HUTCHESON

As I argued in chapter 1, homiletical humor is inextricable from homiletical metaphysics. How much—or even if—preaching ought to *be* funny arises from a preacher's fundamental understanding of what preaching *is*. If we work at it, we can draw a straight line between a preacher's homiletical theology and her view of humor in the pulpit.[3] To illustrate, if you think that preaching is first and foremost a faithful response by the church to God's sovereignty, this will lead to different assumptions about the use of humor in sermons than if you view preaching as the means by

1. Thurman, *Meditations of the Heart*, 73–74.
2. Hutcheson, *Reflections upon Laughter*, 12.
3. On the scope of homiletical theologies see Myers, *Preaching Must Die!*, 1–16.

50

which God calls the wayward to repentance and the lost to salvation. In the former metaphysics, preaching *is* an act of faithfulness to God's originary faithfulness; in the latter metaphysics, preaching *is* an instrumental means to a soteriological end.[4] Now, a preacher who holds to either of these metaphysics of preaching might employ humor or not in his sermons. I'm less concerned with whether (or not) the preacher attempts humor from the pulpit than his reasons for doing so (or not). I'm with Blayne Banting on this, who argues that it is just as important for preachers to consider *why* they ought to be funny and creative as it is to discern *how* to do so.[5] Such reasons point to foundational assumptions about what the preacher understands the purpose of preaching *to be*.

In this chapter, we'll take a look at the assumptions underlying each of the main reasons a preacher might or might not employ humor in the pulpit. To do so, we'll have to proceed cautiously. Preaching is a complex affair. Two preachers could develop and deliver almost identical sermons with very different theological intentions. Likewise, two preachers might preach such wildly different sermons that we would question counting them as part of the same genre of discourse; and yet, these divergent preachers could hold to the same homiletical theology of humor. The challenge, then, will be to paint a history of humor in homiletics broadly enough to capture the predominant perspectives on humor without being reductive or rarifying.

HOMILETICS AND HUMOR: A VERY SERIOUS HISTORY

Western history has always exuded an aura of seriousness. Despite this, Czech novelist Milan Kundera proclaims an "undiscovered comic side to history."[6] A similar sense of seriousness has pervaded the Christian pulpit through the centuries; and yet, I believe there remains an undiscovered comic side to *preaching* as well. There are many reasons for this, but the rationale employed to defend against homiletical humor—and, concomitantly, laughter—boils down to an understanding of the nature of preaching. As Joseph Webb aptly observes, "Whether comedy belongs in the pulpit also depends, strangely enough, on the nature of one's theology. . . . In fact, it is probably changes in theological currents themselves that have permitted the

4. Metaphysics is the branch of philosophy attending to the first principles of Being, identity and change, space and time, causality, necessity, and possibility. Especially following Heidegger, metaphysics is ontotheological.

5. Banting, *With Wit and Wonder*, 2.

6. Kundera, *Art of the Novel*, 125–26.

gradual admission (or readmission) of the comedic into the pulpit."[7] Let's take a brief look at the predominant perspectives for and against sermonic humor through the ages before examining the nuanced reasons contemporary homileticians offer for supporting a chastened form of homiletical humor.

A metaphysics of preaching requires attention to at least three things: 1) the God who summons and empowers preachers; 2) the preacher him-/ her-/themself; and 3) how the preacher's words negotiate the spacing between God's Word and the listeners' epistemological and sensorial worlds.[8] In other words, a metaphysics of preaching is theological, anthropological, and rhetorical. Arguments for and against humor in the Christian pulpit tend to emphasize one of these elements of preaching over the others. They boil down to arguments about the sovereignty of God, theological anthropology, and sermonic rhetoric. Let's look at each of these in turn.

Humoring God

How we regard humor in the pulpit ultimately emerges from a theological position. A theological *Weltanschauung* or worldview precedes preaching as well as humor. This understanding of God ramifies historically in two directions, which we might differentiate according to their divergent eschatologies. The major theological argument against humor in the pulpit (and even the church) operates out of a kind of future eschatology. Such a view proliferates in the writings of the early church fathers. Here the focus is on how Christians ought to behave in preparation for God's future redemption of the world. A second major theological argument defends humor in the pulpit according to a kind of realized eschatology. Here the focus is equally a response to divine agency, but such a theological perspective emphasizes how God in Jesus Christ has *already* turned the world upside down. Accordingly, Christians ought to find humor and laughter abounding in the world of their lived experiences.

Christian theologians have long been suspicious of humor and laughter. The early church fathers derived their negative assessment of laughter

---

7. Webb, *Comedy and Preaching*, xiv.

8. Ordinarily, we would also want to think about the use of Scripture when evaluating a metaphysics of preaching. Despite strong arguments, I remain unconvinced by those who regard the Bible as humorous—at least by our contemporary standards of humor. *Contra* Macy, *Discovering Humor in the Bible,* and Walker, *Illuminating Humor of the Bible.*

from prevailing Greek philosophies, along with Scripture.[9] Among ancient Greek philosophers, Plato was the most influential early critic of humor. He discounted humor under the pretense that it was merely mockery.[10] He saw little virtue in it for human development or education.[11] Humor that expresses malice and scorn toward others was a problem for Plato because it stymied personal and societal development toward the Ideal. So too, humor does not accord with how Scripture teaches us to behave as ethical beings (cf. Eph 4:29; 5:4; Phil 4:8).

As Stephen Halliwell argues in his text *Greek Laughter: A Study of Cultural Psychology from Homer to Early Christianity*, the antihumor and antigelastic view emerged from a fundamental conviction: "laughter denied; laughter deferred."[12] One extreme position held by many church fathers was that this world is the world of pain and tears. Joy, laughter, and humor are reserved for the next world (Luke 6:21; John 16:20; Jas 4:9). Ephrem the Syrian, for example, writes that "laughter expels the virtues and pushes aside the thoughts on death and meditation on the punishment" (cf. Eccl 2:2; 3:1–8; 7:6).[13] And Clement of Alexandria, while valuing the pedagogical influence of Hellenistic culture, nevertheless attacked the stupidity, foolishness, and laughter of pagan religions, declaring, "People who are imitators of ludicrous sensations, or of such as deserve derision, are to be driven from our polity."[14]

What I am associating with a more realized eschatology has guided theologians in a different direction. Steve Wilkens celebrates the use of humor in the pulpit, especially self-deprecating humor, as it indicates our trust in God's forgiveness and our willingness to be vulnerable with our congregants as a faithful response to our trust in God.[15] Thomas Long reminds us that a sense of humor in the pulpit is ultimately a sign of the gospel's

9. On biblical laughter and humor see Arbuckle, *Laughing with God*, 19–41; Friedman, "Humor in the Hebrew Bible"; Morreall, "Sarcasm, Irony, Wordplay, and Humor in the Hebrew Bible"; Iverson, "Incongruity, Humor, and Mark"; and Koester, "Comedy, Humor, and the Gospel of John."

10. In *Philebus*, 48–50, Plato presents the ridiculous (*geloion*) as a kind of vice. The Greek noun *geloion* covers both the comic and jokes. For more on the rich etymology of humor and laughter in Greek, see Halliwell, "Uses of Laughter in Greek Culture." See also Fergusson, "Theology and Laughter," 114.

11. Morreall, "Humor, Philosophy, and Education," 120–31. Cf. Plato, *Laws*, 11.935–6.

12. Halliwell, *Greek Laughter*, 471.

13. Cited in Gilhus, *Laughing Gods*, 69.

14. Clement, *Paedagogus*, ch. 5.

15. Wilkens, *What's So Funny About God?*, 141.

liberating power to free us from our own sense of self-importance.[16] Likewise, Fred Craddock argues that those who criticize humor in the pulpit are more influenced by a Puritan heritage than by the Bible. The value of humor for preaching, Craddock argues, is that it is a form of celebration and an expression of fellowship: "a confession of trust in the creator who made all things as they are and who does not need the protection our humorless piety can afford."[17]

Humoring Humanity

But there were other theological reasons the Early Church Fathers were opposed to laughter, humor, and comedy. Arguments against humor emerged from their theological anthropology, i.e., from their notions of being and behaving before God. John Chrysostom saw humor and laughter as a snare that could trap the unwary participant in sin. Not even approaching the topic of humor, he urged his parishioners to avoid laughter altogether, for laughter gives birth to foul discourse and foul discourse gives birth to foul actions. He reasons, "Often from words and laughter proceed railing and insult; and from railing and insult, blows and wounds; and from blows and wounds, slaughter and murder." To avoid this slippery slope into sin, Chrysostom cautions his listeners to avoid "unseasonable laughter, itself, and the very language of banter; since these things have proved the root of subsequent evils."[18]

Another aspect of our humanity that preoccupied the early church fathers was the connection between the spiritual life and human rationality. Humor and laughter were particularly problematic for those who saw the spiritual life as being advanced through rational means. This perspective found expression in Basil of Caesarea. In his "On the Perfection of the Life of Solitaries" he argued that even if laughter was not aggressive or obscene, it was always irrational and never serious and thus he deems it a fatal flaw. The Christian, he said, "ought not to indulge in jesting; he ought not to laugh nor even to suffer laugh-makers."[19] Basil reinscribes a Platonic bifurcation between mind and body. Since laughter has long been seen as a sign

---

16. Long, *Witness of Preaching*, 9.

17. Craddock, *As One Without Authority*, 91.

18. Chrysostom, "Homily 15 on the Statues," ¶11. See Stenger, "Staging Laughter and Tears," for a critical engagement with Chrystostom's rhetoric in this homily vis-à-vis that of Libanius, a sophist orator who was (possibly) Chrystostom's teacher before he converted to Christianity.

19. Basil of Caesarea, "Letter 22," ¶1.

of the body's unruliness, it's no wonder why it was discouraged in a faith stressing belief.

The theological anthropology of the church has not been univocal on the topic of humor. Early Christians grappled with balancing the benefits of humor against the admonition of the apostle Paul to avoid foolish talk (*morologia*) and coarse jesting (*eutrapelia*). The latter term, *eutrapelia*, however, contrasts with the translation given by Aristotle (and subsequently Thomas Aquinas) as a "good turn," rather than a "bad twisting."[20] In contrast to lewd, scurrilous, and depraved jesting, Aristotle and Aquinas interpret *eutrapelia* as a virtue, a good turn of speech. Aquinas associates it with jocundity and sprightliness, an enjoyment in which the mind is relieved and recreated. He labels the person who exhibits a moderate balance of humor and play *eutrapelos*: a person with a happy disposition who gives his words and deeds a cheerful turn.[21]

Aquinas also addresses laughter and folly in his writings with a degree of ambivalence. As far as defining comedy, Aquinas reiterates Aristotle's claim about the nature of comedy. In his commentary on Aristotle's *De generatione et corruptione,* Aquinas says that comedy concerns itself with "speech about urbane things."[22] In and of itself, this is not a bad thing, provided that it does not intend harm against another person. In the *Summa Theologiae* Aquinas addresses ridicule or derision (*de derisione*) as a species of laughter. Ridicule for Aquinas falls under the purview of sin. He inquires into whether it is a sin distinct from others and if it is a mortal sin. Aquinas answers in the affirmative to both questions.[23] Here the issue is not so much with humor per se than with what one does with humor and what the abuse of humor does to our souls.

A notable exception to theological anthropologies against humor attends to the human capacity for playfulness. Again following the lead of Aristotle, Aquinas regarded mental humor emerging from play as a gift to be celebrated.[24] Play provides us with occasional rest:

> As bodily tiredness is eased by resting the body, so psychological tiredness is eased by resting the soul. As we have explained in discussing the feelings, pleasure is rest for the soul. And

20. Lindvall, *God Mocks,* 28.

21. Aquinas, *Summa Theologiae,* II-II q. 168 a. 2. See also Rahner, "*Eutrapelia.*"

22. Aquinas, "In libros de generatione," 4.50, cited in Rudar, "Nietzsche and Comedy," 23.

23. Aquinas, *Summa Theologiae,* II-II q. 75 a. 1–2.

24. In his *Nicomachean Ethics,* 4.8.9.1128a Aristotle wrote, "Since life also includes relaxation, and in this way we pass our time with some form of amusement . . ."

> therefore the remedy for weariness of soul lies in slackening the
> tension of mental study and taking some pleasure. . . . Those
> words and deeds in which nothing is sought beyond the soul's
> pleasure are called playful or humorous, and it is necessary to
> make use of them at times for solace of soul.[25]

Beyond providing rest for the soul, Aquinas suggests that humor also carries
social benefits. The person who is never playful or humorous acts "against
reason," and so is guilty of a vice.[26]

Others have celebrated the playful aspects of humor on our personhood. In his seminal text on the anthropological significance of play, Johan
Huizinga argues that perspectives throughout the centuries for or against
play share one common component: they all start from the assumption that
play must serve something that is *not* play.[27] In other words, play, as a humorous mode of behavior, serves a psychological and sociological function
beyond itself. But, Huizinga reasons, if play were not a necessary component
of human flourishing, surely some "purely mechanical exercises and reactions" could perform the same function more efficiently. To the contrary,
nature gives us play as a fundamental human capacity. We find a similar
argument for play's noninstrumental value in contemporary homiletics. For
instance, Mary Hinkle Shore writes that play is an intrinsic element of faith.
Play is "enjoyment for its own and for God's sake. On one level, humor in
preaching is about preachers and hearers not taking ourselves so seriously.
On another level, pulpit humor at its best is about enjoying God 'ahead of
time,' and testifying to God's own capacity for play within the context of
God's steadfast love."[28] We find similar arguments in the work of other writers. In his book *Comedy and Preaching,* Webb writes, "The comic persona
is not contrary to the gospel; in fact, the gospel itself needs comic personas
in order for its speaking to be both inviting and invigorating. For those who
have both the courage and the sensitivity to bring the spirit of play and playfulness into the pulpit, the rewards, to both the church and the gospel will
be remarkable indeed."[29] Susan Sparks also commends humor in preaching

---

25. Aquinas, *Summa Theologiae,* II-II q. 168 a. 2.

26. Aquinas, *Summa Theologiae,* II-II q. 168 a. 4: "Anything conflicting with reason
in human action is vicious. It is against reason for a man to be burdensome to others,
by never showing himself agreeable to others or being a kill-joy or wet blanket on their
enjoyment. And so Seneca says, 'Bear yourself with wit, lest you be regarded as sour
or despised as dull.' Now those who lack playfulness are sinful, those who never say
anything to make you smile, or are grumpy with those who do."

27. Huizinga, *Homo Ludens,* 2.

28. Shore, "Leave Them Wanting More," 127.

29. Webb, *Comedy and Preaching,* 137.

as a way to restore that sense of playfulness which we all possess at birth but that gets squeezed out of us as we reach "maturity."[30]

There is a special anthropological argument for humor in the pulpit that appeals to the innate personality of the preacher. We saw this briefly in chapter 1 with the work of David Buttrick. Here the argument runs unidirectionally from the preacher to the sermon; i.e., if the preacher *is* a humorous person, her preaching ought to carry such humor into the pulpit. Ted Smith has done much to spotlight the sociopolitical shift that took place in the early to mid-nineteenth century on this front. Such was a shift from external to internal authority structures.[31] Smith focuses on the preaching practices of Charles G. Finney, who projected a public persona in the pulpit marked by sincerity, habits of speech, and gestures that had been reserved in previous generations for private conversations and intimate relationships. New measures preachers like Finney, Smith argues, "gave up the authority of office and tradition for a new kind of authority better suited to a mass democratic age—what I call the authority of celebrity."[32]

While Finney does not attend to humor specifically as a marker of the preacher's true persona, we see this focus carried out a generation later in the homiletical wisdom of the famed Episcopal preacher Phillips Brooks, and specifically in Brooks's Lyman Beecher Lectures entitled *Lectures on Preaching*. Many are quick to cite Brooks's declaration that humor is a necessary quality for the Christian preacher: "It is one of the most helpful qualities that the preacher can possess. There is no extravagance which deforms the pulpit which would not be modified and repressed, often entirely obliterated, if the minister had a true sense of humor."[33] But rarely do such citations note the context in which this argument was given. This seemingly unequivocal endorsement for humor in the pulpit appears as a point of clarification amid Brooks's critique of "clerical prigs" and "feeble clerical jesters," who defile the church's sacred symbols and doctrines in service of a laugh. This was less a full-throated endorsement of humor than a note that Brooks was not altogether opposed to the use of humor in sermons.

A second point of clarification is needed. Brooks argued against preaching that merely conveys abstract, impersonal dogma. Rather, he saw the preacher as the harbinger of truth *through* his personality. Brooks writes, "The truth must come really through the person, not merely over his lips, not merely into his understanding and out through his pen. It must come

---

30. Sparks, *Preaching Punchlines*, 9.

31. See Smith, *New Measures*, esp. ch. 5.

32. Smith, "Political Theology through a History of Preaching," 25.

33. Brooks, *Lectures on Preaching*, 56–57.

through his character, his affections, his whole intellectual and moral be-ing. It must come genuinely through him."[34] At first blush, it can seem like Brooks is merely inverting the binary preference for truth (i.e., gospel) *over* the preacher's personhood. But for Brooks, the very capacity to communi-cate the truth presupposes an event that has transformed the preacher into a vessel fit for transmitting God's Word to human hearers. "It must be nothing less than the kneading and tempering of a man's whole nature till it becomes of such a consistency and quality as to be capable of transmission."[35] Preach-ers incarnate the gospel through their preaching, Brooks argues, hence their "personalness"—humorous or not—"will cling to it."[36]

All in all, homiletical views of humor emerge from particular theologi-cal anthropologies. Whether the focus is on human sinfulness, the structure of the mind vis-à-vis rationality and play, or the personality of the preacher as a medium for truth, theologians value humor according to their under-standing of humanity. It is important to underscore that these anthropo-logical arguments are no less theological than those we considered in the previous section. In the history of theology, humor emerges variously as a capacity of the self for (self-)transcendence,[37] as a sign of the full humanity of the preacher,[38] and as a marker of the preacher's disposition to discuss serious matters without taking oneself too seriously.[39]

Humoring Discourse

Thus far we've looked at arguments for and against homiletical humor aris-ing from understandings of God and from understandings of humans who are created by and stand before God. Bearing in mind my initial caution

34. Brooks, *Lectures on Preaching*, 8.

35. Brooks, *Lectures on Preaching*, 9. For an excellent treatment of Brooks's recep-tion in homiletics through the reductive formula of "truth through personality" see Anthony, "Christ in Boston."

36. Brooks, *Lectures on Preaching*, 15.

37. "Humor is a proof of the capacity of the self to gain a vantage point from which it is able to look at itself. The sense of humor is thus a by-product of self-transcendence." Niebuhr, "Humor and Faith," 140. In Hyers's words, humor emerges as an "opening up of one's total capacity for wonder and delight, and just plain savoring, in the widest manner possible." Hyers, *Spirituality of Comedy*, 103.

38. Warren Wiersbe argues, "*The whole man must be in the pulpit*, and if this in-cludes a sense of humor, then so be it." Quoted in Wiersbe, *Walking with the Giants*, 197, emphasis original.

39. "We like people who laugh at themselves, because they are saying, 'What I'm talking about is very serious, but I don't take myself too seriously.'" Robinson, *Mastering Contemporary Preaching*, 134.

against treating these theological and homiletical arguments in isolation from one another, let us now focus our attention on the most frequently cited defense of humor in the pulpit, *viz.*, as a mode of sermonic rhetoric. While the dominant perspective through the centuries on the use of humor in preaching has been negative, there are voices of hearty approbation based on the psychosocial and rhetorical effects of humor.

Even those theologians and preachers who are far from advocating *for* humor, many refused to deny it a place in the pulpit. Like Quintilian, Augustine believed in the persuasive power of humor, and sometimes he enlivened his sermons with mischievous witticisms to stir his volatile congregations to raucous laughter.[40] And even as Ambrose followed Basil and Origen in frowning upon humor in the pulpit, he peppered his preaching with "sly, comical touches."[41] The idea here is that humor is permissible inasmuch as it is a rhetorical means to a theological end.

But not all have held the rhetorical benefits of humor as proper to the pulpit. The church's antigelastic and antihumor perspective was renewed in the nineteenth century. Ebenezer Porter, professor of sacred rhetoric and later president of Andover Theological Seminary, wrote that after *simplicity* the second most important quality requisite for effective preaching is *seriousness*. He reluctantly allows for the use of satire in sermons, quickly adding that "it is always dangerous, and almost always mischievous."[42] Concerning levity and clever witticisms in sermons, Porter has this to say: "The preacher trifles in this manner, under the pretense of keeping up the attention of his hearers. But *what* attention does he desire; and for what *purpose*? Not the attention of the theatre or the circus: but the attention of immortal beings, to a message from God. Let him not then degrade his office and himself, by preposterous levity."[43] For Porter, the benefits of humor do not outweigh its deficits. It is unsurprising, then, that Porter's third mark of excellent preaching after simplicity and seriousness is *earnestness.*

Porter's sentiment reflects a widely held perspective in his day that rhetorical wit and popular humor detract from what is true and beautiful. It

---

40. Quintilian, *Orator's Education*, 6.8.35–6; See Rowe, *St. Augustine*, 38, on Augustine's "humorous illustrations"; Torretta, "Preaching on Laughter"; and van Neer, "Didactically Responsible Use of Humour," 551: "Nearly all the evidence is of a negative attitude to humour and laughter on the part of St. Augustine (and all other church fathers), although between the lines one can find glimpses of authentic humour—humour which provokes contrasts and a particular kind of amusement."

41. Ambrose, *De officiis ministrorum*, 16, 1.23.102–3, cited in Dunn-Wilson, *Mirror for the Church*, 88.

42. Porter, *Lectures on Homiletics and Preaching*, 180.

43. Porter, *Lectures on Homiletics and Preaching*, 180.

was a perspective reinforced by Hugh Blair's *Lectures on Rhetoric and Belles Lettres* (1783), which was required reading at Princeton, Harvard, and Yale in the late eighteenth century. Blair, who was both a minister and professor of rhetoric at the University of Edinburgh, recognized that popular rhetors might shape aesthetic trends in one direction or another, but that good taste would always prevail. Blair writes,

> A man of correct Taste is one who is never imposed on by coun-terfeit beauties; who carries always in his mind that standard of good sense which he employs in judging of everything. . . . In the course of time, the genuine taste of human nature never fails to disclose itself, and to gain the ascendant over any fantastic and corrupted modes of Taste which may chance to have been introduced. These may have currency for a while, and mislead superficial judges; but being subjected to examination, by de-grees they pass away; while that alone remains which is founded on sound reason, and the native feelings of men.[44]

For Blair, humor was ultimately a sign of inferior taste and to be avoided in public discourse.

The famed Baptist preacher and homiletician John Broadus presented an ambivalent view of humor in the pulpit. In his *A Treatise on the Prepa-ration and Delivery of Sermons*, which was one of the most widely used introductory homiletics textbooks in America for more than a century, he addresses the rhetorical benefits and challenges of homiletical humor. He was strongly opposed to any *effort* to be amusing and that "anything odd that appears to be calculated, is felt to be incompatible with a genuine seriousness and solemnity."[45] While he acknowledged the benefits of hu-mor to sustain a listener's attention—especially that of children—he wrote, "The humor employed had best be delicate; it may be broad and grotesque, but never coarse or silly. It must be manifestly subordinate to a serious purpose."[46] Humor in the pulpit for Broadus was like oregano: a pinch will go a long way, but a dash will ruin a meal.

Leapfrogging into the twentieth century, John Drakeford argues that employing humor and laughter is a paradoxical strategy to help congregants take things seriously. His *Humor in Preaching* is less about homiletical hu-mor as such than humor as a rhetorical strategy for forging a connection

---

44. Blair, *Lectures on Rhetoric and Belles Lettres*, 29, 40.

45. Broadus, *Treatise on the Preparation and Delivery of Sermons*, 44.

46. Broadus, *Treatise on the Preparation and Delivery of Sermons*, 117. He also ar-gued against imitative gestures (i.e., mimicry) as being "unsuitable to grave discourses, and belong[ing] rather to comedy" (474).

between a preacher and his congregation. Drakeford's argument for humor in the pulpit is strictly instrumental. Despite his discussion of the homiletical benefits of humor, Drakeford cautions, "It is important to remember that a preacher can become too interested in humor, miss the point of his calling, and sink to the role of a jester. . . . Perhaps such preachers are rare, but all preachers must learn to be sensitive to occasions when humor is inappropriate."[47]

The generation of homileticians preceding ours were mostly ambivalent on homiletical humor, but they nevertheless celebrated its rhetorical value. In his seminal text on Black preaching, Henry Mitchell argues that humor "can do much to help both speaker and audience relax and open up to each other. But humor must be in the best of taste and held to a minimum. The telling of jokes is subject to serious question, and only the most chaste and purposeful jokes are likely to be accepted, even though the Black audience is traditionally permissive."[48] James Cox appreciates humor's rhetorical capacity to break the ice, relax inhibitions, and create an attitude of expectancy.[49] There is a pragmatic argument here for employing humor in the pulpit. Stuart Briscoe makes a similar point when he sees humor as providing the mental equivalent of a seventh-inning stretch: "People's minds need a break now and then, and humor can supply it in a way that enhances the sermon. After momentary laughter, people are ready for more content. Or when something disturbs the sermon—such as a loud sneeze—a good-humored retort can bring attention back to the preacher."[50]

In their efforts to help preachers connect the purposes of preaching and their concomitant rhetorical strategies, contemporary homileticians have presented a more nuanced celebration of humor. Luke Powery and Sally Brown offer a helpful typology of a number of rhetorical modalities. Last among these is the *comical*, which they define as a rhetorical approach that capitalizes on humor to make people laugh. Powery and Brown acknowledge, however, that comedic effect is complex and that "[s]ometimes we need to laugh, perhaps to keep from crying in a world that is dying."[51] Let us underscore that while humor has rhetorical benefits, Powery and Brown argue that its use can transcend rhetoric for marginalized persons. Humor proceeds here from a deep theological commitment. Likewise, Frank Thomas underscores the signifying capacity of rhetorical forms

47. Drakeford, *Humor in Preaching*, 93.

48. Mitchell, *Black Preaching*, 116.

49. Cox, *Preaching*, 186.

50. Briscoe, "Interesting Preaching," 388.

51. Brown and Powery, *Ways of the Word*, 15–16.

common to the Black church preaching tradition. In particular, Thomas highlights a rhetorical-humorous technique called *the dozens*. Such use of humor involves verbal sparring between speakers. While it might seem like such humor is all about tearing down the other person to bolster one's sense of superiority, Thomas argues that the use of such humor is nonpersonal. The attack is targeted less at another person than at signifying a fun and playful rhetorical context. Such is "a critical expression of black life in an often-hostile world."[52]

HUMOR THEORY: A VERY SERIOUS EXPLANATION OF WHY WE LAUGH

There is an old expression that the easiest way to ruin a joke is to explain it. While this is true, it can also be incredibly interesting to ask ourselves such questions as: Why do we laugh? What causes some people to laugh and not others? What are the central components of a successful comedy bit or joke? Unsurprisingly, we are far from reaching a definitive consensus around what makes us laugh. Philosopher John Morreall notes that despite thousands of years of debate "there is still considerable difference of opinion about what really defines humor."[53] Agnes Heller argues similarly, asserting that the comical cannot be defined as such, because it manifests in far too many modalities for us ever to arrive at the *essence* of comedy.[54] But this does not stop scholars from trying, and try we must, for getting at our underlying reasons for laughter lends precision to just what it is that is so disturbing or praiseworthy in humor homiletically.

Comedy and humor studies scholars draw upon five main theories to account for how humor works. Each of these theories cuts across several domains of inquiry, including psychology, sociology, and philosophy. Since the word *humor* did not carry connotations of funniness until the eighteenth century, theorists look for other words such as *laughter* and *comedy* to account for the functional efficacy of what we today identify as humor. These are the superiority theory, the incongruity theory, the relief theory, the play theory, and the affect theory.[55]

---

52. Thomas, *Introduction to the Practice of African American Preaching*, 80–81.

53. Morreall, "Conclusion," 217.

54. Heller, *Immortal Comedy*, 15, 204.

55. Let me stress that these are the main theories of humor in the West. Just as humor is culturally conditioned, so too are arguments for why different cultures tend to laugh at certain things over others. In a recent article on the role of cultural difference in humor perception, researchers discovered that Westerners tend to employ maladaptive

The Superiority Theory

The superiority theory is the oldest and most heavily cited reason for disavowing humor in the pulpit. Most often understood through the critiques of humor prevalent in ancient and early modern thinkers, this theory links laughter with the pleasure found in mocking others. This pleasure emerges as a psychosocial reinforcement of another's purportedly inferior social status to us or as a means to reaffirm and enhance an individual or group's sense of superiority over those of different social standing. This theory casts humor in a predominantly negative light, as it focuses on traits most of us would find distasteful. Scorn is unbecoming, and none of us relish opportunities for being laughed at.

The harbinger of the superiority theory of laughter is none other than the father of Western thought: Plato. Plato's thinking here seems to have been influenced by Aristophanes's mockery of Plato's teacher, Socrates, in Aristophanes's comedy *The Clouds*. In the ideal state, Plato said, comedy should be tightly censored and no one should be allowed to make fun of citizens, leaders, or the gods.[56] The idea here is that comedy ought to be avoided because it shows us at our worst, much as tragedy presents us with heroic figures to which we aspire to emulate. While more nuanced than Plato, Aristotle adopted his teacher's wariness of comedy.[57]

Not everyone was opposed to the use of humor to assert one's superiority over others. Thomas Hobbes regarded humor in a positive light. He saw it serving a valuable social function by reinforcing social hierarchies. Hobbes described the feeling expressed in laughter as a moment of "sudden glory" in which we recognize our superiority.[58] Like Plato, Hobbes saw laughter as antisocial and often cruel, but Hobbes celebrated humor as a way to reinforce social systems through class hierarchies, and thereby to reinforce the divine right of the king to rule.

The Incongruity Theory

In the eighteenth century, two alternative theories gained prominence. One of these was the incongruity theory. This theory of laughter focuses less on the psychosocial effects of humor than on the cognitive dissonance we

or aggressive humor, while Easterners tend toward adaptive or affiliative humor. Jiang, Li, and Hou, "Cultural Differences in Humor Perception, Usage, and Implications," 3.

56. Trivigno, "Plato on Laughter and Moral Harm."

57. Aristotle, *Nicomachean Ethics*, 4.8.1127b34–1128a7, and *Poetics*, 1449a34–37.

58. Hobbes, *Leviathan*, 38.

experience when we encounter something out of sorts with our patterns of thinking. When we see a painting of dogs playing poker or adults wearing diapers and sucking on pacifiers, so the theory argues, our minds struggle to reconcile this new data with our preexisting epistemological frameworks. Dogs do not possess opposable thumbs capable of holding cards, nor do they possess the cognitive capacities to gamble (or so we presume). Since a mark of adulthood stands in juxtaposition to that of childhood, when we witness adults dressed up as babies, the incongruity we encounter produces laughter.

The most famous early version of the incongruity theory was posed by Immanuel Kant. He described laughter as an affect caused by "the sudden transformation of a heightened expectation into nothing."[59] Here the end of a joke requires listeners to shift to an absurd second meaning for a word or phrase. This frustrates the desire to understand, Kant said, and is not gratifying to the mind; but the jostling of ideas causes a physical jostling of our internal organs that feels good. As a joke evokes, shifts, and then dissipates our thoughts, we do not learn anything or understand anything better, Kant thinks, and so he finds nothing of intellectual worth in jokes or humor generally. Extrapolating from Kant's premises, Thomas Schultz claims that what we enjoy in humor is not incongruity per se, but *the resolution of incongruity*. With children over the age of six, Schultz says, it is not enough to present them with something incongruous to amuse them. Something in the humor must fit the apparently anomalous element into some conceptual schema. This is precisely what "getting" a joke is. Schultz is even unwilling to call unresolvable incongruity humor—he calls it nonsense. The examples cited by those who insist on the resolution of incongruity are typically jokes in which a word or phrase has a second meaning that emerges in the punch line. Consider the children's riddle:

> Q: *Why can't you starve in the desert?*
> A: *Because of the sand which is there.*

Initially, the hearer of this joke is confronted with the incongruity of an absurd explanation: You can't starve in a place that has sand. But then the hearer notices that "sand which is there" sounds like "sandwiches there." That homophonic awareness resolves the incongruity and allows the answer to make sense in a certain way: In a place with lots of sandwiches, you won't starve.[60]

---

59. Kant, *Critique of the Power of Judgment*, 209.

60. Schultz, "Cognitive-Developmental Analysis of Humor," 12–13, cited in Morreall, "Philosophy of Humor," 569.

Another version of the incongruity theory emerged from the work of Søren Kierkegaard. Unlike Kant, Kierkegaard regarded humor as philosophically significant. He locates the essence of humor in a discrepancy between what is expected and what is experienced, although he calls it contradiction rather than incongruity, writing that "the comical always lies in a contradiction."[61] The violation of expectations is the essence not only of the comical, he says, but also of the tragic. In both comedy and tragedy, some experience contradicts our expectations. The difference is that in the tragic mode, we despair of a way out, whereas in the comic mode, we figure a way out. In these and later versions of the incongruity theory, the core meaning of incongruity is that some thing or some event we perceive or think about violates our mental patterns and expectations.[62] The key to categorizing this violation as comical coincides with whether or not it offers us hope and joy rather than despair and sadness.

We find a similar emphasis in the humor theory of the British philosopher Simon Critchley, who has suggested that humor is produced by a disjunction between the way things are and the way they are represented in the joke, a disjunction "between expectation and actuality."[63] Like Kierkegaard, Critchley sees the philosophical benefits of humor, which he locates in humor's ability to work on us subversively as it produces a "consciousness of contingency." Through this consciousness, argues Critchley, the world is exposed as not naturally given or necessary but capable of being reimagined otherwise.[64] This malleability of the world attributes much power to the comic to help her listeners see the contingency of things. It coincides with an anthropocentric worldview, which situates us as the makers of the world.[65]

61. Kierkegaard, *Concluding Unscientific Postscript*, 413. "The more thoroughly and substantially a human being exists, the more he will discover the comical. Even one who has merely conceived a great plan toward accomplishing something in the world will discover it."

62. Victor Raskin's linguistic theory of humor (*Semantic Mechanisms of Humor*) claims that a joke involves two different frames of reference: one in the setup, the other shown in the punch line. (E.g., *My wife is an excellent housekeeper. When we got divorced, she got the house.*) Prior to this work, Arthur Koestler in *Act of Creation* indicated that a joke involves the juxtaposition of two mutually independent codes. Thus, such forms of episodic or linguistic humor rely upon dichotomous thinking (40).

63. Critchley, *On Humour*, 1.

64. Critchley, *On Humour*, 10.

65. Adam Hearlson names an approach to worship leadership that emphasizes a kind of incongruity that Christian worship aims to subvert. Such liturgical praxis advances a view of the world's complexity without reduction. Hearlson, *Holy No*, 151.

The great Reformed theologian Karl Barth was also a fan of humor in terms of its incongruity. Barth writes,

> Humor arises when we have insight into the contradiction be-tween our existence as children of God and as children of this age, and we become conscious of our actions in a lively way. Humor means a great bracketing of the serious side of the pres-ent. There is humor only in our struggle with the serious side of the present. But we, as children of God, cannot possibly remain entirely serious about and in this struggle. God's future makes itself known as that smile under tears, as that joyfulness in which we can bear the present and take things seriously within the bracket, because the present already carries the future within it.[66]

Here we have a deeply theological argument for humor. For Barth, contra Critchley, humor is a mark of our realization that the so-called "real" world fails to describe the world as it is in and through God's reconciliation and redemption of the created order.[67] From this theocentric worldview, Barth differentiates between genuine and false humor. He associates false humor with that espoused by the superiority theory of humor. Genuine humor is aimed first and foremost at oneself that one "sees the bracket in which one finds oneself." Such humor liberates us from self-aggrandizement and gall. Barth concludes, "Those who laugh at themselves are also allowed to laugh at others and will joyfully also pass the ultimate test of being laughed at themselves—a test that much alleged humor usually fails miserably."[68] Thomas Long puts it this way: "Because God in Christ has broken the power of sin and death, Christian congregations and their preachers are free to laugh at themselves, and they can also laugh at the empty gods of pride and greed. They can mock hell and dance on the grave of death and sin."[69] Here we see the connection between the incongruity theory of laughter and a celebration of humor in the pulpit.

The Relief Theory

The relief theory of laughter melds the psychosocial and cognitive perspec-tives on humor. The argument here is that a comical venting of emotions

---

66. Barth, *Insights*, 6.

67. Critchley is a self-professed atheist. See Critchley, *Faith of the Faithless*, 3.

68. Barth, *Insights*, 6.

69. Long, *Witness of Preaching*, 9.

through a hearty laugh offers a physical and psychological release of tensions.[70] The relief theory says that laughter functions in the nervous system much as a pressure-relief valve works in a steam boiler—it releases pent-up energy. According to a simple version of this theory first espoused by Herbert Spencer, nervous energy naturally leads to bodily movement.[71] When we are angry, for instance, our nervous energy produces small aggressive movements such as clenching our fists or clenching our jaw. Laughter provides a way for us to alleviate some of the pressure such nervous energy produces.

The most prominent proponent of the relief theory was Sigmund Freud. Freud divides our experiences of humor into three categories. He called them *der Witz* (often translated "jokes" or "joking"), the comic, and humor. The laughter produced in all three is a release of nervous energy that has become unnecessary. In *der Witz*, which includes linguistic playfulness such as puns and witty repartee, the superfluous energy is summoned to repress feelings. In the comic mode of release (Freud's second laughter-inducing situation), energy is released through a summons to think. This mode of humor signifies the cognitive strain required to make sense of visual stimuli that defy our lived experience. Comedy scholars today label such humor physical or slapstick comedy. For instance, the frenetic and farcical movements of the Three Stooges appear absurd (and violent) at first glance. They flout our expectations of how a "normal" person might go about performing simple tasks such as changing a tire or painting a fence. When faced with such vaudevillian behavior, Freud says, we "save" the energy we might have spent on understanding the Stooges' movements, and we vent that surplus energy by laughing. And in humor, it is the energy of feeling emotions occurring when an unpleasurable feeling moving toward expression is sublimated into pleasurable laughter or joking remarks (think, here, of jokes used to fill the awkward silence between strangers on an elevator). In telling and hearing jokes, Freud says, we express emotions that we ordinarily repress. The psychic energy released by laughing at such jokes is energy that would have repressed these emotions.[72] The most commonly repressed emotions, according to Freud, are sexual desire and hostility, and that is why so many jokes and witty remarks are often sexual, aggressive, or

---

70. "Encroaching upon prescribed boundaries while playing at the limit, the fun in comedy emerges. The comedic transgression amuses us because we vicariously enjoy the perpetrator's violations while remaining on the side of the law. . . . We are caught at the excess we cannot identify with at the level of the ego, but that resonates at the level of the drive." Gherovici and Steinkoler, eds., *Lacan, Psychoanalysis, and Comedy*, 9.

71. Spencer, "On the Physiology of Laughter," 299.

72. Freud, *Jokes and Their Relation to the Unconscious*, 293–95.

both. In telling such a joke, we bypass our internal censor (i.e., superego) and give vent to our real thoughts and feelings (i.e., id). The psychic energy normally used to do the repressing becomes superfluous and is vented in laughter.

As we observed earlier in the work of Powery and Brown, the relief theory of humor helps us account for the way humor can sometimes function cathartically in minoritized communities. As Paul Beatty suggests, "Humor is vengeance. Sometimes you laugh to keep from crying. Sometimes you laugh to keep from shooting."[73] The relief theory of laughter also helps us make sense of why some minoritized communities find humor in comedy that exploits stereotypes about their race, gender, or ethnicity. Such jokes work to diffuse tension. This is a common feature of Jewish jokes told by Jews about Jews as a way to cope with the psychic pressures of anti-Semitism; in fact, it was his love of Jewish jokes during a particularly anti-Semitic period in Austria's history that prompted Freud to write his *Jokes* book.[74]

The Play Theory

A fourth significant theory of laughter emerged in the twentieth century from animal studies researchers and evolutionary biologists investigating the playful shenanigans of chimpanzees.[75] Around the same time that scientists were uncovering insights from the animal kingdom, a prominent literary history of subversive folk carnivals emerged in France through the translated work of Russian literary theorist Mikhail Bakhtin. Bakhtin's study of pre-modern folk traditions uncovered animal-like antics that suspended hierarchical rank and privileges in the form of corporate play.[76] This theory of laughter deeply influenced Charles Campbell and Johan Cilliers's *Preaching Fools: The Gospel as a Rhetoric of Folly.*

John Morreall is a strong advocate for the play theory of laughter. In his book *Comic Relief: A Comprehensive Philosophy of Humor,* Morreall describes the pattern of humor in the following terms:

---

73. Beatty, ed., *Hokum,* 16.

74. Billig, *Laughter and Ridicule,* 142.

75. See de Waal, *Age of Empathy,* and Provine, *Laughter.* See also Haraway, *When Species Meet,* and Oliver, *Animal Lessons.*

76. Bakhtin, *Rabelais and His World,* and Eco, "Frames of Comic Freedom." For insights into Bakhtin's theory of the carnivalesque and frames of liminality for preaching see Campbell and Cilliers, *Preaching Fools,* 40–43, 203–6, and Lorensen, *Dialogical Preaching,* 95–115.

1. We experience a cognitive shift, a rapid change in our perceptions or thoughts.

2. We are in a play mode rather than a serious mode, disengaged from conceptual and practical concerns.

3. Instead of responding to the cognitive shift with shock, confusion, puzzlement, fear, anger, or other negative emotions, we enjoy it.

4. Our pleasure at the cognitive shift is expressed in laughter, which signals to others that they can relax and play too.[77]

Morreall regards humor as "cognitive play," which predicates that humor is a "non-serious activity" in which "we are not trying to discover the truth or even make sense of what we experience . . . all that matters is the mental jolts are enjoyable."[78]

The Affect Theory

In recent years, scholars have offered theories of laughter that build off the play and incongruity theories. But rather than focusing on the cognitive aspects of play, these scholars focus on the affective atmosphere that enables laughter. This alternative approach owes a debt to more than two decades of groundbreaking work from feminist philosophers and social scientists, who insist that humans—along a continuum with other animal species—are emotionally driven, social, and embodied creatures.[79] In other words, far from an aloof mind perceiving the world at a distance, the self is seen as a process. It is both relational and porous, with various levels of consciousness and felt awareness throughout the body. As Cynthia and Julie Willett rightly observe, "More than just perceiving and thinking subjects, we are also affective agents extended into a biosocial field of often mysterious forces."[80]

The term *affect* signifies more than emotion. Affect melds the ways we feel with the ways we think, indicating a visceral component of our intersectional and social selves. Affect theory roots much of felt experience in the preverbal, unconscious right brain and in the gut. It points to that intuitive perception we have when the atmosphere in the room has shifted. The gut, or enteric nervous system, is also known as the "second brain," as it has more than thirty neurotransmitters and houses 95 percent of the body's

77. Morreall, *Comic Relief*, 50.
78. Morreall, "Humor as Cognitive Play," 252.
79. See Ahmed, *Cultural Politics of Emotion*; Wetherall, *Affect and Emotion*.
80. Willett and Willett, *Uproarious*, 6.

serotonin. In contrast, the term *emotion* points less to the gut than to the semiautonomous capacities for verbal articulation and reflection originating from the left side of the brain.

Given the difficulty of disconnecting one part of the body from another, those who hold to the affect theory of laughter de-emphasize the segmentation between mind and body, intellect and emotion, or perception and intuition. Often contagious, affects transcend mere physical sensations; rather, they are more of an intrapsychic and emotional vibe that is easier to feel than define. Ranging on the one hand from racialized fear to laughter's revitalizing energies on the other, affects carry culturally imbued meanings across porous borders. They travel through discrete and even precise tones, gestures, and rhythms, but they also spread like waves through biosocial networks, and they thus can define the mood of a crowd. As an example, think about how the atmosphere towards Arab Americans shifted after 9/11 or how feelings towards Asian Americans were impacted by Trump's vitriolic rants about "Kung Flu" during the COVID-19 pandemic. Affects like fear or laughter's pleasure might stir up a crowd and sometimes provide genuine comic relief.[81] Consider how a stand-up comedian reads a room to alter its vibes, or how a preacher and organist sense the movement of the Spirit bringing the sermon to a close.

CONCLUSION: RETHINKING HOMILETICAL HUMOR

In his poignant essay "Ministry with a Laugh," Charles Campbell summarizes centuries of theological accretion concerning the role of humor in ministry. Arguing that laughter eludes capture by any one, overarching theory, Campbell asserts that "laughter does indeed break up and crack up; it interrupts all the theories that seek to explain it or get control of it. Laughter is too fluid, too unruly to dogmatism; it fractures whatever systems would seek to contain it."[82] While I agree with Campbell here, when faced with the antigelastic and antihumor perspectives that have dominated much of church history, it can be helpful to direct our demurrals and affirmations of humor with greater precision. In other words, whether we are for or against or ambivalent about the use of humor in the pulpit, it is important to identify our reasons for holding this view. I'm much less interested in getting you

---

81. See Minhaj, *Homecoming King*; Willett and Willett, "Going to Bed White and Waking Up Arab"; and Selim, "Performing Arabness in Arab American Stand-up Comedy."

82. Campbell, "Ministry with a Laugh," 197.

to agree with my theology of preaching than for you to think critically about your theology of preaching.

Campbell advances three forms of laughter for preachers that he labels *incarnation laughter, crucifixion laughter*, and *resurrection laughter*. Each of these perspectives on laughter aligns with general assumptions about the function of humor vis-à-vis core theological convictions. First there's the laughter that "parodies our pretensions" as ministers. Such incarnational laughter abides alongside a particular theological anthropology and a particular perspective on preaching's *raison d'être*. It challenges the simple separation between the funny and the serious. It also admits the personality of the preacher into the pulpit. Such reflexivity opens the preacher/minister to the incongruities abounding in our calling.

A second kind of laughter is ideologically disruptive. Such crucifixion laughter "fractures dogmatic certainties." This view of laughter and humor coincides with an understanding of the gospel as that which challenges our propensities toward ideological rigidity, which shares a border with idolatry. Campbell adds an important caveat here. Such a perspective on humor is more profound that telling jokes in the pulpit or identifying humorous elements in Scripture. "The laughter that breaks up and interrupts is a more encompassing form of laughter; it suggests an orientation for faithful ministry that is deeply rooted not only in the gospel, but also in its ritual appropriation through the centuries."[83] This theological conviction commends a playfulness in the pulpit that transcends the instrumentality undergirding the relief theory of laughter. It does not commend humor for what it can do but for what it is.

Lastly, there is laughter that Campbell labels resurrection laughter. Such laughter frees us from the fear of death. Like the views espoused by Karl Barth, Thomas Long, and Fred Craddock discussed above, resurrection laughter affirms the incongruity manifested in the good news that in the life, death, and resurrection of Jesus Christ the world has been turned upside down. If God in Christ has overcome death itself, how can this radical inversion of the natural state of things lead us to anything but holy laughter? Here it is precisely that the seriousness of God's decision to be for us prompts a humorous outlook on the world. Such a theological perspective also opens a connection between homiletics and the relief theory of laughter. In such a state of awareness, as Freud identifies, "The ego refuses to be distressed by the provocations of reality, to let itself be compelled to suffer. It insists that it cannot be affected by the traumas of the external world; it shows, in fact,

---

83. Campbell, "Ministry with a Laugh," 198.

that such traumas are no more than occasions for it to gain pleasure. This last feature is a quite essential element of humour."[84]

As we proceed in this book, we shall need to bear in mind Campbell's insights about varying kinds of homiletical humor. Whether we are considering the preacher's use of language and its concomitant rhetorical forms (chapter 3), the use of voice and gestures for comedic effect (chapter 6), or engagement with politics (chapter 7), we ought to consider the philosophical and theological commitments harbored therein. Such an expansive and critical outlook on humor in homiletics will further lend itself to critical assessment of the exemplars of stand-up comedy whom I spotlight. Bear in mind as we proceed that I, like you, hold to particular ideological and theological convictions. These convictions guide not only the reception of these comics for homiletics but my inclusion of them in the first place.

84. Freud, "Humour," 162.

Stand-Up Spotlight
Hari Kondabolu
between Humor and Harm

Oppression is pain. And when you tell someone, "We've come a long way,"
you are really telling them to hold on to their pain longer.[1]

—HARI KONDABOLU

H ari Kondabolu is an Indian American stand-up comedian born and raised in Queens, NYC. He holds an MA in human rights from the London School of Economics, and before that he worked for an immigrant rights organization as a part of the AmeriCorps program. Kondabolu's stand-up capitalizes on his liminality and he employs his linguistic mobility and dexterous thought to challenge sociopolitical structures that marginalize and oppress. Though he hates the label "political comedian," among those whom I spotlight in this book, Kondabolu is the one of the most politically focused and critical comics.

Kondabolu's comedy borders on the absurd—not that he himself is an absurdist comic, but that the racial and ethnic disparities and injustices in America are themselves absurd. Kondabolu is no Andy Kaufman. In his 2014 special *Waiting for 2042*, Kondabolu marvels at the absurd claim that he is obsessed with race given all the horrors going on in America. They range from the murder of Trayvon Martin to the tortures taking place in Guantanamo Bay. He says, "Accusing me of being obsessed with talking

1. Kondabolu, *Warn Your Relatives*.

about race in America is like accusing me of being obsessed with swimming when I'm drowning."[2] He's a political comic because racism is political.

CHARGING HUMOR

Culture studies scholar and stand-up comedian Rebecca Krefting presents a helpful designation for the kind of comedy performed by the stand-up comics I spotlight in this book. She calls this kind of comedy "charged humor." This is the kind of comedy performed by those who intentionally produce comedy that is at once humorous while also challenging to social structures of inequality and cultural exclusion. Krefting explains that "charged humor relies on identification with struggles and issues associated with being a second-class citizen and rallies listeners around some focal point be that cultural, corporeal, or racial/ethnic similarities; this requires drawing from personal experience, if not first-hand [then] at least access to, understanding of, or empathy with, those having those experiences."[3] As I noted in chapter 2, I label this *the comical* as a way to differentiate it from mere humor, i.e., that which aims only to get a laugh.

It is not easy to broach such serious topics as racism, misogyny, health care reform, or terrorism in a way that makes people laugh. The challenge is (at least) twofold. First, the comic must distill a complex and potentially divisive issue to its component parts for analysis. This requires deep insight and pedagogical prowess. Second, the comic must find ways to present such *serious* matters in a *humorous* way. In a recent interview, Kondabolu had this to say about his evolution as a comic on this front:

> I think when I got there [the comedy stage] I started to figure out how I could . . . make jokes with hard material and ideas. There were moments where I was didactic and even condescending and that didn't help. I had to actively teach myself that my job was to make people laugh. That's the difference between a guy ranting on stage and a comic. Of course, some people laugh at the face value, which is always a risk when you are using satire.[4]

Note how easy it is for these dual directives to stand in cross-purposes to one another. The impulse towards the comical will be even harder for

2. Kondabolu, *Waiting for 2042*. Note that 2042 is the year that Caucasians are projected to cease being the majority race in America.

3. Krefting, *All Joking Aside*, 5.

4. Kondabolu in Kurian, "Comedian and Filmmaker Hari Kondabolu."

preachers, who must add yet a third imperative to their discourse, *viz.,* that of proclaiming the gospel.

Krefting emphasizes that charged humor is not just about illuminating social justice issues and spurring audience members to action, nor is it simply about attacking individuals and institutions that stand in the way of social justice. Charged humor forges a community out of difference and validates identities among the culturally and legally disenfranchised.[5] Krefting aligns herself most closely with the affect theory of laughter. At its core, charged humor is most concerned with reforming the ways in which audience members think and feel about a particular group of people or a particular sociopolitical issue. Charged comics might employ a number of techniques and comedic styles (e.g., satire, incongruity, sarcasm, play), but at the forefront of their art is a concern for speaking in ways that affirm the inherent worth of all people. Charged humor aims at enacting *cultural citizenship*, which explores how to motivate people to believe and behave in more inclusive and life-affirming ways.[6] Hence, the target of charged humor is simultaneously epistemological (how we think about certain types of people), psychological (how we feel about certain types of people), and sociopolitical (how we structure our society in ways that add value or devalue certain types of people). For instance, in one of Kondabolu's early stand-up bits, he used to read the US citizenship application on stage. He notes that much of it contains arcane facts that few natural born American citizens even know. Such patient exegesis reveals the inequities inherent in American democracy. He says, "For people who don't know, it's like this is what immigrants have to go through to gain status in this country, and it's absurd and something we take for granted as American citizens."[7]

RIDICULE WITHOUT CONTEMPT

As we saw in the last chapter, much of the worry over humor in homiletics emerges from a distaste for ridicule. This, of course, is not unique to Christian theology but pervades the annals of Western thought. Recall that a primary feature of critiques against humor up until the eighteenth century coincided with the superiority theory of humor. It is wrong to derive personal pleasure at another person's expense. There are ethical as well as sociopolitical reasons for this dominant perspective: it is just not worth it

5. Krefting, *All Joking Aside*, 25.

6. On cultural citizenship see Flores and Benmayor, eds., *Latino Cultural Citizenship*, 1–37.

7. Kondabolu, "For Comic Hari Kondabolu, Explaining the Joke IS the Joke."

for our moral well-being or our societies for us to make fun of other people to boost our own fragile egos or bolster the prominence of our group. Kondabolu is a contemporary stand-up comic who takes this critique seriously. In one interview he observes, "There's a lot of things that people find funny that are really just bullying. When people get bullied, there are people that laugh. And I think that is a lot of comedy."[8]

Stand-up that is nothing more than a vehicle to laughter—i.e., comedy with no agenda to politicize issues, unite audience members, or edify the culturally disaffected—is hard enough. But to do so without stooping to ridicule is harder. It's very easy in humor that is socially conscious to engage in ad hominem, but Kondabolu recognizes that individuals operate out of worldviews that precede and predetermine their words and actions. For instance, while Kondabolu makes no efforts to hide his disdain for Donald Trump, the focus of his critique extends beyond Trump. He is concerned about the sociopolitical conditions of possibility whereby Trump could be elected president.[9] This is comedy of a higher order than jibes at the foolishness and bigotry of an individual person.

Race and racism feature prominently in Hari Kondabolu's stand-up. In one of his shows, he was asked by a guy in the audience where he is from. Unsatisfied with Kondabolu's answer that he is from Queens, New York, the man asked where Kondabolu is *really* from, which is code for "why are you not white?" Kondabolu says he was offended that he should be judged by the color of his skin, when his defining trait is not the color but the smoothness of his skin.[10] Kondabolu proceeds to describe his skincare regime in great detail, thereby highlighting the arbitrariness that skin color is a sufficient identity marker.

Preachers can learn a lot from Kondabolu on how to critique systems that devalue certain people according to arbitrary identity markers. Parody is one such rhetorical strategy Kondabolu employs. As we see in the bit about his skincare regime, Kondabolu parodies a centuries-old criterion for racializing people. Kondabolu could have challenged this criterion directly. Instead, he subverts the foundation upon which his taunter bases his racist question through a detailed discussion of his beauty regimen. Parody is a helpful rhetorical strategy for those on the underside of the ascendant power differential. Writing on the comedic agility employed against Hitler during World War II, for instance, Brandon Webb contends that confronting Nazism required "a flexible mode of representation that abandoned the

8. Kondabolu in Sterling, "Feministing Five."

9. Kondabolu, *Warn Your Relatives.*

10. Kondabolu, *John Oliver's New York Stand-Up Show.*

pretense of 'objectivity' and 'truth' for the sly subversion of slapstick and satire" and that because parody disarms, it carries the potential to be more subversive than realism.[11] I see a similar approach in Kondabolu's work.

COLONIZING COMEDY

As an Indian and an American, Kondabolu has a troubled relationship with colonialism. He is at once a subject of colonial rule ethnically, and a more or less passive participant in colonial rule nationally. In one particular routine called "My English Relationship," Kondabolu describes a relationship he had with an English woman. The bit seems to follow a standard trope in stand-up comedy wherein the comic bemoans a failed relationship. He says at the start that everything started great, however as the relationship developed over several months, he grew suspicious of the woman's behavior. He explains, "And then, four months in, she was over at my place four nights a week and I noticed she was telling me what to do, like when to wake up and when to sleep and what to eat." The bit continues along these lines until it reaches its dénouement when Kondabolu realizes "that's when I knew this wasn't love. This English woman was trying to colonize me . . . and of course I did what I was trained to do in such situations. Nothing." Having undercut the traditional failed relationship shtick, Kondabolu proceeds to expound upon the "colonialism" of this dating relationship. Eventually she broke up with him and took lots of things with her (e.g., food, art, self-esteem). And she also left some things behind ("some clothes, and some books . . . and of course an extensive railway system").

A common aspect of Kondabolu's comedic style is to interrupt the flow of the standard setup-punch line structure to parse or offer hermeneutical insight that some of his audience members might miss. He interjects a moment of self-reflexivity into his "My English Relationship" bit, breaking the rhythmic flow of the narrative. "So, uh . . . for the non-South Asians in the audience who didn't understand why there was applause. The British built a really extensive railway system throughout India before they left—and it wasn't so much for transportation for the Indian people . . . it was because it's really hard, of course, to plunder on foot."[12] In defiance of conventional stand-up wisdom, that explaining the joke kills the joke, Kondabolu's discursive footnote about the history of British colonialism in India earns him even more laughs than the punch line itself.

---

11. Webb, "'Hitler Must be Laughed At!,'" 763.

12. Kondabolu, "My English Relationship."

Another way Kondabolu disrupts colonizing ways of thinking is through sarcasm. Sarcasm exploits the tension between discursive denotation and connotation. As such, language is able to work simultaneously on two registers. On one level, his language conveys meaning in a literal sense. This is often labeled *plain speech*. On another level, his words are figurative. Kondabolu begins one bit by asserting that hate crimes are the original terrorism in America. This leads him to discuss the absurdity that millions of dollars are given every year to places very unlikely to face a terrorist threat, rural places like Kansas. His setup goes like this: "The last time Kansas had to deal with terrorism was when a house fell on that witch." Kondabolu then shares that this joke was fact-checked by an audience member once, who informed him that that didn't happen in Kansas, it happened in Oz. The fact-checker goes on to challenge him about terrorism in Kansas, noting that there was a terrorist attack in Overland, Kansas. Hari responds, "No. That is not terrorism, okay? Cause a white dude did the shooting. That's mental health issues. That's completely different. . . . As opposed to a suicide bomber who completely has their shit together."[13] Kondabolu's sarcasm exposes an incongruity emerging from the rhetoric about terrorism in America. In so doing, he helps us to question the logic driving this rhetoric.

TAKEAWAYS FOR STAND-UP PREACHING

Kondabolu has much to offer stand-up preachers, those who approach the comical in and through their preaching. For starters, he showcases a way to embrace one's ethnic identity without resorting to minstrelsy. Kimberly P. Johnson rightly argues that preaching becomes perverted when it belittles, demeans, or oppresses any person or group of people.[14] Few would disagree with her. But the challenge of avoiding such perversion arises when ridicule seems like such a simpler route. Kondabolu refuses, in his mature comedy, to submit marginalized communities to further harm by making fun of their cultures or practices. At the same time, Kondabolu does not approach sociopolitical issues from an objective or neutral position *à la* Bill Cosby or Jerry Seinfeld. To be a Brown man in twenty-first-century America is to always already have a vested interest in making society more equitable and just. This work is not only for people of color. As Andrew Wymer argues, anti-racist preaching is simultaneously anti-cultural preaching inasmuch as white culture continues to dominate. The goal of such preaching

13. Kondabolu, *Warn Your Relatives*.

14. Johnson, *Womanist Preacher*, 5.

is to "eventually render white culture less dangerous to those who are not deemed white."[15]

There is a pedagogical impulse driving Kondabolu's comedy that resonates with the work of Richard Voelz. Arguing for preachers to become critical pedagogues and public intellectuals, Voelz writes, "The preacher-as-teacher seeks to expose, examine, and help listeners assess the social, economic, political, and theological relationships that undergird daily life."[16] Exposition is a necessary first step in this direction. Likewise, Kondabolu does not assume that everyone in the audience will have the same knowledge base he has. He explains that when he engages in "high-end colonialism material," for instance, he feels that exposition is in order. He says,

> I like explaining the references. I feel like, I don't know, maybe again it's me being over-educated, but I do like that. I feel like I'm a cool professor. Maybe I'm not because I just called myself that, but like there's something about OK, maybe I can, you know, because I find these things funny, and I have to find a way for you to think they're funny, and if I have to explain it so you get what I'm talking about and then laugh at the thing I think is funny, then so be it. It might take an extra minute, it might mean that our attention spans have to go back to 1987, but I think it's possible for us to get through a minute setup to get to something else.[17]

Note how even in this NPR interview, Kondabolu presents us with a bit of his comical persona. Analogically, a dad who knows he's telling dad jokes to his kids and makes it clear in the telling that he wants them to know that he knows it's a dad joke, can be endearing. Kondabolu leans into his highbrow, issue-oriented identity, but he finds a way to render that identity on stage in a way that feels engaging and funny.

A further takeaway for stand-up preaching is how Kondabolu models a way to go about what comedy scholar Nicholas Holm labels *reasonable dissent*.[18] By this, Holm bears witness to a tension at the heart of contemporary liberal democracies that constrain our freedom through particular ways of thinking and speaking (i.e., *reasonable* discourse), while expecting us at the same time to exercise our freedom vis-à-vis the very freedom that we are denied. In other words, we are expected to be both reasonable and dissenting. Kondabolu models a way to do this through humor. He helps us to see

15. Wymer, "White Culture, Anti-Cultural Preaching, and Cultural Suicide," 51.

16. Voelz, *Preaching to Teach*, 9.

17. Kondabolu, "For Comic Hari Kondabolu, Explaining the Joke IS the Joke."

18. Holm, *Humour as Politics*, 29–30.

just how unreasonable our so-called reasonable societies are—especially for those who are marginalized and oppressed. By naming the incongruities between the foundational logic of American democracy and the foundational structures that contradict that logic, Kondabolu enables us not only to laugh at the world but to imagine ways to make it a better place for all.

3

Language Games

Standing Up with Words and Forms

A good joke owes as much to its form as to its thought, if not more. The form
may not attract attention to itself as a form, though in a joke it often does.
Yet the joke depends on both its idea and its form, on both together and not
on either of them alone.[1]

—H. GRADY DAVIS

Life doesn't have punchlines.[2]

—BILLY CONNOLLY

Gospel proclamation is impossible without language. The very possibility of *good news* presupposes that we can communicate events and experiences to others. Here I am speaking of language at the most general level of employing signs to signify meanings from one person to another.[3] From the original Gospel writers to preachers today, the task of bearing

1. Davis, *Design for Preaching*, 3–4.
2. Connolly, *Too Old to Die Young*.
3. Following the groundbreaking work of Donyelle McCray, I do not restrict signs to verbal language. See McCray, "On Shrieking the Truth," and "Sweating, Spitting, and Cursing," on the signifying capacities of the body beyond formal language.

witness to God's work among us requires some form of signification. In this chapter we'll be taking a closer look at the varied and nuanced ways stand-up comedians employ language(s) to hilarious and/or cringeworthy effect. Even for "serious" matters, stand-up comedians treat language as a game, a playground for interrogating our assumptions and leading us to consider the world differently. Preachers could learn much from these artists because they open us to different ways of engaging the world around us.

Both stand-up and preaching are types of discourse. They each conform to their respective linguistic conditions and conventions that make them identifiable as such. A different way to think about this is that stand-up and preaching are *systems* of communication that tether speakers and hearers to the comical and the gospel. And, as we have already observed, some comics and preachers blur the borders between the comical and the gospel.[4] These linguistic systems guide our listening in particular ways. The formal structures of stand-up and preaching make each of these modes of discourse incredibly nimble and resilient: everything and everyone are fair game for comedic or homiletical appropriation through these overlapping forms of discourse.

In the last chapter we looked at rhetorical arguments for employing humor in the pulpit. The idea there is that employing jokes, humorous anecdotes, and comical asides make what we are trying to say more interesting and enjoyable. We also saw theologians making a case for homiletical humor out of a profound sense of God's redemptive and liberative work among us—from a comical worldview. Here we will be attending less to why one might employ the humorous or the comical in preaching than how doing so might support our homiletical efforts.

There are deeply theological reasons for attending to the performative capacities of language. Language is the means by which preachers navigate what Mary Catherine Hilkert identifies as a "radical impasse" at the core of human experience, which can lead to hope or despair.[5] John McClure argues that preachers display a communicative competence than can foster deeper ways of understanding. Preachers are potentially more attentive to how language addresses and interpolates its users. In McClure's words,

> They are aware that words and utterances partake of stylizations and intertextual voices and allusions that make them instantiations of conversations and ideologies that precede them and anticipate future response. They know that language that might seem to be immediately and straightforwardly transparent is

4. On the gospel as comedy see Buechner, *Telling the Truth.*
5. Hilkert, *Naming Grace,* 119.

actually part of a larger conversation of ideological struggle about meaning.[6]

Drawing McClure's insights into our current conversation, a theological and cultural ideology always already impacts how preachers will use language and to what ends. Hence, a preacher open to learning from how stand-up comedians use language does so by perceiving an overlapping ideology undergirding certain forms of comedy and certain forms of preaching. Such a preacher recognizes that humorous and comical discourse can foster community through shared laughter. She has likely also recognized a congruency between the comic's and preacher's efforts at facilitating *metanoia*, helping audiences to see the world and others beyond the epistemological and affective constraints that narrow our ways of seeing the world and impede our fellowship with others across modalities of difference.

BA-DUM-BUM AND BEYOND: A BRIEF HISTORY OF AMERICAN STAND-UP

Before we may attend to the use of language(s) in stand-up we need to possess a basic understanding of stand-up's history. I focus here largely on the history of stand-up in America, but one could track similar developments in other contexts.[7] Furthermore, in our globalized contexts and with streaming services like Netflix and HBO Max promulgating content worldwide, the borders between stand-up blurs between contexts and across cultures.

In a recent assessment of the state of the field of humor studies, Bruce Michelson decries humor research that "remains in its decaying orbit around a clutch of doubtful assumptions, chief among them that contrived verbal jokes are the fundamental particles of comic discourse, floating like hydrogen atoms in a near-vacuum of Newtonian entropy, to be isolated and decoded on the basis of perceived semantic incongruity."[8] Michelson highlights not only an outmoded approach taken by some scholars but also a more general assumption that comedy is only about telling jokes. Most stand-up comedians today don't tell a lot of jokes per se. What they do is share their ideas with the audience. These ideas and observations are filtered through the persona of the comic, rendering their words humorous and/ or comical. British comedy coach and actor Logan Murray names the differences from traditional to contemporary stand-up where the comedian

---

6. McClure, *Speaking Together and with God*, 10.

7. E.g., Sunday and Filani, "Playing with Culture"; and Black, "Laughing to Death."

8. Michelson, "Year's Work in American Humor Studies, 2015," 47.

"talks to" an audience, unlike the funny uncle who "talks at" them. Murray writes, "The comic allows free rein to some of the more extreme aspects of his or her personality and hopes that this 'voice' will generate funny ideas."[9] Almost invariably, comics assume a clear perspective on their subject matter, and it is this attitude as much as the bits themselves that generate laughter. En route to crafting effective sermonic punch lines it is helpful to understand how stand-up has changed over the decades.

For the first half of the twentieth century, stand-up comedians performed their acts without referencing their personal lives onstage. From the vaudeville comedians at the start of the century, to the emergence of hole-in-the-wall clubs and family-friendly resorts in the Catskills (a.k.a. the "Borscht Belt") and Black owned and operated comedy clubs in the South (a.k.a. the "Chitlin Circuit"), the comedy stage was a "view from nowhere," to borrow Thomas Nagel's helpful analytic for investigating the social location of knowledge.[10] In the 1950s there were a handful of comics such as Morey Amsterdam and Nipsey Russell who devised their own material, but even these comics conformed to a generic point of view, and without a stamp of personalization, jokes became fodder for pillaging. Many stand-up comics in those days drew their material from the popular joke books of Billy Glason, James Madison, Joe Miller, and Robert Orben, which offered "1001 sure-fire gags for any occasion."[11]

In his history of comedy in America, Kliph Nesteroff describes a major perspectival shift in stand-up that took place during the mid-1950s. This was a transition from the generic to the personal points of view. Prior to this shift, comedy was always about some elusive guy:

> "A guy walks into a bar . . ."
> "Did you hear about the fella who . . ."

Following the acts promulgated by coffeehouse comedians such as Lenny Bruce, Mort Sahl, Jonathan Winters, Jackie "Moms" Mabley, and Dick Gregory, stand-up could no longer hold a joke's protagonist at arm's length. The lines blurred between the stand-up comedian as an objective narrator addressing generic topics and as a *subject* of a joke with a personal stake in its matters of sociopolitical significance. The joke was no longer about some nebulous "fella" who walks into a bar. Now a bit began by declaration: "*I*

---

9. Murray, *Be a Great Stand-Up*, Kindle ed., loc. 862.

10. Nagel, *View from Nowhere*, 1–12.

11. Nesteroff, *Comedians*, 148.

walked into a bar." This new artistic sensibility constituted a massive departure from tradition.[12]

This major shift took place in American stand-up comedy when Mort Sahl took the stage in San Francisco's "the hungry i" in 1953. Saul's casual dress and conversational style signaled a sharp break from the traditional tuxedoed nightclub comedian. As Michael Daube puts it,

> Sahl consciously evoked the guise of a young Intellectual, still dressing as he had when studying city management and traffic engineering at the University of Southern California. The conspicuous newspaper tucked under his arm indicated an intent to occupy the audience with news of the day, and he embraced a colloquial tone resuited to that of a family seated around the kitchen table than that of a professional entertainer and his middle-class audience. Sahl substituted jokes about current events and ostensibly private experiences for the then standard target of mothers-in-law. Rather than interacting with other professionals on-stage, Sahl directly addresses the audience, which serves as the silent partner in a comic dialogue. This allows for a closer relationship between entertainer and audience, predicated on a conversation in the present, and topical enough to include events of the moment.[13]

Of particular note for preachers is this movement toward fostering a deeper sense of intimacy between the comic and her audience, which I discuss in much greater depth in chapter 5 below.

Sahl took credit for this Copernican shift in stand-up, arguing for a new discursive context of "complete freedom" in which the "whole climate has been changed."[14] The new form of stand-up emerging in the late fifties and early sixties came from the comic's purported honesty and from his original thought. Old comedians continued to perform in the old ways in major supper clubs and along the Vegas strip, but there was now a new scene in Greenwich Village venues, San Francisco, and Chicago, that attracted a different kind of crowd who valued the comic's opinions on political issues and who weren't as averse to profanity and taboo topics.[15]

Around the same time Sahl was deformalizing stand-up, a young Jewish comic named Lenny Bruce pushed the intimacy of stand-up in a

12. This transition in stand-up is rendered dramatically in season 1 of *The Marvelous Mrs. Maisel*.

13. Daube, "Laughter in Revolt," 6–7.

14. Nesteroff, *Comedians*, 152.

15. Nesteroff, *Comedians*, 152.

much more radical direction. Bruce's profane truths emerged from our most sacred lies about America, especially its connection with Christianity and whiteness. Even if Sahl was the first in this new wave of stand-up, Bruce was the most controversial. It is one thing to let an audience into your mind as a comic; it is another thing when they find your comical mind offensive. Bruce was the first bona fide shock comic in America. Nothing was out of bounds, and his comedy sets whiplashed the audience from critiques of Christianity to political impersonations to intimate discussions about masturbation.[16]

It is difficult to emphasize enough Bruce's impact on stand-up in America. Both Richard Pryor and George Carlin cite Bruce as their inspiration. Carlin says that after hearing his first Lenny Bruce album, "[i]t let me know there was a place to go—to reach for—in terms of honesty of self-expression. The 1950s was when comedy changed forever for the better. . . . I heard my first Lenny Bruce and my *life* changed."[17] Waxing nostalgic about the comedy of Bruce, journalist Richard Zoglin has this to say:

> He broke down the old set up-punch line structure of stand-up comedy. He held nothing back. Everything got tossed in the performance Mixmaster: social criticism, political commentary, pop-culture satire, snatches of autobiography, sexual confessions, personal gripes, public hectoring, today's headlines, yesterday's trip to the laundry. All of it was out there on stage, raw and unfiltered—everything that he knew, thought, hated, remembered, or could dream up.[18]

This is not to suggest that Bruce never told any jokes; rather, he sprinkled his jokes throughout his sets, with the emphasis less on the power of the joke itself than the worldview it revealed through its performance.

Along with the less formal, more intimate, and more vulgar way of addressing audiences, stand-up comics increasingly forefronted how their lived experiences shaped their take on the world. This was a major feature of Richard Pryor's comedy. Pryor grew up in the years of segregation and began doing comedy in the early 1960s, at the height of the civil rights protests. He wasn't the first crossover Black comedian. Dick Gregory and Redd Foxx had already broken through in white nightclubs. Unlike Bill Cosby, who mostly avoided direct commentary on racial inequality in America, Gregory and Pryor addressed it straight on. Pryor was only three years younger than Cosby, but he seemed of another generation. He didn't ignore race, as Cosby did, or approach it as an abstract sociopolitical issue to be analyzed

---

16. For examples of Bruce's comedy, see Cotkin, *Feast of Excess*, 145–55.

17. Nesteroff, *Comedians*, 150.

18. Zoglin, *Comedy at the Edge*, 12–13.

like Gregory did. Pryor treated white supremacy and the racist structures it supported as unavoidable features of what made him who he was. As Zoglin reports, "He presented a slice of the African American experience that had rarely, if ever, been seen by mainstream white audiences—the hustlers, pimps, junkies, winos, and street preachers he had grown up with—and did it in a way that rang true for black audiences yet was so piercingly human that whites didn't feel excluded."[19]

In the late 1960s, Pryor introduced a new style of stand-up. "Almost single-handedly," wrote James Alan McPherson in the *New York Times Magazine*, "he is creating a new style of American comedy . . . which must be observed and heard at the same time in order to be completely understood and appreciated."[20] Rather than telling jokes, Pryor unfurled long, meandering narratives in which he portrayed the streetwise, earthy dignity and survival skills of characters of the African American underclass. For instance, Pryor describes learning about sex by peeking through keyholes to watch prostitutes at work.[21] Like Jackie "Moms" Mabley, Pryor provided social commentary on the hypocrisies and incongruences that characterize racist thinking.

Pryor and Mabley were not the only comics who fused their lived experiences with their stand-up performances. In her critical analysis of the public presence and comedic performance of Lily Tomlin and her life partner Jane Wagner, Jennifer Reed makes an incisive observation about how the new era of stand-up from the early seventies onward offered deeper nuance for articulating lived experience. "Both humor and queerness depend on a relationship to liminality," Reed notes.[22] In other words, queerness and humor occupy a space between categories and beyond normative constraints. Queerness, for Reed, is "the foregrounding of the insufficiency of heterosexuality to explain the whole world of human relating."[23] Around the same time as Tomlin, Steve Martin was experimenting with new modes of comedic expression. He describes a revolution that took place in his comic direction that moves a step further from the traditional setup-punch line format for stand-up: As his comedic persona emerged, Martin asked himself,

---

19. Zoglin, *Comedy at the Edge*, 43.

20. Cited in Zoglin, *Comedy at the Edge*, 52. "One reason it seemed new is that Pryor had stripped his stand-up comedy almost entirely of jokes." Zoglin, *Comedy at the Edge*, 52–53.

21. Pryor, *Pryor Convictions*, 35.

22. Reed, *Queer Cultural Work of Lily Tomlin and Jane Wagner*, 21.

23. Reed, *Queer Cultural Work of Lily Tomlin and Jane Wagner*, 57.

What if there were no punch lines? What if there were no in-
dicators? What if I created tension and never released it? What
if I headed for a climax, but all I delivered was an anticlimax?
What would the audience do with all that tension? Theoretically
it would have to come out sometime. But if I kept denying them
the formality of a punch line, the audience would eventually
pick their own place to laugh, essentially out of desperation.
This type of laugh seemed stronger to me, as they would be
laughing at something *they chose*, rather than being told exactly
when to laugh.[24]

Fast-forward a few decades and we have the strange new world of alternative comedy made popular by Kathy Griffin, Tenacious D, David Cross,
and Janeane Garofalo. Margaret Cho labels Garofalo the inventor of alternative comedy.[25] There is much to support this, as Garofalo co-created "Eating
It," an alternative comedy cabaret at the now-defunct Luna Lounge in New
York's lower east side. The show ran from 1995 to 2005 and featured such
megastars as Louis C.K., Jim Norton, Rosanne Barr, Patton Oswalt, Marc
Maron, Dave Chappelle, and Sarah Silverman.[26] Cho juxtaposes alternative comedy with observational comedy *à la* Bill Cosby and Jerry Seinfeld,
which subordinates the identity of the comic to the subject matter under
discussion. By contrast, alternative comedy elevates the identity of the joke-
teller and her unique point of view and take on the world. Unlike traditional
contemporary stand-up that boomed in the 1980s, and which emphasizes
the craft of joke-telling, alternative comedy was much more focused on the
comic's persona and authenticity.

Garofalo emphasizes that *alternative* comedy originally referred less to
a deviation in style than in venue.[27] As comedy clubs began closing after the
comedy boom of the eighties lost steam, comics began performing in alternative venues to the traditional comedy club setting. One of the great advan-
tages of the waning interest in comedy clubs was how it created spaces for
comics who deviated from the classic (i.e., white, straight, male) paradigm.

24. Martin, *Born Standing Up*, 111.

25. Note that the label "alternative" for American stand-up comedy differs somewhat from the British version of alternative comedy, which blossomed a decade earlier.
British comedian Tony Allen is credited with coining the term and it became the *de jure*
style of London's Comedy Store in the early eighties. British alternative comedy marked
a style of stand-up that was neither racist nor sexist but free-form, intellectually rigor-
ous, and anarchic. The style is associated with such comics as Jo Brand, Eddie Izzard,
Jimmy Carr, and Stewart Lee. See Lee, *How I Escaped My Certain Fate*, 1–40, for an in-
depth discussion of his journey in and through the alternative comedy scene in the UK.

26. See St. John, "Seinfeld It Ain't."

27. Garofalo interview in Kohen, *We Killed*, 215.

With the comedy club gatekeepers out of the way, new voices emerged on the comedy scene. Suddenly, female comics, LGBTQIA comics, and comics of varying ethnicities were granted a turn at the mic. Because alternative comedy stressed the identity of the performer, stand-up comics were free to embrace their intersectional particularities rather than diminish them.

This history of stand-up comedy in America involves a cast of characters and comedic styles far too broad and complex for such a general introduction as this. The key things to bear in mind as we move forward are that contemporary stand-up is made up of bits, which may or may not include jokes, and that this more expansive mode of discourse requires the comic to take a subjective position with regard to their comedy. Accordingly, some comedians explicitly championed the idea of truth. In a 2004 newspaper article, Richard Pryor was asked whether it's more important for comics to be truthful or to make people laugh. "Truthful, always truthful," he replied, "And funny will come."[28] Shelley Berman—a shining exemplar from the generation that established the ideal of authenticity in stand-up—offers a similar view to that of Pryor, but he identifies truth in relation to the comic themself: "Just as the person onstage is rarely exactly the same as the person offstage, in most cases the truth comedians tell flows easily into fiction."[29]

British stand-up comic and comedy scholar Oliver Double writes that the central idea of contemporary stand-up is that it's about telling the truth.[30] He continues, "Truth is a vital concept in most modern stand-up comedy because of the idea that it is about authentic self-expression. The boundary between offstage and onstage is blurred, and in many cases, the audience believes that the person they see onstage is more or less the same as the person they might meet offstage."[31] The truths told by stand-up comics today are *subjective* truths; in fact, they call into question the very possibility of differentiating between truth's subjectivity and objectivity.

LANGUAGE MATTERS

Contemporary stand-up comics employ language in particular ways. For ease of classification, we can think of a comedy set as being made up of *bits*. A homiletical corollary to a bit is a move.[32] Such incremental units

28. Logan, "Be Truthful—And Funny Will Come."

29. Nachman, *Seriously Funny*, 301.

30. Double, *Getting the Joke*, 160.

31. Double, *Getting the Joke*, 160.

32. See Buttrick, *Homiletic*, 23–36, for a compelling argument for sermonic moves over points.

stand apart from the set through a modicum of thematic consistency. As with effective sermons, a bit or move ought to relate to the whole in some meaningful way. There are essentially three types of stand-up bits: jokes, narrative anecdotes, and verbal asides or rants. A comedic bit renders a comic's outlook on the world. It is through bits that comic personas emerge. Not only do forms of comedic language render a comic's identity, they also engender a certain kind of relationship between the comic and her audience. This relationship is everything. As one commentator puts it, when folks who you don't know or share a sense of humor with try doing a bit on you, it feels like a stranger trying to kiss you.[33]

Comedy comes in many different forms. From slapstick to lyric, from dramatic to visual, comedy often emerges in culturally specific contexts. Much of comedy's *raison d'être* is entertainment, but as long as there has been comedy there have been those who have employed it to address serious sociopolitical issues—both within and beyond a humorous frame.[34] The construct of "social change" in the context of stand-up comedy is far from monolithic; instead, it exists along a continuum that includes such aims as 1) consciousness raising by building public awareness; 2) affective influence by shaping attitudes and behaviors; and 3) direct action by shifting social norms and practices, encouraging public engagement, and influencing policy.[35] Let's take a closer look at how bits employ language to particular ends.

From Setup to Punch Line and Beyond

Before his first appearance on Comedy Central's *The Daily Show with Jon Stewart*, Trevor Noah already had a huge international following. As a biracial man from South Africa, Noah knew well what it meant to live in a country riddled with ideological tensions. He was aware of the dissonance emerging for citizens of a country claiming to embrace principles of democracy and freedom, even as it remained plagued by racial apartheid and state-sanctioned violence against people of color. The comical thrust of Noah's comedy exploits the tensions hardwired into American consciousness to such a degree that we hardly even notice how they shape our beliefs. The comical, as I discussed in chapter 1, gives rise to thought in a humorous

33. Rodrigues, "Thinkpiece About Bits."

34. I use humor, here, as a generic umbrella term intending to elicit laughter. See Attardo, *Linguistics of Humor,* for a thoughtful reflection on the challenge of using terms and taxonomies across fields of study such as philosophy, literary criticism, rhetoric, psychology, linguistics, and so on.

35. Chatoo and Feldman, *Comedian and an Activist Walk into A Bar,* 5.

way. It forces us to see the world with fresh eyes. It achieves this by making us laugh *and* think. Noah enacts the comical brilliantly.

Noah's first joke ever on *The Daily Show* presented stand-up's setup-punch line structure in miniature. "I just flew in," Noah jokes, "and boy are my arms tired."[36] The setup to the joke is situational. Noah asserts that he has just flown in to New York from South Africa. This is a proper setup because it invites the audience to expect some anecdote to follow. The setup, in other words, must invite participation. When Noah tells us he just flew in from South Africa, our immediate follow-up question is to wonder what happened on the flight.

Then comes the punch line: ". . . and boy are my arms tired." The punch line to the joke plays off the polysemic quality of the verbal infinitive "to fly." Noah sets us up by leading us to assume that his assertion that he just flew in involves riding on an airplane. Since, of course, humans cannot fly the way birds and bats can, there is no indication in the setup to alert us to pay attention to the transitive versus intransitive properties of the verb. Because the joke hinges on semantic incongruity, it need not be specific to the individual jokester. Any person from any racial, ethnic, gender, or sexual demographic could tell this joke because it is utterly generic. All one requires to "get" this joke is a knowledge of the dual meaning of the English verb "to fly."

Jon Stewart laughs politely at Noah's throwaway joke, calling it "an oldie but a goodie!" But what Noah says next is much more in line with the structure of contemporary stand-up. Noah's supposed punch line about his arms being tired was actually still part of the setup. Following a beat, Noah presents his real punch line: "No seriously. I've been holding my arms like this since I got here!" (He raises his arms in the "Hands up, don't shoot" surrender pose.) Noah's jabs continue, including confessions that he is more afraid of the police in New York than in Johannesburg and his brief experiences in the US have made him "a little nostalgic for the old days back home." Noah's sharp-witted comparison between US race relations and South Africa's apartheid state speaks jarringly to the persistent reality of racial oppression in America. His punch line strikes a blow to the post-racial narratives that downplay racial injustice. The bit insists that the scourge of racism and its concomitant threat of violence for people of color persists in countless daily manifestations, such as gross wealth inequalities and mass incarceration. As communication and comedy scholar Jonathan Rossing observes, satirical jabs such as Noah's may not dismantle entrenched

36. Noah, "Spot the Africa."

systems of racism; however, "such comedic discourses play a vital role in the struggle against hegemonic racism."[37]

How to Do Things with Jokes

Even as the old school, ba-dum-dum structure features less prominently in contemporary stand-up than it did in the first half of the twentieth century, this does not mean that contemporary comics are done with jokes. The vast majority of contemporary comics move seamlessly between jokes, anecdotes, and asides. But since jokes are what most of us think of when we think about stand-up, it can be helpful to get a handle on how different types of jokes work in different ways.

Sigmund Freud loved jokes.[38] He dedicated an entire book to the topic. Here he draws a fundamental distinction between jokes that employ wordplay and those that employ conceptual play. Freud classified two classes of jokes (*der Witz*): *der Klangwitz* (the joke-sound) and *der Gedankenwitz* (the conceptual joke). The former plays with either homophony or linguistic assonance to produce humor. Freud's "famillionaire" joke is an example of the first type. Here the one-word joke plays off the partial homophony of two words: "familiar" and "millionaire."[39] Here's a more complex example Freud offers of *Klangwitz*:

> A young man who had hitherto led a gay life abroad paid a call, after a considerable absence, on a friend living here. The latter was surprised to see an *Ehering* [wedding-ring] on his visitor's hand. "What?" he explained, "are you married?" "Yes," was the reply, "*Trauring* but true."[40]

As with most sound jokes, much is lost in translation; but with a little help we can still discern what Freud is talking about. In German, the word *Ehering* is a wedding ring. There is also a German expression, *Traurig aber wahr*. This is a colloquialism meaning "sad, but true." Freud removes the word *Ehering* from its matrimonial context by combining it with the adjective *traurig*, which means "sad." In other words, by playing off the phonic similarities between *Trauring* and *traurig*, Freud makes a joke about the sadness of being married. The joke I shared in chapter 2 about how one cannot starve in

---

37. Rossing, "Emancipatory Racial Humor," 615.

38. See Billig, *Laughter and Ridicule*, 139–72, for an in-depth analysis of Freud's theory of humor.

39. Freud, *Jokes and Their Relation to the Unconscious*, 52.

40. Freud, *Jokes and Their Relation to the Unconscious*, 20.

the desert because of the sand which is there/sandwiches there provides an English example of *Klangwitz*.

If the *Klangwitz* rests upon the phonic paradigm of homophony, the *Gendankenwitz* rests upon the semantic paradigm. This is the conceptual joke, which plays less at the level of sound than at the level of logic. To illustrate, Freud tells a joke about salmon mayonnaise (a fancy dish in his Austrian context):

> An impoverished individual borrowed 25 florins from a prosperous acquaintance, with many asseverations of his necessitous circumstances. The very same day his benefactor met him again in a restaurant with a plate of salmon mayonnaise in front of him. The benefactor reproached him: "What? You borrow money from me and then you order yourself salmon mayonnaise? Is *that* what you've used my money for?" "I don't understand you," replied the object of attack; "if I haven't any money I *can't* eat salmon mayonnaise, and if I have some money I *mustn't* eat salmon mayonnaise. Well, then, when *am* I to eat salmon mayonnaise?"[41]

Let's break down this joke like a fraction. This joke conceals its setup behind a syntactic similarity between the two propositions, each of which are logically sound. The first proposition operates at the level of fact, while the second operates at the level of value.

1. Proposition 1: *If a person needs to borrow money, they are not in a position to indulge in fancy food* (literally; they cannot afford it).

2. Proposition 2: *If a person needs to borrow money, they are not in a position to indulge in fancy food* (ethically; they ought not buy it).

The humor of the joke emerges from the tension between the financial state of the poor person and the value judgment of the wealthy person. Both interlocutors present sound logic, but the punch line emerging from the impoverished individual creates a logical absurdity at the semantic level of meaning making: *If a person without money cannot afford salmon mayonnaise, and if a person who has had to borrow money ought not spend money on salmon mayonnaise, then a poor person will never be in a state sufficient to buy salmon mayonnaise.* The structure of the joke conceals a financial state implied by the wealthy benefactor: *Only those who already have the money to enjoy extravagant meals ought to enjoy extravagant meals.*

---

41. Freud, *Jokes and Their Relation to the Unconscious*, 56.

Philosopher Ted Cohen offers us another important analytic for thinking about jokes. He differentiates between a *conditional joke* and a *pure joke*.
A conditional joke is one that can work only with certain audiences and
is typically meant only for those audiences. With a conditional joke the
audience must supply something in order either to "get" the joke or to be
amused by it. That something is the condition on which the success of the
joke depends. A pure joke would be universal, one that reaches everyone
regardless of their cultural particularities or a priori knowledge. A pure joke
presupposes nothing from the audience. Having made this distinction between conditional and pure jokes, Cohen says that there is no such thing as
a *pure* joke. He notes that it is a kind of ideal, but it doesn't exist. At the very
least, the audience will have to understand the language of the joke, and
probably much more. But even if all jokes are conditional, it is still useful to
know just how strongly conditional a particular joke is, and just what kind
of condition is presupposed.[42]

So, Cohen focuses his analysis on conditional jokes, which he further
subdivides into *conditional hermetic* jokes and *conditional affective* jokes.
A hermetic joke is one that requires an audience to have some substantive
knowledge of their topics. Consider this joke:

> Q: *According to Freud, what comes between fear and sex?*
> A: *Fünf.*

Do you get it? It's okay if you didn't. This joke requires prior knowledge of
Freud's psychological theories, of which fear and sex play a major part. But
it also requires that you know German—or at least your German numbers
(*Ein, zwie, drie, fier, fünf, sex* . . .). This is an example of *Klangwitz*, to use
Freud's terminology. It is a sound-joke that operates between the homophony of the English nouns *fear* and *sex* and the German numbers for 4 (*fier*)
and 6 (*sex*).

This little hermetic sound-joke offers insight into the challenges of
employing humor in our preaching. Given the diversity of our congregants
and parishioners, it can be difficult to ensure a sufficient knowledge base
to support a joke's premise. Laughter and joke-telling can foster solidarity,
even between enemies. But, as we all know, if you're the only one in a crowd
who fails to get the joke's humor, it can lead to feelings of alienation. No one
wants to be the odd one out.

A second kind of conditional joke is affective. Typically, these jokes
are understood by many people, but the success of the joke (i.e., its capacity

---

42. Cohen, *Jokes*, 12.

to amuse) depends upon the affective disposition of the audience. Cohen offers the following example of an affective joke.

The thing about German food is that no matter how much you eat, an hour later you are still hungry for power.[43]

This affective joke is also hermetic. It plays off something people sometimes say about Chinese food leaving one hungry after an hour, and its comprehension also requires the listener to know a bit of twentieth-century German history. The joke's capacity for inducing laughter is further conditioned by the affective state of the joke's teller and listener(s). Cohen speculates that this joke might be funnier to Jews than to (non-Jewish) Germans, as it requires feelings of resistance toward the historical instances of some Germans for power at all costs. Kaiser Wilhelm and Adolf Hitler are obvious exemplars here.

Rhythm and Rhyme

Rhythm in comedy is just as important as it is for music. As comedy scholar and stand-up comedian Oliver Double puts it, "Stand-up's backbeat pulses to and fro between performer and punter, the comedian's line followed by the audience's response, a joke-laugh-joke-laugh-joke-laugh rhythm that speeds and slows throughout the show."[44] There is a story told about the great Milton Berle where he once swapped the punch line of a joke for one that made no sense. The relentless rhythm of the gags was such that even this nonsensical, unfunny punch line earned a laugh from the audience.[45] Jerry Seinfeld says much the same thing about the importance of rhythm. In fact, he attributes the success of *Seinfeld* to the stand-up rhythm of the dialogue and a stand-up mindset to the story lines.[46]

Rhythm and rhyme have long been emphasized in African American preaching forms. As Martha Simmons observes, "African-Americans have produced a unique form of preaching whose signature is tonality."[47] In his work on the musicality of Black preaching, William J. Turner Jr. argues for close attention not only to the content of sermons but the tones and cadences in which that content is presented. He writes, "The motion of life in the musical tone struck in preaching is like the dance in the heart of the

43. Cohen, *Jokes*, 21.
44. Double, *Getting the Joke*, 370.
45. Berger, *Last Laugh*, 39.
46. Seinfeld, *Is This Anything?*, 208.
47. Simmons, "Whooping," 864.

preacher, evoking a dance in the heart of the hearer."[48] It would be wrong to associate the tonal qualities of a sermon with sermon delivery alone, even if this is where such tonality is received. Inspired preaching is a word from another world, and music is a native means by which to express the ineffable. "The musicality of preaching supplies what might be seen as a surplus of meaning—which is to say that music adds meaning to the performance of the words. Such music typically produces a mystical and enchanting effect when an audience that is waiting to hear what saith the Lord."[49] Learning from this, stand-up preachers will have to attend to rhythm and rhyme as a way to engage their listeners in the music-like event of the sermon.

SARAH SILVERMAN: BETWEEN CUTENESS AND CRASSNESS

Let's look at a few examples of how one contemporary comic uses jokes to not only make us laugh but to make us think.[50] Sarah Silverman is a Jewish American comic who writes jokes that are at once shocking and thought provoking. Silverman displays a profound respect for the capacities of language to spur laughter. She recounts an early memory in which four-year-old Sarah discovered the power of profanity to elicit laughter. Such language "yielded a strange kind of glory, and I basked in it."[51] She has showed no signs that she's plumbed the proverbial depths of such "glory," which continues to provoke her audiences.

In one of Silverman's best-known controversial jokes, she quips, "I was raped by a doctor, which is a bittersweet experience for a Jewish girl."[52] This joke parsimoniously evokes Jewish stereotypes to engage a taboo topic. The rhetorical shock Silverman achieves through such humor coincides with her presentation of vulnerability. The setup divulges information that is at once intimate and alarming.[53] To hear that someone has endured the horror of rape evokes feelings of sympathy or empathy. It is exactly opposite of what Henri Bergson said was the fundamental condition of laughter, viz., a

---

48. Turner, "Musicality of Black Preaching," 206.

49. Turner, "Musicality of Black Preaching," 201.

50. Aarons and Mierowsky go so far as to label Silverman a public intellectual on the order of Lenny Bruce. Aarons and Mierowsky, "Public Conscience of 'The Chosen People,'" 160.

51. Silverman, *Bedwetter*, 3.

52. Silverman, *Jesus Is Magic*.

53. Linda Mizejewski rightly links Silverman's perceived "edginess" with her wiliness to evoke charged discourses of ethnicity and race. Mizejewski, *Pretty/Funny*, 110.

"momentary anesthesia of the heart."[54] This is the idea that for us to laugh at something or someone, we must not feel for them. If someone trips and falls, for example, most people will respond with care and concern. We can find laughter in the incident only after we realize that the person who fell is not seriously injured. Applying this to Silverman's confession of being raped, the setup moves us out of a comical frame into a serious frame, all the while recognizing the playful contextual frame of the stand-up comedy stage upon which Silverman speaks.

With the punch line comes a twist. This twist comes at the level of *Gedankenwitz*, to borrow Freud's language. It is a conditional-hermetic joke (in Cohen's parlance). To "get" this joke, one must have previous knowledge about the historical stereotype connecting Jews with greed. Silverman combines a horrible thing within any cultural context (rape) with a wonderful thing in a stereotypical patriarchal Jewish context (a young woman marrying a doctor). The joke plays simultaneously at the emotional level and the conceptual level, between abject concern and logical refusal. The joke displays Kant's notion about humor: "Laughter is an affection arising from the sudden transformation of a strained expectation into nothing."[55] But Silverman's joke also challenges Kant's dismissal of humor as offering nothing to the understanding. In our focus on the comical as that which gives rise to thought in a humorous way, we see that Silverman's joke—shocking though it may be—challenges us to think about the complex interplay between sexual violence, ethnic identity, and religion.

Much of Silverman's comedy displays a way with words that forces the audience to hold various sociopolitical commitments in tension. Silverman has been harshly criticized for joking about the Holocaust. In her special *Jesus Is Magic*, Silverman says, "I believe that if Black people were in Germany during World War II, that the holocaust would never have happened. I do. [pause] Or, not to Jews."[56] Let's spend some time unpacking this joke. The setup to the joke trades on the audience's prior knowledge of ethnic violence against Jews by the Nazis and racial violence against Black Americans by white Americans. Silverman draws us into a revisionist scenario in which the holocaust never happened, a scenario especially enticing to her fellow Jews. Like so many of her punch lines, this one is delivered in a flat, matter-of-fact tone that is incongruous with her content. The punch line provokes nervous laughter from her audience by forcing them to hold in tension ethnic oppression in the past and racial oppression that persists in

---

54. Bergson, *Laughter*, 3.

55. Kant, *Critique of the Power of Judgment*, 161.

56. Silverman, *Jesus Is Magic*.

the present. It is only after the joke lands and the audience has responded that the ha-ha can lead to an a-ha. It forces her Jewish American listeners in particular to reconcile their past suffering as a people with the continued suffering of Black people in America. Not only does this joke deconstruct any notion of a post-racial sensibility, it overturns the belief of some Jewish Americans that their historical suffering earns them a get-out-of-jail-free card for concerning themselves with the present-day reality of anti-Black violence. Lissa Skitolsky argues that the preoccupation among Jews regarding the uniqueness and pervasiveness of Jewish suffering in the past fosters "white indifference to or emotional apathy about the pervasive ruthlessness of American genocide against black communities."[57] This joke disrupts such apathy. Silverman addresses it without resolving the complex relationship between gender, race, and class.

Silverman offers other forms of language than jokes in her stand-up. At the end of her 2017 Netflix special, *A Speck of Dust,* she asks if anyone in her audience believes in God. A man named Troy reluctantly raises his hand. She asks him to come down to the front near the stage, and he tells her that he's a Lutheran. Silverman asks a yes/no question: "Would you let God cum in your mouth?" Obviously flustered by the question, the man answers with an unequivocal "No." Silverman is incredulous. She deems it petty that this professed Christian would draw the line at fellatio. She says to the man, "Troy, you're saying, 'God, I know that there's AIDS and rape and famine and genocide and murder. But I know you have a plan, and I am your servant. Unless you're serving cum. And then I'm out.'"[58]

Silverman goes on to marvel at the fact that Abraham was willing to sacrifice his only son as a sign of his faithfulness to God. God, as we know, stayed Abraham's hand just as he was about to murder Isaac. So, Silverman imagines, God next asks he if can cum in Abraham's mouth. Abraham agrees. God cums in his mouth. And Abraham says he thought God was going to stop before he came in his mouth, just like God had stopped Abraham's knife. Silverman concludes, "The Lord works in mysterious ways." Here we have a classic recipe for incongruity emerging from both the structure of Silverman's verbal trap, the loftiness of our perceptions of God, and the lowliness of semen. In other words, the bit forces an uncomfortable choice (for Troy, at least) between his ideology of faith in response to theodicy and a heterosexist ideology in response to fellatio.

57. Skitolsky, "Holocaust Humor and Our Aesthetic Sensibility of American Genocide," 500.

58. Silverman, *Speck of Dust.*

Film and media studies scholar Anthony McIntyre has contributed much to scholarly discourse around the affective charge of cuteness, and particularly its gendered nature based on cultural assumptions, with Silverman serving as a case in point.[59] Cuteness manifests itself inversely to the grotesque. Whereas cuteness attracts our attention, the grotesque repels us. McIntyre writes, "My contention is that cuteness has an inherent tendency to be politically neutralizing: it commonly creates an intimate public that affords respite from the sense of helplessness that pervades contemporary life by (ironically) providing pleasure in aesthetically consuming vulnerability in others." He continues, arguing that Silverman's articulation of cuteness as a staple of her comedic persona stretches the aesthetic of cuteness to the point that its liminality with the grotesque, the sad, and the vulnerable becomes apparent. In so doing, Silverman "not only articulates narratives of emotional precarity in a fresh and engaging way but disrupts the uncritical consumption of cuteness, calling into question the unstated power relations that comprise this aesthetic."[60]

CONCLUSION: WORDS WITHOUT FORMS ARE DEAD

For the past sixty or so years, homiletics has focused on sermonic structure, which is to say that it has stressed linguistic *forms*. This is not to say that homiletics has *only* attended to the structure of sermons, but even those who go against the homiletical flow do so in relation to this flow. In other words, the backlash against the emphasis on forms of sermonic discourse has emerged through emphasizing the content of sermons over and against their forms.[61]

Behind the focus on linguistic forms lies a simple idea: sermons don't just say things; they also do things. Form and content are inseparable. The medium *is* the message, as Marshall McCluhan put it.[62] That is why homileticians have led us to focus on the form and movement of sermons.[63] This attention to the performative capacities of sermons is not particular to preaching. In many allied disciplines, scholars have stressed the interwoven

59. See McIntyre, "Gendering Cuteness," 1–6.

60. McIntyre, "Sarah Silverman," 343–44.

61. E.g., Campbell, *Preaching Jesus,* xi–xii; and Thompson, *Preaching Like Paul,* 1–2.

62. McLuhan, *Understanding Media,* 7–21.

63. As Fred Craddock notes, "Perhaps it will not be taken as irreverent to say that the movement of a sermon is as the movement of a good story or a good joke." Craddock, *As One Without Authority,* 52.

structure of discourse between content and form. Even if the content is pretty much the same, we will receive that content differently if it comes to us in the form of a missive or a sonnet, a story or an essay.

One of the harbingers of what scholars have labeled the "New Homiletic" was a man named H. Grady Davis. His seminal accomplishment was to refocus our attention to the importance of sermonic structure. In his *Design for Preaching*, Davis compared an effective sermon structure to a tree. As living things, trees have a common form that makes its substance recognizable. He urged preachers to structure their sermons like living organisms, with one idea flowing seamlessly into the next just as a tree's roots, trunk, branches, and fruit are all connected.[64] Good structure always seems inevitable. If the structure were different, we would have an entirely different substance. As this pertains to sermon development, if a structure must be imposed on a collection of disparate ideas to form a sermon, then the structure is *wrong*. He writes, "The right form derives from the substance of the message itself, is inseparable from the content, becomes one with the content, and gives a feeling of finality to the sermon."[65]

As the influential Irish preacher R. E. C. Browne once wrote, "Preaching is an art; great art hides the technical ability of the artist and draws no attention to his cleverness. Great art always seems inevitable—the thing could have been said in no other way; it is exuberant and yet controlled by a strength that maintains order without force; it expresses enough to be meaningful and never more than enough."[66] In a similar vein, Thomas Long likens effective form to the silently shifting gears of a car's automatic transmission: "sermon form translates the potential energy of the sermon into productive movement, while remaining itself quietly out of view."[67] Both Browne and Long are right. Great sermons and great stand-up employ form surreptitiously. But this does not make such form invisible. Through careful analysis we may reverse engineer effective stand-up to think more critically and creatively about sermonic form.

Few forms of discourse attend to structure more explicitly than stand-up. Structural concerns in stand-up transpire at a macro and a micro level. Without attention to the movement of a set from one bit to the next, the set will appear chaotic and amorphous. Without attention to the movement of a bit from setup to punch line, there can be no perspectival shift that leads to laughter and/or insight. Stand-up comics play a different language game

---

64. Davis, *Design for Preaching*, 15–16.
65. Davis, *Design for Preaching*, 9.
66. Browne, *Ministry of the Word*, 16.
67. Long, *Witness of Preaching*, 136.

than preachers play; however, in attending closely to their work, we see that these different games play by the same rules.

Stand-Up Spotlight

Dave Chappelle
between Comedy and Critique

I didn't come here to be right;
I just came here to fuck around.[1]

—DAVE CHAPPELLE

Dave Chappelle grew up in Washington, DC and began doing stand-up comedy at the age of fourteen with his ordained Unitarian minister mother driving him to his gigs. He has received numerous accolades for his comedy, including four Emmy Awards for his eponymous sketch comedy show and three Grammy Awards for his comedy specials. In 2019 he received the prestigious Mark Twain Prize for American Humor. Chappelle has been called the "comic genius of America," and *Rolling Stone* ranked him number nine in their "50 Best Stand-Up Comics of All Time."[2] It's hard to imagine a book on stand-up that does not attend to his comedic genius.

But what is it about Chappelle that makes him so special? Media studies scholar Bambi Haggins celebrates Chappelle's lackadaisical candor, sly righteousness, wary hopefulness, and easygoing amiability. Even as he is a provocateur, he nevertheless comes across as "the funny guy on the corner, telling you 'some shit' about life."[3] Chappelle's quintessential talent resides in his ability to deploy common comedic tools to create thought-provoking and compelling juxtapositions that reveal the hypocrisies and injustices of

1. Chappelle, *Bird Revelation*.
2. Powell, "Heaven Hell Dave Chappelle"; Love, "50 Best Stand-up Comics of All Time."
3. Haggins, *Laughing Mad*, 191.

US culture and its sociopolitical institutions. He plays in the uncertainty between what he means and what he says in order to get the audience to laugh. Chappelle's career bears witness to the challenges of such juxtaposition. He walked away from a $50 million deal with Comedy Central due to his worries that his audience members were missing the point of his satirical critiques of racism in America.[4] There's much we could discus about Chappelle's comedy, but the two features most illuminating for stand-up preaching are his playfulness with identity politics and his ideological critiques.

IDENTITY POLITICS

Throughout his long and distinguished comedy career Chappelle has attended to the particularities of identity, particularly racial identity. As a Black man in America, Chappelle has grappled with structural injustice, and he brings this lived experience with him onto the comedy stage—even when there's nothing to laugh about.[5] Much of Chappelle's comedy arises out of incongruity. Like Pryor before him, Chappelle finds such incongruity manifested between America's declared intention to be a place of liberty and justice for all and the grim realities of the systemic oppression of African Americans. We've already witnessed the comedy of incongruity put to great use in the comedy of Dick Gregory and Hari Kondabolu. What makes Chappelle unique is the way he uses his membership in one marginalized group as a means of glossing over and defending his insensitivity to the issues that another group may be facing.[6] Through the comedic juxtaposition of identities Chappelle forces us to grapple with the tensions endemic to those identities.

Beyond shallow jokes about Black people, queer people, and so forth, Chappelle often attends to the logic operating within and across identities. To illustrate, in his 2019 special *Sticks & Stones*, Chappelle names the political consequences that have followed from women's achievement of abortion rights. In the past few years, eight states have responded by passing some of the most strident anti-abortion laws since *Roe v. Wade*. Chappelle does what stand-up comics are supposed to do: he proffers an opinion on a divisive topic. But beyond efforts to get a laugh, Chappelle risks alienating the very people who might laugh at an abortion joke. He asserts that he is neither for nor against abortion. He supports a woman's right to choose what she does with her body, but, by the same logic, he supports a man's right not to

4. Carpenter, *Coloring Whiteness*, 191.
5. See Chappelle's powerful rumination on the murder of George Floyd in *8:46*.
6. Gillota, "Reckless Talk," 15.

have to pay child support. He says, "If you have a dick, you need to shut the fuck up on this one. Their right to choose is their unequivocal right. Gentlemen, that is fair. And ladies, to be fair to us, I also believe if you decide to have the baby, a man should not have to pay. That's fair. If you can kill this motherfucker, I can at least abandon 'em."[7] Notice here what Chappelle is doing. He engages an identity issue that holds dual convictions. Those who would support a woman's right to choose would almost certainly advocate for a man's responsibility to care for his child financially. Chappelle identifies and exploits this tension between rights and responsibilities. What we have in this bit is an act of deconstruction. He affirms the logic at the core of a proposition, then, following that same logic, he opens the proposition to its own deconstruction.

Chappelle's relationship with his self-espoused primary identity marker (i.e., his Blackness) is equally complex. Despite Chappelle's long history of calling out racist policies and perspectives, African American literature scholar Terrence Tucker questions Chappelle's commitment to critiquing white supremacy. Tucker admits that while Chappelle's work is often unprecedented in its conception, it fails to produce a cogent racial analysis. Instead, Tucker charges Chappelle with manifesting "a spirit of ridicule, one that highlights the differences between the races and the privilege that whites enjoy but rarely traces those differences to the fundamental inequality that continues to plague the country."[8]

Let's take a look at an example of Chappelle's treatment of anti-Black racism. A Black man in Texas contracted Ebola and died. Chappelle ponders why this Black man died when two white, American doctors received a "secret serum" and survived. He says, "They just rubbed some Vicks on that n****a's chest. 'Good luck, little buddy.' I knew he wasn't going to make it." Chappelle adds that he read in *The New York Times* that Ebola was the new AIDS. To this he quips, "Here I am, thinking that the old AIDS was working just fine. . . . Isn't it weird that a new disease comes out in the 1980s and it doesn't kill anybody but n****as, fags, and junkies? Isn't that a fucking amazing coincidence that this disease hates everybody that old white people hate?"[9] While this is just one example, it seems to me to challenge the veracity of Tucker's critique. Another example. In *Deep in the Heart of Texas*, Chappelle confronts the persistence of police violence against African Americans, and African American men in particular. But he deflects his critique, stating that Mexicans and Arabs have done a public service to

7. Chappelle, *Sticks & Stones*.

8. Tucker, *Furiously Funny*, 248.

9. Chappelle, *Deep in the Heart of Texas*.

Black people for finding themselves in the police's crosshairs. He says that he has it rough, but a least he can leave a backpack somewhere without having a drone come to kill him.[10] Note that Chappelle is not denying that African Americans face disproportionate discrimination and aggression from the police. That point is beyond debate. At the same time, Chappelle points to an equally problematic bias against Brown people (remember that this special was filmed in Texas). I see Chappelle pointing to a pervasive aspect of white supremacy, which employs varied tactics and rhetoric against non-whites. While distinct, such tactics are no less problematic.

Chappelle has come under scrutiny for his seeming disrespect toward transgender people. In one bit he reflects on Bruce Jenner's gender transition in which she became Caitlyn Jenner. Chappelle concludes,

> Here's my thing. I support anybody's right to be whoever they feel like they are inside. I'm your ally in that. However, my question is to what degree do I have to participate in your self-image? Is it fair that I have to change my whole pronoun game up for this motherfucker? That doesn't make sense. Seriously. If I put on an argyle sweater and I'm like, "Hey, everybody, I feel like a white guy in this sweater, and I want some goddamn respect and a bank loan," that's not gonna work.[11]

Here we may see another aspect of Chappelle's identity politics in action. Note his declaration that he is not against transgender rights. At the same time, he forces us to question the logic undergirding its affirmation. Beyond the politics of pronouns and affirming persons' gender identities, Chappelle holds the debate about transgender identity in critical tension with racial identity. In both cases a person's assigned gender or racial identity corresponds with bodily features. Even as his logic proceeds from a mistaken assumption that gender is a choice, his question is provocative. He forces us to grapple with this tension between gender expression and gender identity vis-à-vis racialized identity markers that remain seemingly out of reach of conscious decision.[12]

---

10. Chappelle, *Deep in the Heart of Texas*.

11. Chappelle, *Deep in the Heart of Texas*.

12. This, of course, overlooks the material attempts to alter one's perceived racial identity through skin creams, hair products, and clothing.

IDEOLOGICAL PROVOCATION

The majority of Chappelle's comedy aims at ideological provocation. In his 2000 HBO comedy special *Killin' Them Softly*, Chappelle narrates a fictional experience he had on a plane while it was being hijacked. Throughout the routine, he plays off of dialects that alternate between defying and reinforcing expectations (e.g., voicing a Chinese terrorist who inexplicably has a Middle Eastern accent; employing linguistic whiteface).[13] Chappelle also resorts to minstrelsy, imagining if terrorists ever did take a Black hostage and what it would sound like to see them reading the terrorist's statement on the news ("They is treating us good. We all chillin' and shit . . .").[14]

The focus of the bit is on participating in media stereotypes in order to subvert them. On scanning the plane to see if there are any Black folks, Chappelle catches the eye of the only other Black passenger on the flight. The two exchange thumbs ups. Chappelle explains that this exchange is woefully misread by white passengers. Slipping into white voice, Chappelle says, "Oh my God, I think those black guys are going to save us." Chappelle's incredulous shake of the head to the audience conveys that the reality of the situation was quite different: the "thumbs up" signified the recognition of the fact that they (the Black passengers) were going to be okay because as he states simply, "Black people are bad bargaining chips."

In his insightful essay "Reckless Talk," comedy scholar David Gillota notes that since Chappelle returned to television after his professional hiatus from comedy, the critical reception of his work has labeled Chappelle's material polarizing. Gillota suggests, however, that this is sort of the point. "Chappelle's humor should be viewed as part of an ongoing process," as "a window into larger cultural debates," rather than as "a fixed and stable ideological position."[15] At his best, Chappelle eludes the confinement of strict ideological positions, suggesting how provocative dialogue and examination may propel a revision to those constraints. Gillota grants that Chappelle's language is "often deliberately offensive," but he sees Chappelle's self-styled "reckless talk" as an intentional tactic designed to unsettle his audience.[16] To be sure, Chappelle's recent Netflix specials have been particularly provocative, displaying insensitivity to members of the #MeToo

---

13. "Linguistic whiteface" is the self-conscious and often exaggerated manipulation of one's vocal qualities (esp. word choice, grammar, and timbre) to suggest that the speaker is white. Carpenter, *Coloring Whiteness,* 24.

14. Chappelle, *Killin' Them Softly*.

15. Gillota, "Reckless Talk," 3.

16. Gillota, "Reckless Talk," 4.

movement and the LGBTQIA community. Indeed, some of Chappelle's commentary is cynical and even downright cavalier.

Nicholas Holm contends that the political capacity of humor's aesthetic arises from its ability to disrupt or disturb the epistemological foundations of society. Shifting, multiplying, and breaking established frames of reference, humor provides new interpretations of the world. This assessment seems applicable to Chappelle's stand-up. Holm is, however, careful to remind his reader that any comic alteration of reality functions politically, but not in any one direction. Comedy can just as easily be made to serve conservative as liberating agendas, and once provocative humor is codified, it begins to function as a social corrective that conserves rather than challenges the established order. Reflecting on Chappelle's racial sketches from his *Chappelle's Show*, Holm writes, "In order for Chappelle's sketches about race to be comic, they therefore need to sustain the power of racial taboos even as they break them."[17] According to Bambi Haggins, comedy is a vehicle for truth. "If one gets an audience laughing, then while their mouths are open, you can shove the truth in," she writes.[18] Contemporary Black comedians, like their predecessors, deliberately combine humor and social critique to "give voice to the jadedly hopeful, politically and pop culturally savvy, and media wary iterations of blackness in post-soul America."[19] Haggins sees Dave Chappelle as the comedian who helped us make sense of America's recent racial boundaries and devotes her longest chapter, "Provocateur in a Strange Land," to Chappelle. A provocateur, in her view, opens up difficult questions that force us to work through the nuances ourselves, rather than promising safe or easy answers. This is certainly true for Chappelle. The question remains whether Chappelle's provocations are in service of the status quo or of an emancipatory ideology.

TAKEAWAYS FOR STAND-UP PREACHING

So, how are we to make sense of Chappelle's stand-up for our homiletical endeavors? At the heart of this debate about Chappelle's recent material is a concern for his ethics. As Oring writes near the end of *Joking Asides*, "Prejudgments about the ethics of laughter and humor influenced attempts to understand the phenomena themselves. Even today, it is difficult to find a paper written on jokes by a philosopher that does not have a substantial

---

17. Holm, *Humour as Politics*, 145.

18. Haggins, *Laughing Mad*, 243.

19. Haggins, *Laughing Mad*, 243.

section devoted to ethical considerations."[20] Steven Benko offers further insight about the ethics of laughter. In conversation with the work of Emmanuel Levinas, Benko encourages us to think about the ways comedy can open us to the other beyond the ideological constraints that can sometimes impede our efforts to be with and for the other. The key question is who is doing the laughing. He writes that only on occasions where the teller and butt of the joke are laughing together do we have an ethical encounter, a genuine opening for community. "The joke teller laughing at herself has become one-for-the-other; the butt of the joke laughing at themselves have become otherwise than they were."[21]

Does Chappelle assist our efforts to be prophetic preachers? In *Preaching Words,* John McClure defines prophetic preaching as "*an imaginative reappropriation of traditional narratives and symbols for the purpose of critiquing a dangerous and unjust present situation and providing an alternative vision of God's future.*"[22] If Chappelle is prophetic, he is prophetic in an oblique and subversive way. His humor leaves much responsibility at the feet of the audience. The question arises for me about whether the prophetic merits of Chappelle's comedy outweigh its priestly costs. In this, his comedy positions him in a vulnerable position alongside the buffoon. I find a deep resonance between Chappelle's brand of stand-up and Adam Hearlson's insights on liturgical subversion. "The buffoon's place on the margin affords him the opportunity to walk a dangerous edge of outright comedy and malevolent attack; after all, how much more marginal can he get? Therefore the *bouffon* [sic] intends to be dangerous; she wants the audience to choke on its laughter. She wants to asphyxiate the audience with her farce."[23]

I am also guided by the work of Thomas Long, who offers a rule for addressing issues of systemic injustice and suffering. Long writes, "If we think we have some insight or wisdom about the theodicy problem, about God, evil, and suffering, but it is not a word that we would want to speak to a sufferer in the depths of loss and grief, then this is a trustworthy sign that this so-called 'wisdom' is not really the gospel, and it should not be spoken at all."[24] This forces me to side against emulating Chappelle in the pulpit inasmuch as the preacher must constantly negotiate between being prophetic and being priestly. But this in no way means that Chappelle has nothing to offer stand-up preachers. Chappelle conceptualizes, through commentary

---

20. Oring, *Joking Asides*, 218.
21. Benko, "Otherwise Than Laughter," 78.
22. McClure, *Preaching Words*, 117.
23. Hearlson, *Holy No*, 45.
24. Long, *What Shall We Say?*, 43.

and example, the stand-up stage as a forum not for ideological consistency or political stability but rather for risk, fluidity, and experimentation. In other words, for Chappelle, a stand-up comedian stands upon the controversial fault lines of his or her culture and uses the stand-up performance to explore or work through contentious issues. This embrace of instability and inconsistency can be termed "reckless talk."[25]

25. Gillota, "Reckless Talk," 4.

4

Narrating Experience
You Can't Make This Stuff Up

What do listeners want and need in sermons? Stories and images.
Not only do we like stories; we live our lives out of them.[1]

—Thomas G. Long

If I want a long boring story with no point to it, I have my life.[2]

—Jerry Seinfeld

We live storied lives. Stories enable us to organize the seemingly random and meaningless data we experience into a unified whole. Stories help us make sense of the world despite its seeming senselessness. In the words of ethicist Alasdair MacIntyre, "Human life has a determinate form, the form of a certain kind of story. It is not just that poems and sagas narrate what happens to men and women, but that in their narrative form poems and sagas capture a form that was already present in the lives which

1. Long, *Witness of Preaching*, 43.
2. Seinfeld and David, "Wallet."

they relate."[3] Another way of saying this is that humans tell stories because that is how we experience the world.

Narrative not only reflects our fundamental experience of the world; it constitutes our selfhood. We narrate ourselves to ourselves and others. By and large, we become the stories we tell ourselves about ourselves. And the obverse of this is equally true: others have the power to shape our self-perception through the ways they narrate our lives. With such power comes commensurate responsibility. The narrative frames within which we make sense of ourselves play a large part in determining our sense of self-worth. They delimit or expand our capacities for imagining alternative ways of being and behaving in the world. Such narrative frames determine whether we find ourselves living out a comedy or a tragedy.

It is no wonder that narrative has proven to be one of the most effective tools in the preacher's homiletical tool belt. The same is true for stand-up comedians. Though the forms and conditions of storytelling in stand-up and preaching differ, both professions draw deeply from the narrative well in their respective crafts. Denominational differences notwithstanding, gospel proclamation intends for something *eventful* to happen in the hearts and minds of the hearers.[4] Even if genuine transformation remains beyond the scope of a preacher's responsibility, preachers preach to effect some change in the world. Otherwise, what is the point? Narrative has become so widely employed in preaching on account of its utility to evoke new perspectives in the hearers' minds, to spur deeper empathy in their hearts, and to catalyze changes in the church and in the world God loves. When a community receives a story from their preacher a kind of transcendence emerges, naming who they can become together. As Thomas Long puts it:

> The capacity of narrative and metaphor to create a common world of experience allows the storyteller/poet to go a long way toward overcoming the dichotomy between individual and community in preaching. In listening to stories and participating in images we are willing, to an extent, to suspend our own concerns in favor of the experience we are having together.[5]

3. MacIntyre, *After Virtue*, 117.

4. This goes back to the first homiletics textbook ever written. In his *De Doctrina Christiania*, Augustine writes, "So the [preacher] who is endeavoring to give conviction to something that is good should despise none of these three aims—of instructing, delighting, and moving his hearers—and should make it his prayerful aim to be listened to with understanding, with pleasure and with obedience." Augustine, *De Doctrina Christiania*, 123.

5. Long, *Witness of Preaching*, 47–48.

Stories foster transformative connectivity. They draw our seemingly disparate and disconnected lives together with those of others. Stories transform us from isolated individuals to members of a community.

NARRATIVE STRUCTURE: IT'S NOT JUST FOR STORYTELLING

Both successful sermons and stand-up sets foster interest and participation. They unfold according to an intuitive structure that imitates listeners' experiences in the world. In his *Poetics,* Aristotle argued that narrative's governing principle is *mimesis.*[6] *Mimesis* (from the Greek *mimeîsthai*) means imitation: a representation of action such that hidden patterns and unexplored meanings may unfold. Stories *imitate* life. The power of stories (*mythoi*) lies in their ability to help us conceptualize the world differently, and thus *mimesis* is inextricable from *mythos.*[7] But this does not mean that all stories function this way. For Aristotle as for us, some stories are bad. Plots wobble, wander, or fall apart altogether. Characters' actions appear disproportionate to their circumstances. As every storyteller knows, imitating life through story is far from simple or straightforward.

Aristotle declared that of all the plots and actions, the episodic plots are the worst. Episodic plots are those in which event follows event without probable or necessary sequence.[8] This holds true for preaching and stand-up. A sermon that presents one declarative utterance after the other is no better at effecting consciousness than a comedy set that moves from joke to joke. That is why preachers and stand-up comedians must attend to the *structure* of their discourse. Even if a sermon or stand-up set contains no stories at all, it may still convey a narrative structure through cohesion between its constitutive parts. This is why many comedians (Chris Rock and Seth Meyers are good examples of this) will tag a refrain from earlier in their set at the very end, creating a sense of completion for the audience.[9]

The most forceful argument for narrative coherence in homiletics emerges from Eugene Lowry. In his influential book *The Homiletical Plot,* Lowry argues that sermonic structure should move from problem to solution, from *itch* to *scratch.* By introducing some ambiguity, imbalance, or

6. Aristotle, *Poetics,* 49b24–28.

7. Critchley, *On Humour,* 16, spots a similar capacity in humor to reveal the situation and indicate how the situation might be changed. He labels this the "messianic power" of laughter.

8. Aristotle, *Poetics,* 1451b35.

9. Rock, *Total Blackout*; Meyers, *Lobby Baby.*

tension, the preacher generates a conflict in the hearts and minds of the congregants; such is the "glue that holds listeners and ideational movement together."[10] Ambiguity and tension foster investment in the listener by tapping into a fundamental human desire for catharsis.

The same structural cohesion holds for effective stand-up, regardless of how many stories (if any) the comic employs. As Judy Carter puts it in her influential text, *Stand-Up Comedy: The Book,* "All stand-up material must be organized into the setup/punch format. If your material isn't organized like this, you're not doing a stand-up. . . . Stand-up comedy is a very specific form of entertainment, consisting of a collection of setups and punches."[11] Even for stream-of-conscious comics like Iliza Shlesinger, Jim Gaffigan, or Sarah Silverman, mimesis abides; their sets imitate our basic human experience of itches (tension) that need to be scratched (release).

Philosopher Richard Kearney argues that we yearn for narrative structure because we experience life as a beginning (at our birth) that moves us ineluctably to an ending (at our death). He writes, "Our very finitude constitutes us as beings who, to put it baldly, are born at the beginning and die at the end. And this gives temporal structure to our lives which seek some kind of *significance* in terms of our past (memory) and forward to our future (projection)."[12] In other words, our existence comes to us pre-plotted. The challenge, of course, is to organize our lived experiences in such a way that the narratives we share tell a story worth telling. Just as we may sometimes experience our lives as boring or pointless—as Jerry Seinfeld names in this chapter's epigraph—unless we intuit some meaning, purpose, or goal in someone else's story, we quickly lose interest.

YOU HAD TO BE THERE: PERSONALIZATION AND PARTICIPATION

In the late 1960s, Richard Pryor introduced a new style of stand-up comedy. Pryor told long narratives in which he portrayed the streetwise, earthy dignity and survival skills of characters of the African American underclass. Like Mabley, Pryor provided social commentary on the hypocrisies and incongruences that characterize racist thinking. Pryor's work continues to influence stand-up comedians; a plethora of African American comedians followed his style. This is demonstrated by *The Original Kings of Comedy.* This movie compiled footage from a 2000 road show that featured comedians

10. Lowry, *Homiletical Plot,* 90.

11. Carter, *Stand-Up Comedy,* 46.

12. Kearney, *On Stories,* 129.

Steve Harvey, D. L. Hughley, Cedric the Entertainer, and Bernie Mac. *The Queens of Comedy*, a female comedy tour film released in 2001, was a spin-off that featured Adele Givens, Laura Hayes, Sommore, and Mo'Nique.[13]

The goal of narration is the same for stand-up as it is for preaching: *to effect a hearing*. To effect such a hearing, Fred Craddock argues, preachers need to establish a certain "posture" that facilitates congregational engagement. Such work calls for two elements: personalization and participation. Personalization sets the listener at ease by making the story about someone other than her. This aspect of effective storytelling establishes distance between the listener and the story's protagonist that is diminished in direct discourse. Such distance is counterintuitive. It does not connote disconnection; rather, it fosters a space between speaker and listener for the listener to decide to invest in the story's resolution.

Personalization in narrative enables preachers to establish distance in two ways. First, narrative establishes distance between the hearer and the message. When a preacher shares a story in a sermon, he preserves the integrity of the message beyond the hearer's subjectivity. Said differently, narrating lived experience names the independence of the message, which in no way depends upon the individual listener for validation. The story I share is *mine*. In sharing it with others, I initiate an altogether different relationship between the content of my preaching and the listener. The preacher says, in effect, "Here is something that did not happen to you. I offer it for your consideration and enjoyment. You do not have to believe any of this." This homiletical posture was a favorite of Friedrich Schleiermacher. In contrast to the homiletical standards dominant in his day, Schleiermacher insisted that preaching should *mediate* a conversation between the biblical text and the minister's congregation. The stuff of mediation for Schleiermacher was the lived experience of the preacher. He argued that the most important component of a sermon is the preacher's *personal investment* in the matter at hand, which does not require congregational assent for its truthfulness.[14] Such a homiletical outlook was markedly different from the "plain style" of preaching that dominated Lutheran and Reformed pulpits in Schleiermacher's day, which took the form of direct discourse on propositional truths.

Craddock associates the second element of distance with a concern for the listener. Craddock explains that narrative offers space for the listener "to reflect, accept, reject, decide. As a listener, I must have that freedom, all the

---

13. *Original Kings of Comedy*; *Queens of Comedy*.

14. For a helpful overview of Schleiermacher's homiletical advances, see Müller, *Homiletik*, 99–122.

more so if the matter before me is of ultimate importance."[15] Paradoxically, the more distance the preacher provides for the listener, the more she fosters participation. Participation invites the listener to overcome the distance, not because the preacher "applied" everything for her, but because the listener has identified with experiences and thoughts relayed in the message that were analogous to her lived experience.[16] In other words, inasmuch as the preacher's story trusts listeners to form their own opinions about the truthfulness of his narration, he invites them into the meaning-making process.

It is not through direct discourse that narrative preaching persuades the listener to accept the preacher's words; rather, by drawing upon a common vocabulary, idiom, imagery, and descriptive detail, the listener receives multiple points of entry to "overhear" the good news and, perhaps, receive it as her own. This point is made most powerfully by Lisa Thompson. Focusing on the experience of African American women preachers, but with a view beyond such gendered and racial particularity, Thompson reminds us that preachers do not preach in a homiletical vacuum. Before the preacher utters a word, congregants have preconceived expectations about how preaching *ought* to sound and look.[17]

Personalization and participation are equally important in stand-up. In her research into the history of stand-up, Susanne Colleary provides a helpful analytic for thinking about the interplay between the comic's selfhood and personhood. From a social analysis perspective, selfhood and personhood differ. Selfhood refers to the interior experience of a subject. Personhood refers to those socially defined aspects that shape one's subjectivity. Both personhood and selfhood are implicated in doing stand-up. They merge in the comedic persona. She calls this the "comic 'I,'" noting how this form of performance transposes the self into the "comic self." Colleary draws upon the work of Irish comic Tommy Tiernan, who describes the comic persona as being "you and yet not you—a part of you but not the whole. It is not a lie, but neither the full truth."[18] It is important that every story the comedian narrates be believable vis-à-vis the comedian's persona. Believability makes authenticity possible. This means that comedians must understand how their audience perceives them, which paves the way toward credibility. Contemporary stand-up plays with the differentiation between the comic as a *self* and as a *persona*.

15. Craddock, *Overhearing the Gospel*, 122.
16. Craddock, *Overhearing the Gospel*, 123.
17. Thompson, *Ingenuity*, 11–22.
18. Colleary, *Performance and Identity in Irish Stand-Up Comedy*, 42, 54.

Even as contemporary stand-up requires personalization, the comedian must navigate the distance between their onstage persona and the audience members in attendance. For a bit to "work" it requires a degree of meaningful *contact* with the listeners. A bit's setup has to "hook" the listener straight away. If the comedian (or preacher) begins by describing situations or settings too far removed from the lived experiences, interests, and concerns of their audience, audience members will lack investment and will not hang around mentally or emotionally for the punch line.

Effective comedians are able to work between personalization and participation. The speaker need not possess the same lived experiences as the listeners. It just has to engage them. To illustrate, consider Ricky Gervais and Ellen DeGeneres. Despite extreme differences in their comic personas—Gervais as a pessimistic misanthrope and DeGeneres as a lighthearted optimist—each has earned millions of dollars for their comedy. Because neither comic comes from money, their ways of being and behaving now differ vastly from how things were for them when they were up-and-coming stand-up comedians. In each of their 2018 Netflix comedy specials, Gervais and DeGeneres find ways to use their current lifestyle to underscore their difference from the vast majority of their audience members.

DeGeneres opens her show *Relatable* by exploiting the tension between her lavish lifestyle and that of everyday Americans. Through her characteristic use of dry irony, she goes into great detail to describe her mundane experience of being mouth-fed by her butler in the solarium, having a bath drawn, pondering her relatability to her audience while gazing out onto her rose garden, and so on.[19] Her description of her posh lifestyle portends to highlight her relatability, but of course her life now contrasts greatly with that of most "normal" people who are not millionaires. This is all part of a long introduction to her main point about how we all tend to stereotype people. In one masterful stroke, DeGeneres exploits her audience members' assumptions about her difference from them to reinforce an argument for her relatability. Coincidently, as the title intimates, the show's theme revolves around this tension between people as types and what we discover when we get to know them as actual people.

Gervais takes a completely different tact. Whereas DeGeneres relies upon her likability, Gervais capitalizes on his disdain for all whom he deems beneath him. His sardonic elitism sets him apart from others, so rather than trying to lessen the distance between himself and his audience, Gervais doubles down. Building off the applause he receives when he steps onto the stage, he asks them to stop clapping because he's "just an ordinary guy, you

19. DeGeneres, *Relatable*.

know, going around talking to people . . . sort of like Jesus in a way . . . but better."[20] He then transitions, telling the audience he decided to title his show *Humanity*. He says, "I don't know why I called it that. I'm not a big fan. I prefer dogs . . . obviously." The rest of the show reinforces his misanthropy, earning laugh after laugh by navigating the play of distance and participation to hilarious effect.

TELL ME A STORY: ELEMENTS OF EFFECTIVE NARRATION

Comedy "works" by tapping into that deep-seated need we humans have for *catharsis*. A world of emotions may emerge between a bit's setup and its punch line, much as the interval between a story's precipitating event and its denouement invites emotional investment. The longer the interval and more palpable the tension, the greater the payoff in terms of emotional (and intellectual) release.

Even as no two stories are identical, they feature common elements that make for quality storytelling. The elements of effective storytelling include emplotment, description, characterization (which includes dialogue and action), and theme. Let's consider each of these in turn. To illustrate each of these elements of effective narration, we'll examine bits from a stand-up comedy show on Comedy Central called *This Is Not Happening*. The show features comedians sharing (true?) stories from their lives. They each have twelve to fifteen minutes to recount some event, so they must be parsimonious with their details. The show has a lot to teach preachers about the elements of effective narration.

Emplotment

Paul Ricoeur defines emplotment as a structuring process, whereby the mind synthesizes heterogenous elements to form a cohesive whole.[21] Every story is made up of multiple incidents. What makes these incidents *events* rather than mere *occurrences* is the cohesion between them and their beginning and ending. Because a story presents concord and discord, emplotment relies upon a reader's or listener's synthetic capacity to string together a succession of incidents into a temporal totality and integrate a story's necessary heteronomy.

20. Gervais, *Humanity*.
21. See Ricoeur, "Life in Quest of Narrative," 21–25.

Every story must begin somewhere. The artistry of storytelling proceeds from the narrator's decision of where to begin because this beginning will accompany successive events in the emplotment process. Successful comedians do this well. Bert Kreischner opens one of his *This Is Not Happening* stories by announcing, "I fought a bear one time."[22] Who isn't interested in learning how that story ends? Joe Rogan tells a story about a time he was caught in a hotel fire.[23] By announcing their subject matter right up front, Kreischner and Rogan "hook" their listeners. Even if nobody in the audience has ever fought a bear or been in a hotel fire, the danger of these situations is immediately apparent. This ratchets up the narrative drive, drawing listeners into the plot. Their openings generate tension between two things we know: 1) Bert Kreischner fought a bear; Joe Rogan was in a hotel fire and 2) because Kreischner and Rogan are necessarily alive (because they are here to tell their story), these harrowing events did not kill them, despite the high probability of death in either situation. The narrative dissonance between these powerful beginnings and their unknown resolution draws the listener into their stories.

In his book *The Art of Fiction*, novelist John Gardner introduces a quality of successful fiction called *profluence*. The word is mostly obsolete in English, but Gardner resurrects it to describe a feeling that a story is going somewhere (the Latin root means "to flow forth"). This is a vital element of emplotment because it does not matter how amazing a story's climax or denouement is if listeners or readers aren't willing to stick it out to the end. Gardner explains that it is of aesthetic necessity that a story contains profluence. This requirement is best satisfied by a sequence of causally related events ending in one of two ways: in resolution, when no further event can take place (the murderer has been caught and hanged, the diamond has been found and restored to its owner . . .), or in logical exhaustion.[24] Effective narration, in preaching as in stand-up, requires profluence.

Especially on account of the hostile nature of some comedy clubs, comedians must craft their stories so that punch lines and funny asides appear along the way to the story's resolution. A fantastic example emerges from the stand-up of Brad Williams. In his *This Is Not Happening* bit, Williams recounts a time he was mistaken for someone else.[25] Williams was born with achondroplasia, which is a form of dwarfism. His seemingly classic case of mistaken identity transpires during a celebrity golf tournament in which he

22. Kreischner, "Battle."
23. Rogan, "Travel."
24. Gardner, *Art of Fiction*, 53.
25. Williams, "Famous."

was mistaken for Jason Acuna, a.k.a. Wee Man of *Jackass* fame. Williams's emplotment displays profluence even as it follows numerous detours: he explains that despite his short stature he is an excellent golfer; that his dad taught him to play golf so he could make stupid dad jokes about his son's "short game"; and how he came to be invited to join in this celebrity golf tournament when he was not, then, a celebrity; and so on. The plot thickens as Williams spots an opportunity to take advantage of his fellow golfers' inability to differentiate between one little person and another. The story moves from punch line to punch line, leading to the climax in which Williams's ruse will be discovered or he will make it through his charade unscathed. As he and his fellow golfers near the end of the course, they come to a hole sponsored by Hooters. One of the servers stops him, announcing that Williams was not Wee Man and that she knows because she once had sex with Wee Man. This is the climax of his story (no pun intended). It is the point at which Williams will either succeed or fail, comedy or tragedy. I'll leave it to you to see how Williams finds resolution in this situation.

Description

Vivid description brings a story to life. An effective narrator will employ description to stir the listener's imagination. Effective description requires the storyteller to provide just enough detail to invite participation. Stephen King describes this well in his book *On Writing*:

> Description begins with the visualization of what it is you want the reader to experience. It ends with your transplanting what you see in your mind into words on the page. It's far from easy. . . . If you want to be a successful writer, you *must* be able to describe it, and in a way that will cause your reader to prickle with recognition. . . . Thin description leaves the reader feeling bewildered and nearsighted. Over description buries him or her in details and images. The trick is to find a happy medium. It's also important to know *what* to describe and what can be left alone while you get on with your main job, which is telling a story.[26]

This advice pertains particularly to preachers and stand-up comedians, as the art of oral/aural narration demands greater concision and focus than written narration.

---

26. King, *On Writing*, 171.

A fantastic example of effective description is displayed by Roy Wood Jr. in his story about an encounter he had with the Dothan Dope Boys.[27] Wood opens with a description of his neighborhood growing up on the West End in Birmingham, Alabama. Wood offers just enough information for the listener to picture what he saw and experienced in his drug-infested neighborhood in the aftermath of white flight. His descriptive narration paints the crack dealers and the meth dealers in a positive light, using his tone and body language to put us in his prepubescent body. This is all a setup for a contrast he makes about the drug dealers he encountered in 2002 in Dothan, Alabama.

Wood explains that as an up-and-coming African American comedian in the South, he didn't have the luxury of being picky about gigs. He followed the "Chitlin Circuit," a designation for comedy clubs and theaters that emerged in the segregated South as venues for Black entertainers to perform. This led him to a show in Dothan hosted by drug dealers. We learn that it was common practice for drug dealers to host comedy shows by pre-selling tickets, using the money to buy a brick of cocaine, flip the brick, and then use the proceeds to pay the comedians. Unfortunately, when Wood and four other comedians arrived for the show, the show's promoter/drug dealer wasn't able to sell his supply. As a result, he wasn't able to pay Wood and his colleagues. He offered to pay them for their stand-up in drugs or he promised to wire them the money after the show via Western Union.

Wood masterfully presents the scene in vivid detail by shifting between direct narration and first-person dialogue as the drug dealer. Wood tells us nothing about this man's appearance, but through his shift in diction, tone, body movement, and inflection he elicits our imagination to fill in the rest of the scene. Other than telling us that they were in a strip club in rural Alabama, the only descriptive detail Wood provides is the make and model of the gun the promoter/drug dealer presents to motivate the comedians into doing their stand-up: a Glock .40, extendo clip. This detail about the type of gun and the fact that it featured an extended magazine says a lot about how serious these drug dealers were that they thought it necessary to supplement the magazine capacity provided by the gun manufacturer to hold more bullets. More bullets = more shooting = more dangerous. Wood doesn't need to tell us what this man was wearing, what kind of hairstyle he wore, how many tattoos he had, etc. What is crucial in Wood's narration is that we understand the stakes as Wood goes on to narrate how he managed to slip away without doing the show or being shot by these Dothan Dope Boys.

27. Wood, "Drugs, Drugs, Drugs."

Characterization

Character manifests itself through dialogue and action. We encounter characters narratively through what they say and do. Here is where the old chestnut "show, don't tell" becomes vital for effective storytelling. Effective storytellers trust the audience to discern a character's inner state of mind and moral constitution by what a character says and what a character does. We learn a lot about a character from how they say what they say, and stand-up comedians rely on inflection, facial expression, bodily gestures, and tone to render a character's, well, character.

An excellent illustration of this comes from Keegan-Michael Key. He shares a story of a time he tried to do a good deed by picking up an apparent homeless man named Jeff and taking him to a nearby shelter.[28] Key encountered this man in a sketchy part of Detroit. He describes his passenger as one who "looked like a cross between a beaten golden retriever and a sad Gary Busey." Quickly the story takes a turn when the man asks Key to stop the car, which Key learns too late is for the purpose of procuring crack cocaine. At the climax of the story, Key narrates how he, as a naive nineteen-year-old, chose to stand up to his bedraggled passenger.

Key says, "So I got really stern, you guys. And I said [sternly], 'Jeff, this is it. I have to be at play practice in two hours. I'm stage managing *Early One Evening* at the Rainbow Bar and Grill." Next thing he knows, Jeff has procured an empty soda can from the floor of Key's car and begins to smoke crack in the passenger seat. Jeff sheepishly responds, "Hope you don't mind." This story's hilarity emerges from the incongruity between what Key offers as a reason for needing Jeff to get out of his car (play practice) and this perilous environment Key strives to navigate. The incongruity shows us how out of place Key was. A second moment of incongruity manifests when Jeff says, "Hope you don't mind," which is absurd for someone like Key. Of course he minds! Here we see how dialogue reveals much about these two characters.

A second revealer of character is action. We learn as much about a character's qualities from what she does as from what she says—in some ways, action is a truer revealer of character because, as the saying goes, *actions speak louder than words*. Along these lines, Kumail Nanjiani shares a story about a transition point in his life as a kid growing up in Pakistan.[29] After grade ten Pakistani students are able to transfer to a different school based on their scores on a series of placement exams. Nanjiani did well on these exams, and so he was invited to attend a more prestigious school

28. Key, "Brain on Drugs."
29. Nanjiani, "Kumail Nanjiani Tries Hard to be Cool."

where the rich kids went. Nanjiani announces his desire to make the most of this transition by becoming one of the "cool kids." He reveals his three-part plan to become cool: 1) walk slower; 2) laugh quieter; and 3) insult better. Already we are waiting for this plan to fall apart, because Nanjiani's comedic persona is very much *not* cool. As the story unfolds, we see how his plan for being accepted by the cool kids fails by the very means he enacted to be cool. His aspirations to coolness vanish when all the cool kids at his school invite him outside only to pelt him with eggs. The discordance between Nanjiani's attempts to be cool and his utter failure to do so renders his character to his audience. Through this narration we come to see how his plan was doomed from the start due to his fundamental lack of coolness.

Theme

Every story worthy of the name *says* something, that is, it says something more than the disparate aspects of the story itself. This something more is called theme. Theme is to story as a thesis is to an essay, with one crucial caveat: theme and story are inseparable. You can't have one without the other. In contradistinction, a thesis may be asserted apart from its essay.

In her book on the craft of fiction writing, Joyce Carol Oates offers a helpful analogy. She compares a story's theme to a bobbin upon which the narrative thread (i.e., plot) is skillfully wound: "Without the bobbin, the thread would fly loose." Quality fiction, Oates continues, cannot be extricated from its theme "except at the risk of reducing it to a mere concatenation of events lacking a spiritual core."[30] To illustrate, Roy Wood Jr. describes his experience of working at Golden Corral as a young man.[31] He goes into great detail describing what it was like for him to work there. One of his co-workers worked the meat cutting station. The man had been formerly incarcerated, and it was clear from the way this man worked and his numerous asides that his number one priority in life was not to return to prison. Wood tells us that the manager of the restaurant took hospitality very seriously. The man encouraged all the employees to join the 100 Club. Those admitted to the 100 Club were Golden Corral workers who managed to learn the names of 100 customers and two of their favorite food items. Wood proudly announces that he eventually earned his way into the 100 Club, but he confesses that there was one customer whose name he never learned because the man was so intimidating. This customer was a body builder. The man came to Golden Corral three times a week and always

30. Oates, *Faith of a Writer*, 119–20.
31. Wood, "Grind."

ordered the same thing: two rotisserie chickens, a pitcher of water, and a slice of carrot cake. (Retuning to description, look at Wood's parsimony here: he leaves it to us to imagine how huge this man must be if he ate like that three times per week.)

As the narration progresses, we hear Wood describe his experience of being arrested for stealing a pair of jeans. After he was processed, finger-prints and all, he entered the jail and came face to face with a man screaming at him for allegedly sleeping with this man's mother. As a scrawny college student, Wood was understandably terrified. He takes his time describing what it felt like to be there, fighting to come to terms with the reality that he would soon be victim to this man's wrath. In terms of narrative drive, this story has it all: vivid description that *shows* the protagonist's environ-ment; tension between characters, who each desire something completely at odds with what the other person wants; and direct discourse that reveals the character's state of mind. We see that the inmate accosting Wood wants justice for his mother (the jail guard informs Wood that while the man had been in jail, someone had in fact abused the man's mother). We see that Wood (like any of us) wants to avoid being throttled by this man. The story's resolution ties the two parts of the story (his hospitality at Golden Corral and his prison experience) together. It turns out that the body builder whose name Wood never managed to remember because he was so intimidating was the one who intervened on Wood's behalf in prison.

Aristotle said stories are compelling to us because they allow us to experience all the emotional turmoil we experience when we are the protag-onists of our own story without having to endure all the real-world conse-quences.[32] When we arrive at a story's resolution, we experience catharsis, that feeling of release that causes the tension driving the story to dissipate. Watching Wood recount his story leads us to crave catharsis. We want to know what happened. We want to know that Wood makes it out of this unscathed.

So, what is the theme of this story? Perhaps you will see this differ-ently, but for me this story speaks to the importance of hospitality, about the power of just being nice to people. Were Wood to have left out his narration of his time as a Golden Corral employee, the manager's 100 Club, or the body builder whose name Wood never obtained, we would not come to rec-ognize for ourselves his theme of hospitality. Joining the Golden Corral 100 Club in Tallahassee, Florida seems 100 miles away from Wood's terrifying encounter with his fellow inmate. It is only by reconciling the incongruity

32. Aristotle, *Poetics*, 1449b21–28.

between these two worlds that we experience both the story's humor and its thematic significance.

IN ALL SERIOUSNESS: STAND-UP AS PROPHETIC INDICTMENT

Stand-up comedians draw upon their lived experience. Because that experience is not always pleasant or happy, many are not afraid to narrate their woes. Comedians do this in one of two ways: either their mishaps and foibles provide the setup for a joke or they become a joke's punch line. Comedians who engage their unfortunate memories reverse the adage that it is better to be laughed with than laughed at. We see this in the comedic style of Richard Pryor and D. L. Hugely—they keep the laughs coming even in their critiques of racial inequality and economic injustice for people of color.

But some comedians subvert the setup-punch line-laugh formula. Rhetorically speaking, these comics strategically supplant a punch line with a kind of prophetic indictment. This is quite brilliant. The audience is expecting a bit's punch line to pay off comedically, i.e., they are expecting to laugh. When the punch line exposes something evil and insidious about the world in which we all live, the silence can be deafening. In playing off the stand-up structure, they challenge their audience to share their indignation by critiquing injustice and/or oppression.

Leading homiletician Frank Thomas offers a similar approach to preaching. He calls these "dangerous sermons," which are sermons aiming to engender a *moral imagination* in a sermon's listeners. Thomas writes, "Far too often, morals and ethics [and humor—I must add] are established based upon the norms of our group. This usually means that if our group does it, it must be moral, and if another group does it, it must be obviously and utterly immoral and wrong." I would argue that this assessment names a foundation not only for ethics but also for comedy. The history of stand-up is replete with examples of comics soliciting laughs at the expense of one people group or another. It plays upon the superiority theory we discussed earlier in the book, which attributes humor to the feeling of superiority we feel when we learn of another's pain or peccadillos. Thomas continues, "This situational ethic is established from a pessimistic, divisive, and combative zero-sum game imagination and worldview. In this mindset, our group must win at all costs, and anyone not of our group must be the loser and enemy, even at the cost of truth, logic, and common sense. This situational ethic is based in the idolatrous and diabolical imagination."[33] Thomas recog-

---

33. Thomas, *How to Preach a Dangerous Sermon*, 52.

nizes the capacity of preaching to exhibit a moral imagination, and we may see such prophetic leadership modeled by some stand-up comedians.

One stand-up comedian who moves between hilarity and critique is Chris Rock. Some of his bits take the form of observational one-liners in the style of Richard Pryor: "Some people say young black men are an endangered species. That ain't true. Endangered species are protected by the government."[34] Rock has always set himself apart in how he moves seamlessly between shock and introspection. In the HBO special *Talking Funny*, Rock states that a laugh is not always his intended reaction to a joke. He likes to keep the audience off-balance, earning groans and boos along with laughs. We see this intention clearly in his Netflix special *Tambourine*.

In *Tambourine* Rock gets brutally honest about his failures as a husband that led to his divorce some years earlier. After announcing this as his topic, he starts to give advice about staying in a relationship. One of his major admonitions about relationships is to avoid competition. He likens this cooperative and collaborative spirit to being a member of a band. The only way to be successful in a band is to recognize your role. "Sometimes you sing lead and sometimes you're on tambourine. And if you're on tambourine, play it right," Rock says. "Play it right. Play it with a fucking smile. 'Cause nobody wants to see a mad tambourine player. That's right. If you're gonna play tambourine, you play that motherfucker right."

The idea of playing the tambourine becomes a refrain at the end of his act that offers serious advice about how to maintain a happy marriage. It's about supporting your partner in their flourishing, rather than forcing them to submit to your whims and desires. Rock confesses,

> Divorce, man. You don't want no parts of this shit, man. And you know, it's my fault 'cause I'm a fucking asshole, man. I'm just . . . I . . . I wasn't a good husband. I wasn't a good husband. I didn't listen. I wasn't kind. True. True. You know? You know, I had an attitude. I thought, "Ah, I pay for everything. I could do what I want." That shit don't fucking work. You know, I just thought I was the shit, man. Uh, I didn't play the tambourine. You gotta play the tambourine. Everybody gotta play the tambourine. I cheated.[35]

Nobody laughed. And of course they didn't because Rock used something intensely personal from his own life as a prophetic indictment against male infidelity and selfishness. Because he was willing to use his failures, he opened his audience to examine their relational experiences.

34. Rock, *Tambourine*.
35. Rock, *Tambourine*.

A frequent target of Rock's ire is white supremacy. In particular, he narrates the ways that whiteness subverts and restricts the flourishing of African Americans. Rock tends to shift rapidly between micro-memoirs and critical commentary. This movement between narrative setup and comical punch line keeps his audience off-balance, which allows him to intersperse prophetic indictment against white privilege by exposing some of its more insidious aspects. We see his prophetic indictment on display in *Bigger and Blacker*.[36] He opens with a brief vignette about how he was waiting for an elevator door to close at his hotel and two white boys in trench coats got on the elevator with him. Rock says he immediately dove out of the elevator. Addressing the epidemic of white kids shooting up their school, he jokes about how he's scared of white kids and that other white kids are going to start asking to go to a Black school just to be safe. In the wake of the Columbine shooting and other less publicized shootings in the late nineties, Rock transposes the debate between mental illness and gun control into the key of white racial privilege.

A more recent example takes aim at the rhetoric defending cops who shoot unarmed Black men as being "just a few bad apples." Rock exposes the problems inherent in this reasoning with examples. "Here's the thing," he says. "I know it's hard being a cop. I know it's hard. I know that shit's dangerous. I know it is, okay? But some jobs can't have bad apples, okay? Some jobs, everybody got to be good. Like . . . pilots. You know? American Airlines can't be, like, 'Most of our pilots like to land. We just got a few bad apples that like to crash into mountains. Please bear with us.'"[37] Rock opines,

> America's insane, man. You gotta get your kids ready for the white man. If you're not, then you're fuckin' up as a parent, okay? I've been getting my kids ready for the white man since they was born, okay? But even before they was born, I've been preparing them for the white man. Yeah. That's right. . . . So everything in my house that's the color white is either hot, heavy, or sharp. So, my kids know when they deal with anything white, they gotta think about that shit. They got to contemplate this shit.
>
> "Ooh. This napkin, okay. Should I wipe my mouth with it or is that what Whitey wants me to do?" . . .
>
> They sit on a white toilet seat, burn their ass. "Daddy, my ass is burning."
>
> "It's white, motherfucker, it's white. That's what Whitey do. He burn yo fuckin' ass. Pay attention!"

36. Rock, *Bigger and Blacker*.
37. Rock, *Total Blackout*.

Shit, when they was little girls, their white onesie weighed
150 pounds.

"Daddy! Dad, it's so heavy. It's so heavy. This hurts. I can't
even stand. I can't even stand."

"It's white, motherfucker, it's white. That's what Whitey do.
He break yo back."[38]

CONCLUSION: A WORD OF WARNING AND HOPE

Fred Craddock argued that in the giving and receiving of a sermon the sermon becomes socially owned by the preacher and her collective hearers.
Inductive, narrative preaching aims to be both democratic and egalitarian.
Inasmuch as congregants are free to hear sermons from their social situations, they become co-constitutive of sermonic meaningfulness.[39] Craddock's inductive method of preaching—of which narrative is a part—frees
the listener to come to her own decision about a sermon's meaningfulness.
Narration requires *participation* between narrator and audience, wherein
the latter is free to join in the movement of the story.

Despite the obvious merits of this approach, there are several dangers
inherent in this homiletic. These dangers transcend matters of technical
mastery. They are deeply theological. First, such necessary participation
risks reinforcing stereotypes and totalizations of a congregation's *others*.
Philosopher Paul Ricoeur stresses the element of persuasion embedded in
narration. Though he has readers in mind, he offers a warning that holds
for listeners as well. Narrators impose a vision of the world on their reader/
listener. This vision is "never ethically neutral, but that rather implicitly or
explicitly induces a new evaluation of the world and of the reader as well."
Accordingly, preachers ought to hold ourselves to a higher moral standard.
Ricoeur concludes, "In this sense, narrative already belongs to the ethical
field in virtue of its claim—inseparable from its narration—to ethical justice. Still, it belongs to the reader, now an agent, an initiator of action, to
choose among the multiple proposals of ethical justice brought forth by the
reading."[40]

Homiletician John McClure argues that inductive preaching assumes
a "relational symmetry" between preacher and congregants or parishioners.
"Preaching relies on a kind of empathic imagination through which preachers and hearers move onto common experiential ground and proceed down

38. Rock, *Total Blackout*.

39. Craddock, *Preaching*, 31–32.

40. Ricoeur, *Time and Narrative*, 249.

a common pathway to specific conclusions. In order for this to work," Mc-Clure adds, "both preachers and hearers must at least tacitly agree that there is symmetry of knowledge and experience between one another."[41] If we are not careful, we can end up reinforcing hegemonic epistemologies that silence different ways of knowing and being. Narratives, as Toni Morrison reminds us, can liberate or enslave the listener/reader. In her book, *The Origin of Others, other* as a category, and *othering* as a practice, are means of estrangement for one's own empowerment. The naming of others *as other* is seldom benign. Othering is insidious because it feigns neutrality while smuggling in hierarchies always already affirmed by those in power.[42] She argues that "because there are such major benefits in creating and sustaining an Other, it is important to 1) identify the benefits and 2) discover what may be the social/political results of repudiating those benefits.[43] This tendency toward homogeneity presents the shadow side of a form of preaching that also has the potential to shine light on alternative ways of being in the world.

Second, as Ruthanna Hooke rightly observes, by employing narrative forms of preaching the preacher abdicates much authority. Hooke worries whether our current cultural moment calls for more authoritative speech from the pulpit than the inductive method often allows. "This is particularly needed," she avers, "if preaching is to recover a public or prophetic voice; a thoroughly democratic sermon cannot easily speak a prophetic word, as the word is almost by definition one that people do not want to hear and may well not arrive at on their own."[44] Hooke's point is especially apropos for stand-up preaching, which aims toward the comical and the humorous.

A third potential danger of narrative preaching emerges from efforts to fit the gospel into ready-made narratives that are too puny to bear the gospel's weight. As Thomas Long avers, "Faithful preaching is not story time; it is instead the spoken word at the epicenter of a community of courageous testimony."[45] I have witnessed the temptation in my preaching along with that of my students to fit the text to a story. Sometimes these testimonies to lived experience draw out the pith of the biblical text. Other times, they constrain the theological and/or sociopolitical impact of the biblical witness. This is a danger that should give us pause as we prepare to proclaim God's Word. A second danger flows from this one. As we have seen in this chapter, so much of the impact potential of narrative depends on a story's

41. McClure, *Other-Wise Preaching*, 51.

42. Morrison, *Origin of Others*, esp. ch. 5.

43. Morrison, *Origin of Others*, 56.

44. Hooke, "Inductive Preaching Renewed," 61.

45. Long, *Preaching from Memory to Hope*, 26.

resolution. Charles Campbell names a tendency for preachers as well as stand-up comics to force a neat and tidy resolution on stories that resist such efforts. Campbell stresses the importance of listening, even to the point of *kenosis,* so that in entering the grotesque gospel we give up our familiar patterns and narrative resolutions.[46]

Bearing in mind these dangers, narrating experience has much to offer stand-up preachers. I think that one of its greatest boons for us and our hearers is its capacity to open us to alternative ways of being and behaving in the world. Exposure to the hearts and minds of others through narration can lead us to recognize our biases and to release them in favor of embracing others. This aspect of narrative goes all the way back to Aristotle. In his *Poetics* Aristotle named two aspects of narrative that continue to work wonders on us. These are *catharsis* and *anagnorisis.* Catharsis can mean emotional release, but its origin is closer to that of purgation or purification. The word appears in Aristotle's earlier works in its medical sense, which bears the idea that ailments were a result of an improper balance of the humors. The second aspect of narrative is that of *anagnorisis.* Aristotle defines this as a change from ignorance to knowledge that accompanies a character's insights arising from a story's denouement.[47]

The great hope I have for narrative, despite its dangers, emerges from the prospect of purging listeners of hate or apathy as a turn from ignorance to knowledge. This is particularly apparent to me in my American context on the issue of race/racism. As Chanequa Walker-Barnes argues, racism is less about our individual feelings and behaviors than it is about an interlocking system of oppression that serves white supremacy.[48] If we have any hope of moving toward racial reconciliation, we need to understand how these structures and systems operate and we need to care enough about these realities to do something about them. She includes the following quote that speaks to the power of narrative to help us recognize these interlocking structures:

> One of the primary issues we must face, especially in this sociopolitical climate, is the need for white people to do the hard work of wrestling with what it really means to be white. . . . The poisonous impact of the narrative of racial difference does not land solely on people of color. The narrative of racial difference has also profoundly affected white people. But unlike people

46. Campbell, *Scandal of the Gospel,* 29.
47. Aristotle, *Poetics,* 1452a.
48. Walker-Barnes, *I Bring the Voices of My People,* 50.

of color, most white people remain completely unaware of the
ways this narrative has affected their sense of identity.[49]

These words of wisdom remind me that so much of what appears to us as
"just the way things are" depends upon narratives that substantiate certain
beliefs and practices. Narratively driven, stand-up sermons hold great potential to subvert such beliefs and practices.

---

49. Walker-Barnes, *I Bring the Voices of My People*, 112, quoting Brenda Salter
McNeil.

Stand-Up Spotlight
Hannah Gadsby
between Deconstruction and
Dehumanization

I'm not here to collect your pity.
I'm here to disrupt your confidence.[1]

—HANNAH GADSBY

Hannah Gadsby burst into the stand-up mainstream in 2018 with her critically acclaimed and Emmy Award-winning Netflix special *Nanette*. Though she has been performing stand-up for many years, it was this special that drew her international attention, largely for the ways she pushed against the constraints of the stand-up genre itself. Reviews of this special earned Gadsby glowing praise from *The New York Times* and *The New Yorker*.[2] Critics celebrated Gadsby's candor about the limits of self-deprecation and the challenges she has suffered privately in order for her to earn a laugh publicly. At the rhetorical apogee of *Nanette* is a disavowal of stand-up itself in which Gadsby uses stand-up comedy to deconstruct stand-up comedy. Not everyone was a fan; in fact, some have challenged its genre-bending, labeling it anti- or post-comedy.[3]

---

1. Gadsby, *Douglas.*

2. See Costa, "Funny, Furious Anti-Comedy of Hannah Gadsby"; and Ryzik, "Comedy-Destroying, Soul-Affirming Art of Hannah Gadsby."

3. Donegan, "Comedian Forcing Standup to Confront the #MeToo Era"; and VanArendonk, "8 Signs You're Watching a Post-Comedy Comedy."

A convention of stand-up—especially for women and LGBTQIA-identifying comics—is to self-deprecate. By denigrating oneself or one's tribe, the comic fosters laughter by making the audience feel superior to the comic. Self-deprecation aligns with the superiority theory of humor, which we examined in chapter 2. This theory emphasizes our tendency to laugh at that which is ugly and/or bad. Stretching all the way back to Plato, the superiority theory presumes a target for laughter. When we laugh at a joke, we are laughing at the butt of the joke, which enables us to take pleasure in our own sense of superiority over the person being described.[4] Some stand-up comics make others the butt of their jokes. But, as Gadsby confesses, she has continuously made herself the butt of her jokes and doing so for more than a decade has extracted a tremendous toll on her as a human being. She says, "There's only so long I can pretend not to be serious."[5]

As with others I've already spotlighted, Gadsby helps us think about our identities and the sociopolitical ideologies that simultaneously make us subjects and subject us. Gadsby further offers a unique mode of deconstructing the discursive norms of stand-up, offering us theological and homiletical insights for thinking about how we name others—both in our world and in the biblical text.

IDENTITY AND IDEOLOGY

Gadsby, like many comics we are studying in this book, forefronts her intersectional identity. Self-presentation is a core feature of contemporary stand-up. By introducing oneself to one's audience, the comic fosters both intimacy and authenticity, which structure one's comedic persona. Such a confessional atmosphere engenders trust, which is vital for establishing the necessary conditions for dialogical engagement and audience investment in what the comic has to say.

One of Gadsby's (self-)defining identity markers is her sexual identity. Early in *Nanette* she addresses her conflicting identities as both a stand-up comic and a lesbian. She has a bit about her sexual orientation and how she doesn't fit well with the Platonic ideal of what a lesbian *ought* to be—as if one's sexuality can be totalized so simplistically. Gadsby is confessional here, telling the truth about her lived experiences. She states that she has received negative feedback from other lesbians about not being lesbian enough in her comedy. From this confession she moves into another well-worn path

---

4. See Plato, *Philebus*, 48–50, and *Republic*, 388e; Aristotle, *Poetics* 5.1449, and *Nicomachean Ethics* 4.8.

5. Gadsby, *Nanette*.

in stand-up: observational comedy. She talks about how she dislikes the rainbow flag as the symbol of LGBT pride. The gay flag, she quips, is "a bit busy."[6] She muses over what sort of comedian can't even make lesbians laugh. Gadsby responds, "Every comedian ever."[7] She names this joke a classic. It's funny, she says, because it's true, and the only people who don't find it funny are her fellow lesbians. After the laughter dies down, Gadsby pivots. She names the rhetorical pickle she's created with this joke: lesbians *have* to laugh at the joke or they prove the point. While its structure suggests that this is the punch line, the punch line of this "classic" joke turns out to be the setup for something much more serious.

The very thing that makes her lesbian joke funny is the reason she wants to quit comedy. She explains that she has built her career out of self-deprecation and that she can no longer withstand the psychic toll it takes on her to be funny. In an article she wrote for *Elle* magazine, Gadsby came to realize, "The world shits on me enough as a fat queer woman from a low socio-economic background. I've got nothing. If I'm not going to speak up for myself, nobody will."[8]

Gadsby forefronts her identity in her stand-up for important reasons. She names the complications of being human that preclude "straight" or uncontradictory behavior. But our lives are messier than that. There is a great deal more truth in ambiguity. We are living at a time when nuance and all the confused intentions, desires, and beliefs that go along with it are considered less a way of understanding human frailty than a failure of accountability. Gadsby aligns her comical persona with her identity—as a neurodivergent (she is on the autism spectrum), gender-nonconforming lesbian.[9] Even as these intersectional identity markers establish her comical persona on stage, they exact a toll from her off stage, and much of her comedy reveals the trauma and absurdities she encounters, mostly from straight, white, neurotypical men.

DISCIPLINARY DECONSTRUCTION

Gadsby's *Nanette* transforms into a commentary on stand-up itself, on what stand-up conceals, and on how it forces the marginalized to participate

6. Gadsby, *Nanette.*

7. Gadsby, *Nanette.*

8. Gadsby, "*Nanette* Isn't a Comedy Show."

9. Ironically, as Sarah Kessler observes, part of Gadsby's notoriety for challenging stand-up reinforces her identity within the "canon of butch respectability." Kessler, "Are You Being Sirred?," 47.

in their own humiliation to elicit the laughter comedy demands. Krefting characterizes *Nanette* as "a feminist-queer metacommentary on comedy."[10] *Nanette* stretches the discursive boundaries of stand-up comedy, so much so that many critics questioned whether it ought to "count" as stand-up at all.[11]

Two major features of Gadsby's comedy style are participation and parody. In other words, she vacillates between participating in the discursive norms of stand-up comedy and parodying those norms as a way to destabilize the genre itself. She follows the expected setup-punch line structure, but just before the punch line she stops. "She doesn't just put her jokes on hold, she excavates them, showing the audience the rotten holes in her humor. She doesn't indict people for laughing, but the subtext is clear. She indicts herself."[12] This has led one comedy critic to write, "To engineer a confrontation with pain and knowledge that, almost as a side effect, exploded the mechanism of stand-up comedy itself."[13]

Another way Gadsby engages in disciplinary deconstruction emerges from her university studies. Gadsby models a way to draw upon what we know as a resource for comedic interventions into politics. Here I am speaking less to the ongoing saga between Democrats and Republicans than to politics as a way of construing power relations between individuals and groups in society. Gadsby was trained as an art historian, and she brings this training into her stand-up. For instance, in *Nanette*, she challenges the continued reverence for Pablo Picasso in light of the #MeToo movement. She says, "They're all cut from the same cloth: Donald Trump, Pablo Picasso, Harvey Weinstein, Bill Cosby, Woody Allen, Roman Polanski. These men are not exceptions, they are the rule. And they are not individuals, they are our stories." She adds that the way we hold these figures in awe despite their moral failings says something disturbing about us. "And the moral of our story is, we don't give a shit. We don't give a fuck about women or children. We only care about a man's reputation."[14] Here she draws upon her disciplinary expertise in art history to make a poignant observation about contemporary victimizers.

The most poignant way Gadsby employs disciplinary deconstruction attends to stand-up itself. She uses stand-up to critique stand-up. Stand-up's imperative to generate resolutions leading to laughter or to ease tensions

10. Krefting, "Hannah Gadsby Stands Down," 165.

11. See Ryzik, "Comedy-Destroying, Soul Affirming Art of Hannah Gadsby"; Als, "Hannah Gadsby's Song of the Self," labels her follow-up Netflix special *Douglas* "solipsism masquerading as art."

12. Gilbert, "*Nanette* Is a Radical, Transformative Work of Comedy."

13. Parker, "Hannah Gadsby's Genius Follow-up to *Nanette*."

14. Gadsby, *Nanette*.

means that it ends up having to ignore the social and political currency of what Cynthia and Julie Willett label "fumerism."[15] Gadsby explains,

> Let me explain to you what a joke is. And when you strip it back to its bare essential components, like, its bare minimum, a joke is simply two things, it needs two things to work. A setup and a punch line. And it is essentially a question with a surprise answer. Right? But in this context, what a joke is, is a question that I have artificially inseminated. Tension. I do that, that's my job. I make you all feel tense, and then I make you laugh, and you're like, "Thanks for that. I was feeling a bit tense." I MADE YOU TENSE. This is an abusive relationship. Do you know why I'm such a funny fucker? Do you? It's because, you know, I've been learning the art of tension diffusion since I was a children [*sic*]. Back then it wasn't a job, wasn't even a hobby, it was a survival tactic. I didn't have to invent the tension. I was the tension.[16]

Nanette was a tremendous hit. As with many hits, people either loved it or hated it. One of the critiques that seems to have affected her most deeply is the argument that in subverting the standards of stand-up, she lost the right to classify herself a stand-up comedian. Gadsby reflects, "In the middle of writing it, I realized my show would be relegated to being 'a one-woman show.' That always happens to women's shows. Nobody would ever say that to a man doing a subversive comedy show or showing his vulnerability on stage. He'd be called a genius pushing the genre."[17] She comes straight at this critique in her 2019 Netflix special *Douglas*. Not only does she list all the ways people have derisively classified her work—as a lecture, a one-woman show, a TED Talk—she parodies each discursive modality in and through her follow-up performance. Gadsby declares, "What this show is, is a metaphorical preposition that explains the relationship between what you think you think you see me think and what I'm genuinely able to think."[18] Such reflexivity offers exciting possibilities for stand-up preachers as well.

---

15. Willett and Willett, *Uproarious*, 28. In their conclusion, the Willetts celebrate Gadsby for creating a new kind of humor in which "anger plus catharsis plus empathy defines the kind of comedy that speaks truth" (152).

16. Gadsby, *Nanette*.

17. Gadsby, "*Nanette* Isn't a Comedy Show."

18. Gadsby, *Douglas*.

TAKEAWAYS FOR STAND-UP PREACHING

Terry Eagleton asserts that comedy exists to disrupt *cosmos*, that sense of the world viewed as a rational, virtuous, beautiful, well-ordered whole.[19] We witness such comedic disruption in the stand-up of Hannah Gadsby. Stand-up is a peculiar discursive modality in that the comic aims to tell the truth about the world without the constraint of telling the whole truth. For this to work there must be a minimal degree of congruence between what the comic tells us about herself and what we believe to be true about her. Her performance and her persona must exhibit and illuminate what it means to be a person in the world, with all its awfulness and lushness. Gadsby does something in her stand-up that we preachers are also called to do. As O. Wesley Allen Jr. argues, preachers could do better at engaging the human condition. This requires preachers to lean in to life's vicissitudes, to embrace sorrow and joy. Allen writes, "No preacher ever brought the gospel to bear on the lives of those in the pews in a way that was truly salvific while wearing floaties and standing in the baby pool of life."[20] In many ways, the world of stand-up comedy is as much a baby pool as the pulpit. There is a tremendous pressure to constrain one's lived experiences to accommodate comedy's discursive norms, i.e., to *be* funny. One of the things that is so instructive about Gadsby's stand-up is the way in which Gadsby works with and against these norms. As Rebecca Krefting observes, "Gadsby uses comedy to interrogate comedy and the ways production and consumption are gendered, among them the pressure placed on women to self-deprecate in order to satisfy gendered cultural values and expectations of femininity."[21]

Another takeaway for preachers from Gadsby's stand-up aligns with what Brad Braxton labels "righteous troublemaking."[22] Such efforts align with the prophetic vocation, a secularized version of which we witness in Gadsby's work. As one critic puts it, "Gadsby's fabled edginess is not so much edginess as excitement at her ability to 'edge' the audience, to walk away or turn off the pleasure switch in order to get to what she considers enlightenment."[23] Such enlightenment, such altered ways of thinking and feeling, is necessary to alter our ways of behaving and belonging. Even

19. Eagleton, *Humour*, 30.

20. Allen, *Preaching and the Human Condition*, 3.

21. Krefting, "Hannah Gadsby," 94. See also Krefting, "Hannah Gadsby Stands Down," and Giuffre, "From Nanette to Nanettflix," 34–38, on how the production and consumption dynamic shifted between Gadsby's live performances and her edited Netflix version.

22. Braxton, "Three Questions about Prophets," 10.

23. Als, "Hannah Gadsby's Song of the Self."

as Gadsby pushes against the conventions of stand-up, she exposes how those conventions reinforce injustice and the feelings of self-worth of those marginalized by particular ways of thinking. Homiletician Melva Sampson emphasizes the importance of preachers embodying redemptive self-love, "redeeming ourselves from who society has seen us as, redeeming ourselves from what we even see ourselves as to the point that we love ourselves unashamedly without apology."[24]

In *Nanette*, Gadsby wants to tell her story properly, without the humiliation she had to endure in order to stay funny. And so, she lays bare her trauma. There's anger, bitterness, and laughter there, but there is mostly truth-telling. Choking up, you hear her say: "Laughter is not our medicine. Stories hold our cure."[25] In her recently published book *Words That Heal: Preaching Hope to Wounded Souls,* homiletician Joni Sancken argues that if we are to take God's healing power seriously, we must be willing to tell the truth about our deepest pains. This is the requisite condition for God's redemption from our wounds, so that "God in Christ can redeem even this pain."[26] Preachers must be willing to tell the hard truths, she writes:

> Exposing dark secrets to the light of Christ can help remove the power of these deep wounds to control lives. Telling the truth in the pulpit about difficult parts of life creates a sense of trustworthiness for the preacher and deepens the relevance of preaching. When survivors hear their truth spoken from the pulpit, it legitimizes their experiences, humanizes them, and highlights their worth to God and the church. When the preacher admits that life is not perfect, it deepens our sense of need before God.[27]

---

24. Cited in Johnson, *Womanist Preacher,* 72.
25. Gadsby, *Nanette.*
26. Sancken, *Words That Heal,* 47.
27. Sancken, *Words That Heal,* 81–82.

5

Staging Identity
On Persona and Authenticity

The stage is a vulnerable place. To people who like you, you're in the spotlight. To those who don't, you're at the center of a target.[1]

—KEVIN HART

The monologue mode of address and the authority accorded the event can make preaching feel artificially formal, creating a sense of distance between preacher and hearers. The use of humor is the preacher's attempt to bridge this gulf.[2]

—RUTHANNA HOOKE

Preachers and stand-up comics face a constant challenge. When they speak from the pulpit or the comedy stage, they speak as themselves, and yet, at the same time, they are speaking as someone else. By this I mean they speak simultaneously as a particular person and as a particular *type* of person. How preachers and comics navigate the distance—however minimal—between their true selves and the expectations that accompany their

1. Hart, *I Can't Make This Up*, 152.
2. Hooke, "Humor in Preaching," 187.

respective roles constitutes their homiletical or comical personae. This is no small task. Among homileticians of late, Lisa Thompson has underscored the difficulty of occupying a particular body and mind in the pulpit amid pressure to conform to received traditions that accompany the performance of preaching—especially for Black women and other marginalized people.[3] Postcolonial homileticians have likewise problematized traditional homiletics that fail to account for the embodied realities of preaching.[4]

Our contemporary social media landscape has added layers of complexity to the task of staging presence. As congregants and comedy fans have greater access to preachers' and comedians' lives outside the spotlight, there is a heightened expectation for their performative personae and private personhoods to align. Casey Sigmon has done much to highlight the challenges and benefits of social media's "technoculture" on the praxis of preaching. She employs the word *technoculture* to name the blurred boundaries between communication technologies and cultures.[5] In the world of stand-up, we saw a clear example of the difficulties this blurring can present for comics when Kevin Hart's homophobic tweets from 2009 resurfaced, creating so much backlash that he pulled out from hosting the Oscars a decade later.[6] What I find most illuminating in Hart's case is the emphasis he placed on his private (purportedly LGBTQIA-affirming) views and his public persona that must constantly work to get a laugh, even at the expense of others.

Staging presence in contemporary technocultures can place as much pressure on preachers as it does for stand-up comics. With greater pressure to display our "authentic" selves in and beyond our preaching, the boundaries between our private and public selves have blurred. With his trademark nuance and subtlety, Ted Smith rightly notes, "The preacher must *display* authenticity in ways that can be received as such. Because the real self is taken to be the ground of authority, performances of authenticity must find ways to display to others what they will see as one's real self."[7] This chapter will attend to ways authenticity and persona emerge in stand-up comedy, gleaning insights for the similar work of preachers.

---

3. Thompson, *Ingenuity,* 5.

4. Kim-Cragg, *Postcolonial Preaching,* 47–66; Kim and Wong, *Finding Our Voice,* 59–60; Kwok, "Postcolonial Preaching in Intercultural Contexts."

5. Sigmon, "Engaging the Gadfly," ch. 3, and "Preaching by the Rivers of Babylon," 129. See also Myers, *Curating Church,* 183–85 and McClure, "Learning from and Transforming the Community-Building Promise," 116, on how social media can provide new ways of being present and sharing identity.

6. Fortin, "Kevin Hart Steps Down."

7. Smith, "Discerning Authorities," 65.

STAND-UP COMEDY: AN INTIMATE AFFAIR

As we saw in chapter 3, Mort Sahl was the first stand-up comic to break out of the abstract and subject-neutral mode of joke telling. He applied his personal opinions and stories from his life as a filter for his comedy. Subject matter in much stand-up comedy today involves material often considered private (e.g., sex, family drama, personal anxieties, and tics). Margaret Cho is a prime example of how a comical persona emerges out of divulging intimate details. Her comedy is known for its sexual explicitness. It draws on intimate physical details linking the otherness of her queer, Korean, female body with challenges against heteronormativity, white supremacy, and patriarchy. Her stand-up routines include descriptions of sex acts with men and women, as well as other intimate details such as her experiences in S&M clubs, colonics, and grooming practices like anal bleaching. By transcending the borders between the private and the public, Cho has built a career as an outlaw persona. As Linda Mizejewski observes, "Cho puts her body where her mouth is, so to speak. Her routines are shocking not so much for liberal use of expletives as for her graphic narrations of her sex life, from her advice on how to hurry a man's orgasm during oral sex to her admission that her favorite sexual act is 'eating ass.'"[8] Now, I think it's safe to say that Cho's subject matter is light-years away from that of most working preachers, but she shows preachers something about our contemporary cultural contexts and the emerging expectations that equate oversharing with authenticity. As the line dividing the public and private self continues to diminish, how are preachers to navigate these pressures?

Walter Benjamin was right to observe that the character revealed on the comedy stage is of an altogether different type than that of persons we encounter off the stage. If we were to hear someone tell the kinds of stories or jokes that are the bread and butter of contemporary stand-up, many of us would revile them, or at minimum, walk away from the joke-teller in disgust. Benjamin writes, "It is never in themselves, never morally, that the actions of the comic hero affect his public; his deeds are interesting only insofar as they reflect the light of character."[9] Bracketing for the moment Benjamin's comment about the irrelevance of a comic's morality (as we have seen in the canceling of Bill Cosby and Louis C.K.), he is right to emphasize that a comic persona is *rendered* in and through a comic's actions. Much as Jesus' persona is rendered by the narration of his words and actions in the

---

8. Mizejewski, *Pretty/Funny*, 126. See also a similar analysis of Richard Pryor's comedy defined as "culturally intimate humor" in Cooper, "Is It Something He Said."

9. Benjamin, "Fate and Character," 310.

Gospels, so too are our homiletical personae rendered by what we do and say in the pulpit.[10]

Canadian sociologist Ian Brodie positions stand-up at the center point along a discursive continuum. The comic overcomes the distance between a purely monologic, unidirectional communication on the one end and a purely dialogic, bidirectional communication on the other.[11] Brodie attributes the possibility for such mediation to the invention of the microphone, which enables communication that places the comic's voice on the same level as that of the audience. With a microphone, the comic is free to speak at a conversational volume, to shout, or to whisper, much as one might at a conversation around the watercooler or kitchen table. Brodie is quick to note, however, that microphones alone cannot establish intimacy between the performer and her audience. "The audience must also know something about the performer, locating her within their own framework. . . . The comedian must interweave the comic bits in her routines with declarative statements or testimonial personal experience narratives which squarely locate her as sharing a core of fundamental precepts with her audience."[12] Comedy coaches all emphasize the importance of finding one's comedic voice.[13] This nebulous and subjective aspect of the performer's performance emerges in a kind of *Gestalt* experience we have of the comic. When a congruence emerges between a comic's personality, embodiment, point of view, comedy material, and performance, we experience them as being authentic.

Brodie argues that contemporary stand-up goes a step further than authenticity. The best stand-up comics engender intimacy between themselves and their audience members. He writes, "My premise is that one of the characteristics of stand-up comedy, and one of the hallmarks of stand-up as a performative genre, is how it tends to be predicated on the *illusion* of intimacy, a disregard for the distancing of the stage."[14] This illusion of intimacy ought to give us pause as preachers. Is preaching an intimate affair, or are we doing something else?

The rhetorical situation of intimacy described by Brodie has homiletical corollaries. St. Augustine's congregational context in Hippo was a raucous space, far closer to contemporary comedy clubs than most churches—especially mainline churches. They routinely applauded. On occasion,

---

10. See Frei, *Identity of Jesus Christ*, 13, and Campbell, *Preaching Jesus,* ch. 8.

11. Brodie, "Stand-up Comedy as a Genre of Intimacy," 160.

12. Brodie, "Stand-up Comedy as a Genre of Intimacy," 170.

13. See Rosenfield, *Mastering Stand-Up*, 236–40; Murray, *Be A Great Stand-Up*, ch. 4; and Carter, *New Comedy Bible,* 171–73.

14. Brodie, "Stand-up Comedy as a Genre of Intimacy," 156.

they might even boo him or shout in protest. "Augustine always kept a close eye on his hearers," writes S. A. H. Kennell, "extending things if they were silent, breaking things off if they applauded."[15] The North African bishop valued spontaneity, and he chastised preachers who wrote sermons out in advance and then read them or performed them from memory. In stressing the importance of intelligibility, Augustine emphasized preaching that establishes deep connections with the hearts and minds of the congregants. He explains that in debates and in public gatherings there is a natural give and take of information. The speaker might be interrupted, either to provide clarification or in contestation. But the sermonic context is altogether different. When decorum eschews interrupting the preacher, it is all the more important that the preacher remain sensitive, and to "come to the aid of the silent listener" by elaborating one's point or rephrasing it until its meaning finds purchase in the minds of the hearers. Augustine adds that "this is not possible for those who deliver prepared or memorized speeches," and only through an intimate appraisal of the congregation's reception might the preacher remain nimble enough to avoid confusion or boredom.[16] Sermon manuscripts frustrate an intimate atmosphere between speaker and listeners. It is no wonder, then, why the vast majority of stand-up comics speak without notes. As stand-up comic and Baptist preacher Susan Sparks argues, "the power is in the eye contact. It's about trust and believability. For a comedian, especially, the kiss of death is to take a five-by-seven index card on stage and read your set. Only rank amateurs do that."[17]

One of the earliest and most influential American homileticians was John Broadus. As we saw in chapter 2, Broadus's homiletical wisdom guided aspiring American preachers for more than a century. Like Augustine, Broadus was a staunch defender of extemporaneous preaching. He vociferously challenged the use of manuscripts in preaching for intruding upon the intimacy of the preaching moment, which relies upon the confluence of the preacher's voice, eye contact, and bodily movements to engender the listener's undivided attention. Beyond pragmatics, there was a theological reason Broadus elevated extemporaneous delivery over manuscript preaching: "How can a man pray that God will guide him through a forest, when he has already blazed the entire path, and committed himself to follow it?"[18] Much closer to our era, Fred Craddock argues that intimacy is not a quality put into a sermon but a quality out of which preaching is done. Here he

---

15. Kennell, "Augustine's Hostile Hearers."

16. Augustine, *De Doctrina Christiana*, 4.10.

17. Sparks, *Preaching Punchlines*, 75.

18. Broadus, *Treatise on the Preparation and Delivery of Sermons*, 429.

focuses on the psychodynamics of orality and its power to socialize and create intimacy. "The human voice, released into a group of persons whose lives are interrelated in many ways, it is an extraordinary force," writes Craddock. "Unlike textuality, orality generates intimacy, in that speaker and listener experience a sense of being on the 'inside' of something very important."[19] Homiletician Carolyn Ann Knight expresses a similar sentiment to Craddock, writing, "Preaching is an act of intimacy, a delicate moment between God and preacher, preacher and people."[20]

Turning again to stand-up comedy, we find marks of intimacy in the comedy of Marc Maron. Maron delivers much of his Netflix special *End Times Fun* seated on a four-legged stool. His wardrobe helps to render his comical persona. He wears a hipsteresque gray vest over a wrinkle-free button up, skinny jeans with rolled cuffs, and reddish-brown boots. He's got the sleeves of his pinstripe button-up pushed to his elbows. This look works well with Maron's salt-and-pepper hair and beard. From his self-presentation and delivery style, Maron's persona takes shape as a hip, fifty-something dude who's baffled by the latest fads and opinions.

Something Maron does exceptionally well is performing a conversation as a way to question so-called wisdom. This is a rhetorical strategy that draws listeners in by establishing distance and inviting participation.[21] Maron sets up one of his bits with a declaration: "You never know when someone's gonna dump some shit in your head and it's gonna ruin your life."[22] He describes a hypothetical day in which you're going about your business when all of a sudden someone asks you,

"Hey, you takin' turmeric?"

"Turmeric? The spice?"

"Yeah, you gotta take that shit."

"Turmeric? The spice that you buy once for this one Indian recipe and never use it again and it stains your wooden spoon? That turmeric?"

"Yeah, you gotta take that shit."

"Why?"

"For inflammation."

Maron's comical persona emerges between his interlocutors. On the one side, he's the postmodern cynic, questioning the plausibility of the latest health fad. On the other side, he's the peddler of faux wisdom, the turmeric pusher. By presenting this in the form of a dialogue, Maron leads the

19. Craddock, *Preaching*, 168–69.
20. Knight, "Preaching as an Intimate Act," 89.
21. Craddock, *Overhearing the Gospel*, 98; Myers, "Method Behind the Mystique."
22. Maron, *End Times Fun*.

audience to identify with both characters. We have all been the unwilling or at least reluctant recipient of faux wisdom (confession: I take turmeric for inflammation). And we've all been the proselytizer for some fad or another, spreading our newfound knowledge as if it were gospel.

Maron exudes irony in this set. He doesn't laugh at his jokes because they aren't really jokes; he's performing the point of view of the skeptic and the critic. Maron questions not only the wisdom of taking turmeric for inflammation, he also questions the source of this wisdom. When Maron's inquisitor discovers that the turmeric guy learned about its value from his trainer, Maron breaks character to offer an aside about the vocation of personal training. He questions any wisdom coming from a guy who didn't really want to be a trainer. Maron casts trainers as tragic figures. They become trainers because they didn't make the team or some other of their dreams and figured that, since they spend a lot of time at the gym anyway, they might as well become a trainer.

Maron slips back into character, adding, "Make sure you get the turmeric with black pepper in it."

"Black pepper, why?"

"Yeah, get the kind with black pepper because it activates it."

The incredulous tone of Maron's character could not be more pronounced. This leads Maron into another aside in which he imagines the origins of this turmeric scam. A couple of vitamin hustlers are wondering what they ought to do with this mound of turmeric that nobody wants, and so they come up with the utterly random idea of combining it with another spice they have lying around. Again, Maron slides from direct discourse with the audience into the characters of these two vitamin hustlers. By highlighting the dubious health benefits of this alchemy, Maron draws attention to how silly this all sounds. His performance benefits from how he seamlessly slides between direct discourse/narration and the characters who play out this scene. Maron mixes showing with telling.

Maron presents preachers with several takeaways for staging presence. First, by donning casual clothes and a laid-back posture, Maron structures the conditions of possibility for intimacy between himself and his audience. His performance shows how a speaker's attire can facilitate or discourage dialogical intimacy. Second, his persona emerges from his strong point of view. This establishes Maron's appearance of authenticity, a self-revelation of who he "really" is.

HOMILETICAL AUTHENTICITY: A VERY BRIEF HISTORY

Selfhood is one of the primary commodities of contemporary stand-up comedy. More important than jokes is the self-presentation of the comic that corresponds with his angle of vision on the world, which Maron so clearly demonstrates in his stand-up. As Phillip Auslander avers, "the comics' personae, as much as their work, become the 'authentic' elements exploited for their commercial potential."[23] To borrow an image from Ferdinand de Saussure, the comic and her performance are like two sides of a sheet of paper; they are indivisible.

While he tends to get associated with the most objectifying perspective on preaching, Karl Barth insisted on the full humanity of the preaching task. In his lectures on homiletics, Barth instructed his students to proclaim God's Word in their own voices and as themselves. He writes, "It is as the persons they are that they have been selected and called. This is what is meant by originality. Pastors are not to adopt a role. They are not to slip into the clothing of biblical characters. That would be the worst kind of comedy."[24] Of central importance here is a minimal discrepancy between the preacher-as-person and the preacher-as-pastor. This wisdom has a long history.

In his landmark study on revivalist preacher Charles G. Finney, Ted Smith maps the rise of sincerity in pulpit and public discourse. We already investigated the connection with this epistemic shift in theological anthropology and the practice of preaching in chapter 2. For preaching to properly kindle the hearts and souls of the populace, the preacher had to *perform* sincerity, that is, preaching needed to publicly reveal a private self that harmonized closely with the public self.[25] Smith goes on to write that "Finney stressed the need for every aspect of preaching to be 'natural,' by which he meant that it should be free from self-consciousness, like action most appropriate to the private sphere. The good preacher felt the right feeling and then spoke and moved in whatever ways came naturally."[26] Finney's stress on preaching that appears natural and uncontrived certainly holds for the performance of contemporary stand-up.

The homiletic impact of this movement toward the public display of private feelings was wide. In his book *Homiletics*, Auburn Theological

---

23. Auslander, *Presence and Resistance*, 132–33.

24. Barth, *Homiletics*, 81–82.

25. Smith, *New Measures*, 189.

26. Smith, *New Measures*, 190.

Seminary professor William G. T. Shedd dismisses elocution for feigning genuine emotion, "the mere delivery of truth." Against this earlier emphasis among his homiletical colleagues toward dispassionate declarations, Shedd argues for preaching that is redolent with ardor and feeling for it is such that "really sets the Christian affections aglow, as speaking in the same spirit to an individual in private intercourse."[27] Around the same time as Shedd, Princeton Theological Seminary professor James W. Alexander expressed a similar sentiment. In his posthumous publication *Thoughts on Preaching*, Alexander has this to say about sermon delivery: "In delivery, learn to know when to dwell on a point; let the enlargement be, not where you *determined* in your closet it should be; but where you feel the spring flowing as you speak *let it gush*. Let contemplation have place *while you speak*."[28] Homiletical authority for Shedd and Alexander situates the preacher in close proximity to his genuine emotions and, accordingly, to those of his congregants.

It will come as no surprise that the homiletical turn toward intimacy in preaching coincided with a turn away from sermon manuscripts. Union Presbyterian Seminary professor Robert Dabney couldn't have put it stronger when he told his preaching students that "reading a manuscript to the people can never, with any justice, be termed preaching."[29] Alexander argues similarly:

> If you press me to say which is absolutely the best practice in regard to "notes," properly so called, that is in distinction from a complete manuscript, I unhesitatingly say USE NONE. Carry no scrap of writing into the pulpit. Let your scheme, with all its branches, be written on our mental tablet. . . . Prepare a skeleton of your leading ideas, branching them off into their secondary relations. This you may have before you. Digest well the subject, but be not careful to choose your *words* previous to your delivery. Follow out the idea with such language as may offer at the moment.[30]

John Broadus held a similar position. "Preaching the gospel can regain its power and success only when the eye in delivery is emancipated alike from the manuscript and the recitation of words committed to memory."[31] Lauding Broadus's gifts for the extempore, one of his seminary students later observed, "[Broadus] assiduously cultivated this habit and developed the

27. Shedd, *Homiletics and Pastoral Theology*, 299.

28. Alexander, *Thoughts on Preaching*, 18. Emphasis original.

29. Dabney, *Sacred Rhetoric*, Lecture XXIII, 328.

30. Alexander, *Thoughts on Preaching*, 151.

31. John Broadus Papers, cited in Dockery and Duke, eds., *John A. Broadus*, 193.

ability to make each person in the audience feel that he was talking directly to him."[32]

Contemporary homileticians and preachers approach the use of sermon manuscripts from a range of perspectives. J. Alfred Smith argues that internalization of the sermon is a requisite for preaching. He writes, "I must internalize the sermon so that it will be alive in my heart and active in my memory." He adds that the written manuscript is not ready for preaching. It must be internalized because the sermon and the preacher must become one in the act of preaching. The sermon is not a speech the preacher has written but "the essence of who the preacher is and what the preacher believes."[33] Cleophus LaRue celebrates the improvisational delivery styles of "intellectual preachers" such as Gardner Taylor, Manuel Scott, E. K. Bailey, and A. Louis Patterson. Such preachers attend carefully to language, finding ways to balance the use of notes or a manuscript with what is going on in the preaching event itself.[34]

Richard Ward stresses the benefits of writing a sermon manuscript. "The ear will teach the eye and the hand what to write and how to arrange the language on a page," notes Ward. "Even as one is writing, one is getting freer from the controlling influence of the page; writing is taking its place in the drama as having a supportive role to play."[35] Jared Alcántara offers a nuanced perspective:

> An improvisational sermon grows out of the inter*play* of tradition and innovation, careful preparation and real-time intuition, and prior planning and contemporaneous interaction. This way of conceiving of the sermon disrupts standard distinctions and binaries. The lines are blurred between preacher and listener(s), scripted and unscripted, tradition and transitioning. Although an established framework exists, so also does freedom, specifically the freedom to "create free spaces within the framework." The playing of the play enfleshes itself at the intersection of convention, intuition, and interaction, and in the free spaces that such an intersection catalyzes.[36]

From this brief survey of homileticians, it is clear that whether a manuscript is used or not, the key to manifesting homiletical authenticity is to use the manuscript in such a way that it does not interfere with the communicative

---

32. Stanfield, ed., *Favorite Sermons of John A. Broadus,* 12.

33. Smith, "How Can They Hear without a Preacher?," 138.

34. LaRue, *I Believe I'll Testify,* 85–86.

35. Ward, "Performing the Manuscript," 239.

36. Alcántara, *Crossover Preaching,* 111.

act performed by preachers and received by congregants. As Frank Thomas teaches us, "Again, these rhetorical processes and skills are not the add-ons of persuasion after one has figured out the rational content of what to say. These rhetorical processes are at the very heart of communication, based in the need and desire to establish identity personhood, social status, and ultimately a place in the human family."[37]

CASE STUDIES IN PERFORMANCE AND PERSPECTIVE

As we have seen, the comedian's identity is vital to the comedy process. Even when comedians perform an exaggerated version of their own identities— as is the case with Joan Rivers or Ricky Gervais—the performance must harmonize with the comic's perspective in order to render the performance authentic. One mark of authenticity pertains to how the comedian relates to their embodiment. An overweight comic may or may not choose to comment on their physique, but they cannot perform as if they are skinny (except ironically). Jim Gaffigan, for instance, features his unhealthy relationship with food as a prominent feature of his act.[38] This is not to cast aspersions on Gaffigan's physique; rather, I aim to suggest that were he to dwell on his penchant for fast food and his disdain for exercise as an objectively skinny man, his comedy would drift from its mark. Whatever the schtick, a comic's "voice" must seem authentic to the identity they embody on stage.

The comedian may make self-deprecating jokes about their appearance, experiences, beliefs, and characteristics as a way to draw attention to their performed identity. Self-deprecating jokes have the potential to critique the culture that creates specific norms and expectations in relation to appearances and identities, while simultaneously criticizing those individuals or groups that subscribe to those particular norms and expectations. Other comedians make jokes about identities that are different from their own. For example, British white male comedian Roy Chubby Brown has established a very successful (and controversial) comedy career making jokes about women and ethnic minorities.

Alternatively, comedians can perform as a particular character that differs from their own identity. Paul O'Grady has performed in drag as his alter ego, Lily Savage, and has made jokes about sex and sexuality from "Lily's perspective."[39] In other cases, such as the various comedic personas

---

37. Thomas, *Introduction to the Practice of African American Preaching*, 80.

38. See the incisive essay by Noland and Hoppmann, "Stop! You're Killing Me."

39. See O'Grady, *At My Mother's Knee*, 132–33.

adopted by Sacha Baron Cohen, the layers of identities are deliberately blurred so that it is not clear which identity, or identities, is being adopted and ridiculed. His comedic persona Ali G, for instance, confused audiences because Ali G's identity was ambiguous. It was unclear whether he was white, Jewish, or Asian. As Robert Saunders argues, Baron Cohen's post-modern performances yield a number of interpretive possibilities: Is he a white man pretending to be a Black man? Is he a white man pretending to be an Asian who is pretending to be Black? Or is he a Jewish man pretending to be an Asian pretending to be a white man pretending to be Black?[40] The un-certainty and fluidity surrounding Ali G's identity has prompted questions about who was impersonating whom and this undecidability has spurred criticisms that Baron Cohen is propagating homophobic, misogynistic, and racist stereotypes.

While some comedians may ensure that they meet these audience ex-pectations, as Sharon Lockyer observes, others can, of course, renegotiate and redefine these expectations. She offers as an example Omid Djalili, a British-Iranian comedian and actor. Djalili often begins his performances by talking in a thick "Middle Eastern" accent. Once the audience is used to this accent and has relaxed into his performance, Djalili then switches to his authentic British accent. In doing so, Omid Djalili subverts stereotypes that some audience members may have about Middle Eastern identities.[41]

Let's take a look at two specific examples of the performance of iden-tity in the work of a pair of comics who have made recent headlines: Ellen DeGeneres and Aziz Ansari. There are several reasons why DeGeneres and Ansari are illuminating for we who would stage our identities homiletically. More than most stand-up comics, DeGeneres and Ansari have emphasized their authenticity across multiple comedic genres. Their respective comedic "voices" come through whether they are performing stand-up, acting in a sitcom, hosting a talk show, or writing a memoir. They thus present us with a persistent picture of who they are on and off stage. Both DeGeneres and Ansari have also made recent headlines specifically where their performed personas seemed at odds with their "true selves." These comics are more than cautionary tales for preachers about the dangers of staging identity. They are not, in my mind, in the same category as other comics such as Bill Cosby and Louis C.K., whose moral reprehensibility so intrudes upon their on-stage personas as to render their art unworthy of consumption by we who denounce abuses of power to victimize women.[42] DeGeneres and Ansari

40. Saunders, *Many Faces of Sacha Baron Cohen*, 57–82.
41. Lockyer, "Identity," 377–78.
42. Cf. Willard, *Why It's OK to Enjoy the Work of Immoral Artists*.

present us with a morally ambiguous picture that is far more illuminating for preachers, many of whom (myself included) struggle to hold ourselves to an ethical ideal while we remain fully aware of our foibles, fallenness, and culpability with white supremacist and (hetero)sexist systems.

Ellen DeGeneres: Authentically Gay

Few stand-up comics have worked harder to present themselves as authentically themselves than Ellen DeGeneres. Throughout her successful career as a comic, actor, and talk show host, Ellen has presented herself as both nice and funny. As an observational comic, she takes great joy in finding humor in the mundane moments of life. "Ellen DeGeneres is not famous for being famous. She is famous for being herself . . . for conveying authenticity under the banner of a comedic Ellen-ness in which her perceived genuineness functions as the mortar that holds the house of Ellen together."[43] In her stand-up as well as her highly successful career as a talk show host, Ellen presents a persona that is at once naïvely childlike and potently perceptive. She moves seamlessly between playful asides and thought-provoking insights the way she might talk at a dinner party with family. Part of the joy we receive from Ellen is that of feeling like she's just one of our friends, telling us the truth about herself as we move through life together.

A major feature of identity for contemporary persons is our sexual identity. Especially in America, which abides in the tension between puritanical privation and libidinal excess, being forthright with one's sexual desires is a mark of authenticity.[44] For Ellen, this sexual economy is critical to her authenticity quotient. Some have gone so far as to label her "America's lesbian sweetheart" and "public lesbian number one."[45] Ellen has constructed a persona rooted in "realness," which is seemingly unconcerned with any resulting financial consequences. In an interview published in *The New York Times,* Ellen contrasts herself with Oprah. Contrary to Oprah, whom Ellen regards as "very business minded," Ellen states, "I'm just that way. I'm happy my show is successful. But I am also content just to be me."[46] By explicitly

43. Weber and Leimbach, "Ellen DeGeneres's Incorporate Body," 304.

44. Eve Sedgwick describes the process of coming out about one's sexuality as simultaneously "compulsory and forbidden." Sedgwick, *Epistemology of the Closet,* 70. Cf. Ross, "Beyond the Closet as Raceless Paradigm," 163: "this narrative of progress carries the residue, and occasionally the outright intention, born within evolutionary notions of the uneven development of the races from primitive darkness to civilized enlightenment."

45. Tonello, "America's (Lesbian) Sweethearts"; and Reed, "Ellen DeGeneres."

46. Barnes, "Easy, Breezy, Trending."

eschewing capitalist motivations, Ellen redoubles her persona as the one who is *authentically* herself—no matter the credits or debits she incurs.

Ellen managed to harness the negative energy generated from her public outing as a lesbian into financial success. In the fall of 1996, word leaked that the character of Ellen Morgan, a bookstore manager, might acknowledge that she was a lesbian, making *Ellen* the first prime-time sitcom to feature a gay leading character. Over the next six months, ABC relentlessly encouraged the hype, with DeGeneres herself fueling the fire by joking in television interviews that her character was "Lebanese" and resisting attempts to clarify her own sexuality beyond that of her character on the show. A week before the episode aired, DeGeneres made a well-publicized "coming out" of her own, appearing on the cover of *Time* magazine under the headline "Yep, I'm Gay."[47] An interview with Diane Sawyer on ABC's *20/20* ran on April 25, during the all-important "sweeps week" for the network.

When her eponymous show was canceled, Ellen returned to stand-up. She went back on the road to test material that would eventually constitute her HBO special *The Beginning*, which aired in 2000. She reports the different crowds who now gathered to hear her perform. "I would say that ninety percent of the audience was gay and ten percent were straight. I lost all of my straight fans because everyone thought I was going to be some militant lesbian comedian and talk about rainbow flags."[48] Here we may discern a tension around staging identity. Sometimes just "being oneself" takes an emotional and financial toll.

Gender and sexuality studies scholars Brenda Weber and Joselyn Leimbach argue that Ellen is able to appeal to so many audiences across so many mediated platforms due to the perceived authenticity of her "incorporate body." This term designates a specific fashioning of the self that combines and fuses together hybridities of desire and identity under a single sign of authenticity.[49] This frame of analysis bears witness to Ellen's intersectional identity and its alignment with neoliberal capitalism. In other words, Ellen's purported authenticity, and especially her nonthreatening lesbianism that does not disrupt the heteronormative status quo, coincides with the neoliberal logics of self-determination. Being who one is can carry financial rewards, as it has for Ellen. Mizejewski further notes how Ellen's identity is characterized by a certain "leakiness," a Bakhtinian term that names the slippages out of categories and definitions. Such leakiness is mediated by her

47. Handy, "Roll Over, Ward Cleaver."
48. DeGeneres interview in Kohen, *We Killed*, 207.
49. Weber and Leimbach, "Ellen DeGeneres's Incorporate Body," 307.

blonde, blue-eyed whiteness along with her advocacy for play, generosity, and kindness.[50]

In 2020, Ellen's authenticity came into serious question as former staff members on her talk show and celebrities began to challenge Ellen's perception as unfailingly kind and generous. This led to the circulation of two scathing reports that *The Ellen DeGeneres Show* was a toxic work environment where producers sexually harassed junior staffers—all with Ellen's knowledge.[51] I am uninterested in weighing in on this debate about Ellen's meanness or kindness. What I find most illuminating about this story for preaching is the tension it spotlights between one's public persona and personal practices. The tension is key. It is only because Ellen presents herself as so unfailingly kind that her persona cannot abide charges that call her kindness into question. Preachers ought to recognize that we, too, exude a particular persona in and through our preaching. We'd do well to learn from Ellen's media/identity crisis.

Aziz Ansari: Authentically Feminist

Aziz Ansari is an Indian American comic who hails from Columbia, South Carolina, and much of his stand-up comedy and acting roles have capitalized on the cultural distance manifesting between his dual identities. Yet, even as his South Asian heritage is obvious in his embodiment, his comedy does not resort to mimicry or to making jokes about tuk-tuks and curry.[52] Beyond his ethnic identity, Ansari's stand-up routines focus much more on the challenges of dating and finding love amid the recent rise of technological phenomena like Twitter, Tinder, and Instagram. Ansari's work on this is not only funny but insightful. He moves beyond surface features to challenge the unspoken ethical norms that underlie online interactions.

Like many contemporary comics, Ansari's humor manifests through incongruity. But much of Ansari's comedy emerges from affective rather than cognitive incongruity. As Steven Benko and Eleanor Jones note, "Ansari is an effective comedian not just because of his skill with words but also because of the atmosphere he creates by playing in the space created by the different cultures he intersects with."[53] Ansari capitalizes on the incongruity that manifests between his purported identity as a feminist and the

---

50. Mizejewski, *Pretty/Funny*, 197.

51. For a timeline and commentary on how these events unfolded see Abad-Santos, "How Ellen DeGeneres's Façade of Kindness Crumbled."

52. Ansari, *Premium Blend*.

53. Benko and Jones, "That's Way Too Aggressive a Word," 100.

technocultural systems that can disempower women. He presents himself as an all-around good guy, who genuinely wants to avoid harming others. At the 2016 Golden Globes, where he received the coveted Best Actor award for his work on *Master of None*, Ansari wore all black as a show of solidarity with the #MeToo movement.

A mark of Ansari's comedy is its charged or progressive orientation. Like many of the stand-up comics spotlighted in this book, Ansari approaches what I identify as *the comical*: the use of humor to challenge the ways we think and feel. While he is funny and makes use of his fair share of jokes, his humor is much more oriented to cultural critique than at getting a laugh at all costs. He capitalizes in particular on the absurdities of misogyny in contemporary politics and culture. He presents himself as a likeable, vulnerable, and sensitive man. His feministic authenticity is reinforced by his book *Modern Romance: An Investigation*, which he co-wrote with NYU sociologist Eric Klinenberg. Ansari's "voice" comes through in the book as that of one who empathizes with and understands the complexities of contemporary womanhood. Accordingly, he has taken strong stances against "bro culture." Through the use of sarcasm and irony, Ansari points out the inconsistencies redolent in patriarchal systems and structures and he leverages these inconsistencies to combat the very ideologies that perpetuate women's marginalization. For example, in his 2013 Netflix special *Buried Alive* Ansari discusses the absurd phenomenon of "dick pics," where a man sends a picture of his genitals to someone through text or email.[54] He asks how such a bizarre phenomenon became so commonplace. To highlight the absurdity of this invasive act, Ansari imagines how hard it must have been for guys to do this before camera phones and cell phones. He says, "Thirty years ago, if I went up to some woman and I was like, 'Hi. I recently took some photos of my penis. And I just got 'em developed, and some of the shots look fantastic." Following a volley of laughs, Ansari returns to direct discourse to assert that if he mailed these pictures to a woman back then, he would have been arrested that very day. While Ansari doesn't come right out and say this, in his oblique, comical way he is labeling dick pics a form of sexualized violence that ought to be criminalized.

In 2018 an article appeared on the *babe.net* website entitled "I Went on a Date with Aziz Ansari. It Turned Into the Worst Night of My Life."[55] This article accused Ansari of sexual misconduct. The online magazine published a pseudonymous tale from "Grace," who recounted in vivid detail a date she had with Ansari the previous fall. The article describes Ansari

54. Ansari, *Buried Alive*.
55. Way, "I Went on a Date with Aziz Ansari."

as sexually aggressive, pressuring Grace to perform sexual acts against her wishes. The article painted a dissonant picture of Ansari from the one he had spent years cultivating. The piece immediately went viral, prompting calls to #CancelAnsari and for others to question whether the encounter was anything more than "a date that went badly."[56] Ansari admitted that the encounter had occurred but that he believed everything was consensual.[57]

Grace's story produced a tidal wave of opinions. A central feature of these pieces was to hold men accountable for their actions against women. The question was less about whether Ansari did anything wrong (he confessed as much) than it was about whether he deserved to be #canceled for his actions. At the crux of the debate was a value judgment about Ansari's character. Did his actions behind closed doors render his onstage persona void? In other words, did his actions against one woman contradict his actions for all women?

Some feminist comedy scholars and journalists have asked important questions about staging identity, wondering if Ansari "subconsciously created a character based upon his real-life dark side or if that character was separate from his tactless but noncriminal actions."[58] Others have focused less on what Ansari did or didn't do on his date with Grace and more on what problems and possibilities this incident incites about how to talk about sexual misconduct in the public square.[59] While I share these questions and concerns, where I find Ansari's fall from grace most illuminating for preaching centers on his persona. Unlike many stand-up comics who have faced similar allegations, Ansari has elected to use his platform on Netflix to speak directly into the scandal and to seek forgiveness for the harm he caused Grace and his fans.[60] Such an act of public contrition is necessary for a comic such as Ansari. Unlike Louis C.K., whose comic persona is that of a sexist misanthrope, who thinks himself above the audience, Ansari must restore our trust in him as a person off stage before we will be able to buy his act on stage.

56. See Tholmer, "People Are Having Very Different Reactions"; Flanagan, "Humiliation of Aziz Ansari"; North, "Aziz Ansari Story Is Ordinary"; and *All Things Considered*, "Fine Line Between a Bad Date and Sexual Assault."

57. Thomas, "Aziz Ansari Responds to Sexual Assault Claim."

58. Oppliger and Mears, "Comedy in the Era of #MeToo," 166.

59. See North, "Aziz Ansari Actually Talked," and "Louis C.K. and Aziz Ansari Have an Opportunity for Redemption."

60. Ansari, *Right Now*.

CONCLUSION: LET'S GET PERSONAL

A challenge persists for preachers and comics: how much of our authentic selves are we willing to reveal through our performances? Because preachers interact with the same group of people in and out of the pulpit, we perform under tighter restrictions than stand-up comics. We destroy our credibility if we behave too differently in private, public, and pulpit spaces. Comics have an advantage over preachers here in that most of their audience members know only what the comic chooses to reveal about themselves—either on stage or through social media. The person who preaches must align with the person our congregants or parishioners understand us to be. We must decide, then, just how much of our true selves we are willing to show in our preacherly personas.

I am blessed in my work at Columbia Theological Seminary to teach preaching with my friend and colleague Anna Carter Florence. One thing she stresses to our preaching students every year is for us to keep God the subject of our preaching. There is a temptation, she argues, to change the subject to ourselves. This is largely a defense mechanism. We worry that if we say what we believe God wants us to say, our listeners will think differently about us. When preachers do this, we rob our congregants or parishioners of an opportunity to hear the Word of God enfleshed among us. Carter Florence goes a step further, and this next point sits uncomfortably—even paradoxically—with the first: when we make God the subject of our preaching, the preacher will be laid bare in the sermon. This means that the more we focus on God, the more personal our preaching becomes. In her words, "The sermon is personal. Interpretation is personal. You cannot engage a text and emerge without a limp or a scar or some other trace of what the text did to you. And when you preach after such an encounter, *that* is what the congregation will see."[61]

What I take from this is that staging identity is not so much about sharing all our peccadillos and preferences than it is about bringing our full selves to the task of preaching. When we open ourselves to the God at work in the text and in our lives, we cannot help but get personal. I think we sometimes overthink authenticity to the point that we are focused more on image management than we are about just being ourselves. We needn't worry so much about performing ourselves in the pulpit. Instead, we should perform an encounter between God's Word and God's people. When we do this, authenticity and intimacy will take care of themselves.

61. Carter Florence, "Preaching and the Personal," 12.

Stand-Up Spotlight
Wanda Sykes
between Invective and Irony

That's what you gotta do.
You gotta hum a negro spiritual to keep from killing somebody.[1]

—WANDA SYKES

Wanda Sykes is a comedic genius. After more than twenty years, Sykes has solidified her status as one of the most incisive and hilarious comics of all time. She has won many awards and accolades for her comedy, including an Emmy in 1999 for her work on *The Chris Rock Show*. Her style of comedy has earned her a loyal following across multiple demographics. Historicizing Sykes as part of the Black comedy elite and a crossover success with white audiences, Bambi Haggins situates Sykes within Black comedy as someone who has "crafted a distinct comic persona that, onstage, has the potential to reach and appeal to multiple audiences without contorting her voice or diluting the content of the comedy."[2] Sykes follows in the footsteps of Jackie "Moms" Mabley, taking up the mantle of the storyteller as truth-teller.

In 2008, at a rally in opposition to Proposition 8, a California resolution seeking to reverse the legalization of same-sex marriage, Sykes officially came out as lesbian. Her comedy debunks myths that we are living in a post-racial or post-gay cultural context. She challenges the platitude that "it gets better" and other narratives that align with neoliberal, capitalist,

1. Sykes, *What Happened, Ms. Sykes?*
2. Haggins, *Laughing Mad*, 175.

white, heteronormative values.[3] Charging audiences to think more critically about the ways queer and Black people in America experience history and progress, Sykes's post-coming out performances are works of discursive and temporal subversion in which she deconstructs notions of linear, progressive improvement, notions that silence the multiplicities of Black queer womanhood and mythologize US citizenship as moving toward some teleological utopia.[4]

INTERSECTIONAL RHETORIC: IRONY AND SATIRE

Irony is a major feature of Sykes's stand-up. Long valued for its subversive potential, irony is viewed by many as an essential part of the modern critical spirit. Irony holds capacities for subverting political ideologies.[5] A helpful overview of irony as a rhetorical tool comes from Umberto Eco: "irony asserts the contrary of that which is considered to be the case, and is effective only if the case is not explicitly asserted. Irony means saying '~ p' when, on the contrary 'p' is the case. But if one asserts '~ p' and immediately afterword informs one's interlocutor that 'in fact, as you know, p is the case,' the ironic effect is destroyed."[6] So the key is to invert meaning without divulging that you are doing so. In choosing to employ irony as a medium of expression Sykes places trust in the audience. It requires advanced cognitive abilities to detect irony. Such requires listeners to discern the critical gap between the literal target of the joke and the figurative one. In using irony, Sykes confronts the powers that be obliquely. Doing so risks that the audience will fail to understand what she's doing, that they will miss or misplace the point she's trying to make.

One of Sykes's most famously ironic bits involves a hypothetical scenario in which women have detachable pussies. She opens the bit with a direct assertion of the psychological toll it takes on girls when they learn that they have something that everybody wants. Without a hint of sarcasm in her tone, she talks about this in terms of its convenience. Sykes muses that she would never have to worry again about going out alone at night. If she could

---

3. See Goltz, "It Gets Better," on this LGBT anti-suicide campaign.

4. See Wood, *Cracking Up*, ch. 3 for a deep dive into how Sykes's comedy "cracks up time."

5. Cynthia Willett writes that an "authentic democratic politics" will employ "the vital play of *irony* against hubris." Willett, *Irony in the Age of Empire*, 94. Others blame the phenomenon of irony for the rise of a cynical bad faith in contemporary culture. See Booth, *Rhetoric of Irony*, ix.

6. Eco, "Frames of Comic Freedom," 5.

just leave her pussy at home, potential assailants would be foiled before any aggression could even transpire. She acts out this scenario, saying to her late-night attacker, "Uh! Sorry. I have absolutely nothing of value on me. I am pussyless."[7] Note that the irony of this imagined encounter only works on a figurative level because of the epistemological framework structured by heteronormative, misogynistic values. As Debra Ferreday contends, rape culture is "a complex social phenomenon that is not limited to discrete criminal acts perpetrated by a few violent individuals but is the product of gendered, raced and classed social relations that are central to patriarchal and heterosexist culture."[8] On the surface, Sykes's scenario is both absurd and hilarious, so much so that her audience can't stop laughing; but in order to laugh at the joke, we have to understand a deeper, more sinister reality coming through Sykes's critique.

Beyond the pervasive threat of male aggression, Sykes names some additional perks of having a detachable pussy, namely, that it would facilitate some real bonding, some "real sisterhood" between women. She plays out another scenario in which she is on a date with a man. Things are heating up between them, and Sykes calls a female friend late at night. She says, "Look! Do me a favor. Run by my house and grab my pussy. . . . It's in the shoebox on the top shelf." The crowd goes nuts with laughter. Even as this part of the bit affirms women's sexual desire, it doesn't erase the competing desire to leave her pussy at home in the first place.

Lastly, Sykes's bit bears witness to a danger in employing irony. She speculates that having a detachable pussy would give guys "some perks too." After she decides to leave her pussy at home at the behest of her male partner, she returns home to find it "all bent out of shape." Her partner responds shiftily: "Uh . . . some of the fellas stopped by . . ."[9] Sykes presents this in an ironic contradiction between heterosexual male desire and the threat of male violence against women. She invites her audience to participate in her oblique attack on toxic masculinity without making them the explicit target ("Ladies, you know you can't trust them."). Even as her bit empowers women to enjoy their bodies without fear of violence, her irony smuggles in an indictment against a Black male contingent through her mimicry of a Black man's voice. Thus, while she challenges one oppressive social structure, she bolsters another. In aiming her irony at a Black man, she runs the risk of reinforcing a prejudice in American culture that associates Black

7. Sykes, *Sick and Tired*.

8. Ferreday, "*Game of Thrones*, Rape Culture, and Feminist Fandom," 22. See also Cox, "Standing Up against the Rape Joke."

9. Sykes, *Sick and Tired*.

men with sexual violence. This is a problem. While the primary premise of the bit targets the objectifying male gaze, she ends up targeting a second group, with its own complicated history. The secondary premise stems from white patriarchal postbellum rhetoric that sought to legitimate the lynching of Black men by insisting they were a threat to white women. While acknowledging this problematic, Willett and Willett write, "By turning male humor inside out, she takes her own property back. With a nod, she gives back power to the pussy and eroticizes that old maternal wisdom that also allows her to put her house back in order."[10]

Much of Sykes's post-coming out work plays on themes of Black visibility and queer identity vis-à-vis the white, heteronormative gaze. She frequently plays with stereotypes that get attached to Black female and queer bodies. She openly confronts not just racist oppression and misogyny but the unexamined hostility gays and lesbians receive from some African American communities.[11] Her humor disrupts flows of power and the boundaries and hierarchies that circumscribe these flows as she mocks them. One of the ways she embraces the complexity of her intersectional identity is through satire.[12]

In a famous bit in which she essentializes queerness and Blackness for comical effect, Sykes grapples with the multiple levels of power and powerlessness at work on her Black, queer body. She declares with conviction, "It's harder being gay than it is Black."[13] The setup for this joke, purposefully anti-intersectional, reveals the confusing, conflicting feelings of racial progression paired with homophobic regression. After announcing her recent marriage, she says she had to come out in defiance of Proposition 8. She confesses, "I had to say something cuz I was so hurt and I was so fuckin' pissed." She names the disjunction between President Obama's election to the presidency and Prop 8 passing in California. Without pause, she continues: "It is harder. It's harder being gay than it is being Black. Cuz there's some things I had to do as gay that I didn't have to do as Black. I didn't have to come out Black. I didn't have to sit my parents down and tell them about my Blackness."[14] Sykes adds, "I didn't have to sit them down: 'Mom, Dad I gotta tell y'all something. Hope y'all still love me. I'm just gonna say it. Mom, Dad: I'm Black.'" Playing her mother, Sykes exclaims, "Oh no, Lord

10. Willett and Willett, *Uproarious*, 32.

11. Sykes, "Comic Wanda Sykes"; and Lawrence, "Funny and Proud."

12. See Finley, "Black Women's Satire as (Black) Postmodern Performance."

13. Sykes, *I'ma Be Me*.

14. See Dunning on how interraciality invokes a historical narrative about the constant renegotiation of Blackness throughout the history of the United States. Dunning, *Queer in Black and White*, 16.

Jesus, not Black!" while wailing melodramatically. Sykes turns her back to the audience and outstretches her arms yelling to God, "Anything but Black, Jesus! Give her cancer, Lord, give her cancer! Anything but Black, Lord!" Turning, Sykes continues in her mother's voice, "No. No. You know what it is? You been hanging around Black people . . . they twisted your mind!" [15]

As Katelyn Hall Wood observes, "Through this performative exchange, Sykes satirizes coming out of the closet to reveal its social and political constructedness. The processual script of coming out, when substituted with Blackness, is revealed to be ridiculous. Coming out is not inherently liberatory, nor might it offer the Black lesbian body freedom."[16] In essence, Sykes's satire asks her audience to imagine beyond the "matrix of domination" that keeps democratic freedoms in deadlock across multiple axes of being.[17] By satirizing a stereotypical coming out confession, she transposes her Blackness onto her queerness. In so doing, she testifies to the intersectional complexities and consequences of power dynamics within African American cultures for LGBTQIA-identifying people, especially within religious cultural contexts.[18]

COMIC RAGE AND THE POLITICS OF POLITICS

Performance studies scholar Philip Auslander offers us a helpful analytic for assessing Sykes's brand of stand-up. Rather than thinking in outmoded dichotomies between comedy and rage, Auslander attends to the ways that certain female comics perform "Fem-Rage." Such a framework helps us see beyond conventional wisdom that juxtaposes comedy and rage. Here rage is turned into comedy, even as comedy exposes the rage that motivates it.[19] Similarly, Terrence Tucker identifies Sykes as "one of the newer and most

---

15. Religious humor, as Beretta E. Smith-Shomade points out, plays an important role in the history and culture of the Black church. She notes that while the Black church is not homogeneous, it has played a central role as an institution in the lives of African Americans and is often a featured subject of Black humorists. She adds that humor in church or about church serves to "alleviate religious anxiety" and functions as a challenge to overly rigid notions of respectability. Ultimately, she writes, "the job of the black church is found not only in the bosom of Jesus but also in the belly laugh of its members and outliers." Smith-Shomade, "'Don't Play with God!,'" 334, 335.

16. Wood, *Cracking Up*, 98.

17. Hill Collins, *Black Feminist Thought*, 247–51.

18. Sedgwick describes the process of coming out about one's sexuality as simultaneously "compulsory and forbidden." Sedgwick, *Epistemology of the Closet*, 70. Cf. Ross, "Beyond the Closet as Raceless Paradigm," 163.

19. Auslander, "Brought to You by Fem-Rage."

consistent voices in comic rage."[20] We see this comic rage carried out in both the micro- and macro-political levels.

By attending to her development as a comic and social critic, we may see how she has grown in her performance of comical rage. For instance, her 2003 special *Tongue Untied* begins with Sykes addressing politics.[21] By starting with politics, a realm long denied to women, Sykes distinguishes herself from other female comics who steer clear of politics. After four segments in which she addresses political issues (a critique of George W. Bush's engineering of war and his manipulation of fears about weapons of mass destruction), Sykes turns to topics that are more traditional in the work of women comedians; namely, issues involving gender and sexuality. However, she approaches these topics in surprising ways. In her 2006 comedy special *Sick and Tired* she offers a scathing critique of the Bush administration, but Sykes rarely places herself inside the world of her material. Reminiscent of Dick Gregory's comedy, she distances herself from the object of her critique. She proclaims in a joke about racial profiling, for instance, "When we see a white man running down the street, we think, 'He must be late!'"[22]

Fast-forward a few years and we see Sykes's political comedy take a different tack. She satirically imagines Barack Obama's internal monologue and provides some anticipation for his later shift to a more performatively masculine style in her 2009 stand-up special, *I'ma Be Me*. In it, she describes what she notes as Obama's looser and more casual posture and walking style after the 2008 election. She notes, "He didn't do that shit during the campaign, did he? Naw, he was stiff as a motherfucker during the campaign! It's like he was counting that shit down in his head, like, 'OK, 1, 2, wave, smile, 1, 2, wave, smile. Whatever you do, do not touch your penis. Touch your dick, it's all over. Do not touch your dick."[23] Not only does this bit speak to the double standard to which President Obama was held, it also provides a kind of psychic release. Even as Sykes takes aim at the political system, her actual target is the system of anti-Black racism that caused President Obama to have to modulate his body because, as Sykes puts it in repeated punch line throughout this special, "White people are lookin' at you!"[24] This confronts the complexities of racial visibility before the white gaze. Sykes's assertion aligns with the relief theory of laughter, which we discussed in chapter 2. It was first outlined in 1709 by Lord Shaftesbury, in which he argued, "The

---

20. Tucker, *Furiously Funny*, 254.

21. Sykes, *Tongue Untied*.

22. Sykes, *Sick and Tired*.

23. Sykes, *I'ma Be Me*.

24. Sykes, *I'ma Be Me*.

natural free spirits of ingenious [people], if imprisoned or controlled, will find out other ways of motion to relieve themselves in their constraint; and whether it be in burlesque, mimicry, or buffoonery, they will be glad at any rate to vent themselves and be revenged upon their constrainers."[25] Even as Sykes employs mimicry and buffoonery, this does not erase the rage fomenting beneath the service of her bit.

TAKEAWAYS FOR STAND-UP PREACHING

Sykes offers many comical tactics that can prove helpful for working preachers. The first and most obvious aspect of her performances emerge from her negotiation of audience expectations of her as a Black, queer woman. Preachers and congregants carrying epistemological assumptions into pulpit and pew. There is no homiletical tabula rasa. There can be no phenomenological reduction thorough enough to remove a preacher's expectations of her congregants and her congregants' expectations of her. In this way, every act of proclamation involves "riffing" off these expectations. At the same time, as Lisa Thompson argues, authentic proclamation calls for the preacher to claim her preacherly voice in and against these epistemological structures. "The location of black women in both their communities and the wider world places demands upon their voices in the work of overcoming obstacles to have their truth received. In preaching, black women have the task of deciding how they will or will not negotiate expectations about their abilities to speak and offer valid speech for the sake of the entire community."[26] Because white, male bodies have dominated proclamatory discourse for centuries, Thompson's study displaces these dominant bodies by unapologetically focusing on the ministries of Black women. She reveals an alternative theological anthropology that structures the preaching of Black women a priori. "The preacher, even as she occupies her particular body and uses words within a particular space, is constantly in tension with received traditions of how a sermon takes shape and is performed and the look of the bodies that carry out its performance."[27] Sociopolitical biases can delegitimize women as legitimate bearers of gospel proclamation even before they utter a single word. Sykes, too, performs against a historical backdrop that has privileged the voices of straight, white men. Rather than denying this, Sykes leans into her culturally conditioned, intersectional

---

25. Shaftesbury, "Sensus Communis," 34.

26. Thompson, *Ingenuity*, 12.

27. Thompson, *Ingenuity*, 5.

complexity. She embraces her identity to subvert the powers and principalities that would discount her ways of knowing and behaving.

The second takeaway I see emerges from the first. This is her growing affirmation of her selfhood. Even as she acknowledges the challenges that have accompanied her coming out as a lesbian, marriage to a white woman, and becoming a mother of two white kids, Sykes names the beauty inherent in her embodiment. Sykes exhibits what Otis Moss III labels a "second sight" that emerged from the Africanization of preaching amid the horrors of chattel slavery. Such preachers approached the gospel "with an eye upon the existential tragedy manufactured by a false anthropology and demented theology. The preacher witnessed a country claiming equality yet birthed in the blood of a holocaust of red and black bodies."[28] There is something similar going on in Sykes's stand-up that is at once life-affirming and rebellious. The preacher whom Moss lifts up as an exemplar of prophetic wisdom bears a likeness to Sykes. Sykes embodies a kind of "blues sensibility" that does not deny or ignore the suffering she has endured, but refuses to grant it the final word.

28. Moss, *Blue Note Preaching*, 15.

6

Bodies Matter

On Voice and Gesture

*If God made the body, and the body is dirty,
the fault lies with the manufacturer.*[1]

—LENNY BRUCE

*The message and the messenger are experienced together by the listeners. It
goes without saying, therefore, that the person of the preacher can be an asset
or a liability, even a contradiction, to the preaching event.*[2]

—FRED CRADDOCK

Stand-up and preaching are embodied acts. There can be no comedy
without a comic. There can be no proclamation without a proclaimer.
This seems obvious enough, though the Western church has tended to favor a preacher's capacity to disseminate ideas over and above *his* embodied
realities (and I emphasize the preacher's sex here. To be a male preacher is
to not have to talk about or even acknowledge one's preaching body; this

---

1. Quoted in Zoglin, *Comedy at the Edge*, 7.
2. Craddock, *Preaching*, 212.

has never been the case for female preachers).[3] Sure, preachers wield words, but without some *body* preaching fails to exist. Accordingly, homiletics cannot ignore or diminish the incarnational aspects of preaching and the role it plays in our communication. As philosopher Judith Butler argues, "No act of speech can fully control or determine the rhetorical effects of the body which speaks."[4] Butler calls this unpredictable quality the "excess" of speech. Whether behind a pulpit or on a comedy stage, our bodies and voices "speak" just as much as the words we use.

Whereas many preachers strive to hide their bodies—shrouding them in dark robes, distracting viewers from them with variegated stoles, hiding them behind massive pulpits—many comics embrace their bodies. Comics recognize that the body and its many vicissitudes and quirks provide some of the best material for stand-up. Indeed, many comics confess that childhood or adolescent dissatisfaction with their bodies spurred their comedic genius. Sarah Silverman became funny as a way to detract from her bed-wetting.[5] Kevin Hart attributes his comedic development to his diminutive stature. "As the little guy, you have a choice to make if you want to be popular," writes Hart. "You can be the tough guy and overcompensate for your mini-me self or you can be the funny guy and accept your size. An added incentive for choosing the latter is that it's hard for someone to punch you while they're laughing. I chose to be the funny guy."[6] Hart's admission supports Lawrence Mintz's ethnographic observation that stand-up comics are "defective" in some bodily way, and that contemporary comics exploit their perceived defects to elicit pity. Through these bodily significations, the comic earns a reprieve from traditional social expectations.[7] Comics acknowledge what their bodies are saying, and rather than shrinking from such discourse, they embrace it for comedic effect.

Beyond a comic's perceived bodily deficiencies, many comics have had to grapple with their embodiment of otherness. Like most rhetorical spaces, the comedy stage is dominated by white, straight men. Comics of color, female comics, and LGBTQIA-identifying comics have not had the luxury of ignoring their racialized, gendered, and sexualized bodies. Many comics have leaned into their identities, exploiting their marginalization as a

3. Lammers Gross, *Women's Voices in the Practice of Preaching*, writes, "There is a war on women's bodies. Media representations of women's bodies, traditional gender norms, and the pervasive reality of physical and sexual abuse has led to disconnect women from their bodies" (48–49).

4. Butler, *Excitable Speech*, 155.

5. Silverman, *Bedwetter*, 3.

6. Hart, *I Can't Make This Up*, 67.

7. Mintz, "Stand-Up Comedy as Social and Cultural Mediation," 74.

central part of their comic personas. For instance, Yasser Fouad Selim writes about the way post-9/11 Arab American comics such as Maysoon Zaid and Ahmed Ahmed *performed* their Arabness by exploiting Arab stereotypes as a way to sublimate fear and hostility.[8]

Comedy marvels in bodily difference and the body's tendency to muck up our otherwise lofty and noble aspirations. But even when our bodies seem to betray our oral/aural discourse, they are still communicating in ways that transcend what we are saying. In a series of fascinating articles on bodily excesses that both emerge from and exceed speech, Donyelle McCray writes of a "strange holiness" preaching bodies exude. McCray focuses on sweating, spitting, cursing, and weeping as extralinguistic signs bearing witness to and revealing the gospel in and through holy speech.[9] She writes, "The gravity of the [preaching] moment presses on the preacher and draws a truth out of the preacher's body."[10] Preaching and stand-up bear witness to alternative truths in and through their respective speaking bodies. Preachers can learn much from stand-up comics about how our embodied, intersectional identities might work in tandem with voice and gesture to enhance sermonic performance and to foster an intimate environment for gospel proclamation.

COMEDIC PERSONA AND PASTORAL PERFORMANCE

One of the things most comedians do that preachers tend not to do is draw attention to themselves in ways that are integral to their act. We looked at this phenomenon in detail in the last chapter. Comedians know that they are the subject of their performance; preachers believe that God is the subject of their preaching. Karl Barth argued that preaching ought to be a "selfless human word, a human word which will not say this or that in a spirit of self-assertion but devote itself only to letting God's own Word say what must be said."[11] Such a theology seems to challenge the quest for homiletical insight from stand-up comics about the art of self-presentation. And yet, Barth was also the one who taught us that "one cannot speak of God without speaking of [humanity]."[12] James Cone picked up on Barth's insistence on

8. Selim, "Performing Arabness in Arab American Stand-up Comedy."

9. See McCray, "Sweating, Spitting, and Cursing," and "On Shrieking the Truth," 106–7.

10. McCray, "Sweating, Spitting, and Cursing," 53.

11. Barth, *Church Dogmatics*, I/2, 764.

12. Barth, *Humanity of God*, 56.

the Divine-human connection in the person of Jesus Christ, the Word made flesh, which was the focus of his 1965 doctoral dissertation, "The Doctrine of Man in the Theology of Karl Barth." In his mature theology, Cone, following Barth, argued that "the only legitimate starting point for theology is the man Jesus who is the revelation of God."[13] But Cone reasoned that to take this Jesus seriously we must accept his incarnation in its sociohistorical context. By so doing, Cone could not follow Barth in ignoring Jesus' racialized identity. Hence, "the sole purpose of God in our theology is to illuminate the black condition so that black people can see that their liberation is the manifestation of [God's] activity. We believe that we can learn more about God and, therefore, about man, by examining black people as they get ready to do their thing . . ."[14]

Elizabeth Johnson recognized a similar point of theological insight to that of Cone; except rather than focusing on Jesus' sociopolitical marginalization in terms of his racial identity, Johnson attends to his sexual identity and its sociopolitical capacities. Johnson writes,

> The fact that Jesus of Nazareth was a man is not in question. His maleness is constitutive of his personal identity, and as such, it is to be respected. His sex is intrinsic to his historical person as are his race, class, ethnic heritage, culture, his Jewish religious faith, his Galilean village roots, and so forth. The difficulty arises, rather, from the way this one particularity of sex, unlike the other historical particularities, is interpreted in sexist theology and practice. Consciously or unconsciously, Jesus's maleness is lifted up and made essential for his christic function and identity.[15]

The same truths Cone and Johnson observe offer a theological rationale for attending to other marginalized identities, which makes the comic's embodied performance a potential site of revelation for preaching—not merely to earn a laugh, but for deeply theological reasons.

Some homileticians attend closely to the theological underpinnings of pastoral performance. Jana Childers, for instance, has done much to disabuse preachers of a pejorative understanding of performance. She argues that the aversion some preachers have for performance arises from its connotations with inauthentic preaching. But she reminds us that no matter how much we strive to preach "authentically," we are still performing. In her words, "Once a preacher is in front of a congregation, she or he is performing. The only question is, is it better to be aware of, and therefore able

13. Cone, *Black Theology of Liberation*, 23.
14. Cone, *Black Theology of Liberation*, 90.
15. Johnson, "Redeeming the Name of Christ," 118–19.

to exercise some control over, the performance? . . . Paradoxically, the key to authentic preaching is found in the notion of 'honest performance.'"[16] By attending to matters of bodily performance, preachers can wrestle with what authenticity or honesty looks like for them; i.e., how much of their *true* identity should emerge from a sermon?

All preaching exhibits a particular point of view. From a post-Enlightenment perspective, preachers present a picture of the world that aims to correspond with reality (even if this reality is the upside-down reality Jesus labeled the kingdom of God). Much preaching takes place in the indicative mood, naming the way things *are*—even when life seems to suggest the opposite. Preachers proclaim, and in their proclamation, they reveal a perspective. It is small wonder that preachers who benefit from the status quo in terms of race, ethnicity, gender and sexual identity, sexual orientation, class, and ability have a vested interest in maintaining the world as we know it. This is not rocket science, and we might point to Maslow's hierarchy of needs to measure the degree to which a preacher's subjecthood and identity factor into his preaching. No conspiracy theory is needed to substantiate the claim that a preacher's degree of intersectional privilege shapes their homiletical outlook. As Andrew Wymer argues in his case for a cultural posture of critically white homiletical identity and praxis, such anti-racist preaching will also be anti-cultural inasmuch as the dominance of whiteness benefits white preachers.[17]

The obverse side of this coin is equally true. Preachers whose social identity contributes to their marginalization and oppression are more likely to preach against those powers and principalities that militate against their full humanity. Their claims to be treated with dignity and respect arise from their negative experiences. This is why prophetic preachers tend to emerge from the crucible of injustice. When they know firsthand how sociopolitical forces conspire against one or more aspects of their personhood, how can they not proclaim (literally cry out, *pro-clamare*) the good news as a word of hope for the hopeless, a word calling for repentance for the powerful and humility from the proud? But before we rush in to paint a glossy varnish on this situation, it is important to consider the words of HyeRan Kim-Cragg. She reminds us that it's not that homileticians and preachers who are not straight, white, able-bodied, and male have some superpower on account of their embodied otherness; rather, because of the "invisibility of whiteness" that structures homiletical theory and praxis, such homileticians and preachers have been forced to locate themselves vis-à-vis these normative

---

16. Childers, *Performing the Word*, 48.

17. Wymer, "White Culture, Anti-Cultural Preaching, and Cultural Suicide," 51.

power structures.[18] My experience bears witness to this. I was well into my career in homiletics before I realized how many structures and systems—especially my seminary and doctoral education—were engineered for people with my identity markers to thrive.

Susan Sparks is both a Baptist preacher and a stand-up comedian. In her delightful book *Preaching Punchlines: The Ten Commandments of Comedy*, Sparks stresses the importance of risking vulnerability to present our authentic personalities in our preaching. In fact, Sparks argues *against* putting on masks to hide our true selves for fear of judgment.[19] This is equally true for preaching and stand-up. In an insightful essay, Ruthanna Hooke acknowledges the truth in the adage, "they didn't come here to see you" (i.e., the preacher). She nevertheless argues that "it is important that this personal element in preaching be present in a way that enhances rather than detracts from the ultimate goal of encountering God."[20] Performance is a part of life. We perform all the time (as parents, friends, lovers, etc.). Such performance can add to our self-understanding, leading us to a deeper enjoyment of ourselves in relation to others. At the same time, performance can inhibit our becoming, forcing us to constrain our identities to accommodate others' expectations of us.

A helpful definition of stand-up is that it is a "laughter-inducing performance that meets the expectations of the audience in a novel way."[21] Of course, sometimes the best comedy elicits laughter by *defying* audience members' expectations. I wonder if we might think of preaching along similar lines, as a *gospel-inducing performance*. Childers prefers the term *performance* over the safer term, *delivery*. A delivery is mechanical and transactional. It connotes much less vitality than performance. She writes, "*Performance* is a term that neatly encompasses both the mechanical and the organic aspects of the preaching moment, both the human and the divine."[22] Its theological corollary is *incarnation*. In performing the sermon, we incarnate the gospel. This calls upon preachers to think deeply about the oral and visual dynamics of our preaching.

18. Kim-Cragg, "Invisibility of Whiteness," 29.

19. Sparks, *Preaching Punchlines*, 60.

20. Hooke, "Personal and Its Others in the Performance of Preaching," 24.

21. Brodie, "Stand-Up Comedy," 735.

22. Childers, "Preacher's Performance," 214.

RHETORICAL BODIES: A VERY WHITE, STRAIGHT, MALE HISTORY

Historically, whatever attention homiletics has paid to embodiment it inherited from classical rhetoric. Whenever histories of homiletical rhetoric were written, they tended to omit other sources of influence beyond ancient Greece and Rome. Frank Thomas enumerates the predominant reasons for this omission, which includes the oral transmission of African American rhetoric, the apprenticeship model of education in the Black church, a Western intellectual bias that fails to take African American rhetoric seriously, and a failure to study African American preaching in the guild of homiletics.[23] This is why the history of pulpit rhetoric is so white.

The first century BCE text *Rhetorica ad Herennium* breaks the training of an orator into five parts: invention, arrangement, style, memory, and delivery. Beginning here, and continuing in the rhetorical instruction of Cicero and Quintilian, delivery comes last.[24] When it comes to delivery, classical rhetoricians regarded attention to bodily gestures as supplements to the persuasive logic of an orator. Quintilian wrote, "All emotional appeals necessarily lose their force if they are not kindled by the voice, facial expression, and demeanor of practically the entire body."[25] But it is important to note that Quintilian's ideal Roman orator was isomorphic with "the man of standing," that is, a man of means and virtuous character, the man "always already authorized so to express himself and the man to whom one must listen."[26]

For classical orators, attention to bodily gestures and vocal patterns was pragmatic. If rhetoric is the art of persuasion, and if persuasion is at once logical and emotional, then it makes good sense to employ one's bodily capacities in service of persuasion. Gestures and vocal inflections provoke the emotions of one's listeners, rendering them more amenable to a speaker's message. Even Cicero confessed his susceptibility to gestures employed by skilled orators. He conceded to another orator that "your wagging finger made me tremble with emotion."[27] Attention to bodily performance for Roman rhetoricians centered on gestures made with the eyes and with the hands. These subtle uses of one's body superseded other bodily gestures, especially those of mimicry or acting out a motion described in words.

23. Thomas, *Introduction to the Practice of African American Preaching*, 16–17.

24. *Rhetorica ad Herennium*, 1.2.3. defines delivery as "the graceful regulation of voice, countenance, and gesture"), cited in Edwards, "'Hypokritēs' in Action," 15.

25. Quintilian, *Orator's Education*, 11.3.2.

26. Gunderson, "Discovering the Body in Roman Oratory," 171.

27. Cicero, *De oratore*, 2.188.

Ancient sources mention examples such as suggesting a sick person by imitating the posture of a doctor bending over to take the pulse of a patient or miming a musician by making string-plucking motions as if playing the lute. Classical rhetoricians deemed such overtly theatrical gestures inappropriate, especially for formal orations about serious matters.[28]

In what is ostensibly the first homiletics textbook ever written, Augustine appropriates Roman rhetoric for Christian teaching and preaching. In Book 4 of *De Doctrina Christiana*, Augustine stresses virtuous living and a clear assertion of biblical wisdom over eloquence. He discusses three styles of eloquence: the subdued style, which is adequate; the temperate style, which is elegant; and the majestic style, which is forcible. He is quick to add that "the man [*sic*] who cannot speak both eloquently and wisely should speak wisely without eloquence, rather than eloquently without wisdom."[29] Augustine says nothing about the role of the body in delivery, which is unsurprising when we consider that Augustine preached *ex cathedra*, i.e., he sat while preaching, which was a mark of his office. It is clear, however, that Augustine preached with careful attention to congregational reception. The church at Hippo was a lively fellowship, as earlier noted. Augustine's congregants often shouted with emotion, clapped to indicate agreement with what was being said, and cried when moved to conviction over sin. It seems that his homiletical context was not much different from the atmosphere in some comedy clubs. By way of example, the transcription of his Sermon Ninety-Six includes congregational interjections: "Alluring is the world, but more alluring is the One by whom the world was made. [The congregation here begins cheering.] What did I say? What is there to start cheering about? Look, the problem (in the biblical text) has only just been laid out, and you've already started cheering."[30]

African American preachers have carried into the present the wisdom from the North African bishop of Hippo. Teresa Fry Brown writes, "Black preachers traditionally have had a love of the poetic power of language. The articulation of the sacred 'word of God' can free persons to weep away their pain for shouts with cathartic joy." She attends here to much more than diction or elocution. Rather, "Black preachers' rhetoric, communication channel, imagery, poetics, style, metaphor, simile, intonation, pregnant pausing, self-disclosure, message-intent body movement, and facial expression at times relay more faith information than vocalizations."[31] The late,

28. Aldrete, *Gestures and Acclamations in Ancient Rome*, 35.

29. Augustine, *De Doctrina Christiana*, 4.28.

30. Sermon 96.4, quoted in Harmless, ed., *Augustine in His Own Words*, 133.

31. Fry Brown, "Reestablishing the Purpose and Power of the Preached Word," 97.

great preacher and civil rights activist Prathia Hall offers similar insights, reminding us not to dissociate the voice from the body. She argues that "the pronunciation, intonation, rhythm, in singsong modulations in my voice can only be captured by the voice, not by the mere choice of words. Yet my repetition of certain words and phrases gives greater power and effectiveness to voicing themes of suffering and celebration. This is important in facilitating a 'listening' imagination."[32]

Bodies matter beyond formal methods of rhetoric. Due to the post-Cartesian dualities between body and mind and between subject and object—along with the church's two-thousand-year discomfort with bodies—much of the history of preaching has ignored embodied realities such as race, gender, sexuality, and ability. Recent work in homiletics has done much to overcome this scant attention to bodies and embodiment in preaching. Kwok Pui-lan contributes a postcolonial framework for thinking about the performative dynamics of preaching. She writes, "Through speech act and gestures, the preacher as performer seeks to act or consummate an action, to construct new realities, and to perform or signal possible new identities."[33] In a similar vein, Kim-Cragg advances an interdisciplinary, intercultural, and interreligious approach to preaching that not only attends to the preacher's body, but also the bodies in the pews. She is right to teach us that many of these bodies are marked according to their intersectional otherness vis-à-vis dominant (i.e., white, heteronormative, ableist, Christian) culture.[34]

COMEDIC VARIATIONS ON VOICE AND GESTURE

We have attended to the fact that before a preacher or comic speaks, their bodies are already saying things. For both comedic and preacherly performance, there is an "excess" of speech we can neither ignore nor deny. Those who experience marginalization on account of their race, gender, ability, or sexual orientation cannot ignore the ways in which their embodiment shapes their performance. In one sense, bodily performance is passive, requiring nothing from the performer than to ascend to that "vulnerable place" of which Kevin Hart speaks.[35] In another sense, bodily performance is active. Preachers and comics *decide* how to use their bodies to say things

32. Hall, "Encountering the Text," 65.

33. Kwok, "Postcolonial Preaching in Intercultural Contexts," 11. Cf. Travis, *Decolonizing Preaching*, 44.

34. Kim-Cragg, "Unfinished and Unfolding Tasks of Preaching."

35. Hart, *I Can't Make This Up*, 152.

and do things. Let's look at two examples of how stand-up comics utilize their voices and bodies to enhance the reception of their content. We'll look at stand-up sets from *Saturday Night Live*'s Leslie Jones and from Ramy Youssef, the titular character from the Hulu dramedy *Ramy*.

Leslie Jones: Big, Loud, and Proud

In her 2020 Netflix special *Time Machine,* Leslie Jones offers an intriguing case study on embodying comedy.[36] First off, it is important to note Jones's physicality on the stage. She is six feet tall, and her spiked-up hair easily adds another six inches to her stature. She is an African American, able-bodied woman in her fifties, and she displays no trepidation in embracing her age and culture, which provide amusing fodder for her stand-up. She wears form-fitting black jeans with several tasteful rips and frays cut into the legs. She wears a black T-shirt featuring the side profile of Nipsie Hussell, a famous West Coast rapper from the early 2000s, who was gunned down in 2019. In stark contrast to Jones's dark skin, dark hair, dark jeans, and dark T-shirt, Jones sports a beige knee brace. Of course, she could have worn this *under* her jeans, but part of Jones's performance centers on her age. The knee brace takes on semiotic value, signifying her comfort with her body and enhancing rather than detracting from her embodied stand-up.

She has this one bit about attending an after-party at the Grammys in the nineties. Let's look at how her performance supports her comedic efforts. Jones begins the bit with a casual, laid-back tone, mentioning that one of her friends was always able to get her and her friends into such events. To set up the context, she says, "There was different stars back then," followed by a middle finger to the entire audience and a stern expression. This earns a spate of laughs. Coupling this assertion with flipping off the audience she says without saying, "Yeah, I know I'm older than you. Deal with it." Jones mentions that LL Cool J was there, which earns many cheers from the audience, but still she maintains her casual pacing back and forth across the stage. She then tells the audience that Tevin Campbell was there, too. This earns far fewer cheers than the LL Cool J reference. Playing off the mixed reception she receives, she observes, "White people are like, 'Who the fuck is Tevin Campbell, bitch?'" Then she says, "Black people are like, '*Can we taa-a-alk for a minute*?'" Jones proceeds to sing the chorus from one of Campbell's more popular songs. The audience members who know the song join in singing.

36. Jones, *Time Machine.*

What is interesting here is Jones's commitment to the Campbell reference. She merely mentions LL Cool J, who is the more widely familiar reference, but she performs Tevin Campbell (body rolls and all). Her body language and vocal patters transform into that of Campbell. This performance sets itself against the casual tone Jones exuded in her background description to this story from her past. Jones then drops out, allowing the audience to finish the chorus. She jumps and shouts with excitement, exclaiming, "There's some old Black motherfuckers in the house!" Jones's performance and jubilation earn another round of laughs, but what is even more important is that she's hooked the audience. The more completely she commits to recounting this story, the more deeply invested the audience becomes in finding out what happened at the Grammys after-party. The older Black members of her audience are on the inside with her. They share this cultural and historical understanding. At the same time, the other, mostly white, audience members who do not get this reference are put in the position of feeling excluded. They, too, invest in the story because nobody wants to be the odd one out. She concludes her set up by saying, "White people are like, 'We still don't know that shit. Sing some Bon Jovi, bitch!'" Jones concludes with a concession that draws the outsiders back into the know. "But that's the only song he had anyway, white people, I'm just sayin.'"

Next comes the transition: "And I was in my best hoe attire." She picks up the speed of her pacing, preening, and posing, working the stage like a runway model. Jones is no longer the casual storyteller. She has transformed herself back into her twenty-something body. She fully commits to this performance, which paints a vivid picture of her at this glamorous party. She wore a red dress, and Jones's sensual description of the dress invites us to imagine what she looked like. Jones also tells us she had her new, freshly attached ponytail from that morning. She then holds the wired microphone at a distance from the back of her head to show us what the ponytail looked like. Jones describes her stilettoes by tiptoeing across the stage. She confesses that she had borrowed these shoes from her friend, and Jones's feet were too big for them. She twists her facial features from a smile to a wince, adding comedic momentum to her narration.

This leads her to the story's climax. None other than Prince arrives at the party. To illustrate her plan to get with Prince (to "out hoe these hoes"), Jones kicks off her imaginary stilettoes and proceeds to dance for Prince to his "Gett Off." She embodies the sensuality of Prince, again embracing her body and affirming her sexuality. The punch line to the story comes when Jones confesses, "That Sade ponytail flew straight off."

There are many takeaways from Jones's performance. For starters, she regards her body and voice as accompaniments to her logical and affective content. She has a large frame, and rather than downplaying her size, she embraces her long arms, legs, and torso to enhance her bit about the Grammy party. She also establishes distance between herself and her audience (especially with the Tevin Campbell song), which paradoxically invites greater participation from the audience. She sets herself apart from those younger than herself. This establishes solidarity with folks who are close to her age. This rhetorical move also sets the rest of the audience in a state of not wanting to be left out. In other words, they *want* to participate. This investment is crucial for the second half of the bit, where she narrates the process of going all out to impress at a party. Lastly, she commits to her narration. She doesn't just *tell* us about her dance for Prince. She *shows* us her dance. In doing so, Jones simultaneously self-deprecates and affirms her beauty.

Ramy Youssef: Subtle, Quiet, and Confused

Ramy Youssef is an Arab American comic who presents himself with great subtlety. With his backward baseball hat, loose-fitting untucked shirt with the sleeves rolled up, and faded jeans, Youssef looks more like a guy you'd run into at the lumber section at Home Depot or to help a friend move a couch from his basement apartment than a comedian with his own show on Hulu and an HBO special. But this only adds to Youssef's presentation of easy authenticity.

In addition to his look, Youssef's minimalist body movement and soft-spoken voice adds to the feeling of discursive intimacy. He makes you feel like you are just two friends having a chat over a Belgian beer at a backyard cookout or sipping lattes together at an overpriced coffee shop in a hip, urban section of town. Youssef's subtle use of his voice and gestures draw attention to the funny stories and comical observations that make up his sets. He's so quiet and laid back in his performance it invites you to lean in to what he has to say.

In his *Feelings* special he performs a bit about his father.[37] Without resorting to minstrel stereotypes, he describes his father as a prototypical American immigrant with a strong work ethic and a DIY mentality. Along the way to the punch line of this bit, he adds several twists to the setup to earn a few laughs along the way. For instance, he explains that his father taught himself everything from plumbing to auto repair, just so he would never have to pay another man to do it. He says, "His nightmare would be to hand money to another man and look him in the eye."

37. Youssef, *Feelings*.

Youssef narrates how in just ten years his father went from being a busboy to the manager of a hotel. He adds that the hotel happens to be in New York City, and the owner of the hotel happens to be Donald Trump. Youssef grew up with a photo of his father and Trump shaking hands. He explains that for a young Arab kid, whoever is friends with your dad is your uncle. Youssef pauses to allow a spate of laughter from the audience. With a dubious tone, Youssef says that as he's watched the news over the last few years, he thought to himself, "Uncle Donald?" The interrogative mood of Youssef's punch line is key. His soft-spoken tone enhances the impact of his question because it plays in multiple ways at once. By inflecting his question, Youssef could signify a sense of surprise (i.e., that his "uncle" is the President of the United States). The question could also signify incredulity that this man whom Youssef grew up admiring could proliferate such hatred toward people like the very man he made manager of one of his hotels. Trump's Muslim ban is incongruous with a man Youssef grew up admiring.

Youssef never raises his voice. Other than a few casual hand gestures for emphasis, he does little with his body. His delivery could not be more different from Jones's ebullient and effusive narration of her experience with Prince at the Grammys after-party. What is key for both Jones and Youssef is that their narrative delivery resonates with their comedic personas. Each of them appears authentic to the person they present themselves to be. Despite their wildly different modes of vocal and gestural discourse, both comics narrate their lived experiences in a way that seems authentic to their personhood and personality. As such, they model for preachers how we might employ our bodies and voices in ways that arise from our unique personalities and experiences. They teach us that there is no one way to perform and that the decisions we make about bodily movement on stage, modulation of volume, pitch, and tone, how much we use our hands and to what effect, and how we navigate silence and stillness all have a part to play in our communication of the message God has given us to proclaim.

STAGING BODILY PRESENCE

As we have seen, stand-up comics draw attention to their bodily presence in service of eliciting laughter and insight. It would be a mistake, however, to label them narcissistic attention seekers obsessed over their bodies. As our bodies are one of the first things people notice when we move into the spotlight, our bodies are already communicating before we open our mouths. As Jennifer Copeland rightly notes, "Since bodies cannot be excluded from an analysis of any oral communication, and especially not from preaching, a study of preaching must incorporate the body's real presence in the pulpit. To deny the presence of a gendered body is to perpetuate the bifurcation of the human being into polarized categories . . ."[38] There is a corollary to this insight in stand-up. Simply by dint of being onstage, female comics, queer comics, and comics of color trouble a form of domination by occupying spaces historically confined to white, straight men in stand-up. They perform, as Joanne Gilbert propounds, a "rhetorical marginality" that, unlike sociological marginality, "may actually empower."[39] It is imperative, then, as we study what stand-up comics can teach preachers that we attend not only to how they use their vocal and physical gestures to enhance their performance but also to the signifying capacities of their bodies as bodies.

In her book *Pretty/Funny: Women Comedians and Body Politics*, Linda Mizejewski notes the gender dynamic of stand-up performances in which women must grapple with their visual presentation vis-à-vis the male gaze. This transpires either through subversion or elision. Male comics, by contrast, are not subject to this judgmental, gendered gaze because their attire, their bodies, and their comportment are less scrutinized than are those of female comics.[40] The same could be said about female preachers. Virginia Purvis-Smith opens her phenomenological study on gender and homiletical aesthetics by observing, "When a clergywoman preaches from a pulpit, she enters a space which has particular aesthetic value, for this space has been occupied and its character defined by male presence for centuries."[41] Purvis-Smith sheds fresh light on the homiletical dimensions of gender and sex, arguing that these aspects transcend slight modifications in rhetoric and gesture, but extend to the formation of an entirely new aesthetic. Maxine Walaskay, in an earlier study, addresses several aspects of aesthetic value in pulpit discourse, examining even the gendered complexities related to "pulpit garb" and the impact clothing decisions bear upon perception of the speaker's authority.[42] More recently, Amy McCullough has revived attention to clothing and other aesthetic considerations such as jewelry and makeup that female preachers must negotiate in their pulpit performances.[43]

Mizejewski challenges the cultural assumptions that militate against women in comedy, operating out of what she labels a "pretty versus funny"

38. Copeland, *Feminine Registers*, 68.

39. Gilbert, *Performing Marginality*, 6.

40. Mizejewski, *Pretty/Funny*, 14.

41. Purvis-Smith, "Gender and the Aesthetic of Preaching," 224.

42. Walaskay, "Gender and Preaching." She concludes, "My hunch is that, even if [congregants] like what they hear, they feel ambiguous about what they see" when a woman preaches (11).

43. McCullough, *Her Preaching Body*, esp. 62–95.

epistemological bias. Nowhere is this epistemology more overt than in Christopher Hitchens's infamous diatribe baldly titled, "Why Women Aren't Funny." In the article, Hitchens goes so far as to declare women and humor "antithetical."[44] In *The Promise of Happiness,* Sarah Ahmed articulates the caricature of the feminist killjoy: "Feminists are typically represented as grumpy and humorless, often as a way of protecting the right to certain forms of social bonding or of holding onto whatever is perceived to be under threat."[45] Thanks to the pioneering efforts of comics such as Jackie "Moms" Mabley, Lilly Tomlin, and Kathy Griffin, contemporary female stand-up comics have found clever ways to challenge this feminist stereotype. Along with the other female comics I spotlight in this book, we may witness this performance of feminine/feminist humor in the work of Margaret Cho and Nikki Glaser.

Margaret Cho: Queering Bodily Identities

Embracing both her queerness and Koreanness, Cho resists and subverts the American ideal of feminine beauty. Cho's backstory is important here. In her early twenties, Cho catapulted to stardom in the short-lived ABC sitcom *All-American Girl* (1994–1995). She'd been performing stand-up for five years and had perfected the persona of a rebellious American daughter of Korean immigrants. This was what captured the attention of the ABC executives. When it came time to begin filming, those same executives who spotted Cho demanded she lose thirty pounds before the first episode was set to begin filming—just two weeks away! The sudden weight loss led to Cho's hospitalization with kidney failure, yet she continued to diet through the first season. Despite her efforts, Cho received incessant criticism from the tabloids. In her 2001 memoir, Cho confesses that the failure of *All-American Girl* confirmed her worst thoughts about herself: that she was too unattractive and too Asian to fit in with the ideal of feminine American beauty. Rather than yearning to live up to this impossible ideal of photo-shopped, American femininity, Cho embraced her otherness as a strength rather than a hindrance. *I'm the One That I Want* subverts American racism and the tyranny of unrealistic body ideals for women. "I have been a long-time perpetrator of hate crimes against myself, and I am turning myself in. I have had enough," confesses Cho. Later she speaks of the self-inflicted harm she endured as a result of hating her body. She says that fat is a feminist

44. Hitchens, "Why Women Aren't Funny."
45. Ahmed, *Promise of Happiness,* 65.

issue. "Weight is not just about our bodies. It's about how we feel about ourselves. It affects every decision we make."[46]

Cho has much to say about the inverse correlation in stand-up between a woman's purported attractiveness and her chances at making it as a comedian. She says, "I think for women in comedy, it's really hard if you're pretty. If you're pretty, you just can't work." She goes on to explain that when she was younger, she was "really fat." She attributes some of her early success to her body type, which granted her "some kind of weird authority" because no one wants to listen to a comic who comes across as superior to her audience.[47] At the same time, Cho was never shy about asserting her sexual desires. In the early days, she reports, she wore a lot of "Madonna-wannabe old lingerie kind of stuff." She received pushback for being both fat and overly flirtatious. She kept being told she was too sexual, even when she didn't think she was doing anything.

When Cho came out as queer several things happened. For starters, she began to emphasize her queerness to subvert rigid definitions of sexuality according to the gay/straight binary. On the one hand, she says it was easier being a queer woman than it was for queer/gay men in the late nineties. Especially because Cho was open about her attraction to women and men, she earned a reception from male comics along with her audience. She reports that the crowd most hostile to her sexuality was lesbians. She says, "Lesbians were like, 'Well, you're not completely gay, so you don't really count. You can't be one of us unless you are all the way one of us.'"[48]

Jennifer Foy discusses how female comics who use sexual humor converge two points of female subversion: humor and sexual aggression. In "fooling around" on stage (with its double connection to comedy and sex), they risk damaging the relationship with their audiences, which they need to preserve to get the desired response, i.e., laughter. To some extent, the preservation of this complicated relationship is dependent on persona management.[49] As Cho came to accept the beauty of her body by resisting the unconscious image of American femininity thrust upon her, Cho grew increasingly direct in her stand-up about the need for women to free themselves from the cultural brainwashing that makes them feel physically unacceptable. Cho calls for a revolution from the dominant culture's negative messages about women's bodies urging conformity of appearance and behavior. She argues that self-esteem is revolutionary and a challenge to

46. Cho, *I'm the One That I Want*, 91, 206.
47. Cho interview in Kohen, *We Killed*, 181.
48. Cho interview in Kohen, *We Killed*, 187.
49. Foy, "Fooling Around," 712.

shallow norms of society. "Stand-up comedy offers space to speak to the complexity of our identities," as Rebecca Krefting argues.[50] Cho's politicized content and comedy style—her attention to social issues relevant to women, LGBTQ folks, Asian Americans, and people of color, and her adroit shifts into accents and characters representing these groups—allows her to perform in ways that resist classification within any group.

Nikki Glasser: Abjecting Beauty

Nikki Glaser conforms to the very image of American feminine beauty that Cho nearly died trying to attain. Tanned, white, blonde, and fit, Glaser seems to lack the obvious physical defects that elicit audience sympathy and participation. Recall Lawrence Mintz's argument discussed earlier in this chapter that stand-up comics are "defective" in some bodily way, and that contemporary comics exploit their perceived defects to elicit pity.[51] But for Glaser, it is precisely this societal expectation regarding her prototypical beauty that causes her so much psychological distress. If she presents a "defect" to the audience, it is a defective sense of self inscribed in her unconsciously through the male gaze and media. In a 2020 interview with Conan O'Brian, O'Brian puzzles over the fact that Glaser is a very attractive person and yet a major component of her comedy is the faults she finds with her body. Glaser responds, "I wish I could just accept myself, but I just really have low self-esteem because I was born a woman."[52]

Glaser is known for her willingness to talk openly about her body and sexuality. A trademark of her style is her nonchalance, even when speaking about the most intimate matters. While most preachers wouldn't last long at their churches if they focused on their genitalia, we may still learn a lot about homiletical embodiment from Glaser in the ways she simultaneously participates and subverts feminine stereotypes.

In a bit about how she behaved at the beginning of a romantic relationship, Glaser says she felt like she put Spanx on her personality.[53] In another bit she opens by asserting that men wield a tremendous power over women by offering even the most innocuous compliment.[54] She confesses that she attempted stand-up for the first time fifteen years ago. When a hot guy approached her after the show and complimented her gifts in stand-up, she

50. Krefting, "Margaret Cho's Army," 273.

51. Mintz, "Stand-Up Comedy as Social and Cultural Meditation," 74.

52. Glaser, "Nikki Glaser Doesn't Mind a Micropenis."

53. Glaser, *Perfect*.

54. Glaser, *Bangin'*.

decided then and there to do stand-up for the rest of her life. From this she tells the audience that she craves compliments because she was an ugly child. Growing up with a beautiful sister, Glaser developed a belief that she was unattractive. At one point in her set, Glaser says that people would literally stop her mom to tell her that Glaser's sister should be a model. Glaser says, "They wouldn't see me at first, so I would emerge from behind my mom's legs like Nosferatu saying, 'What should I be?'" In mimicking Nosferatu, Glaser employs her voice and her mimetic gifts to sound and look like the ugly child she perceived herself to be.

Glaser displays through her relationship with her body what John Limon labels *abjection*. The abject indicates what cannot be subject or object to you. It is that part of yourself that is not entirely part of you and yet it is not entirely apart from you. Limon explains, "When you feel abject, you feel as if there were something miring your life, some skin that cannot be sloughed, some role (because 'abject' always, in a way, describes how you act) that has become your only character. Abjection is self-typecasting."[55] Limon investigates the ways that contemporary stand-up is a way of avowing and disavowing abjection. He points to an "essential abjectness" in stand-up. He says that "all stand-ups are abject insofar as they give themselves over to the stand-up condition, which is a noncondition between nature and artifice. (They are neither acting nor conversing, neither in nor out of costume.) Reality itself, in the way of the abject, keeps returning to the stand-up comedian, who throws it off in the form of jokes."[56] We see this in Glaser's comedy in the way she talks about her gender and sexuality, which holds a liminal position for her. She presents her body as both a site of desire and revulsion. Even as she conforms to the very gender and racial stereotypes that shaped so much of Cho's adolescent loathing, Glaser's comical persona identifies these bodily features as a blessing and a curse.

CONCLUSION: LET'S GET PHYSICAL

In this chapter we have attended to the ways contemporary stand-up comics employ their bodies to enhance their performance. The body, as we have seen, is not a neutral bystander on the comedy stage or behind the pulpit. Bodies speak, and just like our human languages—structured as they are by cultural conventions—our bodies communicate according to the ways they work with and against those conventions. As Charles Rice avers, "The particular vehicle of the word is a [person] whose humanity is the medium

55. Limon, *Stand-Up Comedy in Theory*, 4.
56. Limon, *Stand-Up Comedy in Theory*, 105.

of the message. As such a medium, the greatest responsibility the preacher has is to reveal [their] humanity. The promise of preaching depends for its realization not upon the minister's conventional saintliness or even [their] talents, but upon [their] personhood."[57] Such homiletical wisdom calls upon us to attend to our embodied personhood as a constitutive component of our proclamation.

If our bodies are the medium for the gospel message, then it is imperative that we pay attention to what messages our bodies are sending in our efforts to communicate the gospel. Lisa Thompson has written much to remind us that our "fleshy parts" are not value neutral. She rightly observes that "[w]e have assigned more value to some people over and against others. Our inequitable assessments of human worth are often broken down along the lines of those matters associated with the fleshy parts of our lives, whether or not we acknowledge those breakdowns. Divisions and disproportionate power in relationships exist along those same lines."[58] For stand-up preachers this means that we need to understand the ways our bodies mark us with particular privileges and problems. We also ought to find creative ways to use our gendered, racialized, sexually oriented, and variously abled bodies in ways that call out for just and equitable valuation of *all* bodies.

Even as our bodies speak before we might want them to, we also have agency over our bodies. The stand-up comics we've considered in this chapter offer us many insights on this front. Accordingly, we ought to recognize the performative capacities of our particular bodies, leveraging our voices, facial expressions, and physical gestures to signify toward new ways of thinking and feeling. This bodily performativity transcends our mere materiality. Ruthanna Hooke asserts that our preacherly bodies are sites where the Holy Spirit enters our lives and transforms us: "in allowing the personal into preaching, as the place that the Spirit breathes into and transforms, we create the possibility for performances that transgress and disrupt established norms so that a new identity can be shaped within us." Our bodies, in other words, can become sites of holy mischief, wreaking havoc on the systems and structures that try to restrict our capacities for being and behaving. She concludes her argument by saying, "As we offer the personal, and then allow it to be transformed through the performance of this other (the text, and God in the text), we become our essential selves and at the same time are inspired by the divine breath and participate in the

---

57. Rice, *Interpretation and Imagination*, 76.
58. Thompson, *Preaching the Headlines*, 33.

becoming flesh of the divine Word."[59] Hooke's homiletical wisdom resonates with that of the great American revivalist preacher Charles G. Finney, who once said, "A minister should always feel deeply his subject, and then he will suit the action to the word and the word to the action, so as to make the full impression which the truth is calculated to make."[60] Such efforts to marry deep feeling with action in words call for special attention to one's voice and embodied gestures. What this achieves, for both comedians and preachers, is an experience of intimacy between the speaker and her audience.

59. Hooke, "Personal and Its Others," 42, 43.
60. Quoted in Smith, *New Measures,* 190.

Stand-Up Spotlight
Hasan Minhaj
between Identification and
Alienation

The last thing a comic wants is to be taken seriously. But I can tell you this: You hear people say, "There's so much suffering in the world—jokes are inappropriate." I say hunger is inappropriate. Poverty is inappropriate. Lies and hypocrisy from governments, that's inappropriate.[1]

—HASSAN MINHAJ

Hasan Minhaj is an Indian American stand-up comedian and political news commentator who focuses on the complex of ethnicity, religion, pop culture, and politics on a global scale. He came to notoriety as a *Daily Show* correspondent in 2014. His 2017 Netflix stand-up special *Hasan Minhaj: Homecoming King* and his subsequent weekly news show *Patriot Act* have cemented his comic persona as that of a hip millennial attuned to societal injustice and determined to challenge the insidious structures that marginalize and minimize otherness.

Minhaj's ethnic identity is an important part of his comedy, but in his later work he focuses more on his Brownness and the complicated ways in which his skin color marks his otherness in white supremacist America while at the same time marking his otherness from other others such as African Americans, Arabs, and Latinx people. *Homecoming King* narrates Minhaj's experience in navigating his love life in high school. Alongside this dominant narrative are Minhaj's family members. He shows how his

1. Minhaj, *Stand Up Planet.*

parents' experiences as immigrants shaped their expectations of him, form-
ing him indelibly. He explains,

> My dad is from that generation like a lot of immigrants where
> he feels like if you come to this country, you pay this thing like
> the American Dream tax, right? Like you're gonna endure some
> racism, and if it doesn't cost you your life, well, hey you lucked
> out. Pay it! There you go, Uncle Sam. But for me, like a lot of us,
> I was born here. So, I actually have the audacity of equality. Life,
> liberty, pursuit of happiness. All men created equal. It says it
> right here, I'm equal. I'm equal! I don't deserve this.[2]

He presents himself as a prototypical second-generation Indian American,
making frequent references to his taste in food, fashion, and film. Throughout his special he slides seamlessly between English and Hindi, providing
translations for his non-South Asian audience. This creates volleys of laughter that unites his diverse audience members in their common humanity. At
the same time, Minhaj never resorts to minstrelsy. He embraces his cultural
identity while resisting the temptation to mimic affected Indian accents to
earn a cheap laugh.[3]

MODULATING MOVEMENT AND MEANING

Minhaj situates his personal history within a broader sociopolitical context.
He names the subtle and not so subtle forms of racism he experiences on
a daily basis, calling out the myriad ways that white people negotiate their/
our dominance at the expense of people of color. Minhaj facilitates the narration of his lived experiences and his explication of fraught sociopolitical
situations through frequent shifts in tone. At one minute he is animated,
kinetic, and loud. At the next he is somber, pensive, and quiet. At one point
in *Homecoming King* Minhaj's bombast gives way to a whispered grief as
he details the antagonism his family faced in the wake of 9/11, including
anonymous hate calls, graffitied racial slurs, theft, and the vandalism of their
car.

> And I know 9/11 is a super touchy subject. I understand. Be-
> cause when it happened, everyone in America felt like their
> country was under attack. But on that night, September 12th,

2. Minhaj, *Homecoming King*.

3. Krefting, *All Joking Aside*, 198: "Minstrelsy can earn an easy laugh or offer a way
of building community or something else, depending on the setting, audience compo-
sition, the comic, and their intentions."

it was the first night of so many nights where I felt like my family's love and loyalty to this country was under attack. And it always sucks. As immigrants, we always have to put on these press releases to prove our patriotism. We're always auditioning, like "We love this country, please believe me."[4]

Here we witness Minhaj's comical brilliance at full stretch. By juxtaposing fears and hopes of post-9/11 Brown people in America, Minhaj fosters empathy across multiple axes of identity.

He normalizes his otherness even as he challenges racial stereotypes about the sexuality of South Asian men. At the climax of *Homecoming King* we learn what happens between him and his white girlfriend. He vividly recaps the sense of adolescent longing leading up to the prom; how he defied his parents by sneaking out of his room, fervently biked over to her house in his freshly pressed tux, and upon arrival, discovered another boy—a white boy—already there placing a corsage on his date's wrist. Minhaj's movement here is quite brilliant. By drawing on universal feelings of first love and crushing heartbreak, he appeals to everyone in the audience who has their own heartbreak story. Having drawn everyone in, his story illuminates the insidious and unjust incongruities surrounding both public and private value judgements based on race. Such concrete narration from Minhaj's point of view positions the listener to see the world through his eyes. He structures through his narrative emplotment what Aristotle identifies as *catharsis* and *anagnorisis*, which we discussed in chapter 5.[5] The story's climax forces the audience to face up to the realities of racism on a personal level. Such metanoia dovetails into Minhaj's counternarrative that treats the same realities on a national level.

While Minhaj speaks at length about racialization and racism, he takes the time to admit his relative privilege as a Brown man in North America:

"Awww, you couldn't go to prom with a white girl?" Who gives a fuck? At least your spine isn't getting shattered in the back of a police wagon, the way it's happening to my African American brothers and sisters in this country to this day. So this is a tax you have to pay for being here? I'll pay it. "I can't date your daughter." I don't give a fuck, Uncle Sam. Take it . . . For every Trayvon Martin or Ahmed the clock kid, there are shades of bigotry that happen every day between all of us. Because we're

4. Minhaj, *Homecoming King*.
5. Aristotle, *Poetics*, 1452a.

too afraid to let go of this idea of the Other. Someone who's not
in our tribe, you're Other.[6]

Minhaj models a sophisticated awareness of his intersectional identity and
the challenges and privileges his identity markers generate. On the one hand,
his Brownness makes him a target for discrimination. On the other hand,
Minhaj recognizes that his racial identity provides him with social privilege
and protects him from the systemic racism and police brutality endured by
Black people. In this moment, he manages to speak to his own experiences
without dismissing or taking away from the oppression of others, a self-
awareness crucial to building communities in the face of subjugation.

Minaj's racial and ethnic humor creatively exposes, destabilizes, and
dissents against the prevailing power structures and identity constructions
that sustain racial oppression at unconscious levels. His material departs
from traditional stand-up in that it avoids cartoonish accents and ethnic
characterizations. He neither speaks on behalf of other groups nor does he
rely on cheap comedic tricks to elicit laughter at the expense of marginalized
communities. This conscious effort "not to push down on groups that are already being objectified" shapes the meaningfulness of Minhaj's stand-up.[7]
Instead, he employs a powerful moment from his boyhood to foreground a
multifaceted counternarrative of Brownness that resists stereotypes of religious fanaticism and violence.

By weaving his story into the fabric of American culture, Minhaj fosters solidarity across strata of difference. His universal story of unrequited
love encourages resonance, while his particular story of being a Brown man
in post-9/11 America fosters understanding and empathy. Enhancing his
nuanced storytelling is the show's production. The stories and visuals work
together to elicit an affective response from the audience. Viewers can see
his wide-eyed surprise and feel his anger due to the unique cinematography
that frequently has Minhaj addressing the camera directly. He also uses a
mix of photos and video clips projected on a huge screen behind him to
cushion his material, which is peppered with hundreds of sharp pop culture
references. His rapid-fire delivery, use of relevant analogies and metaphors,
and compelling, quieter moments of vulnerability create a sense of realism
and encourage contemplation beyond the immediate comedic context.
Minhaj transcends racial difference by inviting people to connect over
common issues, as many of the subjects he touches on—religious tensions,
generational divisions, and bicultural identity—are applicable to numerous
migrant communities. He also does not use his experiences to diminish or

6. Minhaj, *Homecoming King.*
7. Minhaj interview in Caniesco, "Daily Show's Hasan Minhaj."

erase the oppression of other groups. Along with his marginalization he acknowledges his privilege, which, despite his racialization as a terrorist threat, protects him from attack. By focusing on similarities over differences, Minhaj taps into the audience's shared humanity, compassion, and empathy to build intimacy with them rather than alienate them.

CRITICAL PUBLIC PEDAGOGY

Minhaj's stand-up material is emancipatory in that it provokes a deeper, more sophisticated engagement with issues like racial identity and the access it provides or denies to power and privilege. In so doing, Minhaj unveils the character of domination. He uses laughter, visual aids, lightheartedness, and narrative prowess to make serious points. He models what political theorist Amber Day and others label "satiractivism" by drawing awareness to issues alongside educative commentary that promotes critical, public consciousness and an impulse to contest sociopolitical injustices.[8] In this manner, humor provides pedagogical possibilities for solidarity by fostering cross-racial understanding and inspiring coalitions toward counter-hegemonic struggle. He reminds us that we do not live in a post-racial or egalitarian cultural context.

Rhetorical studies scholar Jonathan Rossing also tackles the post-race myth in his scholarship. Rossing explains how comedians like Minhaj use an "emancipatory racial humor" as a pedagogical tool to expose the ways dominant narratives reinforce racial hegemony. This liberated and liberating form of racial humor provides counternarratives, creates community, and undermines the specious notion of a post-racial society, which discounts issues of racial oppression and social and political injustice. Rossing explains that he uses the term emancipatory racial humor to describe these comic discourses because it brings to the forefront cognitive and affective strategies that challenge dominant ways of construing reality. Thus, it bears the potential to promote critical comical resistance and reflection about racial oppression, which in turn may transform audiences' perspectives and belief systems.[9] The counternarratives that this humor produces, Rossing argues, have three pedagogical functions:

8. Day, *Satire and Dissent*, 94; McClennen and Maisel, *Is Satire Saving Our Nation?*, 1–20.

9. Rossing, "Emancipatory Racial Humor as Critical Public Pedagogy," 615.

1. They reveal the "character of the oppression." Critical humor exposes the dominant meaning-making practices that legitimize existing power relations.

2. Counterhegemonic racial humor offers defiant "counteraction to oppression." It does this by providing a forum where counternarratives might gain a hearing.

3. Emancipatory racial humor features "cunning, inventive retaliation" that interrogates the assumptive, naturalized racial constructions that privilege whiteness at the expense of those who are not white.[10]

Minhaj's emancipatory humor drives his efforts on *Patriot Act*. The show set itself apart from other entertainment news shows such as *Full Frontal with Samantha Bee, The Daily Show with Trevor Noah,* and *Last Week Tonight with John Oliver* in terms of tone, aesthetic, and format. For starters, Minhaj remains standing throughout his show. This ties him more to the primary performative mode of stand-up than that of news correspondents and political pundits. Smart, satirical, and bristling with righteous indignation, these shows pull off deep dives into current events to expose the hypocrisy and injustices perpetrated by politicians, corporations, and sociopolitical institutions. *Patriot Act* felt different, argues Joshua Rivera, because of the tone Minhaj added to his commentary and critique. He writes, "*Patriot Act* was *already* mad, and it knew you were, too. It wasn't interested in getting you riled up about something new, but all that shit you already slog through to get through the day? The show wanted to break that stuff down to its disparate parts and tell you what could be done about it."[11]

In addition to its tone, the aesthetic of *Patriot Act* was distinct. Everything from Minhaj's casual, urban-chic attire to the hip-hop beats accompanying his entrance on stage, to the use of visual aids and graphics made it distinct. At times Minhaj presents as a cheeky university professor with bomb-ass visual arts and tech skills. The show won several awards, including a Peabody Award for excellence in journalism and an Emmy for outstanding motion design. Minhaj has leaned into his comical persona as a "watchdog comedian," challenging Prime Minister Narendra Modi and his manipulation of the Indian elections, political corruption in Brazil, and the violent drug war in the Philippines. In an interview, Minhaj defended his commitment to fighting for civil liberties across the globe.[12]

10. Rossing, "Emancipatory Racial Humor as Critical Public Pedagogy," 620.
11. Rivera, "Goodbye to Patriot Act."
12. Elsayed, "Interview with Hasan Minhaj."

TAKEAWAYS FOR STAND-UP PREACHING

There is much to glean from Hassan Minhaj for stand-up preaching. I will focus on two aspects of his work that set him apart from the other comics I spotlight in this book. The first thing that jumps out when you come to his stand-up with a critical eye is the way he opens the genres of stand-up and political satire to novel possibilities. In her important work on reimagining the generic conventions of sermons, Donyelle McCray pushes us to blend multiple forms of discourse to rethink frameworks for prophetic speech. Such genre-bending ought to aim at more than novelty for novelty's sake, nor should it be used to avoid grappling with difficult issues from the pulpit. Genre-bending sermons, McCray argues, help us reimagine authority structures, wherein the preacher emerges as a sage, bearing witness to an archive of communal stories, rituals, and practices to express the faith in new ways.[13]

With the aid of McCray's scholarship, we may bear witness to the ways Minhaj enacts a bit of genre-bending. For starters, he employs visuals like no other contemporary stand-up. This use of visual technologies not only supports the pedagogical impulse of his comedy, it also offers him alternative registers upon which to weave counternarratives that deconstruct dominant and dominating narratives. Both *Homecoming King* and *Patriot Act* employ visuals and theatricality in unique ways. Their primary purpose is to support Minhaj's explication of complex matters ranging from anti-Islam xenophobia to the complexities of the US electoral system to Amazon's economic dominance despite the company's unjust labor practices. In all his work, Minhaj presents information to his audiences in service of bolstering their awareness and personal investment in matters of social injustice.

Another way he bends the generic borders of stand-up is in the way he employs personal narratives as forms of critical comical resistance. In *Homecoming King* he blurs the line between stand-up and autobiography. Minhaj's special relies much more heavily on personal stories than jokes. This does not set him that far apart from the other comics I spotlight in this book. What does set him apart is how he holds various narratives in tension with one another, showing us through his narration how the personal is always political.

The second takeaway I wish to mention pertains to a warning I issued in this book's introduction about the risks one bears in challenging powerful structures with comedy. In his book *Surviving a Dangerous Sermon* Frank Thomas acknowledges the difficult realities facing preachers who choose to

---

13. McCray, "Playing in Church," 12.

speak out on matters of sociopolitical injustice. He names the serious consequences of this calling, including sleepless nights, ridicule, isolation, threats, and even physical violence. Thomas writes, "Preaching dangerous sermons is a difficult choice, and the choice should be made with eyes wide open."[14] Thomas is right, and one of the things I've tried to do as I made a case for the why and the how of stand-up preaching is to make these difficulties evident in the work of stand-up comics. Minhaj is a case in point of this danger.

In a 2018 episode of *Patriot Act*, Minhaj spoke out against the Saudi Arabian government for a number of recent acts of injustice. In particular, Minhaj criticized the Saudi Crown Prince Mohammed bin Salman for the alleged role he played in the killing of prominent journalist and vocal critic Jamal Khashoggi at the Saudi consulate in Istanbul. Minhaj also criticized the Saudi government for its devastating war in Yemen and its deplorable crackdown on women's rights advocates. The Saudi government responded by requesting the episode be removed from Netflix, as it violated the kingdom's anti-cybercrime laws criminalizing the production and transmission of digital material impinging on the monarchy's religious values and public morals. Netflix complied.[15] While it seemed removing the episode on Saudi Arabia was the end of the incident, Netflix later decided to cancel *Patriot Act*.[16] Though Netflix has not admitted why exactly they decided to cancel the show, speculation has focused on the Saudi episode and Minhaj's criticism of Netflix for pulling the episode.[17] Here we see a passionate advocate for justice speaking truth to power, only to have that power turned against him. It is a sobering reminder of just what is at stake in critical comical discourse.

14. Thomas, *Surviving a Dangerous Sermon*, 96.
15. See Khalil and Zayani, "De-Territorialized Digital."
16. Porter, "Patriot Act with Hasan Minhaj Canceled at Netflix."
17. Gonzalez, "Hasan Minhaj's 'Patriot Act' Canceled at Netflix."

7

Just Joking
Preaching the Political and the Profane

I'm not interested in making everybody laugh. I'm more interested in making everyone learn. I want some people to feel uncomfortable. I want them to shift in their seats. I want to make some people cry.[1]

—AMANDA SEALES

Very plainly and simply, a dangerous sermon is a sermon based in the preacher's moral imagination that upends and challenges the dominant moral hierarchy that operates in the church and/or cultural context of the preaching event.[2]

—FRANK THOMAS

Jokes are political. As we have seen in the preceding chapters, jokes work within and against power structures. "Every joke is a tiny revolution," George Orwell wrote. "Whatever destroys dignity, and brings down the mighty from their seats, preferably with a bump, is funny."[3] He goes on to

1. Seales in Fox, "Amanda Seales Is Not for Everyone."
2. Thomas, *Surviving a Dangerous Sermon*, xvii.
3. Orwell, "Funny, but Not Vulgar," 284–85.

argue that for a joke to be funny it must not actually offend anyone. It is hard to imagine that such joking that aims at a revolution, even a tiny one, can take place without offending those who hold the power, those whose dignity is destroyed.

Many jokes are also profane. The Latin word for profane (*profānus*) literally means "outside of the temple." Profanity emerges from the idea that to employ a word outside its religious context was out of bounds. Today's common profanities are traditionally religious in nature, as in "God damn" or "Jesus Christ." Paradoxically, profanity doubles the connection between the profane and the sacred. M. Conrad Hyers argues that the comical is the link that bridges the gap between profanity and sacrality: "In this very act of profanation, the comic leap into nonsense points in its own nonsensical way to the mystery of the sacred, the mystery of being itself, which cannot simply be reduced to logical syllogisms and rational forms, the mystery which cannot be exhausted by priestly definitions and delineations, which cannot be contained and ordered by [humanity]."[4] For profanities to be truly profane, the connotation of a word must be irreverent, which requires a priori value structures that stipulate what counts as irreverent. Profanity is determined by the whims of those in power and by the power structures that demarcate their exercise of power.[5] A profanity, therefore, is a form of rebellion against someone or something in power, typically of that which is spiritual, excremental, or sexual in nature (e.g., "shit" or "fuck"). These examples reflect a rebellion against value structures—a rebellion against religion and a rebellion against the prim, high culture concerned with hiding bodily functions and sexual desires.

Joking, as a "tiny revolution," can serve political and moral purposes. Comedy can help us challenge sociopolitical structures that marginalize certain people groups and oppress others. As Chatoo and Feldman argue,

> When it comes to social justice issues, particularly issues that can seem removed from everyday life—such as climate change or global poverty—one of the foremost challenges to public engagement is getting people to pay attention in the first place. In today's media environment, where myriad messages—and issues—compete for our increasingly fragmented attention, comedy can cut through the clutter, promoting attention to topics that otherwise may be eclipsed from public view.[6]

4. Hyers, "Dialectic of the Sacred and the Comic," 71–72.
5. Mohr, "Defining Dirt," 271.
6. Chatoo and Feldman, *Comedian and an Activist Walk into A Bar*, 41–42.

Comedy, in other words, can foster awareness even as it exposes incongruities between what we profess to believe and our behaviors that might belie those beliefs. In this final chapter, we'll look specifically at the challenges and opportunities joking presents for preaching toward justice.[7] We'll also examine some of the ways stand-up comics can help us navigate precarious topics and challenge political structures, both of which might call for a lighter touch than direct, prophetic discourse may allow.

COMEDY IS NO LAUGHING MATTER

Even as we recognize the ways comedy can spur our listeners to regard themselves, others, and the planet in fresh ways, it is not without its dangers. Recall that the earliest critiques of comedy arose from its capacity to lead us astray ethically. Aristotle resisted comedy because it presents people as worse than they ought to be. By highlighting their ridiculousness, it reduces them as fit to be mocked. Aristotle remarks that comedy represents the actions of the base because laughter (*tò geloîon*) and the comic element to which it is connected is an aspect of "baseness" (*tò aiskhrón*).[8] This was the element in comedy that Hobbes found so delightful. The "sudden glory" that arises from comedic laughter is that by which we apprehend "some deformed thing in another, by comparison whereof we applaud ourselves for being morally or intellectually superior."[9]

When comedy targets a particular kind of person and encourages us to laugh at their base actions and opinions, the laughter it produces in us can bypass any moral instruction it might hold. In so doing, it loses any propaedeutic function. As Wylie Sypher cautions, "One of the strongest impulses comedy can discharge from the depths of the social self is our hatred of the 'alien,' especially when the stranger who is 'different' stirs any unconscious doubts about our own beliefs." Sypher goes on to say that the comedian "can point out our victim, isolate him from sympathy, and cruelly expose him to the penalty of our ridicule."[10] We must take great care in attempting

---

7. Justice is an ambiguous concept, as it can signify distributive, procedural, retributive, or restorative justice. Each of these, in turn, is context dependent. By *just joking* in this chapter's title I mean joking that aims at equity and restoration. As André Resner puts it in his argument for *just preaching*, "A faith driven by the biblical vision realizes that in a world that continues to compromise fair treatment of human beings based on color, ethnicity, or socioeconomic status that God, and all of God's creation, is being compromised at the same time." Resner, *Just Preaching*, xx.

8. Aristotle, *Poetics*, 1449a34–37.

9. Hobbes, *Leviathan*, 125.

10. Sypher, "Meanings of Comedy," 242.

comedy—especially from the pulpit—that we do not misdirect our comedy to "punch down" or belittle those who are already marginalized on account of their identity markers. Comedy that is reactive or conservative finds its audience all too willing to laugh to bolster the status quo and buttress the self-esteem and power structures of the majority.

A second risk in employing comedy as a tool for approaching justice is that comedic laughter can cause us to make light of situations and circumstances that we ought to take more seriously. In a recent interview Slovenian psychoanalytic philosopher Alenka Zupančič recounts a joke from the times of Apartheid in South Africa:

> A violent fight starts on a bus between black people sitting in the back and white people sitting in front. The driver stops the bus, makes everybody get out, lines them up in front of the bus, and yells at them: "Stop this fight immediately! As far as I'm concerned, you are all green. Now, those of the lighter shade of green please get on the bus in front, and those of the darker shade, at the back."[11]

What this joke exposes, Zupančič suggests, is how humor can function to neutralize difference and thereby perpetuate discrimination. This is a critique shared by those who advocate for the importance of identity politics, who worry that efforts to overcome gender binaries through non-gender binary markers such as "queer" or "third sex," or efforts to eradicate racial distinctions in service of some "color-blind" or "post-racial" utopia sometimes function like the color "green" in the Apartheid joke.[12] If we forget or decide to let go of the concept of sexual or racial difference in this radical sense, we risk ending up like the passengers of this bus: declared non-racial, all the while continuing to be judged on the basis of an identity marker that can be used to discriminate. As my Columbia Theological Seminary colleague Chanequa Walker-Barnes argues, any push toward reconciliation between those of different races cannot succeed if it is presupposing a faulty understanding of racial constructs and the machinations of white supremacy. Color-blind racism—with its call for the symmetrical treatment and obliteration of all racial identities—misses the persistence of anti-Black racist structures and practices.[13]

---

11. Zupančič, "Philosophy or Psychoanalysis?," 450.

12. Cf. Thomas, *Surviving a Dangerous Sermon*, 8: "Identity politics is the working gospel of taking seriously one's ethnicity, gender, race, or social location as an interpretive lens through which to view the biblical text and hence construction of theology."

13. Walker-Barnes, *I Bring the Voices of My People*, 63.

A third risk of attempting comedy pertains to its capacity to manipulate others. This, of course, has its personal benefits. As stand-up comedian and actress Amy Schumer notes, cracking jokes was a way to get out of trouble while she was growing up. She discovered that whether it was teachers catching her talking in class or cops finding her with beer in her backpack on the beach, "it always felt like my only way to get home free was to make everyone laugh. It always dismantled the power structure within seconds. Being funny was my ultimate hustle!"[14] Schumer's examples might seem rather innocuous on a micro-level, but on a macro-level the consequences of comedic manipulation can be dire. M. Conrad Hyers notes that in Stalinist Russia comedies were permitted, and even encouraged, by the government. Yet they were of a certain, carefully censored type. The Soviet State encouraged comedies that targeted capitalistic countries and democratic values. In Hyers's words, "This use of the comic simply reinforces the underlying tragic vision of life and its doctrinaire rigidity. We laugh at others as a way of justifying ourselves and our condemnation of those who disagree with us."[15]

It's easy to dismiss such use of comedy in a totalitarian sociopolitical situation, but the comedy connected with carnivals can also be used to manipulate and enforce conformity. Recall that Mikhail Bakhtin proffered the carnivalesque as the model for comedic interventions against the powers and principalities and that this lampooning and lambasting impulse is one of its major attractions to homiletician Charles Campbell. Campbell writes, "We are the Body of Christ when we become a grotesque, carnivalesque community that defies the world's categories and liberates people from the rankings and norms and prohibitions of the established order."[16] This is a noble goal, but it presupposes that the carnivalesque can sufficiently defy and liberate. Howard Jacobson offers a counterpoint, inquiring into the "essential conservatism" of carnivals. His questions ought to give us pause: "For all its escapades at the edges of our reverence and decency, is it not the first ambition of festive laughter (and maybe of all laughter) to corral the wayward back into conformity? To draw the eccentric back into the circle?"[17] Henri Bergson comes to a grim conclusion about comedic laughter of this sort. "By laughter," Bergson argues, "society avenges itself for the liberties taken with it . . . Always rather humiliating for the one against whom it is directed, laughter is really and truly a kind of social 'ragging.'" Bergson ultimately concludes that "laughter cannot be absolutely just. Nor should it

14. Schumer, *The Girl with the Lower Back Tattoo*, 100.

15. Hyers, *And God Created Laughter*, 114–15.

16. Campbell, *Scandal of the Gospel*, 87.

17. Jacobson, *Seriously Funny*, 201.

be kind-hearted either. Its function is to intimidate by humiliating."[18] It is hard to reconcile this with justice.

A final caution in approaching the comical in our preaching toward justice gets at the ultimate sociopolitical function of comedy. Follow my logic here. If the ultimate goal of just preaching is to make the world a more equitable place, and if people need to change their hearts and minds to imagine a more equitable world, and if comedy holds the potential to change people's hearts and minds, then why all these cautions? Well, not everybody accepts the premise that comedy *can* lead to tangible social change.[19] Let's look briefly at two arguments that ought to give us pause about the possibility of just (i.e., justice-oriented) joking.

The first form of this argument against the sociopolitical impact of comedy is aesthetic. Critical theorists such as Theodor Adorno and Jacques Rancière question whether forms of artistic expression can actually make the world a better place. Addressing the politics of aesthetics today, Rancière counts the joke as a dialectical form of aesthetic dissensus. He argues that in the joke, the conjunction of heterogeneous elements is staged as a tension or polarity but that this tension dissipates as soon as we realize that what the joke-teller is saying is nothing more than a harmless game.[20] Here we may recall Kant's description of comedic laughter as an emotion produced by "the sudden transformation of a heightened expectation into nothing."[21] A joke's incongruity producing nothing but laughter in its punch line diffuses any political action potential of the joke. Adorno says that, politically speaking, a successful work of art "is not one which resolves objective contradictions in a spurious harmony, but one which expresses the idea of harmony negatively by embodying the contradictions pure and uncompromised, in its innermost structure."[22] The idea here is that the aesthetic work ought not resolve the tension. Rather, it is only through unresolvable tension that people might take to the streets in protest against the status quo, which the joke often presupposes in its setup.

The second form this argument against comedy takes is economic. It is linked with the aesthetic critique in terms of dissipating a tension that might prompt actual social change. It is also apropos for our consideration of the

18. Bergson, *Laughter*, 198.

19. John Morreall writes, "When we want to evoke anger or outrage about some problem, we don't present it in a humorous way, precisely because of the practical disengagement of humor. Satire is not a weapon of revolutionaries." Morreall, *Comic Relief*, 101.

20. Rancière, "Contemporary Art and the Politics of Aesthetics," 46.

21. Kant, *Critique of the Power of Judgment*, 209.

22. Adorno, *Prisms*, 32.

action potential of stand-up comedy. Critical theorists like Adorno force us to grapple with the ways stand-up has been commodified economically and culturally.[23] When stand-up becomes a veritable commodity, just another moment for sublimation rendered by the "culture industry," it has lost its subversive edge. In his *Aesthetic Theory* Adorno argues that when comedy becomes a way to redirect critical potential towards amusement rather than intervention against the conditions of contemporary thought, it makes us complacent to the repulsive sociopolitical conditions of contemporary existence.[24] Any stand-up that makes it onto cable networks or streaming platforms (e.g., Netflix, HBO, Comedy Central) has already been vetted by those who wield cultural and economic capital. No matter how subversive the stand-up seems, so the argument goes, it is not subversive enough to ameliorate injustice in any radical sense.

A number of scholars and comics share Adorno's misgivings. Christie Davies argues against the sociopolitical efficacy of joking, asserting that they have "no significant material consequences." Davies continues, "Vigorous political rhetoric, a stirring sermon, a persuasive advertisement, a well-placed lie, a piece of malicious gossip are all uses of words that are infinitely more powerful than jokes." [25] For her, jokes achieve nothing that could not be attained in other non-humorous ways to greater rhetorical effect. Despite his misgivings about the sociopolitical efficacy of comedy, Nicholas Holm holds out hope that comedy can achieve a particular form of political logic he labels "reasonable dissent." But he remains wary about some forms of comedy that neither appeal to reason nor fan the flames of dissent.[26] Performance studies scholar Kate Fox confronts this dissonance between comedic and serious frames. She recognizes that discursive performativity is far more complicated than scholars like to think. Her argument tracks with the one I've been making throughout this book against the binary logic that separates the humorous from the comical and the serious from the playful. Fox advances a new word to describe the fusion of the comical and the humorous: *humitas*. Humitas is a portmanteau that melds *humor* with *gravitas*. She argues convincingly that humor and seriousness can operate within the same performative frame, which is evidenced by each of the stand-up comics spotlighted in this book. She writes, "When humour is used as more

23. Some stand-up comics such as Steve Martin, and more recently Chelsey Peretti (*One of the Greats*) and Maria Bamford (*The Special Special Special!* and *Old Baby*) recognize the commodification of stand-up and push against it in their subversive performances. See Wuster, "Comedy Jokes," and Gillota, "Beyond Liveness."

24. Adorno, *Aesthetic Theory*, 64.

25. Cited in Quick, *Why Stand-Up Matters*, 203.

26. Holm, *Humour as Politics*, 29–30.

than mere cloak or distraction or disguise, its potential to really shift the terms of the homogenized and monological discourse on politics, culture and academia is huge, interesting and risky."[27] Let's turn now to see how such *humitas* might guide stand-up preaching.

COMEDY AS CRITICAL RESISTANCE

In a recent think piece for *The Atlantic*, Megan Garber suggests that comedians have recently begun to play the role of public intellectuals.[28] Looking at the work of stand-up comics such as John Oliver and Amy Schumer, she celebrates comedy's capacity for "productive subversion." Garber shows how contemporary stand-up comics employ the comical both to enlighten the public and to cause offense. Such "creative destruction" enables people to broach taboo topics that might otherwise be precluded at the risk of offending the fragile sensibilities of the populous. Preachers may likewise play the role of public intellectuals, engaging the political and the profane. We see clarion calls for such an approach to preaching in the work of Richard Voelz and Frank Thomas.[29] Whether it is through stand-up or preaching, such uses of the comical aim at more than mere laughter or entertainment. "Joking is not just about moving an audience to laugh; joking is about moving an audience to see things and people differently."[30]

The critical function of comedy goes all the way back to its origin. Aristophanes once wrote that, like tragedy, "comedy has a sense of duty, too."[31] Here Aristophanes challenges the popular notion in his day that only tragedy could deal with serious matters such as morality and politics. Here at the beginning of comedy we find a comedic intervention against tragedy as the sole means of modeling just citizenry. Plato, too, thought that any comedy worthy of public consumption would need to be ethically informative and thereby action guiding. He calls these the epistemic and practical benefits of comedy. Plato set clear restrictions on comedy to be truth tracking, that is, to communicate the truth about what is worthy of ridicule and what such ridiculous speech and action are like.[32] As Franco Trivigno adds, "On this view, then, laughter is truth functional; that is, it is committed

27. Fox, "Humitas," 96.

28. Garber, "How Comedians Became Public Intellectuals."

29. See Voelz, *Preaching to Teach*; Thomas, *How to Preach a Dangerous Sermon*.

30. Benko and Jones, "That's Way Too Aggressive a Word," 105.

31. Aristophanes, *Acharnians*, 496. See also Silk, *Aristophanes and the Definition of Comedy*, 40–41.

32. Plato, *Laws*, 11.935–36.

to a claim about something's being ridiculous, and that claim may be true or false. These claims are not merely aesthetic, determined by the tastes of the agent, but claims about value—about what is virtuous and vicious— and these are determined by the moral reality."[33] Plato was all for comedy that exposed falsehoods, but he struggled to find any examples in his day of comedy that didn't imitate the worst kind of social existence, making it ethically unworthy of imitation by its viewers. Plato deemed it both just and highly appropriate to laugh at the enemies of virtue and goodness; but Plato argued that no citizen, no free man, ought to ever perform comedy. Comedy was to be performed only by slaves and foreigners, for it was impossible, Plato thought, that one could imitate vice without being personally corrupted by it. "Because the citizens will laugh at these imitations of vice without having themselves to imitate them, they can learn about vice with the appropriate ethical distance. Further, since they will laugh together at these vicious figures, they will reinforce or consolidate their shared social rejection of vice."[34] His argument notwithstanding, let's recall that Plato's platitudes presuppose a society structured on the systematic subjugation of some for the benefit of others. This makes his argument dubious.

Part of the role public intellectuals take on—whether on the comedy stage or behind the pulpit—is that of helping their audience to develop capacities to discern virtue from vice. This critical function facilitates the possibility of resisting vice at a personal and systemic level. The word *resistance* can refer to both emancipation and domination. Workers who unionize *resist* the interests of management to consider profits above workers' safety and fair compensation. Management might, in turn, *resist* efforts to unionize to keep pace with stockholders' financial expectations. Here's where the modifier "critical" becomes so important. As David Couzens Hoy argues, critique is what makes it possible for us to differentiate between emancipatory resistance and resistance that has been co-opted by oppressive forces.[35]

Homiletics has long had those who advocate for preaching's capacity for critical resistance. James Harris writes that because there are so many advocates of maintaining the status quo "there is an urgent need for effective preaching that is truthful, indicting, confrontational, straightforward— a radically simple strategy that will be heard and acted upon rather than alienating—preaching that will challenge and transform the prevailing power structures that tend to oppress minorities, women, and the poor."[36] In

---

33. Trivigno, "Plato on Laughter and Moral Harm," 29.

34. Trivigno, "Plato on Laughter and Moral Harm," 30.

35. Hoy, *Critical Resistance*, 2.

36. Harris, *Preaching Liberation*, 38.

critical conversation with Fred Craddock, Adam Hearlson offers a similar argument, but he adds a caveat. While he recognizes that indirect discourse (*à la* narrative or jokes) can invite people into new ways of being in the world, Hearlson argues that "the ignored do not need indirect speech, they need direct speech. Those who have ears to hear have not heard a word in a long time, because those who have a place to speak have ignored them."[37] The question for preaching that seeks justice is whether the more indirect, less straightforward mode of comical discourse can provide prophetic challenge without forsaking priestly comfort.

PLAYING POLITICS: MODELS OF INTERSECTIONAL COMICAL RESISTANCE

Marc Maron offers a sobering point about the current state of politics in America and the challenges it presents stand-up comics. "Political humor, now that it's become such a farce, it's hard to outdo it."[38] Maron is talking about the state of political comedy in the wake of Trump's presidency. Prior to the 2016 presidential election, the words and actions of politicians and pundits provided a steady stream of material for stand-up. There seems to be a minimal comical quotient where politics is concerned; i.e., it is only when politics is taken seriously that stand-up can expose the humorous element that "serious" politicians would seek to occlude.

Patton Oswalt suggests that the reason stand-up comedians pick on politicians is almost like a prayer: "Hey, could you maybe not steer us off of a cliff? But the only way I can maybe keep you on it is to make you look ridiculous so you'll stop what you're doing."[39] While I resonate with Oswalt's impulse here, it suggests what we might label *puny politics*. This is a way of engaging politics that targets politicians and policy makers *as people*. It is the sort of comedy that revels in George W. Bush's gaffes or Donald Trump's hair. This is what we find in the comedy of late-night hosts such as Stephen Colbert and Jimmy Kimmel. Much of their comedic monologues attack individual people rather than opening deliberative discourse concerning the complexities of politicians' actions. Seeing clips of Trump with toilet paper stuck to the bottom of his shoe or President Biden tripping as he climbs the stairs to Air Force One might make us chuckle, but the humor it produces only reinforces our ideological positions. It aligns with the superiority theory of laughter. Against this we might identify comedy oriented toward

37. Hearlson, *Holy No*, 30.
38. Maron, "Politics Aside."
39. Oswalt, "Politics Aside."

potent politics. The goal here is to expose the incongruities and affective implications of political policies and ideals. This moves us into a different comedic frame that emerges from the incongruity and affect theories of laughter, which I presented in chapter 2.

This distinction I am making between puny and potent politics tracks with the argument of Alenka Zupančič on the political consequences of comedy. Zupančič argues that when the target of comic critique is a person who possesses all the defects and foibles as the rest of us, such humor cannot be considered political—even if the butt of the joke happens to be a politician. Only when the central premise of humor is built upon engagement with questions of knowledge, power, and judgments about the status of real-world behaviors, can it properly be labeled *political*. Like me, she's interested in the kind of humor that can actively intervene in political discourse in a way that goes beyond the ridicule of one's opponents. It's not simply the case that one will only "get" the joke if one already shares the joke's underlying political perspective, but also that in "getting" the joke—i.e., interpreting it correctly—the hearer might become aware, or even convinced, of the political issues at stake. Such playing with politics can thus be considered "true comedy" in Zupančič's terms, because it explores rather than denigrates the abstract ideals of politics. As Holm observes. "Rather than locating humour in the mismatch between the ideal universal category of politics and the flawed subjects who inhabit and enact that category, humour here arises from fidelity between the actions of subjects and the demands of the wider system."[40] Accordingly, Zupančič refers to ad hominem jokes as "false comedy" because they leave universal categories of the political "fundamentally untouched in their abstract purity."[41]

There are a number of reasons we might play in and with politics in our preaching. The first reason is pragmatic in that it works alongside the function of humor on our thoughts and opinions. We all tend to resist ideas that clash with our beliefs and opinions. There is a direct correlation between our vested interest in an idea and our level of critical engagement with arguments about it. But with humor, our attention and interest are directed at "getting" the joke. So, cognitively speaking, we are focused more on the joke itself than the underlying argument that might impel it, thereby reducing our motivation and ability to counter-argue. Consistent with this idea, researchers have found that late-night political jokes, compared to non-humorous versions of the same jokes, produced more thoughts aimed

40. Holm, *Humour as Politics,* 83.
41. Zupančič, *Odd One In,* 31.

at humor comprehension and appreciation, and less negative thoughts directed at message arguments.[42]

Jeffrey Israel offers a second reason we might approach politics from a comical perspective. In his recently published book *Living with Hate in American Politics and Religion,* Israel argues for the importance of humorous play as a way to foster connection across modes of difference. He writes that "[t]ime and space that is set aside for this kind of play with the elements of culture that may be indefensible, crude, irrational, or unreasonable is crucially important to living well with the interminable emotional legacies of historic injustice."[43] Such space is not about purgation nor is it merely palliative. It is not a safe space to blow off some steam or to inure people with spectacle as a way to anesthetize them to injustice. Rather, Israel argues that "the idea is that flourishing—living well—for many of us will involve activating, engaging, performing, expressing, and otherwise perpetuating nasty, rancorous words, ideas, and emotions in the context of play."[44] Political humor can engender such a critical space.

Terrence Tucker offers a third benefit for playing with politics. Tucker's work centers on the ways stand-up and literary comics rage against systems of injustice. He draws an important distinction here between *comic defiance* and *comic critique.*[45] Only the latter contributes critical commentary on unjust structures, especially those of structural racism. Tucker associates comics such as Richard Pryor, Whoopi Goldberg, and Chris Rock with comic critique. Comics such as Eddie Murphy and Andrew Dice Clay embody mere defiance. The former use profanity as a tool for critical comical resistance. The latter employ profanity just to get a laugh.

Black feminist scholar bell hooks has identified humor as a form of political weaponry suitable for subverting claims to a "post-gendered" or "post-racial" cultural context.[46] Joking that is just resists more than jokes about ethnic, racial, and sexual others. Such comedy forces us to consider how in appropriating others' patterns of speech we might reinforce denigrating stereotypes. For instance, in a recent article examining the use of linguistic and ethnic media stereotypes in everyday speech, researcher Sylvia Sierra shows how speakers employ media stereotypes to construct "their humourous individual identities and their shared cultural and ethnic

42. Young, "Privileged Role of the Late-Night Joke."

43. Israel, *Living with Hate in American Politics and Religion,* 17.

44. Israel, *Living with Hate in American Politics and Religion,* 17.

45. Tucker, *Furiously Funny,* 242.

46. hooks, "Keynote Speech."

identities via the 'others' they voice."[47] Sierra conducted playback interviews with her research participants, who revealed their surprise and sometimes their dismay that they were employing stereotypes. There is strong evidence that humor grants legitimacy to stereotypes regarding racial groups, more so when it adheres to conventional racial narratives. Jokes about Asian women being bad drivers or of the "angry Black woman," for example, resonate with audiences because they do not deviate from the ideological framing that supports them.[48]

As playing politics can be difficult to discuss in abstraction, let's look at two examples of contemporary stand-up performers who approach the comical as a way to challenge unjust sociopolitical structures. I selected each of these exemplars for the ways they highlight the intersectional complexities of critical comical resistance. Trevor Noah offers a perspective on how to use satirical humor to address macropolitical problems. Amanda Seales shows us ways to address micropolitical issues through storytelling and sarcasm.

Trevor Noah: Satire vs. Systemic Injustice

Long before he was tapped to become Jon Stewart's replacement on Comedy Central's *The Daily Show*, Trevor Noah had made a name for himself as a stand-up comic in his home of South Africa and abroad. Noah's intersectional identity has shaped his comedy in particular ways, and this insider-outsider status grounds his comical point of view.[49] He was born to a white Swiss father and a Black Xhosa mother, and a lot of his humor stems from the way his body was considered illegal as the product of one Black parent and one white parent during Apartheid South Africa.[50] He describes how his family couldn't even walk down the street together. Noah states that his father would have to wave to him from the other side of the road "like a creepy pedophile." If they came across the police, his mom would have to drop his hand and pretend she had no idea who he belonged to, like he was "a bag of weed."[51]

One of Noah's performance strategies is to make shrewd observations about US racial discourse couched in the feigned ignorance of an outsider.

47. Sierra, "Linguistic and Ethnic Media Stereotypes in Everyday Talk," 186.

48. Green and Linders, "Impact of Comedy on Racial and Ethnic Discourse"; Pérez, "Racist Humor."

49. Meyer, *You Laugh But It's True.*

50. Noah, *Son of Patricia.*

51. Noah, "Trevor Noah: Live at the Apollo."

Noah displays great skill in transitioning between the voices of a vast array of characters from many different cultural backgrounds, and he uses this to gain credibility with his audience to counter his outsider status. A joke that exemplifies the comic power of Noah's feigned ignorance, coupled with an informed deconstruction of American racial discourse, is his KKK bit:

> When I was in Tennessee, I stumbled across an organization known as the Ku Klux Klan. You heard of them? Worst magic show ever. Guy gave me a pamphlet [*with a white, Southern accent*], "Come and see the Grand Wizard! The Grand Wizard!" [*In his normal voice*] Didn't do one trick. Not even one trick. I mean, I noticed a few Black people disappear, but that's not magic. That's just Reaganomics. I wasn't impressed.[52]

The joke highlights Noah's performative strategy: equal parts innocent and studied. It enables him to couch a critique of American racism in its overt forms (the KKK) while simultaneously critiquing American racism in its less obvious but equally pernicious forms (the economic disenfranchisement of African Americans under Ronald Reagan's sociopolitical agenda). Noah follows up with a second observation. He muses,

> The whole name is wrong. They got that, as you know, from Ancient Greece, it was *Kúklos Adelphôn*, meaning a "circle of brothers." Which is wrong for two reasons: one, if your sole purpose as an organization is to hate Black people, don't you find it strange that you've now named yourself the circle of brothers. And secondly, did they realize that in Ancient Greece, circles of brothers were doing very different things?[53]

Noah's seamless transition from Reaganomics to the etymology of the KKK deconstructs overt anti-Black racism in two ways. First, by playing with the Greek word *adelphôn* he riffs off the semantic linkage between brothers in ancient Greece and in contemporary African American parlance. In both instances, the signifier *brothers* stretches beyond a biological relationship between two males. This conceptual joke destabilizes the virulent anti-Black agenda of the KKK. Second, Noah employs a hermetic conceptual joke (to use Cohen's terminology, which I discussed in chapter 3). The joke requires certain knowledge from the listener to "get" the joke. In ancient Greece close fellowship between *adelphoi* often included sexual acts. By hearkening back to this historical-cultural detail, Noah forces the hypermasculine structure of the KKK into tension with its sexually fluid origins. He implies,

52. Noah, *African American.*
53. Noah, *African American.*

in other words, that the KKK is gay, which would presumably trouble the homophobia that also marks the KKK.

This bit links a series of jokes targeting racism in America. Notwithstanding the merits of "punching down" at an organization like the KKK, we must attend to a problematic feature of Noah's bit. Even as his topic for prophetic indictment is racism in its structural (Reaganomics) and interpersonal (KKK) guises, he also targets gay men. I want to give Noah the benefit of the doubt considering his many other pro-LGBTQIA comments. I want to label this a slipup. Nevertheless, Noah displays insensitivity to the ways that accusations of gayness coincide with ridicule. This situation merits a callback to a line from W. Kamau Bell that I shared in the introduction. Bell argues, "Some jokes are like a shotgun blast, where a bunch of pellets come out and hit whoever's in the area."[54] Recall how Bell redoubled his efforts to make his jokes "target focused" once he became aware of this. I draw our attention to Noah's problematic joke to remind us of how tricky just joking can be. I also want to avoid the temptation to give progressive comics like Noah a pass even when they perpetuate toxic stereotypes.

One of the techniques that Noah uses with particular efficacy is his oral prowess. For my money, he's the best at mimicking other languages and character vocalizations. It helps that Noah is fluent in six languages. Throughout his stand-up career he has built his comic routine into other languages to perform in other countries using their native tongues and to expose something about the cultures of those dialects he mimics.[55] Noah does an excellent job of avoiding minstrelsy in taking on the voices of others. Through the lenses of anthropological linguistics, humor studies, and media studies, Kendra Calhoun studies subversive comics who employ anti-hegemonic humor, by which they are obligated to convey that they do not subscribe to the ideologies they present. Calhoun argues that this type of humor poses complexities that humor that reaffirms and reifies the status quo does not.[56] Citing the comic legacies of Dick Gregory and Richard Pryor as important influences on contemporary Black performers, she notes that African American comedy has become far more capacious and encompasses humor that is by turns explicit or "subtle," social or "personal," realistic or "outlandish"—all of which she maintains are effective means of challenging mainstream stereotypes of the racial other.

To better understand the performative significance of Noah's vocalizations, Faedra Chatard Carpenter offers us helpful terminology to analyze

54. Bell, *Awkward Thoughts of W. Kamau Bell*, 173.
55. Meyer, *You Laugh But It's True*.
56. Calhoun, "Vine Racial Comedy as Anti-Hegemonic Humor," 28.

aural racial signifiers, such as "aural whiteness" and "aural Blackness," and "linguistic whiteface." These technical elements in speech signify racial associations based on learned behavior. She writes, "Factors such as word choice and dialect are often the clues that guide a listener to draw conclusions about the speaker's race, but rather than being racially determined, these choices and patterns are evidence of one's acculturation, experience, and environment."[57] In Noah's *Afraid of the Dark* special, he discusses the way voice changes perceptions: "I like accents because I'm always impressed by how much power they have over us, over our minds. When someone speaks in a certain way, it changes how we feel about that person. For good and for bad."[58] In turn, Noah subverts our cultural norms with the stealth of a practiced comic, but also keeps our eyes and ears trained on what he's doing at all times: dissecting power and privilege through jokes.

Noah is probably best known in the US for hosting *The Daily Show with Trevor Noah*. Like other satirical news shows such as *Full Frontal with Samantha Bee* and *Last Week Tonight with John Oliver*, Noah blurs the boundaries between journalism and entertainment and those dividing political reporting from stand-up comedy. Noah has capitalized on his ability "to get across a sharp point of view in an ingratiating manner,"[59] to tackle divisive political issues such as police brutality against African Americans and immigration reform. For instance, in 2017 Noah discussed Colin Kaepernick's dropping to one knee during the National Anthem in protest of police brutality. Noah joked about when would be the "right time to protest" for African Americans, suggesting "right before lunch" or "on their own time." He compares the NFL protests to the civil rights movement, musing over what would have happened if Rosa Parks had elected to protest segregation on Montgomery's buses at home from her couch instead. "Hey Rosa, why you protesting on the bus? People have places to be. Take the bus to your house. Sit down on your couch. And boom! Racism solved."[60]

Noah has another satirical bit on *The Daily Show* about Trump's calls for increased border security with threats of closing the border between the US and Mexico. Noah splices "actual" news stories into his comical commentary.

> Noah: In case you were wondering, shutting down the US-Mexico border wouldn't just hurt the hombres down south, no. There will also be more painful consequences here in the US,

57. Carpenter, *Coloring Whiteness*, 198.
58. Noah, *Afraid of the Dark*.
59. Zinoman, "For Daily Show Successor, Another Dust-Up."
60. Noah, "When Is the Right Time for Black People to Protest."

because economists have warned that a closed border would affect five million American jobs and over 600 billion dollars in trade. Yeah, and if you think a border shutdown won't affect you because you don't live or work around the border, well, you might want to think again.

MSNBC Reporter: The US, listen to this, would run out of avocados in three weeks if President Trump shuts down the border with Mexico.

Noah: Do you hear that? That's the sound of yoga moms all over America freaking out right now. [Noah shifts to linguistic whiteface] "Where will I get my healthy fats?" [Shifts back to his normal voice] So, once again, Donald Trump has shown there's no problem he can't make twice as bad.[61]

If the second-wave feminist motto that *the personal is political* is true, then Noah inverts this logic to show how *the political is personal*. This avocado bit is more than a throwaway joke. It's an indictment of the kind of people who might dismiss the real-world consequences of Trump's xenophobic policies because they don't seem to affect them personally.

Amanda Seales: Womanist Micropolitics

Amanda Seales has worn many hats. She's been a recording artist, a VJ, a rapper, an actress, and a cultural commentator since the 1990s. She has a master's degree in African American studies with a concentration in hip-hop from Columbia University and she employs this training to humorous and incisive effect. Her work highlights the challenges African American women face in the US in the overlapping oppressions of racism and sexism. Seales blends music, social commentary, and TED Talk-styled self-help into her stand-up. In a 2019 interview, she stated that in a world of fake news and post-truth, comedians are "the last bastion of truth and reality."[62] Her stand-up is political, biting, intersectional, and steeped in Black feminist aesthetics.

Seales offers us a way to engage the political at a micro level. As Katelyn Hale Wood writes, "As the #MeToo movement gained momentum, Black feminist comics have extended their performances to critique the misogyny and sexual violence within the world of comedy."[63]

61. Noah, "Trump Exacerbates America's Immigration Crisis."
62. Seales interview in Fox, "Amanda Seales Is Not for Everyone."
63. Wood, *Cracking Up*, 127–8.

Seales's stand-up celebrates Black femininity vis-à-vis white supremacy and androcentrism. She offers a comical iteration of what bell hooks labels "political solidarity between women."[64] Like hooks, Seales recognizes the primacy of struggling against racist, sexist structures on an individual and collective level. In her 2019 special *I Be Knowin'*, Seales creates comedy that simultaneously honors and celebrates Black women and Black culture in the US and is unapologetic in its critique of power systems. As one critic observed, "*I Be Knowin'* can feel as much like going to church or a pep rally as it can feel like a night out at the comedy club. But when Seales is testifying, you just want to keep hearing her preach."[65]

In an Instagram stories-styled introduction, she iterates who her special is for and who it's not for. She says, "Now y'all keep asking me, 'Amanda, who is this special for?' And I keep tellin' y'all, 'It's for my sisters!' But it's comedy, so it's really for everybody." A beat later, she amends her previous statement, admitting, "Okay, maybe not for everybody." She continues:

> Everybody except for racists, rapists, sexists, misogynists, narcissists, ya know, folks that are just callin' the cops on Black folks who are just livin' our lives? Yeah, it ain't for you. It ain't for fuck boys or trif gals, or that one ex who still ain't paid you that money back he owed you? Uh uh. No laughs for them. It ain't for Trump voters, or coons, or people who believe that white men can't be terrorists. It ain't for homophobes, or transphobes, or xenophobes. (You know that wall is some bullshit. Hmmm.) It ain't for bullies. It ain't for poachers. It ain't for abusers. And even people who keep asking me, "Amanda, can I pick your brain?" No! It ain't for dudes who want head, but don't wanna eat no pussy! It ain't for you. [sigh] It also is not for people who don't take care of their kids, and it ain't for people who take their shoes and socks off on planes! Who raised you?[66]

With this, Seales walks on stage to a reception of raucous applause.

This foregrounding structures the rhetorical trajectory of her set. She leans in to what philosopher Charles Mills calls an "alternative epistemology," one that embraces ways of knowing that defy the dominant and dominating epistemologies proffered by straight, white men as the objective or neutral way of adjudicating truth.[67] In this vein, Seales offers much that is worthy of our attention, but I want to focus on two bits in particular. We

64. hooks, "Sisterhood," 125.
65. McCarthy, "Amanda Seales."
66. Seales, *I Be Knowin'*.
67. Mills, *Blackness Visible*, 21–39.

might classify the first bit as street wisdom and the other as office wisdom. Both bits name the challenges Black women face in the US on a daily basis because of their gender and race.

Seales made national headlines several years ago when she got into a heated debate with a white, straight man on CNN on the issue of cat-calling. Her interlocutor, whom she describes as "the whitest white man of whitery," insisted that women should be flattered by catcalling because "all women love getting compliments from men in the street."[68] She says, "If I'm in Brooklyn at midnight, and a Jamaican man appears from the shadows . . . " Seales begins to perform undulating body rolls. She holds each hand in a gun shape, pointing her index and middle fingers toward the audience. "Sweetness," she says with a thick Jamaican accent. She stresses the sibilant sound of the word, imitating a snake's hiss. "Ya look like a vanilla ice cream." Seales dangles her microphone from her crotch, swings it back and forth like a penis. Then, tossing and catching the mic, she continues in her affected Jamaican accent, "Me wan' lick yaaaaa." Switching back to her own, serious voice, she declares, "That's not a compliment. That's a threat."

To continue her point, Seales moves to another New York borough. She says, "If I'm in Harlem and some brothas pause their dice game. And they like [Here she switches into an accent that mimics that of an urban, Black male.] "'Yawww! Shorty rockin' rough and stuff with one afro puff and the jacket and the pants with the da da da da da on it, I see you, Maaa! What's really good?' [in normal voice] Yeah, that's not a compliment. It's an observation." Her bit builds in frustration. "Then, they want you to smile! [in a Harlem accent] 'Why you mad? Let me see dem pearly whites. Yo, why you ain't smiling, Ma?'" Resuming her normal voice, Seales responds with gritted teeth. "You know why I'm not smiling? Cuz I just spent the last twenty minutes in a public bathroom fashioning a makeshift maxi pad out of a long-ass CVS receipt. Just so I don't gotta walk around here lookin' like a dire wolf bit me in the pussy! You still tryin'a holla, n*gga, what's up?"[69]

With this bit, Seales shows rather than tells all that is problematic with catcalling. She displays how this form of address is not a compliment, and she holds this in tension with the realities of being a woman in the modern world. These gender challenges notwithstanding, Seals fosters some racial tensions in this bit that seem to undercut her point. By opening this bit by stressing the race of her CNN interlocutor who had the "caucasity" to mansplain catcalling to her, she shifts the focus from gender to race. This

68. Abad-Santos, "Man Tried to Mansplain Catcalling on CNN."

69. Seales, *I Be Knowin'*.

ambiguity is exacerbated by her two exemplars of catcalling, both of whom she presents as Black.

The second insightful account of micropolitics transpires in an office. Seales prefaces her verbatim by declaring that there are two types of white people: those that happened to be white and white people. The former, whom she labels *Hannahs*, "know and understand that there ain't no truth to whiteness." They understand that it was created for the sole purpose of oppression. Hannahs know to use their privilege to give access to those who don't have access to that privilege. *Beckys*, on the other hand, "believe the lie that whiteness makes them better. They actually think it makes them supreme. And if you believe that something that was created for the sole purpose of oppressing others makes you better, then you ain't shit."[70]

Seales implicates both well-intentioned and ill-intentioned white women throughout her bit because both iterations of white femininity have been protected in unhealthy ways. She compares this protection to kids who aren't exposed to germs, causing their immune systems not to develop properly. She says, "White women and women who happen to be white ain't been exposed to criticism, so now they all fragile and they be cryin' all the goddamn time. And now, all of uuuuus [i.e., Black women] gotta deal with that shit. Every day at work." Signaling the pervasiveness of white women's fragility and the problematic behaviors it inaugurates, Seales sets out to restore a semblance of equilibrium in professional settings: "Right now there is a woman benefiting from white privilege who is storming into a break room in a huff." Seales quickly walks across the stage with wide strides, fists at her sides, head turned down in an affected pout. Sighing dramatically, Seales shifts into a particularly high-pitched, nasally version of linguistic whiteface: "Did you see Renita? Last week, she had an adorbs pixie cut. And today [pause] she showed up with dreadlocks!" Seales pauses again, feigning tears and pouting. "And I didn't recognize her on the elevator. And now she thinks I'm a racist!" Seales throws her hands in the air in mock exasperation. She turns to rest her forehead on the microphone stand, burying her face in the crook of her arm to conceal her overblown embarrassment.

Returning to her normal voice, Seales shows us how this incident has impacted Renita, saying, "She is aware, but she don't care!" She flips her imaginary dreadlocks out of her face for effect.

> She ain't got time to care. Cuz she's composing an email that she has now written four times, and had to delete, delete, delete, delete, delete. Cuz she was tellin' the truth, but it's gonna send her to HR. Cuz now she has to employ that whole other language

70. Seales, *I Be Knowin'*.

that any Black person who is attempting to excel in this country has had to learn. We all have had to learn duality, so that we can talk on the block and in the boardroom, just to protect y'all. Cuz y'all done turned passive-aggression into a synonym for professionalism![71]

With comedic insight into a concrete example of the sort of microaggressions Black women must grapple with in professional settings, Seals models an approach to just joking that is simultaneously hilarious and indicting. It offers relief to her audience members who may have endured similar encounters with "Beckys" in their own work environments. It is a display of what Philip Auslander labels "fem-rage," and it comes close to what Donna Allen identifies in the rhetoric of emancipatory praxis and performed identity emerging from shamans and certain exemplars of womanist proclamation.[72] It is no wonder, then, why Sean McCarthy says that "when Seales is testifying, you just want to keep hearing her preach."[73]

CONCLUSION: JOKING WITH GOD

A persistent problem we have faced throughout this book pertains to the bifurcation of playful and serious discourse. In much work in humor studies, scholars insist on a "comic frame" as a necessary condition for the possibility of humor.[74] The stand-up stage is one such frame. The pulpit, by contrast, is framed by a seriousness that can preclude the comical or the humorous. In the work of stand-up comics such as Trevor Noah and Amanda Seales we have a model of just joking that blurs divisions between playfulness and politics. Each in their own way, they bear witness to what I label the comical. Through the use of humor they force us to think and feel in ways that can spur us to resist the power structures that frustrate the flourishing of those who've been denied equitable cultural citizenship.

Steven Benko and Eleanor Jones argue that comedy and the laughter it produces are only ethical to the extent that they redraw the boundaries between people groups so that we become more inclusive and just.[75] Here we have humor that is used as more than a mere cloak or distraction or disguise. Such humor has the potential to repair breaches and restore

71. Seales, *I Be Knowin'*.

72. Auslander, "Brought to You by Fem-Rage"; Allen, *Toward a Womanist Homiletic*, 36, 85.

73. McCarthy, "Amanda Seales."

74. Huizinga, *Homo Ludens*, 10, calls this the "magic circle."

75. Benko and Jones, *That's Way Too Aggressive a Word*, 110.

relationships. Of course, this presupposes a particular theology in which the church understands its calling to be with and for the marginalized and oppressed. Lisa Thompson's insight about the ultimate intention behind a willingness to speak out on current events, to "preach the headlines," guides us here. She argues that such work is about determining those matters in the sociopolitical arena that impinge upon what is of ultimate concern for Jesus followers and "proclaiming out of that conviction for the sake of living according to those convictions."[76]

Thompson's work highlights the importance of tethering teaching with persuasion. To change how we behave, we must first change how we believe. As the driving impetus behind the comical, just joking adds a modicum of delight to our teaching and persuasion. Such laughter-inducing levity does not stand in opposition to teaching and persuading. Rather, at its best, just joking offers a path to critical comical resistance that just might offer our congregants or parishioners the space they need to imagine the world otherwise.

76. Thompson, *Preaching the Headlines*, 117.

Stand-Up Spotlight

John Oliver
between Seriousness and Stupidity

I like the balance between seriousness and stupidity. I think I would get depressed if I was gonna start doing just one of them.[1]

—JOHN OLIVER

John Oliver is a British American stand-up comic turned late-night news host. He combines his wry sense of humor with over-the-top digressions to produce comedy that is informative, critical, and silly. Early in his comedy career he was a staple of the Edinburgh Fringe Comedy Festival, a nesting ground for British alternative comedy. Oliver served as a correspondent for *The Daily Show with Jon Stewart*. For four years he hosted a Comedy Central show called *John Oliver Presents*, where he used his platform to introduce marginalized comedic voices to a wider audience (including Harry Kondabolou, whom I spotlighted above). Much of Oliver's comedy career has focused on matters of sociopolitical significance, and he engages such topics with a clear orientation toward justice. This topical and perspectival bent places him in company with the other stand-up comics I've spotlighted in this book. Oliver is most famous for his weekly "entertainment politics" show on HBO, *Last Week Tonight with John Oliver*.[2]

1. Hiatt, "John Oliver Takes on the Trump Era."
2. Jones, *Entertaining Politics*, argues against rigid binary constructions that obscure the interconnectedness of media-politics and popular culture (13).

STAND-UP JOURNALISM

Oliver presents us with a form of communication that media studies scholar Geoffrey Baym labels "discursive integration," where news, politics, and entertainment are no longer distinct modes of discourse but have become inseparable.[3] Media and political scholars debate whether we ought to consider comedic news a new form of political journalism or "fake" news.[4] It is important to distinguish the political humor arising from comedic news shows such as those hosted by Stephen Colbert, Trevor Noah, Samantha Bee, W. Kamau Bell, and John Oliver from other "fake news" presented as actual journalism. Given the rise of *actual* fake news following the 2016 presidential election cycle, it can be difficult to measure the veracity of current news content. Julia Fox argues that a more fruitful direction would be to delineate how comedic (not fake) news programs present us with two types of (real) public discourse. They offer journalism and political satire in the same show.[5] Fox's research team studied the relationship between jokes and facts in the main stories from the 2017 episodes of *Last Week Tonight*. They found that nearly three times as many facts in the main stories were presented by Oliver than other, traditional news sources. Oliver is also unique among late-night political news hosts in that he does not exclusively rely on traditional news sources for content; rather, through investigative journalism he functions as the discursive authority in the main stories on his show.[6] For their efforts, Oliver and his team have received the Peabody Award for excellence in journalism.

A crucial feature of journalism is to provide facts to citizens, especially those that politicians and corporations seek to hide, distort, or deny. Unlike traditional journalists, who avoid offering their personal opinions on current events—at least in theory—Oliver presents his material from a strong point of view. For instance, in an episode that aired on March 21, 2021, Oliver's feature story was about plastics.[7] Oliver provides a crucial history of our relationship to plastics in America. As he presents us with data about this topic he does little to hide his perspective on the issue. His function is to challenge the manufactured ideology that the individual consumer is responsible for recycling and reducing waste for the good of the environment. Through a mix of farce and critical analysis, he shows how big corporations

3. Baym, "The Daily Show," 261.

4. See Jones, "'Fake' News versus 'Real' News," and *Entertaining Politics*, 185–205. See also McChesney, "Foreword," 1–2.

5. Fox, "Journalist or Jokester?," 29.

6. Fox, "Journalist or Jokester?," 36.

7. Oliver, "March 21, 2021: Plastics."

like Coca-Cola have conspired with state and national governments to keep the steady flow of plastics happening—all the while making us feel like if we would just do a better job recycling, we wouldn't have a plastic land mass the size of Texas floating in the Pacific Ocean.

As much as his progressive perspective, Oliver's stand-up journalism (if I may call it that) offers us another feature to consider. Oliver's show has been labeled "the most fact-checked comedy show in the history of television."[8] Unlike facts, which are considered to have intrinsic characteristics about an external reality, jokes have no intrinsic characteristics. To speak of facts requires ostensive reference to a reality that exists beyond the discourse itself. A joke, by contrast, depends mostly on its context to evoke humor in the mind of the receiver while they cognitively process the joke. A joke does not have to be true in a propositional sense. It is because of their contextual contingency that jokes lose so much in translation or explanation. In presenting facts alongside jokes, Oliver keeps his audience on their toes.

Another way Oliver is closer to stand-up comics than journalists revolves around his identity. As we discussed in chapter 5, comics stage their identity through their comical personas. Oliver names his intersectional identity to temper or embrace his ideological slant on the news. Oliver's stand-up and comedic journalism capitalizes on his outsider status as a Brit and his insider status as an American *immigré*. At the same time, he is well aware that the US and the UK are mired in imperialism and colonialism and are complicit in many of the world's problems. Rather than attempting to hide or ignore his ethnic, racial, sexual, and gender identities, Oliver takes pains to articulate how his intersectional identity shapes his interpretation of the world. In part, he employs his identities for comedic effect. But there are also important political reasons for naming his identity. Consider his episode on Asian Americans that aired in mid-2021. In light of anti-Asian sentiments connected with COVID-19 and the recent wave of violence targeting Asian Americans, Oliver asserts that we are long overdue to have an honest conversation about Asian Americans in America. With this lead-in Oliver offers an important caveat, "Before we start, I fully recognize the history of white people on TV generalizing confidently about this subject isn't great." He goes on to show examples of this from video clips from the eighties, where white news anchors speak of Asian Americans in a blatantly reductive way.[9]

8. Hiatt, "John Oliver Takes on the Trump Era."

9. Oliver, "June 6, 2021: Asian Americans." There is a homiletical corollary to this in Kim-Cragg, "Invisibility of Whiteness."

FOR RHETORICAL EFFECT

A prominent feature of late-night comedy news shows is ad hominem. Rather than attacking someone's ideas or actions, you attack them as a person. While this might play to one's demographic base, recall that this is the very kind of comedy that the early church fathers, Plato, and Aristotle opposed. But Oliver does something else, which is much more in line with the incongruity theory of humor. He uses satire and parody more to draw our attention to problematic policies and practices than personalities. For instance, when then-Vice President Mike Pence was pushing hard to challenge LGBTQIA rights, Oliver took aim at Pence obliquely though parody.

In 2018 Pence's daughter Charlotte Pence had just written a children's book entitled *Marlon Bundo's A Day in the Life of the Vice President*. The fictional book starred Marlon Bundo, which is the name of Mike Pence's real pet rabbit. Jill Twiss, a writer on *Last Week Tonight*, wrote a parody children's book entitled *A Day in the Life of Marlon Bundo*. In Twiss's book Marlon Bundo happens to be gay, and the story centers around Bundo's same-sex romance with a rabbit called Wesley. Oliver promoted Twiss's book on his show and followed it up with a running segment meant to challenge Mike Pence's homophobia. The parody version of Marlon Bundo and Oliver's commentary was about challenging the ways in which Pence's religious ideology was shaping public policy.[10] Through parody Oliver moves beyond ad hominem, even if he does little to hide his personal disdain for Pence. The Marlon Bundo segments are both a parody of a children's book and a productive counterproposal to the message Pence was pushing.

Another important rhetorical feature of Oliver's comedy is satire. Satire intends to provoke a change in thinking, perception, or belief—even a repentance of the old way of thinking, perceiving, believing—by mimicking rhetorical forms.[11] Oliver provokes such metanoia through a chaotic combination of smart, substantive satire and absurd asides that often have little or nothing to do with the important issue Oliver is talking about. Russell Peterson makes an important distinction that informs our analysis of Oliver's brand of comedy. Peterson differentiates between *satire* and *pseudo-satire*. Satire points out hypocrisy and functions as a form of cultural and political criticism accessible to the average citizen. This is not to be confused with pseudo-satire, which is personality-driven and mocks the appearances and

---

10. Oliver, "March 18, 2018: Marlon Bundo."

11. Caron, *Satire as the Comic Public Sphere,* 22: "*Satire* names those comic artifacts that actualize the potential and distill it within a laughter-provoking presentation. Thus *satire* names a mode of comic speech associated with the ridiculous, while humor signifies a mode associated with the ludicrous."

personality quirks of politicians. Real satire solicits laughter aimed at others and sometimes ourselves (when we are complicit) in order to expose a larger systemic fault or flaw. Satire nourishes our democracy, while pseudo-satire is like fast food: popular, readily available, tasty, but ultimately unhealthy.[12]

Nicholas Holm makes a similar distinction between political jokes and jokes about politics. He writes that when comedians ridicule Trump's false bravado or Bush's stupidity, or when the HBO political sitcom *Veep* reveals the petty motivations that lurk below the surface of electioneering, the humor produced may not be considered political in any critical sense. "These are not political jokes; they are jokes about politics," writes Holm. "Consequently, any political valence attributed to such instances of humor is misplaced when they rely upon mockery of individual failing and the policing of middle-class social mores, rather than the subversion or critique of political institutions and processes, let alone structures of power."[13]

SATIRACTIVISM

Scholars debate the sociopolitical efficacy of late-night news shows such as *Last Week Tonight*. In what Don Waisanen labels "advocacy satire" and Sophia McClennen and Remy Maisel label "satiractivism," some scholars find satire to be politically efficacious.[14] Others disagree. James Caron, for instance, argues that the performative qualities of "truthiness satire" and "satiractivist speech" should *not* be claimed as either political speech or political action. "Such speech . . . may have the rhetorical effect of a protest, but it is not equivalent to protest in the street."[15] Likewise, Hennefeld and her coauthors write, "It is doubtful that political satire can still defend democratic values in the age of 'post-truth,' election cyberhacking, and the appropriation of 'fake news' as authoritarian disinformation."[16]

Regardless of its ultimate impact, none can deny that Oliver's comical approach to current events draws attention to stories that we might otherwise miss. Oliver moves beyond the distanced irony that constitutes much political comedy news shows, calling for hope even after the most seemingly hopeless news stories. He employs political humor to take action on behalf of disadvantaged individuals or groups, lending force to their voices

12. Peterson, *Strange Bedfellows*, 22–23.

13. Holm, *Humour as Politics*, 82.

14. McClennen and Maisel, *Is Satire Saving Our Nation?*, 1–20. See also Day, *Satire and Dissent*, 94.

15. Caron, "Quantum Paradox of Truthiness," 165.

16. Hennefeld et al., "In Focus," 138; Kersten, "America's Faith," 312.

to make direct interventions into public affairs. Oliver offers many examples of explicit calls for his audience to take action. I'll mention two of them.

The first intervention focuses on the issue of net neutrality.[17] In 2014 the FCC was considering two options for net neutrality. The FCC proposed permitting fast and slow broadband lanes, which would compromise net neutrality. The FCC was also considering reclassifying broadband as a tele-communication service, which would preserve net neutrality. After Oliver's episode spurred a surge of comments supporting net neutrality, the FCC voted to reclassify broadband as a utility in 2015. Oliver opens the segment in his trademark silly fashion by noting all the amazing things the Internet allows us to do—like buying coyote urine (Oliver shows the Amazon page for this product). Oliver jokes that the only combination of two words in the English language inciting more boredom than "net neutrality" are "featur-ing Sting" (the British pop star). Net neutrality is the principle whereby all Internet data has to be treated equally. The proposed changes by the FCC would enable telecommunications companies to allow big tech companies like Netflix to pay to have their content delivered more quickly to consum-ers, thereby squelching the competition. Having explained what is at stake in the proposed net neutrality legislation, Oliver offered it a more legitimate name: "Preventing Cable Company Fuckery." Oliver then mobilized his viewers to direct their comments about this proposed bill to the FCC. The FCC received nearly 800,000 comments, which led them to later ditch the bill. The impact of Oliver's episode led some to label him "the firebrand activist we're looking for."[18]

A favorite strategy of Oliver's is trolling, and his intervention into net neutrality calls upon Internet trolls explicitly to use their powers for good. Amber Davisson and Mackenzie Donovan focus on Oliver's rhetorical ap-propriation of trolling in *Last Week Tonight*. The authors suggest that these trolling techniques provoke "responses from both the target of the trolling and from the audience that wants to participate in the trolling."[19] *Last Week Tonight*'s trolling techniques function rhetorically to amplify attention and engage the audience in social activism. Though the impact of this technique frequently employs the kind of ad hominem attacks that drift from political comedy to comedy about politics (to borrow Holm's vocabulary), this tactic succeeds in getting audience members involved in political issues. In the second iteration of the net neutrality debate under the Trump administra-tion, Oliver encouraged trolling of Ajit Pai, the new chairman of the FCC

17. Oliver, "June 1, 2014: Net Neutrality."
18. McDonald, "John Oliver's Net Neutrality Rant."
19. Davisson and Donovan, "'Breaking the News on a Weekly Basis,'" 513.

who was leading the charge to end net neutrality. Despite these efforts, the Trump-led FCC was able to remove the net neutrality rules enacted under the Obama administration, revealing that trolling as a strategy for satiractivism has its limits.[20]

A second example of how Oliver's comedy aims at more than eliciting laughter but to effect real-world change transpired during an episode on the insidious and pervasive practice of bail bonds.[21] Oliver provided concrete data about how bail bonds worked in New York City in a predatory manner against people who are economically disadvantaged. Not only did Oliver provide a historical background into bail bonds, but he spotlighted concrete abuses in his own city. The function of this segment wasn't just to provide history, it wasn't just to increase awareness in the moment, but it led to concrete action in the public square. Like the net neutrality episode, Oliver opened his segment on bail bonds cheekily. "Jail can do for your actual life what being in a marching band can do for your social life," he joked. "Even if you're just in for a little while, it can destroy you." The episode ended with a call to action, and subsequently his viewers put so much pressure on New York City Mayor Bill de Blasio that he began to reform the bail bond process in the city. One key to the effectiveness of this call to action was its specificity. Oliver told his viewers exactly what he wanted them to do. "Increasingly," Oliver averred, "bail has become a way to lock up the poor, regardless of guilt." Aided by sound research, a compelling ethical argument for procedural justice, and a call to action, results emerged.[22]

TAKEAWAYS FOR STAND-UP PREACHING

In many ways, while it is performatively and rhetorically distinct from stand-up as such, *Last Week Tonight* is closer to what preachers do in the pulpit than that of a lot of the stand-up comedians we've been investigating. Following the weekly news cycle, Oliver produces a thoroughly researched news segment that is much more aligned with the kind of thoughtful preparation that preachers undertake. One might say that Oliver "preaches the headlines," to borrow the title from Lisa Thompson's book.[23] He uses a teleprompter to deliver his material, which frees him from having to memorize an hour's worth of content each week. Few preachers preach without notes or a sermon manuscript, so we may also study how Oliver uses such aids

20. Oliver, "May 7, 2017: Net Neutrality 2."
21. Oliver, "June 7, 2015: Bail Bonds."
22. Kaufman, "John Oliver Gets Results!"
23. Thompson, *Preaching the Headlines*.

without sacrificing the atmosphere of intimacy and authenticity stand-up comics engender. As opposed to the general workflow of contemporary stand-up, which builds material that is tested and refined over the course of many months or years en route to a televised special, Oliver's workflow is like a preacher's in that he gets one shot to present his material. Lastly, unlike many stand-up specials, Oliver's weekly take on current events presents us with a clear focus, function, and call to action, which aligns with how many preachers are taught to structure their sermons.

I've been deeply influenced by Long's argument that sermons need more than a focus (what the preacher is trying to say). Sermons also carry a function. The function is what the sermon is trying to do.[24] Sermons can provide comfort, can challenge our actions or ways of thinking, they can teach, and so on. In my introductory preaching class, my students sometimes struggle to differentiate between what the sermon is doing and what the preacher wants the people to do. When we lay Long's focus and function framework on Oliver's comedy, we see that many of his main segments are as complex and compelling as a strong sermon.

Another takeaway for preachers arises from the movement or flow of his comedy. Oliver is a master of comedic non sequitur. Here the humor emerges from absurd asides and exegetical witticisms that offer the audience a mental and emotional break from his serious topics. These non sequiturs range from silly rants to critical commentary to trolling public officials whom he calls out for some act of injustice. One of the really special things Oliver does as he moves between goofy jokes and thoughtful analysis is that his shifting rhetorical styles allow him to discuss topics that rarely find a place in stand-up (e.g., SLAPP suits, the US electoral college, big coal, payday lending, police violence). Oliver presents us with fresh ways to discuss certain topics that we preachers might also be loath to engage, topics that are not all that engaging or exciting to most congregants (e.g., transubstantiation, atonement theories). We might shy away from some important theological topics for fear of losing the attention or interests of people, fear of getting too "in the weeds."

Lastly, Oliver models a form of comedy we might label *hopeful pragmatism*. In America's political landscape it can sometimes seem hopeless that positive change can result from our efforts. As a result, a lot of stand-up comics peddle in nihilism. But even when Oliver engages the darkest and most insurmountable topics, his engagement is always in the service of making the world a better place. It's these grace notes amid horrible situations

24. See Long, *Witness of Preaching*, ch. 3.

that can mobilize people to take action. It can empower us to believe that the world can be a better place.

Conclusion

To Tell the Truth

To preach, you can't be in your right mind. You have to be a little out of it, to be perfectly frank. Because there isn't anything that's going to dislocate you more than the grace of God.[1]

—Anna Carter Florence

Telling the truth may get you hell, but it also gets you into heaven.[2]

—Richard Pryor

Preachers face a perennial struggle. In the interplay between Scripture, our congregational or parish contexts, and the world, we seek to be pastoral and prophetic. Even though these two homiletical modalities are often presented in binary fashion, they fall along a spectrum. The more pastoral and affirming a sermon, the less prophetic; the more prophetic, the less comforting. This fundamental tension emerges from the competing natures of prophetic and pastoral sermons. A word of challenge is often at odds with a word of comfort. Even as we know this strains against the pragmatics of rhetoric, we may wish to fold this spectrum in half, to lay the prophetic and pastoral on top of one another such that the difference between them dissipates. We want to preach sermons that are *both* pastoral *and* prophetic. We want our preaching to make the world God loves a better, more just place

---

1. Carter Florence, "Preacher as One 'Out of Your Mind,'" 151.
2. Worth, *Lenny Bruce*, 49.

for everyone, *and* we want to do this without having to face an emergency session or deacon's meeting after every sermon.[3]

As we have seen throughout this book, stand-up comedy can serve preachers well on our quest to meld prophetic sermons with pastoral sensitivity. The kind of stand-up I've spotlighted inaugurates shared laughter, helping us overcome boundaries and barriers between ourselves and others. It can also spur awareness, insight, and action. It can aid us in the transformation of our hearts and minds so we may recognize what is at stake in the ways we live our lives. It is not without its risks, about which I've tried to be forthcoming throughout this book; but these risks are worth it for stand-up preachers. Any preaching worthy of the name is risky. Why not have a little fun along the way?

COMILETICAL METAPHYSICS: HOPES AND HANG-UPS

In his recent book *Art and Preaching,* Sunggu Yang argues that homiletics is long overdue for a metaphysical makeover. We have focused for far too long on the *what* and the *how* of preaching that we have neglected the *who* and the *why.*[4] Though he doesn't include stand-up comedy to support his proposal for holistic-artistic preaching, I believe stand-up offers another possible mode of aesthetic encounter. By attending to the *who* of the stand-up comic, we have opened some affinities and divergences with that of the preacher. We have focused in particular on the ways stand-up comics narrate their lived experiences (chapter 4) and "stage" their identities through comical personas (chapter 5). We've also discussed how the bodies of preachers and comics shape how listeners receive their respective messages (chapter 6). Their language games overlap in interesting ways (chapter 3), especially at a formal level—even if the kind of language most stand-up comics employ would undoubtedly get a preacher fired.

Even more insight emerges from a critical consideration of the *why* of stand-up preaching. Yang makes a compelling case for preaching that generates aesthetic-holistic encounters between the preacher, the biblical text, and contemporary art forms (e.g., architecture, fashion, film, drama). In this encounter with the *mysterium tremendum,* the Word of God overwhelms the preacher as it did Isaiah in the temple (Isa 6:1–8). The focus

---

3. Leah Schade helpfully suggests facilitating a deliberative dialogue with congregants in preparation for preaching on controversial topics. Schade, *Preaching in the Purple Zone,* 79.

4. Yang, *Art and Preaching.*

shifts from understanding the propositional content to be preached to that of enjoying and participating in a noumenal experience that is more intuitive than rational. As we have seen, many of the historical objections to the humorous operates from a resistance to laughter's irrationality (chapter 2). I have argued in favor of the affective capacities of the comical (chapter 1) as a path to *metanoia*. It is only when our hearts and minds are receptive to change that we can engage the political (chapter 7). Comedy holds unique opportunities for homiletics to render open-ended or fluid encounters with God and world that expose the incongruities manifesting between the phenomenal and noumenal. Such encounters potentiate a change of hearts and minds.

In their treatment of comedy as a pathway to social change, Caty Borum Chatoo and Lauren Feldman synthesize interdisciplinary theories and research about the effects of comedy on social civic and political challenges. They locate four common forms of comedy's influence at the audience level: 1) increasing message and issue attention; 2) disarming audiences and lowering resistance to persuasion; 3) breaking down social barriers; and 4) stimulating sharing and discussion.[5] What preacher would not desire to accomplish such tasks through her preaching? This quadripartite functionality offers ways for us to think comiletically, that is, to think homiletically about comedy. Such an angle of vision presses us back into questions about the metaphysics of preaching. Rather than foreclosing upon any one metaphysics, Chatoo and Feldman's analytic returns us to fundamental questions about preaching's ends and essence. If preaching and comedy are alternative discursive pathways to the truth, we might benefit from discerning where these pathways converge.

FINAL TAKEAWAYS FOR STAND-UP PREACHING

Here at the end of the book, there are a few points to reiterate and a few cautions to stress. It can be tempting to focus on the transcendent capacities of the humorous, on its ability to set us apart from our troubles, to relieve us of the existential anguish we encounter in our day-to-day lives. This is a mistake. As Simon Critchley reminds us, "Humor does not redeem us from this world, but returns us to it ineluctably by showing that there is no alternative. The consolations of humor come from acknowledging that this is the only world and, imperfect as it is and we are, it is only here that we can make a difference."[6] Despite Critchley's disavowal of any world beyond

5. Chatoo and Feldman, *Comedian and an Activist Walk into A Bar*, 36–58.
6. Critchley, *On Humour*, 17–18.

the material world, his insight highlight's humor's potential for all but those who hold to a pie-in-the-sky-by-and-by theology.

Humor doubles our connection to our bodily realities, to the *humus* that animates our passions and links us with the blood, sweat, and tears of ourselves and others. By showing us the folly of the world, humor does not deliver us from that folly by turning our attention elsewhere; rather, it calls on us to face the folly of the world and change the situation in which we find ourselves. At its best, humor does not make us feel superior to one another. It tethers us to an essential materiality we share with all creatures. And in drawing our hearts and minds back to our inherent lowliness, humor reminds us that the customs and conventions that govern our ways of believing, behaving, and being are not necessary. We can make the world a better place. We can imagine the world otherwise. And this is good news for preachers.

Second, theologians have worried over the temptation to make ourselves the star of our sermons. Joseph Webb, for instance, opened his *Comedy and Preaching* book by saying, "Still, it should be said that the preacher is not, nor should he or she be, a comedian. Few preachers, however funny they are, can match the best of the professional comedians who make us all laugh at some time or other."[7] Webb is right. Most of us are not as funny as professional comedians. If we were, perhaps we would be doing that rather than preaching. But even as Webb strives to temper our expectations about our own comedic potential, this does not mean we ought to shrug our shoulders and step back into the pulpit with the paltry vim and vigor of the priest performing the wedding at the end of *The Princess Bride* ("Mawidge . . .").

Stand-up comics are not born. They are made. They work at their craft much as we preachers do. Comparing us to contemporary stand-up comics can leave us disheartened. We might watch a few Netflix or HBO specials and think to ourselves, "I could never be as funny as her. I shouldn't even bother trying." Most preachers, I speculate, at one point or another felt the same way about preachers and preaching. We watch an Anna Carter Florence, a Tom Long, or a Frank Thomas sermon, and we might just as easily bemoan our homiletical inferiority. Part of what makes a master in any profession is their ability to make what they do look so easy. Preaching is a gift of the Spirit. But it is also a practice we can develop over time with concerted effort. The same goes for comedy. So, don't lose heart. Practice. Make mistakes. Laugh at yourself. Improve.

---

7. Webb, *Comedy and Preaching*, xiv.

Comedy is a means of persuasion as well as instruction and entertainment. It holds the capacities to accomplish Augustine's homiletical trifecta: to teach, to delight, and to persuade. These are the marks of effective rhetoric. Together they constitute eloquence. To teach is a necessity, because what's the point of saying anything if your interlocutor doesn't understand you? Preaching toward delight secures your listener's attention. It matters little how accurate and astute your instruction is if nobody bothers to pay attention. Persuasive speech compels them to act, and if you can achieve this, you ought to consider it a triumph. Augustine concludes, "The eloquent divine, then, when he is urging a practical truth, must not only teach so as to give instruction, and please so as to keep up the attention, but he must also sway the mind so as to subdue the will."[8] But, unlike Cicero, from whom Augustine borrows in this pericope, Augustine sees neither the wisdom nor the eloquence originating solely in the preacher. Playing on the word *orator* as one who speaks *and* one who prays, Augustine says a preacher must become a person of prayer before they become a person of words.[9] And the reason why the preacher must pray is so the Holy Spirit will provide the eloquence for divine truths to be spoken and received.

It is a mistake to separate comedy from spirituality. Such a bifurcation aligns with one that is just as insidious: separating the spiritual from the political. As M. Conrad Hyers puts it, "To understand comedy is to understand humanity. Among the defining characteristics of the human spirit is a capacity for laughter, humor, revelry, and setting things in common perspective."[10] Hyers stresses that even as such a humorous disposition draws us into deeper contact with our humanity, it draws us deeper into our spirituality and our polity. He argues convincingly for a dialectical understanding of the comical and the sacred, linking the two with the political arena. Hyers avers that the sacred and the comical require one another to avoid distortion of both of them. "As in the case of the king, if the sacredness of his person and role is taken too seriously to the exclusion of laughter the door is opened to absolutism and despotism; but if the laughter does not presuppose a certain seriousness and sacrality, the door is opened to political chaos and social disruption."[11] Hyers's wisdom applies whether we are talking about monarchy or democracy. It matters little whether sovereignty is invested in a sole person (*à la* Hobbes) or whether the people are sovereign (*à la* Rousseau). Either way, the comical supervenes between a

---

8. Augustine, *De Doctrina Christiana*, 4.12. Cf. Cicero, *De oratore*, 21.

9. Augustine, *De Doctrina Christiana*, 4.15.

10. Hyers, *Spirituality of Comedy*, 1.

11. Hyers, "Dialectic of the Sacred and the Comic," 69.

seriousness that leads to tyranny or a levity that leads to anarchy. Blessed is the community that holds these in balance.

Another blessing of stand-up preaching arises from the cathartic, unifying effects of corporate laughter. Emory University primatologist Frans de Waal reminds us that laughter inaugurates a more fundamental link between human and nonhuman animals than humor does, specifically in the former's capacity to constitute social relationships. "Our supernoisy barklike displays announce mutual liking and well-being. The laughter of a group of people broadcasts solidarity and togetherness, not unlike the howling of a pack of wolves."[12] When we expose a community to the humorous, we open a window to transcendence that we all may look through. If preachers can evoke laughter from our congregants, we wrest from them cognitive and affective control. Such a momentary release draws a congregation's attention to their embodied, corporate existence and, depending on your perspective, to our need or capacity for redemption and reconciliation. Thus, what we borrow from them rhetorically, we return to them with interest socially and spiritually.

Lastly, humor provides preachers and churchgoers with the fortitude to face the world in its manifold messiness. In his farewell remarks to the graduating class of 1973, Princeton Theological Seminary president James McCord argued that a minister's sense of humor stands in direct proportion to three things: 1) the size of their world; 2) the stakes on which they are willing to risk their life; and 3) their faith in God's sovereignty over the powers and principalities of this world.[13] McCord was addressing a group of future ministers struggling to find their footing amid tectonic sociopolitical shifts. The Vietnam War was still raging, while the wars on poverty and racism were fizzling. On top of this, the US Congress was filing articles of impeachment against Richard Nixon for his infamous Watergate scandal. With pastoral sensitivity, McCord recognized that the ministerial journey would not be an easy one for these graduates. Nevertheless, he commended humor as the virtue most befitting a Christian minister. Humor is a divine quality bequeathed to we who are created in God's image (cf. Ps 2:4a). Humor is our primary weapon against dictatorial regimes. Instead of thinking of the line that separates good (ethical) humor from bad (unethical) humor as somehow external to us, we ought to begin with the idea that what constitutes the line between good and bad humor is our orientation toward other people: "what we see when we face them and how we understand our responsibility for that visage."[14]

12. de Waal, *Mama's Last Hug*, 69–70.

13. McCord, "Farewell Messages," 49.

14. Benko, "Otherwise Than Laughter," 72.

Works Cited

Aarons, Debra, and Marc Mierowsky. "Public Conscience of 'The Chosen People': Sarah Silverman in the Wake of Lenny Bruce." *Comedy Studies* 8, no. 2 (2017) 154–66.

Abad-Santos, Alex. "How Ellen DeGeneres's Façade of Kindness Crumbled." *Vox*, August 7, 2020. https://www.vox.com/21357113/ellen-degeneres-canceled-mean-backlash-toxic-workplace.

———. "A Man Tried to Mansplain Catcalling on CNN. He Was Rightfully Side-Eyed to Death." *Vox*, November 3, 2014. https://www.vox.com/xpress/2014/11/3/7149495/catcalling-viral-video-cnn.

Abernathy, Ralph David. *And the Walls Came Tumbling Down: An Autobiography.* New York: Harper & Row, 1989.

Acham, Christine. *Revolution Televised: Prime Time and the Struggle for Black Power.* Minneapolis: University of Minnesota Press, 2004.

Adorno, Theodor W. *Aesthetic Theory.* Translated and edited by Robert Hullot-Kentor. New York: Continuum, 1997.

———. *Prisms.* Translated by Samuel and Shierry Weber. Cambridge, MA: The MIT Press, 1983.

Ahmed, Sarah. *The Cultural Politics of Emotion.* Edinburgh: Edinburgh University Press, 2004.

———. *The Promise of Happiness.* Durham, NC: Duke University Press, 2010.

Alcántara, Jared E. *Crossover Preaching: Intercultural-Improvisational Homiletics in Conversation with Gardner C. Taylor.* Downers Grove, IL: IVP Academic, 2008.

Aldrete, Gregory S. *Gestures and Acclamations in Ancient Rome.* Baltimore: The Johns Hopkins University Press, 1999.

Alexander, James W. *Thoughts on Preaching: Contributions to Homiletics.* London: Hamilton, Adams, and Co., 1864.

All Things Considered. "The Fine Line Between a Bad Date and Sexual Assault: 2 Views On Aziz Ansari." NPR, January 16, 2018. https://www.npr.org/2018/01/16/578422491/the-fine-line-between-a-bad-date-and-sexual-assault-two-views-on-aziz-ansari.

Allen, Donna E. *Toward a Womanist Homiletic: Katie Cannon, Alice Walker, and Emancipatory Proclamation.* New York: Peter Lang, 2013.

Allen, O. Wesley, Jr. *Preaching and the Human Condition: Loving God, Self, and Others.* Nashville: Abingdon, 2016.

Allen, Ronald J., and O. Wesley Allen Jr. *The Sermon without End: A Conversational Approach to Preaching.* Nashville: Abingdon, 2015.

Als, Hilton. "Hannah Gadsby's Song of the Self." *The New Yorker*, July 22, 2019. https://www.newyorker.com/magazine/2019/07/29/hannah-gadsbys-song-of-the-self.

Ansari, Aziz. *Buried Alive*. Directed by Dylan Southern and Will Lovelace. Netflix, 2013.

———. *Premium Blend*. Season 9, Episode 3. Comedy Central, February 3, 2006.

———. *Right Now*. Directed by Spike Jonze. Netflix, 2019.

Ansari, Aziz, and Eric Klinenberg. *Modern Romance: An Investigation*. New York: Penguin, 2015.

Anthony, Benjamin J. "Christ in Boston: The Death and Afterlife of Phillips Brooks." PhD diss., Vanderbilt University, 2015.

Apatow, Judd. *Sick in the Head: Conversations about Life and Comedy*. New York: Random House, 2016.

Aquinas, Thomas. *The Summa Theologiae*. Translated by Fathers of English Dominican Province. London: Catholic Way, 2011.

Arbuckle, Gerald A. *Laughing with God: Humor, Culture, and Transformation*. Collegeville, MN: Liturgical, 2008.

Aristophanes. *Acharnians; Knights*. Translated by Jeffrey Henderson. Loeb Classical Library 178. Cambridge, MA: Harvard University Press, 2014.

Aristotle. *Nicomachean Ethics*. 3rd ed. Translated by Terence Irwin. Indianapolis: Hackett, 2019.

———. *Poetics*. Translated by Stephen Halliwell. Loeb Classical Library 199. Cambridge, MA: Harvard University Press, 1995.

Attardo, Salvatore. *The Linguistics of Humor: An Introduction*. Oxford: Oxford University Press, 2020.

Augustine. *De Doctrina Christiana*. Edited and translated by R. P. H. Green. Oxford: Clarendon, 1995.

Auslander, Philip. "'Brought to You by Fem-Rage': Stand-Up Comedy and the Politics of Gender." In *From Acting to Performance: Essays in Modernism and Postmodernism*, 108–25. London: Routledge, 1997.

———. *Presence and Resistance: Postmodernism and Cultural Politics in Contemporary American Performance*. Ann Arbor, MI: The University of Michigan Press, 1994.

Bakhtin, *Rabelais and His World*. Translated by Helene Iswolsky. Bloomington, IN: Indiana University Press, 1984.

Baldwin, Charles Sears. "Saint Augustine on Preaching (*De Doctrina Christiana*, IV)." In *The Rhetoric of St. Augustine of Hippo: De Doctrina Christiana and the Search for a Distinctly Christian Rhetoric*, edited by Richard Leo Enos and Roger Thompson, 187–203. Waco, TX: Baylor University Press, 2008.

Baldwin, Lewis V. *Behind the Public Veil: The Humanness of Martin Luther King Jr.* Minneapolis: Fortress, 2016.

Bamford, Maria. *Maria Bamford: Old Baby*. Directed by Jessica Yu. Netflix, 2017.

———. *Maria Bamford: The Special Special Special!* Directed by Jordan Brady. Netflix, 2012.

Banting, Blayne A. *With Wit and Wonder: The Preacher's Use of Humour and Imagination*. Eugene, OR: Resource, 2013.

Barnes, Brooks. "Easy, Breezy, Trending: Ellen DeGeneres, TV and Twitter Hit, Ready to Host Oscars." *New York Times*, January 17, 2014. http://www.nytimes.com/2014/01/19/arts/television/ellen-degeneres-tv-and-twitter-hit-ready-to-host-oscars.html?_r=0.

Barnes, Mike. "Dick Gregory, Trailblazer of Stand-Up Comedy, Dies at 84." *The Hollywood Reporter*, August 19, 2017. https://www.hollywoodreporter.com/news/dick-gregory-dead-stand-up-comedy-legend-civil-rights-activist-was-84-1004479.

Barth, Karl. *Church Dogmatics*, I/2. Edited by G. W. Bromiley and T. F. Torrance. Translated by G. W. Bromiley. Edinburgh: T. & T. Clark, 1975.

———. *Church Dogmatics*, III/2. Edited and translated by G. W. Bromiley and T. F. Torrance. Edinburgh: T. & T. Clark, 1968.

———. *Church Dogmatics*, III/3. Edited and translated by G. W. Bromiley and T. F. Torrance. Edinburgh: T. & T. Clark, 1960.

———. *Homiletics*. Translated by Geoffrey W. Bromiley and Donald E. Daniels. Louisville: Westminster John Knox, 1991.

———. *The Humanity of God*. Translated by John Newton Thomas and Thomas Wieser. Louisville: John Knox, 1996.

———. *Insights: Karl Barth's Reflections on the Life of Faith*. Edited by Eberhard Busch. Translated by O. C. Dean Jr. Louisville: Westminster John Knox, 2009.

Basil of Caesarea. "Letter 22." In *Nicene and Post-Nicene Fathers, Second Series*, vol. 8, edited by Philip Schaff and Henry Wace, translated by Blomfield Jackson. Buffalo, NY: Christian Literature Publishing Co., 1895.

Baym, Geoffrey. "The Daily Show: Discursive Integration and the Reinvention of Political Journalism." *Political Communication* 22 (2005) 259–76.

Beatty, Paul, ed. *Hokum: An Anthology of African-American Humor*. New York: Bloomsbury, 2006.

Belafonte, Harry, with Michael Schnayerson. *My Song: A Memoir*. New York: Alfred A. Knopf, 2011.

Bell, W. Kamau. *The Awkward Thoughts of W. Kamau Bell: Tales of a 6'4", African American, Heterosexual, Cisgender, Left-Leaning, Asthmatic, Black and Proud Blerd, Mama's Boy, Dad, and Stand-Up Comedian*. New York: Dutton, 2017.

Benjamin, Walter. "Fate and Character." In *Reflections: Essays, Aphorisms, Autobiographical Writings,* edited by Peter Demetz, translated by Edmund Jephcott, 304–11. New York: Schocken, 1986.

———. *Understanding Brecht*. Translated by Anna Bostock. London: Verso, 2003.

Benko, Steven A. "Otherwise Than Laughter: Levinas and an Ethics of Laughter." In *Ethics in Comedy: Essays on Crossing the Line*, edited by Steven A. Benko, 71–83. Jefferson, NC: McFarland & Co., 2020.

Benko, Steven A., and Eleanor Jones. "That's Way Too Aggressive a Word: Aziz Ansari, Comedy of Incongruity, and Affectively Charged Feminism." In *Ethics in Comedy: Essays on Crossing the Line*, edited by Steven A. Benko, 99–112. Jefferson, NC: McFarland & Co., 2020.

Berger, Phil. *The Last Laugh: The World of Stand-Up Comics*. New York: Cooper Square, 2000.

Bergson, Henri. *Laughter: An Essay of the Meaning of the Comic*. Translated by Cloudesly Brereton and Fred Rothwell. New York: Macmillan, 1912.

Berlant, Lauren, and Sianne Ngai. "Comedy Has Issues." *Critical Inquiry* 43 (Winter 2017) 233–49.

Billig, Michael. *Laughter and Ridicule: Towards a Social Critique of Humour*. London: SAGE, 2005.

Black, Steven P. "Laughing to Death: Joking as Support Amid Stigma for Zulu-Speaking South Africans living with HIV." *Journal of Linguistic Anthropology* 22 (2012) 87–108.

Blair, Hugh. *Lectures on Rhetoric and Belles Lettres.* Vol. 1. Dublin: Whitestone, 1783.

Booker, Vaughn A. "'Deplorable Exegesis': Dick Gregory's Irreverent Scriptural Authority in the 1960s and 1970s." *Religion and American Culture* 30, no. 2 (Summer 2020) 187–236.

Booth, Wayne C. *A Rhetoric of Irony.* Chicago: The University of Chicago Press, 1974.

Braxton, Brad R. "Three Questions about Prophets: Who, Why, and How?" *The African American Pulpit* 11, no. 4 (Fall 2008) 8–10.

Briscoe, Stuart. "Interesting Preaching." In *The Art and Craft of Biblical Preaching: A Comprehensive Resource for Today's Communicators,* edited by Haddon Robinson and Craig Brian Larson, 385–89. Grand Rapids: Zondervan, 2005.

Broadus, John A. *A Treatise on the Preparation and Delivery of Sermons.* Philadelphia: Nelson S. Quiney, 1870.

Brodie, Ian. "Stand-Up Comedy." In *Encyclopedia of Humor Studies,* edited by Salvatore Attardo, 734–37. Los Angeles: SAGE, 2014.

———. "Stand-Up Comedy as a Genre of Intimacy." *Ethnologies* 30, no. 2 (2008) 153–80.

Brooks, Phillips. *Lectures on Preaching.* Grand Rapids: Kregel, 1989.

Brothers, Michael A. *Distance in Preaching: Room to Speak, Space to Listen.* Grand Rapids: Eerdmans, 2014.

Brown, Sally A., and Luke A. Powery. *Ways of the Word: Learning to Preach for Your Time and Place.* Minneapolis: Fortress, 2016.

Browne, R. E. C. *The Ministry of the Word.* London: SCM, 1953.

Buchanan, John M. "Punch line: Sermonic joke telling is a precarious business." *The Christian Century,* August 9, 2003. https://www.christiancentury.org/article/2003-08/punch-line.

Buechner, Fredrick. *Telling the Truth: The Gospel as Tragedy, Comedy, and Fairy Tale.* New York: HarperCollins, 1977.

Butler, Judith. *Excitable Speech: A Politics of the Performative.* New York: Routledge, 1997.

Buttrick, David. *A Captive Voice: The Liberation of Preaching.* Louisville: Westminster John Knox, 1994.

———. *Homiletic: Moves and Structures.* Philadelphia: Fortress, 1987.

———. *Preaching Jesus Christ: An Exercise in Homiletic Theology.* Eugene, OR: Wipf and Stock, 2002.

Calhoun, Kendra. "Vine Racial Comedy as Anti-Hegemonic Humor: Linguistic Performance and Generic Innovation." *Journal of Linguistic Anthropology* 29, no. 1 (2019) 27–49.

Campbell, Charles L. "Ministry with a Laugh." *Interpretation: A Journal of Bible and Theology* 69, no. 2 (2015) 196–208.

———. *Preaching Jesus: New Directions for Homiletics in Hans Frei's Postliberal Theology.* Grand Rapids: Eerdmans, 1997.

———. *The Scandal of the Gospel: Preaching and the Grotesque.* Louisville: Westminster John Knox, 2021.

———. *The Word Before the Powers: An Ethic of Preaching.* Louisville: Westminster John Knox, 2002.

Campbell, Charles L., and Johan H. Cilliers. *Preaching Fools: The Gospel as a Rhetoric of Folly*. Waco, TX: Baylor University Press, 2012.

Caniesco, Roni. "Daily Show's Hasan Minhaj on *Stand-Up Planet*." *Wear Your Voice*, June 3, 2016. https://www.wearyourvoicemag.com/funny-first-gens-take-world-interview-hasan-minhaj-stand-planet/.

Carlin, George. "Napalm, Silly Putty, and Human Nature." Interview with David Jay Brown in *Conversations on the Edge of the Apocalypse*, 187–202. New York: Palgrave MacMillan, 2005.

Carlin, George, with Tony Hendra. *Last Words: A Memoir*. New York: Free, 2009.

Caron, James E. "The Quantum Paradox of Truthiness: Satire, Activism, and the Postmodern Condition." *Studies in American Humor* 4, no. 2 (2016) 153–81.

———. *Satire as the Comic Public Sphere: Postmodern "Truthiness" and Civic Engagement*. State College, PA: Penn State University Press, 2021.

Carpenter, Faedra Chatard. *Coloring Whiteness: Acts of Critique in Black Performance*. Ann Arbor, MI: University of Michigan Press, 2014.

Carpio, Glenda R. *Laughing Fit to Kill: Black Humor in the Fictions of Slavery*. Oxford: Oxford University Pres, 2008.

Carroll, Noel. *Humour: A Very Short Introduction*. Oxford: Oxford University Press, 2014.

Carter, Judy. *The New Comedy Bible: The Ultimate Guide to Writing and Performing Stand-Up Comedy*. Oceanside, CA: Indie Books International, 2020.

———. *Stand-Up Comedy: The Book*. New York: Random House, 1989.

Carter Florence, Anna. "Preacher as One 'Out of Your Mind.'" In *Slow of Speech and Unclean Lips: Contemporary Images of Preaching Identity,* edited by Robert Stephen Reid, 144–53. Eugene, OR: Cascade, 2010.

———. "Preaching and the Personal." In *Preaching and the Personal*, edited by J. Dwayne Howell, 11–18. Eugene, OR: Pickwick, 2013.

———. *Preaching as Testimony*. Louisville: Westminster John Knox Press, 2007.

Caudill, Abbie, and Julie A. Woodzicka. "Funny Business: Using Humor for Good in the Workplace." *Humor: International Journal of Humor Research* 30, no. 1 (2017) 43–62.

Champion, Jared N., and Peter C. Kunze, eds. *Taking a Stand: Contemporary US Stand-Up Comedians as Public Intellectuals*. Oxford, MS: The University of Mississippi Press, 2021.

Chappelle, Dave. *8:46*. Directed by Julia Reichert and Steven Bognar. YouTube, 2020. https://www.youtube.com/watch?v=3tR6mKcBbT4.

———. *The Age of Spin*. Directed by Stan Lathan. Netflix, 2017.

———. *The Bird Revelation*. Directed by Stan Lathan. Netflix, 2017.

———. *Deep in the Heart of Texas*. Directed by Stan Lathan. Netflix, 2017.

———. *Killin' Them Softly*. Directed by Stan Lathan. HBO, 2000.

———. *Sticks & Stones*. Directed by Stan Lathan. Netflix, 2019.

Chatoo, Caty Borum, and Lauren Feldman. *A Comedian and an Activist Walk into A Bar: The Serious Role of Comedy and Social Justice*. Oakland, CA: University of California Press, 2020.

Childers, Jana. *Performing the Word: Preaching as Theater*. Nashville: Abingdon, 1998.

———. "The Preacher's Performance." In *The New Interpreter's Handbook of Preaching*, edited by Paul Scott Wilson, 213–14. Nashville: Abingdon, 2008.

Childers, Jana, and Clayton J. Schmit, eds. *Performance in Preaching: Bringing the Sermon to Life*. Grand Rapids: Baker Academic, 2008.

Cho, Margaret. *I'm the One That I Want*. New York: Random House, 2001.

Chun, Elaine W. "Ideologies of Legitimate Mockery: Margaret Cho's Revoicings of Mock Asian." *Pragmatics* 14, nos. 2–3 (June 2004) 263–89.

Chrysostom, John. "Homilies on the Statues." In *Nicene and Post-Nicene Fathers*, vol. 9, edited by Philip Schaff, translated by W. R. W. Stephens. Buffalo, NY: Christian Literature Publishing Co., 1889.

Cicero. *De oratore*. Translated by H. Rackham. Loeb Classical Library 348. Cambridge, MA: Harvard University Press, 1960.

Cilliers, Johan. "Prophetic Preaching in South Africa: Exploring Some Spaces of Tension." *Dutch Reformed Theological Journal* 54, nos. 1 and 2 (2013) 1–15.

Clement of Alexandria. *The Paedagogus*. In *Ante-Nicene Fathers*, vol. 2. edited by Alexander Roberts, James Donaldson, and A. Cleveland Coxe, translated by William Wilson. Buffalo, NY: Christian Literature Publishing Co., 1885.

Cohen, Ted. *Jokes: Philosophical Thoughts on Joking Matters*. Chicago: The University of Chicago Press, 2001.

Colleary, Susanne. *Performance and Identity in Irish Stand-Up Comedy: The Comic 'I.'* New York: Palgrave MacMillan, 2015.

Collins, Ronald K. L., and David M. Skover. *The Trials of Lenny Bruce: The Fall and Rise of an American Icon*. Naperville, IL: Sourcebooks, 2002.

Cone, James H. *A Black Theology of Liberation*. Maryknoll, NY: Orbis, 2010.

———. "The Doctrine of Man in the Theology of Karl Barth." PhD diss., Northwestern University, 1965.

Connolly, Billy. *Too Old to Die Young*. Directed by Steve Brown. Rykodisc, 2004.

Cooper, Evan. "Is It Something He Said: The Mass Communication of Richard Pryor's Culturally Intimate Humor." *Communication Review* 10, no. 3 (2007) 223–47.

Copeland, Jennifer E. *Feminine Registers: The Importance of Women's Voices for Christian Preaching*. Eugene, OR: Cascade, 2014.

Costa, Cassie da. "The Funny, Furious Anti-Comedy of Hannah Gadsby." *New Yorker*, May 2, 2018. www.newyorker.com/culture/culture-desk/the-funny-furi-ous-anti-comedy-of-hannah-gadsby.

Cotkin, George. *Feast of Excess: A Cultural History of the New Sensibility*. Oxford: Oxford University Press, 2015.

Cox, James. *Preaching*. San Francisco: Harper & Row, 1985.

Cox, Lara. "Standing Up against the Rape Joke: Irony and Its Vicissitudes." *Signs: Journal of Women in Culture & Society* 40, no. 4 (2015) 963–84.

Craddock, Fred B. *As One Without Authority*. Rev. and expanded ed. St. Louis: Chalice, 2001.

———. *Overhearing the Gospel*. Rev. and expanded ed. St. Louis: Chalice, 2002.

———. *Preaching*. Nashville: Abingdon, 1985.

Crawford, Evans. *The Hum: Call and Response in African American Preaching*. Nashville: Abingdon, 1995.

Critchley, Simon. *The Faith of the Faithless: Experiments in Political Theology*. London: Verso, 2012.

———. *On Humour*. London: Routledge, 2002.

Dabney, Robert L. *Sacred Rhetoric; or A Course of Lectures on Preaching*. Richmond, VA: Presbyterian Committee of Publication, 1870.

Dagnes, Allison. *A Conservative Walks Into a Bar: The Politics of Political Humor*. New York: Palgrave Macmillan, 2012.

Dalimore, Arnold. *C. H. Spurgeon*. Chicago: Moody, 1984.

Dance, Daryl Cumber, ed. *Honey, Hush! An Anthology of African American Women's Humor*. New York and London: W. W. Norton & Company, 1998.

Daube, Matthew. "Laughter in Revolt: Race, Ethnicity, and Identity in the Construction of Stand-Up Comedy." PhD diss., Stanford University, 2009.

Davis, H. Grady. *Design for Preaching*. Minneapolis: Fortress, 1958.

Davisson, Amber, and Mackenzie Donovan. "'Breaking the News on a Weekly Basis': Trolling as Rhetorical Style on Last Week Tonight." *Critical Studies in Media Communication* 36, no. 5 (2019) 513–27.

Day, Amber. *Satire and Dissent: Interventions in Contemporary Political Debate*. Bloomington, IN: Indiana University Press, 2011.

Deeg, Alexander. "Disruption, Initiation, and Staging: The Theological Challenge of Christian Preaching." *Homiletic* 38, no. 1 (June 2013) 3–17.

DeGeneres, Ellen. *Relatable*. Directed by Joel Gallen and Tig Notaro. Netflix, 2018.

Dessau, Bruce. *Beyond a Joke: Inside the Dark World of Stand-Up Comedy*. London: Arrow, 2012.

de Waal, Frans. *The Age of Empathy: Nature's Lessons for a Kinder Society*. New York: Random House, 2009.

———. *Mama's Last Hug: Animal Emotions and What They Tell Us about Ourselves*. New York: W. W. Norton & Company, 2019.

Dockery, David S., and Roger D. Duke, eds. *John A. Broadus: A Living Legacy*. Nashville: Broadman, 2008.

Donegan, Moira. "The Comedian Forcing Standup to Confront the #MeToo Era." *New Yorker*, June 28, 2018. https://www.newyorker.com/culture/culture-desk/the-comedian-forcing-stand-up-to-confront-the-metoo-era.

Double, Oliver. *Getting the Joke: The Inner Workings of Stand-Up Comedy*. 2nd ed. London & New York: Bloomsbury, 2014.

Drakeford, John W. *The Humor in Preaching*. Grand Rapids: Zondervan, 1986.

Dunning, Stefanie K. *Queer in Black and White: Interraciality, Same Sex Desire, and Contemporary African American Culture*. Bloomington, IN: Indiana University Press, 2009.

Dunn-Wilson, David. *A Mirror for the Church: Preaching in the First Five Centuries*. Grand Rapids: Eerdmans, 2005.

Dying Laughing. Directed by Lloyd Stanton and Paul Toogood. Gravitas Ventures, 2016.

Eagleton, Terry. *The Function of Criticism*. New ed. London: Verso, 2005.

———. *Humour*. New Haven: Yale University Press, 2019.

Eco, Umberto. "Frames of Comic Freedom." In *Carnival!*, edited by Thomas A. Sebeok, 1–10. Berlin: Walter de Gruyter, 1984.

Edgar, Brian. *Laughter and the Grace of God: Restoring Laughter to Its Central Role in Christian Spirituality and Theology*. Eugene, OR: Cascade, 2019.

Edwards, Mike. "'Hypokritēs' in Action: Delivery in Greek Rhetoric." *Bulletin of the Institute of Classical Studies* Supplement 123 (2013) 15–25.

Ellis, Iain. *Humorists vs. Religion: Critical Voices from Mark Twain to Neil DeGrasse Tyson*. Jefferson, NC: McFarland & Company, 2018.

Elsayed, Danya. "Interview with Hasan Minhaj." *IGNITE*, April 19, 2018. https://ignitestudentlife.com/interview-with-hasan-minhaj/.

Farmer, David John. "Medusa: Hélène Cixous and the Writing of Laughter." *Administrative Theory & Praxis* 23, no. 4 (December 2001) 559–72.

Fergusson, David. "Theology and Laughter." In *The God of Love and Human Dignity: Festschrift for George Newlands,* edited by Paul Middleton, 107–16. London: T. & T. Clark, 2007.

Ferreday, Debra. "*Game of Thrones,* Rape Culture, and Feminist Fandom." *Australian Feminist Studies* 30, no. 83 (2015) 21–36.

Filani, Ibukun. "On Joking Contexts: An Example of Stand-up Comedy." *Humor: International Journal of Humor Research* 30, no. 4 (2017) 439–61.

Finley, Jessyka. "Black Women's Satire as (Black) Postmodern Performance." *Studies in American Humor* 2, no. 2 (2016) 236–65.

Flanagan, Caitlin. "The Humiliation of Aziz Ansari." *The Atlantic,* January 14, 2018. https://www.theatlantic.com/entertainment/archive/2018/01/the-humiliation-of-aziz-ansari/550541/.

Flores, William V., and Rina Benmayor, eds. *Latino Cultural Citizenship: Claiming Identity, Space, and Rights.* Boston: Beacon, 1997.

Fortin, Jacey. "Kevin Hart Steps Down as Oscars Host After Criticism Over Homophobic Tweets." *New York Times,* December 6, 2018. https://www.ny-times.com/2018/12/06/arts/kevin-hart-homophobic-tweets.html.

Foucault, Michel. *History of Madness.* Edited by Jean Khalfa. Translated by Jonathan Murphy and Jean Khalfa. London: Routledge, 2006.

Fox, Jesse David. "Amanda Seales Is Not for Everyone." *Vulture,* July 8, 2019. https://www.vulture.com/2019/07/amanda-seales-good-one-podcast.html.

Fox, Julia. "Journalist or Jokester? An Analysis of *Last Week Tonight with John Oliver.*" In *Political Humor in a Changing Media Landscape,* edited by Jody C. Baumgarner and Amy B. Becker, 29–45. Lanham, MD: Lexington, 2018.

Fox, Kate. "Humitas: Humour as Performative Resistance." In *Comedy and Critical Thought: Laughter as Resistance,* edited by Krista Bonello Rutter Giappone et al., 83–100. London: Rowman & Littlefield, 2018.

Foy, Jennifer. "Fooling Around: Female Stand-Ups and Sexual Joking." *The Journal of Popular Culture* 48, no. 4 (2015) 703–13.

Frei, Hans W. *The Identity of Jesus Christ, Expanded and Updated Edition: The Hermeneutical Bases of Dogmatic Theology.* Eugene, OR: Cascade, 2013.

Freud, Sigmund. "Humour." In *The Standard Edition of the Complete Psychological Works of Sigmund Freud, XXI,* translated by J. Strachey et al., 160–66. London: Hogarth Press, 1961.

———. *The Interpretation of Dreams.* Penguin Freud Library 4. Harmondsworth: Penguin, 1990.

———. *Jokes and Their Relation to the Unconscious.* Penguin Freud Library 6. Harmondsworth: Penguin, 1991.

Friedman, Hershey H. "Humor in the Hebrew Bible." *Humor: International Journal of Humor Research* 13, no. 3 (2000) 257–85.

Fry Brown, Teresa L. "The Action Potential of Preaching." In *The Purposes of Preaching,* edited by Jana Childers, 49–66. St. Louis: Chalice, 2004.

———. "Reestablishing the Purpose and Power of the Preached Word through Black Church Studies." In *The Black Church Studies Reader,* edited by Alton B. Pollard III and Carol B. Duncan, 91–99. New York: Palgrave Macmillan, 2016.

————. "Prophetic Truth-Telling in a Time of Fatigue and Fragmentation." In *Questions Preachers Ask: Essays in Honor of Thomas G. Long*, edited by Scott Black Johnston, Ted A. Smith, and Leonora Tubbs Tisdale, 126–40. Louisville: Westminster John Knox, 2016.

Fuentes Morgan, Danielle. *Laughing to Keep from Dying: African American Satire in the Twenty-First Century*. Urbana, IL: University of Illinois Press, 2020.

Fulford, Larry. "The Complete and Utter Loss of Time." In *The Dark Side of Stand-Up Comedy*, edited by Patrice A. Oppliger and Eric Shouse, 305–15. New York: Palgrave Macmillan, 2020.

Gadsby, Hannah. *Douglas*. Directed by Madeleine Parry. Netflix, 2020.

————. *Nanette*. Directed by Jon Olb and Madeleine Parry. Netflix, 2018.

————. "*Nanette* Isn't a Comedy Show. It's a Sledgehammer." *Elle*, July 26, 2018. https://www.elle.com/culture/movies-tv/a22564399/hannah-gadsby-nanette-netflix/.

Garber, Megan. "How Comedians Became Public Intellectuals." *The Atlantic*, May 28, 2015. https://www.theatlantic.com/entertainment/archive/2015/05/how-comedians-became-public-intellectuals/394277/.

Gardner, John. *The Art of Fiction: Notes on Craft for Young Writers*. New York: Vintage, 1991.

Gelb, Arthur. "Comic Withers Prejudice Cliches: Dick Gregory Aims Shafts at Negroes as well as Whites Show at Blue Angel is Offered without Trace of Rancor." *The New York Times*, March 20, 1961. https://www.nytimes.com/1961/03/20/archives/comic-withers-prejudice-cliches-dick-gregory-aims-shafts-at-negroes.html.

Gervais, Ricky. *Humanity*. Directed by John L. Spencer. Netflix, 2018.

Gherovici, Patricia, and Manya Steinkoler, eds. *Lacan, Psychoanalysis, and Comedy*. Cambridge: Cambridge University Press, 2016.

Gilbert, Joanne. *Performing Marginality: Humor, Gender and Cultural Critique*. Detroit: Wayne State University Press, 2004.

Gilbert, Kenyatta R. *The Journey and Promise of African American Preaching*. Minneapolis: Fortress, 2011.

Gilbert, Sophie. "Daniel Sloss Shows How Comedians Should Talk About Assault." *The Atlantic*, November 6, 2019. https://www.theatlantic.com/entertainment/archive/2019/11/daniel-sloss-and-rape-jokes/601360/.

————. "*Nanette* Is a Radical, Transformative Work of Comedy." *The Atlantic*, June 27, 2018. https://www.theatlantic.com/entertainment/archive/2018/06/nanette-is-a-radical-brilliant-work-of-comedy/563732/.

Gilhus, Ingvild Saelid. *Laughing Gods, Weeping Virgins: Laughter in the History of Religion*. London: Routledge, 1997.

Gillota, David. "Beyond Liveness: Experimentation in the Stand-up Special." *Studies in American Humor* 6, no. 1 (2020) 44–61.

————. "Reckless Talk: Exploration and Contradiction in Dave Chappelle's Recent Stand-Up Comedy." *Studies in Popular Culture* 42, no. 1 (Fall 2019) 1–22.

Gimbrell, Steven. *Isn't That Clever: A Philosophical Account of Humor and Comedy*. New York: Routledge, 2020.

Giuffre, Liz. "From Nanette to Nanettflix: Hannah Gadsby's Challenge to Existing Comedy Convention." *Comedy Studies* 23, no. 1 (2021) 29–39.

Glaser, Nikki. *Bangin'*. Directed by Nicholaus Goossen. Netflix, 2019.

————. "Nikki Glaser Doesn't Mind a Micropenis." CONAN on TBS, March 11, 2020. https://www.youtube.com/watch?v=l9krQrndKSw.

———. *Perfect*. Directed by Ryan Polito. Comedy Central, 2016.

Goltz, Dustin. "It Gets Better: Queer Futures, Critical Frustrations, and Radical Potentials." *Critical Studies in Media Communication* 30, no. 2 (2013) 135–51.

Gonzalez, Sandra. "Hasan Minhaj's 'Patriot Act' Canceled at Netflix." *CNN*, August 18, 2020. https://www.cnn.com/2020/08/18/entertainment/hasan-minhaj-patriot-act/index.html.

Green, Aaryn L., and A. Linders. "The Impact of Comedy on Racial and Ethnic Discourse." *Sociological Inquiry* 86, no. 2 (2016) 241–69.

Gregory, Dick. *Callus on My Soul: A Memoir*. With Shelia P. Moses. New York: Dafina, 2003.

———. *Defining Moments in Black History: Reading Between the Lies*. New York: Amistad, 2017.

———. *Dick Gregory's Bible Tales, with Commentary*. New York: Stein and Day, 1974.

———. "Foreword." In *African American Humor: The Best Black Comedy from Slavery to Today*, edited by Mel Watkins, xi–xvi. Chicago: Lawrence Hill, 2002.

———. "Gregory at the Hungry I club in San Francisco," www.huntleyarchives.com, video 1097974.

———. *Mo'Funny: Black Comedy in America*. Directed by Yvonne Smith. HBO, 1993. https://www.youtube.com/watch?v=doq7GUKCg9Y.

———. *No More Lies: The Myth and Reality of American History*. New York: Amistad, 2021.

Gregory, Dick, with Robert Lipsyte. *n*gger: An Autobiography*. New York: E. P. Dutton and Company, 1964.

Griffiths, Trevor. *Comedians*. New York: Faber & Faber, 1987.

Gunderson, Erik. "Discovering the Body in Roman Oratory." In *Parchments of Gender: Deciphering the Bodies of Antiquity*, edited by Maria Wyke, 169–89. Oxford: Oxford University Press, 1998.

Gutiérrez, Catalina Argüello, Hugo Carretero-Dios, Guillermo B. Willis, and Miguel Moya Morales. "'It's Funny if the Group Says So': Group Norms Moderate Disparaging Humor Appreciation." *Humor: International Journal of Humor Research* 31, no. 3 (2018) 473–90.

Haggins, Bambi. *Laughing Mad: The Black Comic Persona in Post-Soul America*. New Brunswick, NJ: Rutgers University Press, 2007.

Hall, Prathia L. "Encountering the Text." In *Power in the Pulpit: How America's Most Effective Black Preachers Prepare their Sermons*, edited by Cleophus J. LaRue, 59–66. Louisville: Westminster John Knox, 2002.

Halliwell, Stephen. *Greek Laughter: A Study of Cultural Psychology from Homer to Early Christianity*. Cambridge: Cambridge University Press, 2008.

———. "The Uses of Laughter in Greek Culture." *The Classical Quarterly* 41, no. 2 (1991) 279–96.

Handy, Bruce. "Roll Over, Ward Cleaver: And Tell Ozzie Nelson the News. Ellen DeGeneres is Poised to Become TV's First Openly Gay Star. Is America Ready or Not?" *Time*, April 14, 1997. https://time.com/vault/issue/1997-04-14/page/77/.

Haraway, Donna J. *When Species Meet*. Minneapolis: University of Minnesota Press, 2008.

Harmless, William, ed. *Augustine in His Own Words*. Washington, DC.: The Catholic University of America Press, 2010.

Harris, James H. *Preaching Liberation*. Minneapolis: Fortress, 1995.

Hart, Kevin. *I Can't Make This Up: Life Lessons*. New York: Simon & Schuster, 2017.

Hearlson, Adam. *The Holy No: Worship as a Subversive Act*. Grand Rapids: Eerdmans, 2018.

Heller, Agnes. *Immortal Comedy: The Comic Phenomenon in Art, Literature, and Life*. Lanham, MD: Lexington, 2005.

Hennefeld, Maggie, Annie Berke, and Michael Rennett. "In Focus: What's So Funny about Comedy and Humor Studies?" *JCMS: Journal of Cinema and Media Studies* 58, no. 3 (2019) 137–42.

Hiatt, Brian. "John Oliver Takes on the Trump Era: The *Rolling Stone* Interview." *Rolling Stone*, February 17, 2017. https://www.rollingstone.com/tv/tv-features/john-oliver-takes-on-the-trump-era-the-rolling-stone-interview-126096/.

Hilkert, Mary Catherine. *Naming Grace: Preaching and the Sacramental Imagination*. New York: Continuum, 1997.

Hill Collins, Patricia. *Black Feminist Thought: Knowledge, Consciousness, and the Politics of Empowerment*. New York: Routledge, 2009.

Hitchens, Christopher. "Why Women Aren't Funny." *Vanity Fair*, January 1, 2007. https://www.vanityfair.com/culture/2007/01/hitchens200701.

Hobbes, Thomas. *Leviathan*. Edited by J. C. A. Gaskin. Oxford: Oxford University Press, 2008.

Hogan, Cait. "The Ethics of 'Rape Jokes.'" In *The Dark Side of Stand-Up Comedy*, edited by Patrice A. Oppliger and Eric Shouse, 277–92. New York: Palgrave Macmillan, 2020.

Hokenson, Jan Walsh. *The Idea of Comedy: History, Theory, Critique*. Madison, NJ: Fairleigh Dickinson University Press, 2006.

Holm, Nicholas. *Humour as Politics: The Political Aesthetics of Contemporary Comedy*. Cham, Switzerland: Palgrave Macmillan, 2017.

Hooke, Ruthanna B. "Humor in Preaching: Life Touched by Grace." *Word & World* 32, no. 2 (Spring 2012) 187–89.

———. "Inductive Preaching Renewed." In *The Renewed Homiletic*, edited by O. Wesley Allen Jr., 58–62. Minneapolis: Fortress, 2010.

———. "The Personal and Its Others in the Performance of Preaching." In *Preaching and the Personal*, edited by J. Dwayne Howell, 19–43. Eugene, OR: Pickwick, 2013.

hooks, bell. "Keynote Speech: Feminist Transgressions." National Women's Studies Association Conference, November 14 2014. http://www.nwsa.org/.http://old.nwsa.org/pastconferences#2014.

———. "Sisterhood: Political Solidarity Between Women." *Feminist Review* 23, no. 1 (1986) 125–38.

Hoy, David Couzens. *Critical Resistance: From Poststructuralism to Post-Critique*. Cambridge, MA: The MIT Press, 2004.

Hutcheson, Francis. *Reflections upon Laughter, and Remarks upon the Fable of the Bees*. Glasgow: R. Urie, 1750.

Huizinga, Johan. *Homo Ludens*. New York: Harper, 1970.

Hyers, M. Conrad. *And God Created Laughter: The Bible as Divine Comedy*. Atlanta: John Knox, 1988.

———. "The Dialectic of the Sacred and the Comic." *CrossCurrents* 19, no. 1 (Winter 1968–69) 69–79.

———. *The Spirituality of Comedy: Comic Heroism in a Tragic World*. New Brunswick, NJ: Transaction, 1996.

Israel, Jeffrey. *Living with Hate in American Politics and Religion: How Popular Culture Can Defuse Intractable Differences*. New York: Columbia University Press, 2019.

Iverson, Kelly R. "Incongruity, Humor, and Mark: Performance and the Use of Laughter in the Second Gospel." *New Testament Studies* 59, no. 1 (January 2013) 2–19.

Izadi, Elahe. "The New Rock Stars: Inside Today's Golden Age of Comedy." *The Washington Post*, June 3, 2017. https://www.washingtonpost.com/graphics/2017/lifestyle/inside-comedys-new-golden-age/.

Jacobson, Howard. *Seriously Funny: From the Ridiculous to the Sublime*. New York: Viking, 1997.

Jiang, Tonglin, Hao Li, and Yubo Hou. "Cultural Differences in Humor Perception, Usage, and Implications." *Frontiers in Psychology* 10, no. 123 (2019) 1–8.

Johnson, Elizabeth A. "Redeeming the Name of Christ." In *Freeing Theology: The Essentials of Theology in Feminist Perspective*, edited by Catherine Mowry LaCugna, 115–38. San Francisco: HarperSanFrancisco, 1993.

Johnson, Kimberly P. *The Womanist Preacher: Proclaiming Womanist Rhetoric from the Pulpit*. Lanham, MD: Lexington, 2017.

Jones, Jeffrey P. "'Fake' News versus 'Real' News as Sources of Political Information: The Daily Show and Postmodern Political Reality." In *Politicotainment: Television's Take on the Real*, edited by Kristina Riegert, 129–49. New York: Peter Lang, 2007.

———. *Entertaining Politics: Satiric Television and Political Engagement*. 2nd ed. Lanham, MD: Rowman and Littlefield, 2010.

Jones, Leslie. *Time Machine*. Directed by David Benioff. Netflix, 2020.

Kant, Immanuel. *Critique of the Power of Judgement*. Edited by Paul Guyer. Translated by Paul Guyer and Eric Matthews. Cambridge: Cambridge University Press, 2000.

Kaufman, Scott Eric. "John Oliver Gets Results! New York City to Change Bail Requirements for Low-Level Offenders." *Salon*, July 8, 2015. https://www.salon.com/2015/07/08/john_oliver_gets_results_new_york_city_to_change_bail_requirements_for_low_level_offenders/.

Kaveny, Cathleen. *Prophecy without Contempt: Religious Discourse in the Public Square*. Cambridge, MA: Harvard University Press, 2018.

Kearney, Richard. *On Stories*. London: Routledge, 2002.

Kennell, S. A. H. "*Vt adhuc habeat fides nostra reprobatores*: Augustine's Hostile Hearers." In *Augustin, philosophe et prédicateur: Hommage à Goulven Madec; Actes du colloque international organisé à Paris les 8 et 9 septembre 2011*. Collection des Études Augustiniennes, Série Antiquité 195, edited by Isabelle Bochet, 343–52. Paris: Institut d'Études Augustiniennes, 2012.

Kennison, Sheila M., and Rachel H. Messer. "Humor as Social Risk-Taking: The Relationships Among Humor Styles, Sensation-Seeking, and Use of Curse Words." *Humor: International Journal of Humor Research* 32, no. 1 (2019) 1–21.

Kersten, Holger. "America's Faith in the Laugh Resistance: Popular Beliefs About Political Humor in the 2016 Presidential Elections." *Humor* 32, no. 2 (2019) 299–316.

Kessler, Sarah. "Are You Being Sirred? Work in Progress, *Nanette*, *Douglas*, and the New Butch Middlebrow." *Film Quarterly* (Spring 2021) 46–55.

Key, Keegan-Michael. "Brain on Drugs." *This Is Not Happening*, Season 1, Episode 1. Directed by Eric Abrams. Comedy Central, January 17, 2015.

Khalil, Joe F., and Mohamed Zayani. "De-Territorialized Digital Capitalism and the Predicament of the Nation-State: Netflix in Arabia." *Media, Culture & Society* 43, no. 2 (2021) 201–18.

Kierkegaard, Søren. *Concluding Unscientific Postscript to Philosophical Fragments.* Vols. 1–2. Edited and translated by Howard V. Hong and Edna H. Hong. Princeton, NJ: Princeton University Press, 1982.

Kim, Eunjoo Mary. *Christian Preaching and Worship in Multicultural Contexts: A Practical Theological Approach.* Collegeville, MN: Liturgical, 2017.

Kim, Matthew D. *Preaching with Cultural Intelligence: Understanding the People Who Hear Our Sermons.* Grand Rapids: Baker Academic, 2017.

Kim, Matthew D., and Daniel L. Wong. *Finding Our Voice: A Vision for Asian North American Preaching.* Bellingham, WA: Lexham, 2020.

Kim-Cragg, HyeRan. "Invisibility of Whiteness: A Homiletical Interrogation." *Homiletic* 46, no. 1 (2021) 28–39.

———. *Postcolonial Preaching: Creating a Ripple Effect.* Lanham, MD: Lexington, 2021.

———. "Unfinished and Unfolding Tasks of Preaching: Interdisciplinary, Intercultural, and Interreligious Approaches in the Postcolonial Context of Migration." *Homiletic* 44, no. 2 (2019) 4–17.

King, Stephen. *On Writing: A Memoir of the Craft.* New York: Pocket, 2000.

Kingford, Josh. "How to Film Stand Up—with Jerrod Carmichael." *YouTube,* March 21, 2021. https://www.youtube.com/watch?v=HjH8oztEiPI.

Knight, Carolyn Ann. "Preaching as an Intimate Act." In *Power in the Pulpit: How America's Most Effective Black Preachers Prepare their Sermons,* edited by Cleophus J. LaRue, 89–100. Louisville: Westminster John Knox, 2002.

Koester, Craig R. "Comedy, Humor, and the Gospel of John." In *Word, Theology, and Community in John,* edited by John Painter, R. Alan Culpepper, and Fernando F. Segovia, 123–42. St. Louis: Chalice, 2002.

Koestler, Arthur. *The Act of Creation.* London: Hutchinson and Co., 1964.

Kohen, Yael. *We Killed: The Rise of Women in American Comedy: A Very Oral History.* New York: Sarah Crichton, 2012.

Kondabolu, Hari. "For Comic Hari Kondabolu, Explaining the Joke IS the Joke." *NPR,* April 21, 2014. https://www.npr.org/2014/04/21/305509473/for-comic-hari-kondabolu-explaining-the-joke-is-the-joke.

———. "My English Relationship." *YouTube,* April 8, 2010. https://www.youtube.com/watch?v=IIxutnYm6Tg.

———. *John Oliver's New York Stand-Up Show.* Season 1, Episode 2. January 15, 2010.

———. *Waiting for 2042.* Kill Rock Stars, 2014.

———. *Warn Your Relatives.* Directed by Bobcat Goldthwait. Netflix, 2018.

Kondabolu, Hari, and Ajay Kurian. "Comedian and Filmmaker Hari Kondabolu on Comedy, Culture and Maintaining Your Integrity." *Cultured,* March 11, 2021. https://www.culturedmag.com/comedian-and-filmmaker-hari-kondabolu-on-comedy-culture-and-maintaining-your-integrity/.

Kondabolu, Hari, and Anna Sterling. "The Feministing Five: Hari Kondabolu and Janine Brito." *Feministing,* July 7, 2012. http://feministing.com/2012/07/07/the-feministing-five-hari-kondabolu-and-janine-brito/.

Kongerslev, Marianne. "'Good Comedy Can Upset People': A Conversation with Bobby Wilson of the 1491s." *Studies in American Humor* 6, no. 2 (2020) 341–54.

Krause, Adam Michael. *The Revolution Will Be Hilarious & Other Essays.* Porsgrunn: New Compass, 2018.

Krefting, Rebecca. *All Joking Aside: American Humor and Its Discontents.* Baltimore: The Johns Hopkins University Press, 2014.

———. "Hannah Gadsby: On the Limits of Satire." *Studies in American Humor* 5, no. 1 (2019) 92–102.

———. "Hannah Gadsby Stands Down: Feminist Comedy Studies." *JCMS: Journal of Cinema and Media Studies* 58, no. 3 (2019) 165–70.

———. "Margaret Cho's Army: 'We Are the Baddest Motherfuckers on the Block.'" In *Hysterical! Women in American Comedy,* edited by Linda Mizejewski and Victoria Sturtevant, 273–302. Austin, TX: University of Texas Press, 2017.

———. "Savage New Media: Discursive Campaigns For/Against Political Correctness." In *The Joke Is on Us: Political Comedy in (Late) Neoliberal Times,* edited by Julie Webber-Collins, 245–266. Lanham, MD: Lexington, 2019.

Kreischner, Bert. "Battle." *This Is Not Happening,* Season 1, Episode 2. Directed by Jeff Tomsic. Comedy Central, January 26, 2015.

Kundera, Milan. *The Art of the Novel.* Translated by Linda Asher. Rev. ed. New York: Harper & Row, 2000.

Kurian, Ajay. "Comedian and Filmmaker Hari Kondabolu on Comedy, Culture and Maintaining Your Integrity." *Cultured,* March 11, 2021. https://www.culturedmag.com/article/2021/03/11/comedian-and-filmmaker-hari-kondabolu-on-comedy-culture-and-maintaining-your-integrity.

Kwok, Pui-lan. "Postcolonial Preaching in Intercultural Contexts." *Homiletic* 40 no. 1 (2015) 9–20.

Lammers Gross, Nancy. *Women's Voices in the Practice of Preaching.* Grand Rapids: Eerdmans, 2017.

LaRue, Cleophus J. *I Believe I'll Testify: The Art of African American Preaching.* Louisville: Westminster John Knox, 2011.

Latta, Robert L. *The Basic Humor Process: A Cognitive-Shift Theory and the Case against Incongruity.* Berlin: Mouton de Gruyter, 1998.

Lawrence, Stratton. "Funny and Proud: Wanda Sykes Grows into Her Role as Comedy's Activist." *Post and Courier,* October 10, 2012. https://www.postandcourier.com/charleston_scene/latest_headlines/funny-proud-wanda-sykes-grows-into-role-as-comedy-s-activist/article_969288f8-d462-5a79-8029-2d4e0cbe58od.html.

Lee, Stewart. *41st Best Stand-up Ever.* Directed by Michael Cumming. Real Talent, 2008.

———. *How I Escaped My Certain Fate: The Life and Deaths of a Stand-Up Comedian.* London: Faber and Faber, 2010.

Lichtenstein, Jesse. "Soweto's Stand-up Son: Can Trevor Noah's Comedy Cross the Atlantic?" *Newsweek,* June 18, 2012.

Lichter, S. Robert, Jody C. Baumgartner, and Jonathan S. Morris. *Politics Is a Joke! How TV Comedians are Remaking Political Life.* New York: Routledge, 2018.

Limon, John. *Stand-Up Comedy in Theory, or, Abjection in America.* Durham, NC: Duke University Press, 2000.

Lindvall, Terry. *God Mocks: A History of Religious Satire from the Hebrew Prophets to Stephen Colbert.* New York: NYU Press, 2015.

Lischer, Richard. *The Preacher King: Martin Luther King Jr. and the Word that Moved America.* Oxford: Oxford University Press, 2020.

Lockyer, Sharon. "Identity." In *Encyclopedia of Humor Studies*, edited by Salvatore Attardo, 377–78. Los Angeles: SAGE, 2014.

Logan, Brian. "Be Truthful—And Funny Will Come." *The Guardian*, August 9, 2004. https://www.theguardian.com/film/2004/aug/09/comedy.edinburghfestival2004.

Long, Thomas G. *Preaching from Memory to Hope*. Louisville: Westminster John Knox, 2009.

———. *What Shall We Say? Evil, Suffering, and the Crisis of Faith*. Grand Rapids: Eerdmans, 2011.

———. *The Witness of Preaching*. 3rd ed. Louisville: Westminster John Knox, 2016.

Lorensen, Marlene Ringgaard. *Dialogical Preaching: Bakhtin, Otherness, and Homiletics*. Arbeiten zur Pastoraltheologie, Liturgik und Hymnologie, Book 74. Göttingen: Vandenhoeck & Ruprecht, 2013.

Lorenz, Konrad. *On Aggression*. Nashville: Abingdon, 2002.

Love, Matthew. "50 Best Stand-up Comics of All Time." *Rolling Stone*, February 14, 2017. https://www.rollingstone.com/culture/culture-lists/50-best-stand-up-comics-of-all-time-126359/.

Lowry, Eugene L. *The Homiletical Plot: The Sermon as Narrative Art Form*. Expanded ed. Louisville: Westminster John Knox, 2001.

Lundblad, Barbara K. *Transforming the Stone: Preaching Through Resistance to Change*. Nashville: Abingdon, 2001.

Luria, Sarah B., John Baer, and James C. Kaufman, eds. *Creativity and Humor*. Cambridge, MA: Academic, 2019.

MacIntyre, Alasdair. *After Virtue*. Notre Dame, IN: University of Notre Dame Press, 1981.

Macy, Howard R. *Discovering Humor in the Bible: An Explorer's Guide*. Eugene, OR: Cascade, 2016.

Maron, Marc. *End Times Fun*. Directed by Lynn Shelton. Netflix, 2020.

———. "Politics Aside." *The History of Comedy*, Season 1, Episode 8. CNN, August 13, 2017.

Martin, Steve. *Born Standing Up: A Comic's Life*. New York: Scribner, 2007.

McCarthy, Sean L. "Amanda Seales: *I Be Knowin'* on HBO: Not for the 'Insecure' Folks, but Rather, About Them." *Decider*, January 29, 2019. https://decider.com/2019/01/29/amanda-seales-i-be-knowin-hbo-review/.

McChesney, Robert W. "Foreword." In *The Stewart/Colbert Effect: Essays on the Real Impacts of Fake News*, edited by Amarnath Amarasingam, 1–2. Jefferson, NC: McFarland, 2011.

McClennen, Sophia A. "The Joke Is On You: Satire and Blowback." In *Political Humor in a Changing Media Landscape*, edited by Jody C. Baumgartner and Amy B. Becker, 137–56. Lanham, MD: Lexington, 2018.

McClennen, Sophia A., and Remy M. Maisel. *Is Satire Saving Our Nation? Mockery and American Politics*. New York: Palgrave Macmillan, 2014.

McClure, John S. "Learning from and Transforming the Community-Building Promise of Social Networking Services." In *Questions Preachers Ask: Essays in Honor of Thomas G. Long*, edited by Scott Black Johnston, Ted A. Smith, and Leonora Tubbs Tisdale, 113–25. Louisville: Westminster John Knox, 2016.

———. *Preaching Words: 144 Key Terms in Homiletics*. Louisville: Westminster John Knox, 2007.

————. *Other-Wise Preaching: A Postmodern Ethic for Homiletics*. St. Louis: Chalice, 2001.

————. *Speaking Together and with God: Liturgy and Communicative Action*. Lanham, MD: Lexington/Fortress Academic, 2018.

McClymond, Michael J., ed. *Encyclopedia of Religious Revivals in America*. Vol. 2. Westport, CT: Greenwood, 2007.

McClymond, Michael J., and Gerald R. McDermott. *The Theology of Jonathan Edwards*. Oxford: Oxford University Press, 2012.

McCord, James I. "Farewell Messages by the President of the Seminary to the Classes 1973 and 1974." *The Princeton Seminary Bulletin* 67, no. 1 (Winter 1975) 48–51.

McCullough, Amy P. *Her Preaching Body: Conversations about Identity, Agency, and Embodiment Among Contemporary Female Preachers*. Eugene, OR: Cascade, 2018.

McCray, Donyelle C. "On Shrieking the Truth: Mary and Proclamatory Wailing." *Interpretation* 75, no. 2 (April 2021) 102–11.

————. "Playing in Church: Insights from the Boundaries of the Sermon Genre." *Liturgy* 36, no. 2 (2021) 11–17.

————. "Sweating, Spitting, and Cursing: Intimations of the Sacred." *Practical Matters* 8 (April 2015) 52–62.

McDonald, Soraya Nadia. "John Oliver's Net Neutrality Rant May Have Caused FCC Site Crash." *The Washington Post*, June 4, 2014. https://www.washingtonpost.com/news/morning-mix/wp/2014/06/04/john-olivers-net-neutrality-rant-may-have-caused-fcc-site-crash/.

McGowan, Todd. *Only a Joke Can Save Us: A Theory of Comedy*. Evanston, IL: Northwestern University Press, 2017.

McGraw, James R. "Meet the Turkey General." In *The Shadow that Scares Me*, by Dick Gregory, 26–33. New York: Pocket, 1968.

McIntyre, Anthony P. "Gendering Cuteness." In *The International Encyclopedia of Gender, Media, and Communication*, edited by Karen Ross, 1–6. London: John Wiley & Sons, 2020.

————. "Sarah Silverman: Cuteness as Subversion." In *Hysterical! Women in American Comedy*, edited by Linda Mizejewski and Victoria Sturtevant, 325–47. Austin, TX: University of Texas Press, 2017.

McLuhan, Marshall. *Understanding Media: The Extensions of Man*. Cambridge, MA: The MIT Press, 1994.

McMickle, Marvin A. *Where Have All the Prophets Gone? Reclaiming Prophetic Preaching in America*. Cleveland, OH: Pilgrim, 2019.

Mendhurst, Andy. *A National Joke: Popular Comedy and English Cultural Identities*. London: Routledge, 2007.

Meredith, George. "On the Idea of Comedy and the Uses of the Comic Spirit." In *George Meredith's Essay on Comedy and Other* New Quarterly Magazine *Publications: A Critical Edition*, edited by Maura C. Ives, 114–45. Lewisburg, PA: Bucknell University Press, 1998.

Meyer, David Paul. *You Laugh But It's True*. Day 1 Films, 2011.

Meyers, Seth. *Lobby Baby*. Directed by Neal Brennan. Netflix, 2019.

Michelson, Bruce. "The Year's Work in American Humor Studies, 2015." *Studies in American Humor* 3, no. 1 (2017) 46–121.

Middleton, Jason. "A Rather Crude Feminism: Amy Schumer, Postfeminism, and Abjection." *Feminist Media Histories* 3, no. 2 (April 2017) 121–40.

Mills, Charles W. *Blackness Visible: Essays on Philosophy and Race*. Ithaca, NY: Cornell University Press, 1998.

Minhaj, Hassan. *Homecoming King*. Directed by Christopher Storer. Netflix, 2017.

———. *Patriot Act*. Directed by Richard Preuss and others. Netflix, 2018–2020.

———. *Stand Up Planet*. Directed by David Munro. KCETLink Media and Kontent Films, 2014.

Mintz, Lawrence E. "Stand-Up Comedy as Social and Cultural Mediation." *American Quarterly* 37, no. 1 (1985) 71–80.

Mitchell, Henry H. *Black Preaching: The Recovery of a Powerful Art*. Nashville: Abingdon, 1990.

Mizejewski, Linda. *Pretty/Funny: Women Comedians and Body Politics*. Austin, TX: University of Texas Press, 2014.

Mohr, Melissa. "Defining Dirt: Three Early Modern Views of Obscenity." *Textual Practice* 17, no. 2 (2003) 253–75.

Morreall, John. *Comedy, Tragedy, and Religion*. Albany, NY: State University of New York Press, 1999.

———. *Comic Relief: A Comprehensive Philosophy of Humor*. Malden, MA: Wiley-Blackwell, 2009.

———. "Conclusion." In *Humor in the Arts: New Perspectives*, edited by Vivienne Westbrook and Shun-liang Chao, 217–20. Abingdon: Routledge, 2019.

———. "Enjoying Incongruity." *Humor* 2, no. 1 (1989) 1–18.

———. "Humor and Emotion." *American Philosophical Quarterly* 20, no. 3 (1983) 297–304.

———. "Humor and the Conduct of Politics." In *Beyond a Joke: The Limits of Humour*, edited by Sharon Lockyer and Michael Pickering, 63–78. New York: Palgrave Macmillan, 2005.

———. "Humor as Cognitive Play." *JLT Articles* 3, no. 2 (2009) 241–60.

———. "Humor, Philosophy, and Education," *Educational Philosophy and Theory* 46, no. 2 (2014) 120–31.

———. *Humor Works*. Amherst, MA: Human Resource Development, 1997.

———. "Philosophy of Humor." In *Encyclopedia of Humor Studies*, edited by Salvatore Attardo, 566–70. Los Angeles: SAGE, 2014.

———. "The Rejection of Humor in Western Thought." *Philosophy East and West* 39, no. 3 (July 1989) 243–65.

———. "Sarcasm, Irony, Wordplay, and Humor in the Hebrew Bible: A Response to Hershey Friedman." *Humor: International Journal of Humor Research* 14, no. 3 (2001) 293–301.

Morrison, Toni. *The Origin of Others*. Cambridge, MA: Harvard University Press, 2017.

Moss, Otis, III. *Blue Note Preaching in a Post-Soul World: Finding Hope in an Age of Despair*. Louisville: Westminster John Knox, 2015.

Müller, Hans Martin. *Homiletik: Eine evangelische Predigtlehre*. Berlin: Walter de Gruyter, 1996.

Murray, David P. "Serious Preaching in a Comedy Culture." *Puritan Reformed Journal* 3, no. 1 (2011) 328–38.

Murray, Logan. *Be a Great Stand-Up*. 2nd ed. Kindle ed. Blacklick, OH: McGraw-Hill, 2010.

Myers, Jacob D. *Curating Church: Strategies for Innovative Worship*. Nashville: Abingdon, 2016.

————. "The Method Behind the Mystique: A Brief Appraisal of Fred Craddock's Narratology." *The Expository Times* 132, no. 1 (Oct 2020) 18–23.

————. *Preaching Must Die! Troubling Homiletical Theology.* Minneapolis: Fortress, 2017.

Nachman, Gerald. *Seriously Funny: The Rebel Comedians of the 1950s and 1960s.* New York: Pantheon, 2003.

Nagel, Thomas. *The View from Nowhere.* New York: Oxford University Press, 1986.

Nanjiani, Kumail. "Kumail Nanjiani Tries Hard to be Cool." *This Is Not Happening Presents: Fisticuffs.* Online Exclusives, Episode 25. Directed by Jeff Tomsic. Comedy Central, February 4, 2014.

Nesteroff, Kliph. *The Comedians: Drunks, Thieves, Scoundrels and the History of American Comedy.* New York: Grove, 2015.

Niebuhr, Reinhold. *Discerning the Signs of the Times: Sermons for Today and Tomorrow.* New York: Charles Scribner's Sons, 1946.

————. "Humor and Faith." In *Holy Laughter: Essays on Religion in the Comic Perspective,* edited by M. Conrad Hyers, 135–41. New York: Seabury, 1969.

Noah, Trevor. *Afraid of the Dark.* Directed by David Paul Meyer. Netflix, 2017.

————. *Son of Patricia.* Directed by David Paul Meyer. Netflix, 2018.

————. "Spot the Africa." *The Daily Show with Jon Stewart.* Comedy Central, December 5, 2014. https://www.youtube.com/watch?v=AHO1a1kvZGo.

————. *Trevor Noah: African American.* Directed by Ryan Polito. Netflix, 2013.

————. "Trevor Noah: Live at the Apollo." *Live at the Apollo.* Directed by Paul Wheeler. BBC One. S9 E1, November 22, 2013.

————. "Trump Exacerbates America's Immigration Crisis." *The Daily Show,* April 4, 2019. https://www.youtube.com/watch?v=ZmOKKY9shiQ.

————. "When Is the Right Time for Black People to Protest?" *The Daily Show,* September 25, 2017. https://www.youtube.com/watch?v=4-Gx23vHoCE.

Noland, Carey Marie, and Michael Hoppmann. "Stop! You're Killing Me: Food Addiction and Comedy." In *The Dark Side of Stand-Up Comedy,* edited by Patrice A. Oppliger and Eric Shouse, 129–50. New York: Palgrave Macmillan, 2020.

North, Anna. "Aziz Ansari Actually Talked about Sexual Misconduct Allegations Against Him Like an Adult." *Vox,* February 13, 2019. https://www.vox.com/2019/2/13/18223535/aziz-ansari-sexual-misconduct-allegation-me-too.

————. "The Aziz Ansari Story Is Ordinary. That's Why We Have to Talk about It." *Vox,* January 16, 2018. https://www.vox.com/identities/2018/1/16/16894722/aziz-ansari-grace-babe-me-too.

————. "Louis C.K. and Aziz Ansari Have an Opportunity for Redemption. They're Squandering It." *Vox,* January 9, 2019. https://www.vox.com/2019/1/9/18172273/louis-ck-comeback-parkland-aziz-ansari-metoo.

Oates, Joyce Carol. *The Faith of a Writer: Life, Craft, Art.* New York: HarperCollins, 2004.

O'Grady, Paul. *At My Mother's Knee . . . and Other Low Joints.* London: Bantam, 2008.

Oliver, John. "March 18, 2018: Marlon Bundo." *Last Week Tonight with John Oliver,* Season 5, Episode 5, HBO.

————. "March 21, 2021: Plastics." *Last Week Tonight with John Oliver,* Season 8, Episode 6, HBO.

————. "May 7, 2017: Net Neutrality 2." *Last Week Tonight with John Oliver,* Season 1, Episode 11, HBO.

———. "June 1, 2014: Net Neutrality." *Last Week Tonight with John Oliver*, Season 1, Episode 5, HBO.

———. "June 6, 2021: Asian Americans." *Last Week Tonight with John Oliver*, Season 8, Episode 4, HBO.

———. "June 7, 2015: Bail Bonds." *Last Week Tonight with John Oliver*, Season 2, Episode 11, HBO.

Oliver, Kelly. *Animal Lessons: How they Teach Us to Be Human*. New York: Columbia University Press, 2009.

Oppliger, Patrice A., and Kathryn Mears. "Comedy in the Era of #MeToo: Masking and Unmasking Sexual Misconduct in Stand-Up Comedy." In *The Dark Side of Stand-Up Comedy*, edited by Patrice A. Oppliger and Eric Shouse, 151–72. New York: Palgrave Macmillan, 2020.

The Original Kings of Comedy. Directed by Spike Lee. HBO, 2000.

Oring, Elliott. *Joking Asides: The Theory, Analysis, and Aesthetics of Humor*. Boulder, CO: Utah State University Press, 2016.

Orwell, George. "Funny, but Not Vulgar." In *The Collected Essays, Journalism and Letters of George Orwell, Vol. 3: As I Please, 1943–1945*. Edited by Sonia Orwell and Ian Angus, 283–88. New York: Harcourt Brace Jovanovich, 1968.

Oswalt, Patton. "Politics Aside." *The History of Comedy*, Season 1, Episode 8. CNN, August 13, 2017.

Peretti, Chelsea. *One of the Greats*. Directed by Lance Bangs. Netflix, 2014.

Parker, James. "Hannah Gadsby's Genius Follow-up to *Nanette*." *The Atlantic*, June 25, 2019. https://www.theatlantic.com/entertainment/archive/2019/06/hannah-gadsbys-new-live-show-douglas-review/592471/.

Pérez, Raúl. "Racism without Hatred? Racist Humor and the Myth of 'Colorblindness.'" *Sociological Perspectives* 60, no. 5 (2017) 956–974.

———. "Racist Humor: Then and Now." *Sociology Compass* 10, no. 10 (2016) 928–38.

Peterson, Russell. *Strange Bedfellows: How Late-Night Comedy Turns Democracy into a Joke*. New Brunswick, NJ: Rutgers University Press, 2008.

Plato. *Laws, Volume II: Books 7–12*. Translated by R. G. Bury. Loeb Classical Library 192. Cambridge, MA: Harvard University Press, 1926.

———. *Statesman; Philebus; Ion*. Translated by Harold North Fowler and W. R. M. Lamb. Loeb Classical Library 164. Cambridge, MA: Harvard University Press, 2015.

———. *Republic, Volume I: Books 1–5*. Edited and translated by Christopher Emlyn-Jones, William Preddy. Loeb Classical Library 237. Cambridge, MA: Harvard University Press, 2013.

Porter, Ebenezer. *Lectures on Homiletics and Preaching, and on Public Prayer; together with Sermons and Letters*. New York: Jonathan Leavitt, 1834.

Porter, Rick. "Patriot Act with Hasan Minhaj Canceled at Netflix." *The Hollywood Reporter*, August 18, 2020. https://www.hollywoodreporter.com/tv/tv-news/patriot-act-with-hasan-minhaj-canceled-at-netflix-4047572/.

Powell, Kevin. "Heaven Hell Dave Chappelle." *Esquire*, April 30, 2006. https://www.esquire.com/entertainment/movies/a11122/esq0506chappelle-92/.

Powery, Luke A. *Dem Dry Bones: Preaching Death, and Hope*. Minneapolis: Fortress, 2012.

Protevi, John. *Political Affect: Connecting the Social and the Somatic*. Posthumanities, vol. 7. Minneapolis: University of Minnesota Press, 2009.

Provine, Robert P. *Laughter: A Scientific Investigation.* New York: Viking, 2001.

Pryor, Richard. *Bicentennial N*gger.* Produced by David Banks. Warner Bros, 1976.

———. *Pryor Convictions: And Other Life Sentences.* Reprint ed. Los Angeles: Rare Bird, 2018.

Purvis-Smith, Virginia. "Gender and the Aesthetic of Preaching." In *A Reader on Preaching: Making Connections,* edited by David Day, Jeff Astley, and Leslie J. Francis, 224–29. London: Routledge, 2016.

The Queens of Comedy. Directed by Steve Purcell. HBO, 2001.

Quick, Sophie. *Why Stand-Up Matters: How Comedians Manipulate and Influence.* London: Bloomsbury, 2015.

Quintilian. *The Orator's Education, Volume V: Books 11–12.* Edited and translated by Donald A. Russell. Loeb Classical Library 494. Cambridge, MA: Harvard University Press, 2002.

Rahner, Hugo. "*Eutrapelia*: A Forgotten Virtue." In *Holy Laughter: Essays on Religion in the Comic Perspective,* edited by M. Conrad Hyers, 185–97. New York: Seabury, 1969.

Rancière, Jacques. "Contemporary Art and the Politics of Aesthetics." In *Communities of Sense: Rethinking Aesthetics and Politics,* edited by Beth Hinderliter, William Kaizen, Vared Maimon, Jaleh Mansoor, and Seth McCormick, 31–50. Durham, NC: Duke University Press, 2009.

Raskin, Victor. *Semantic Mechanisms of Humor.* Studies in Linguistics and Philosophy 24. Dordrecht: D. Reidel, 2011.

Raymond, Emilie. *Stars for Freedom: Hollywood, Black Celebrities, and the Civil Rights Movement.* Seattle: University of Washington Press, 2015.

Reed, Jennifer. "Ellen DeGeneres: Public Lesbian Number One." *Feminist Media Studies* 5, no. 1 (2005) 23–36.

———. *The Queer Cultural Work of Lily Tomlin and Jane Wagner.* New York: Palgrave Macmillan, 2013.

Resner, André, ed. *Just Preaching: Prophetic Voices for Economic Justice.* St. Louis: Chalice, 2003.

Rice, Charles L. *Interpretation and Imagination.* Philadelphia: Fortress, 1970.

Ricoeur, Paul. "Life in Quest of Narrative." In *On Paul Ricoeur: Narrative and Imagination,* edited by David Wood, 20–33. London: Routledge, 1991.

———. *Time and Narrative.* Vol. 3. Translated by Kathleen Blamey and David Pellauer. Chicago: The University of Chicago Press, 1988.

Rivera, Joshua. "Goodbye to Patriot Act, a Comedy Show that was a Different Kind of Angry." *The Verge,* August 20, 2020. https://www.theverge.com/2020/8/20/21377250/patriot-act-hasan-minhaj-show-canceled-netflix.

Robinson, Haddon. *Mastering Contemporary Preaching.* Portland, OR: Multnomah, 1989.

Rock, Chris. *Bigger and Blacker.* Directed by Keith Truesdell. HBO, 1999.

———. *Bring the Pain.* Directed by Keith Truesdell. HBO, 1996.

———. *Dying Laughing.* Directed by Paul Toogood and Lloyd Stanton. Gravitas Ventures, 2016.

———. *Rock This!* New York: Hyperion, 2000.

———. *Roll with the New.* Produced by Prince Paul. Dreamworks, 1996.

———. *Tambourine.* Directed by Bo Burnham. Netflix, 2018.

———. *Total Blackout.* Directed by Bo Burnham. Netflix, 2021.

Rodrigues, Austin. "A Thinkpiece About Bits (Not a Bit)." *Vulture,* November 18, 2014. https://www.vulture.com/2014/11/a-think-piece-about-bits-not-a-bit.html.

Rogan, Joe. "Travel." *This Is Not Happening,* Season 1, Episode 7. Directed by Jeff Tomsic. Comedy Central, March 13, 2015.

Rosenfield, Stephen. *Mastering Stand-Up: The Complete Guide to Becoming a Successful Comedian.* Chicago: Chicago Review, 2017.

Ross, Marlon. "Beyond the Closet as Raceless Paradigm." In *Black Queer Studies: A Critical Anthology,* edited by E. Patrick Johnson and Mae Henderson, 161–89. Durham, NC: Duke University Press, 2005.

Rossing, Jonathan P. "Critical Race Humor in a Postracial Moment: Richard Pryor's Contemporary Parrhesia." *Howard Journal of Communications* 25, no. 1 (2014) 16–33.

———. "Dick Gregory and Activist Style: Identifying Attributes of Humor Necessary for Activist Advocacy." *Argumentation and Advocacy* 50, no. 2 (2013) 59–71.

———. "Emancipatory Racial Humor as Critical Public Pedagogy: Subverting Hegemonic Racism." *Communication, Culture, & Critique* 9 (2016) 613–32.

Rowe, Trevor. *St. Augustine: Pastoral Theologian.* London: Epworth, 1974.

Rudar, Michael Christian. "Nietzsche and Comedy: Provocative Laughter Amidst a Tragic Philosophy." PhD diss., Duquesne University, 2014.

Ryzik, Melena. "The Comedy-Destroying, Soul-Affirming Art of Hannah Gadsby." *New York Times,* July 24, 2018. www.ny-times.com/2018/07/24/arts/hannah-gadsby-comedy-nanette.html.

Sancken, Joni. *Words That Heal: Preaching Hope to Wounded Souls.* The Artistry of Preaching. Nashville: Abingdon, 2019.

Saroglou, Vassilis, and Lydwine Anciaux. "Liking Sick Humor: Coping Styles and Religion as Predictors." *Humor: International Journal of Humor Research* 17, no. 3 (2004) 257–77.

Saucier, Donald A., et al. "'What Do You Call a Black Guy Who Flies a Plane?': The Effects and Understanding of Disparagement and Confrontational Racial Humor." *Humor: International Journal of Humor Research* 31, no. 1 (2018) 105–28.

Saunders, Robert A. *The Many Faces of Sacha Baron Cohen: Politics, Parody, and the Battle Over Borat.* Lanham, MD: Lexington, 2014.

Schade, Leah D. *Preaching in the Purple Zone: Ministry in the Red-Blue Divide.* Lanham, MD: Rowman and Littlefield, 2019.

Schumer, Amy. *The Girl with the Lower Back Tattoo.* New York: Gallery, 2016.

Seales, Amanda. "Amanda Seales's Catcalling." *Good One: A Podcast About Jokes.* July 8, 2019. https://www.globalplayer.com/podcasts/episodes/7DraGBX/.

———. *I Be Knowin'.* Directed by Stan Lathan. HBO, 2019.

———. *Small Doses: Potent Truths for Everyday Use.* New York: Abrams, 2019.

Sedgwick, Eve Kosofsky. *Epistemology of the Closet.* 2nd ed. Berkeley, CA: University of California Press, 2008.

Seinfeld, Jerry. *Is This Anything?* New York: Simon & Schuster, 2020.

Seinfeld, Jerry, Chris Rock, Ricky Gervais, and Louis C.K. *Talking Funny.* Directed by John Moffitt. HBO, 2011.

Seinfeld, Jerry, and Larry David. "The Wallet." *Seinfeld,* Season 4, Episode 5, September 23, 1992.

Selim, Yasser Fouad. "Performing Arabness in Arab American Stand-up Comedy." *American, British and Canadian Studies* 23, no. 1 (December 2014) 77–92.

Shaftesbury, Lord. "Sensus Communis: An Essay on the Freedom of Wit and Humour in a Letter to a Friend." In *Characteristics of Men, Manners, Opinions, Times,* edited by Laurence E. Klein, 29–69. Cambridge: Cambridge University Press, 1999.

Shedd, William G. T. *Homiletics and Pastoral Theology.* Edinburgh: William Oliphant & Co., 1867.

Shore, Mary Hinkle. "Leave Them Wanting More: Humor in Preaching." *Word & World* 32, no. 2 (Spring 2012) 124–31.

Shouse, Eric, and Patrice Oppliger. "Sarah Is Magic: The (Post-Gendered?) Comedy of Sarah Silverman. *Comedy Studies* 3, no. 2 (September 2012) 201–16.

Sierra, Sylvia. "Linguistic and Ethnic Media Stereotypes in Everyday Talk: Humor and Identity Construction Among Friends." *Journal of Pragmatics* 152 (2019) 186–99.

Sigmon, Casey Thornburgh. "Engaging the Gadfly: A Process Homilecclesiology for a Digital Age." PhD diss., Vanderbilt University, 2017.

———. "Preaching by the Rivers of Babylon: How an Exile from Pulpit and Pew Can Change White Preaching on the Other Side of the Pandemic." *Interpretation* 75, no. 2 (2021) 123–33.

Sigurdson, Ola. "Emancipation as a Matter of Style: Humour and Eschatology in Eagleton and Žižek." *Political Theology* 14, no. 2 (2013) 235–51.

Silk, M. S. *Aristophanes and the Definition of Comedy.* Oxford: Oxford University Press, 2000.

Silverman, Sarah. *The Bedwetter: Stories of Courage, Redemption, and Pee.* New York: Harper, 2010.

———. *Jesus Is Magic.* Directed by Liam Lynch. Showtime, 2005.

———. *A Speck of Dust.* Directed by Liam Lynch. Netflix, 2017.

Simmons, Martha. "Whooping: The Musicality of African American Preaching Past and Present." In *Preaching with Sacred Fire: An Anthology of African American Sermons, 1750 to the Present,* edited by Martha Simmons and Frank A. Thomas, 864–84. New York: W. W. Norton & Company, 2010.

Skitolsky, Lissa. "Holocaust Humor and Our Aesthetic Sensibility of American Genocide." *Journal of Aesthetics and Art Criticism* 77, no. 4 (2019) 400–511.

Sloss, Daniel. *Dark.* Directed by Ryan Polito. Netflix, 2018.

———. *Jigsaw.* Directed by Daniel Sloss. Netflix, 2018.

———. *X.* Directed by Daniel Sloss. HBO, 2019.

Smith, J. Alfred. "How Can They Hear without a Preacher?" In *Power in the Pulpit: How America's Most Effective Black Preachers Prepare Their Sermons,* edited by Cleophus J. LaRue, 133–40. Louisville: Westminster John Knox, 2002.

Smith, Ted A. "Discerning Authorities." In *Questions Preachers Ask: Essays in Honor of Thomas G. Long,* edited by Scott Black Johnston, Ted A. Smith, and Leonora Tubbs Tisdale, 55–72. Louisville: Westminster John Knox, 2016.

———. "Political Theology through a History of Preaching: A Study in the Authority of Celebrity." *Homiletic* 42, no. 1 (2017) 18–34.

———. *The New Measures: A Theological History of Democratic Practice.* Cambridge: Cambridge University Press, 2007.

Smith-Shomade, Beretta E. "'Don't Play with God!': Black Church, Play, and Possibilities." *Souls: A Critical Journal of Black Politics, Culture, and Society* 18, nos. 2–4 (2016) 321–37.

Sparks, Susan. *Preaching Punchlines: The Ten Commandments of Comedy.* Macon, GA: Smyth & Helwys, 2019.

Spencer, Herbert. "On the Physiology of Laughter." In *Essays on Education, Etc.,* 290–309. London: Dent, 1911.

Spurgeon, Charles. *Lectures to My Students.* Grand Rapids: Associated Publishers, undated.

———. *The New Park Street Pulpit.* Grand Rapids: Baker, 2007.

St. John, Warren. "Seinfeld It Ain't." *New York Times,* January 29, 2006. https://www.nytimes.com/2006/01/29/fashion/sundaystyles/seinfeld-it-aint.html.

Stanfield, Vernon Latrelle, ed. *Favorite Sermons of John A. Broadus.* New York: Harper Bros., 1959.

Stenger, Jan R. "Staging Laughter and Tears: Libanius, Chrysostom and the Riot of the Statues." In *Greek Laughter and Tears: Antiquity and After,* edited by Margaret Alexiou and Douglas Cairns, 166–86. Edinburgh: Edinburgh University Press, 2017.

Sterling, Anna. "The Feministing Five: Hari Kondabolu and Janine Brito." *Feministing,* July 7, 2012. http://feministing.com/2012/07/07/the-feministing-five-hari-kondabolu-and-janine-brito/.

Strickland, Michael. "Brimstone and Treacle: Charles Spurgeon's Humor in the Teaching of Preaching." *Homiletic* 39, no. 2 (2015) 21–29.

Sunday, Adesina B., and Ibukun Filani. "Playing with Culture: Nigerian Stand-up Comedians Joking with Cultural Beliefs and Representations." *Humor: International Journal of Humor Research* 32, no. 1 (2019) 97–124.

Sykes, Wanda. "Comic Wanda Sykes." Radio Interview, *Fresh Air,* August 1, 2019. https://www.npr.org/programs/fresh-air/2019/08/01/747288552/fresh-air-for-aug ust-1-2019-comic-wanda-sykes.

———. *I'ma Be Me.* Directed by Beth McCarthy-Miller. HBO, 2010.

———. *Sick and Tired.* Directed by Michael Drumm. Image Entertainment, 2006.

———. *Tongue Untied.* Directed by Paul Miller. Comedy Central, 2003.

———. *What Happened, Ms. Sykes?* Directed by Liz Patrick. Epix, 2016.

Sypher, Wylie. "The Meanings of Comedy." In *Comedy,* edited by Wylie Sypher, 193–255. Garden City, NY: Doubleday, 1956.

Tholmer, Jessica. "People Are Having Very Different Reactions to the Aziz Ansari Sexual Assault Story." *hellogiggles.com,* January 15, 2018. https://hellogiggles.com/celebrity/aziz-ansari-sexual-assault-reactions/.

Thomas, Frank A. *How to Preach a Dangerous Sermon.* Nashville: Abingdon, 2018.

———. *Introduction to the Practice of African American Preaching.* Nashville: Abingdon, 2014.

———. *Surviving a Dangerous Sermon.* Nashville: Abingdon, 2020.

———. *They Like to Never Quit Praisin' God.* Rev. and expanded ed. Cleveland, OH: Pilgrim, 2013.

Thomas, James M. *Working to Laugh: Assembling Difference in American Stand-Up Comedy Venues.* Lanham, MD: Lexington, 2015.

Thomas, Megan. "Aziz Ansari Responds to Sexual Assault Claim." *CNN,* January 16, 2018. https://www.cnn.com/2018/01/15/entertainment/aziz-ansari-responds/index.html.

Thompson, James W. *Preaching Like Paul: Homiletical Wisdom for Today.* Louisville: Westminster John Knox, 2001.

Thompson, Lisa L. *Ingenuity: Preaching as an Outsider.* Nashville: Abingdon, 2018.

————. *Preaching the Headlines: Possibilities and Pitfalls*. Working Preacher 6. Minneapolis: Fortress, 2021.

Thurman, Howard. *Meditations of the Heart*. Boston: Beacon, 1999.

Tonello, Michael. "America's (Lesbian) Sweethearts." *HuffPost*, June, 24, 2007. https://www.huffpost.com/entry/americas-lesbian-sweethea_b_53502.

Torretta, Gabriel. "Preaching on Laughter: The Theology of Laughter in Augustine's Sermons." *Theological Studies* 76, no. 4 (2015) 742–64.

Trahair, Lisa. *The Comedy of Philosophy: Sense and Nonsense in Early Cinematic Slapstick*. Albany, NY: State University of New York Press, 2007.

Travis, Sarah. *Decolonizing Preaching: The Pulpit as Postcolonial Space*. Lloyd John Ogilvie Institute of Preaching Series 6. Eugene, OR: Cascade, 2014.

Trivigno, Franco V. "Plato on Laughter and Moral Harm." In *Laughter, Humor, and Comedy in Ancient Philosophy*, edited by Pierre Destrée and Franco V. Trivigno, 13–34. Oxford: Oxford University Press, 2019.

Tubbs Tisdale, Leonora. *Prophetic Preaching: A Pastoral Approach*. Louisville: Westminster John Knox, 2010.

Tucker, Terrence T. *Furiously Funny: Comic Rage from Ralph Ellison to Chris Rock*. Gainesville, FL: University of Florida Press, 2020.

Turner, William J., Jr. "The Musicality of Black Preaching: Performing the Word." In *Performance in Preaching: Bringing the Sermon to Life*, edited by Jana Childers and Clayton J. Schmit, 191–210. Grand Rapids: Baker Academic, 2008.

VanArendonk, Kathryn. "8 Signs You're Watching a Post-Comedy Comedy." *Vulture*, May 8, 2018. https://www.vulture.com/2018/09/post-comedy-taxonomy.html.

van Neer, Joost. "Didactically Responsible Use of Humour in St. Augustine's 'Sermo' 53, 12–14." *Augustiniana* 54, no. 1/4 (2004) 551–88.

Voelz, Richard. *Preaching to Teach: Inspire People to Think and Act*. Nashville: Abingdon, 2019.

Walaskay, Maxine. "Gender and Preaching." *Christian Ministry* 13, no. 1 (January, 1982) 8–11.

Walker, Steven C. *Illuminating Humor of the Bible*. Eugene, OR: Cascade, 2013.

Walker-Barnes, Chanequa. *I Bring the Voices of My People: A Womanist Vision for Racial Reconciliation*. Grand Rapids: Eerdmans, 2019.

Ward, Richard F. "Performing the Manuscript." In *The New Interpreter's Handbook of Preaching*, edited by Paul Scott Wilson, 236–39. Nashville: Abingdon, 2008.

Watkins, Mel. *On the Real Side: A History of African American Comedy*. New York: Simon & Schuster, 1994.

Way, Katie. "I Went on a Date with Aziz Ansari. It Turned Into the Worst Night of My Life." *Babe.net*, January 13, 2018. https://babe.net/2018/01/13/aziz-ansari-28355.

Webb, Brandon. "'Hitler Must be Laughed At!': The PCA, Propaganda and the Perils of Parody During Wartime." *Historical Journal of Film, Radio and Television* 39, no. 4 (2019) 749–67.

Webb, Joseph M. *Comedy and Preaching*. St. Louis: Chalice, 1998.

Weber, Brenda R., and Joselyn K. Leimbach. "Ellen DeGeneres's Incorporate Body: The Politics of Authenticity." In *Hysterical! Women in American Comedy*, edited by Linda Mizejewski and Victoria Sturtevant, 303–24. Austin, TX: University of Texas Press, 2017.

Wetherall, Margaret. *Affect and Emotion: A New Social Science Understanding*. London: Sage, 2012.

White, E. B. *A Subtreasury of American Humor.* New York: Capricorn, 1980.

Wiersbe, Warren. *Walking with the Giants.* Grand Rapids: Baker, 1976.

Wilkens, Steve. *What's So Funny About God? A Theological Look at Humor.* Downers Grove, IL: IVP Academic, 2019.

Willard, Mary Beth. *Why It's OK to Enjoy the Work of Immoral Artists.* New York: Routledge, 2021.

Willett, Cynthia. *Irony in the Age of Empire: Comic Perspectives on Democracy and Freedom.* Bloomington, IN: Indiana University Press, 2008.

Willett, Cynthia, and Julie Willett. "Going to Bed White and Waking Up Arab: On Xenophobia, Affect Theories of Laughter, and the Social Contagion of the Comic Stage." *Critical Philosophy of Race* 2, no. 1 (2014) 84–105.

———. *Uproarious: How Feminists and Other Subversive Comics Speak Truth.* Minneapolis: University of Minnesota Press, 2019.

Willett, Cynthia, Julie Willett, and Yael D. Sherman. "The Seriously Erotic Politics of Feminist Laughter." *Social Research* 79, no. 1 (Spring 2012) 217–46.

Williams, Brad. "Famous." *This Is Not Happening,* Season 4, Episode 3. Directed by Eric Abrams. Comedy Central, February 17, 2018.

Willimon, William H. *Proclamation and Theology.* Nashville: Abingdon, 2005.

Wilson, Paul Scott. "A Homiletical Theology of Promise: More Than One Genre?" In *Toward a Homiletical Theology of Promise,* edited by David Schnasa Jacobsen, 69–86. Eugene, OR: Cascade, 2018

———. *Preaching as Poetry: Beauty, Goodness, and Truth in Every Sermon.* Artistry of Preaching. Nashville: Abingdon, 2014.

Wittgenstein, Ludwig. *Culture and Value.* Chicago: The University of Chicago Press, 1984.

Wong, Ali. *Ali Wong: Baby Cobra.* Directed by Jay Karas. Netflix, 2016.

———. *Ali Wong: Hard Knock Wife.* Directed by Jay Karas. Netflix, 2018.

Wood, Katelyn Hall. *Cracking Up: Black Feminist Comedy in the Twentieth and Twenty-First Century United States.* Iowa City, IA: University of Iowa Press, 2021.

Wood, Roy, Jr. "Drugs, Drugs, Drugs." *This Is Not Happening,* Season 3, Episode 11. Directed by Eric Abrams. Comedy Central, February 1, 2019.

———. "Grind." *This Is Not Happening,* Season 4, Episode 13. Directed by Eric Abrams. Comedy Central, February 15, 2019.

Worth, Marvin. *Lenny Bruce: Let the Buyer Beware.* Los Angeles: Shout! Factory, 2004.

Wuster, Tracy. "Comedy Jokes: Steve Martin and the Limits of Stand-Up Comedy." *Studies in American Humor* 3, no. 14 (2006) 23–44.

Wymer, Andrew. "'Either a Killer or a Suicide': White Culture, Anti-Cultural Preaching, and Cultural Suicide." *Liturgy* 35, no. 3 (2020) 45–53.

Yang, Sunggu. *Art and Preaching.* Eugene, OR: Cascade, forthcoming.

Young, Andrew. *An Easy Burden: The Civil Rights Movement and the Transformation of America.* New York: HarperCollins, 1996.

Young, Dannagal G. "The Privileged Role of the Late-Night Joke: Flooring Humor's Role in Disrupting Argument Security." *Media Psychology* 11, no. 1 (2008) 119–42.

Youssef, Ramy. *Ramy Youssef: Feelings.* Directed by Chris Storer, 2019.

Zinoman, Jason. "For Daily Show Successor, Another Dust-Up." *New York Times,* April 10, 2015. https://www.nytimes.com/2015/04/10/arts/television/daily-show-trevor-noah-controversy-twitter.html.

Zoglin, Richard. *Comedy at the Edge: How Stand-up in the 1970s Changed America.* New York: Bloomsbury, 2009.

Zupančič, Alenka. *The Odd One In: On Comedy.* Cambridge, MA: The MIT Press, 2008.

———. "Philosophy or Psychoanalysis? Yes, please!" *Crisis & Critique* 6, no. 1 (March 2019) 434–53.

Subject and Name Index

9/11, 33, 70, 166, 185–7
ABC (American Broadcasting Company), 151, 178
Abernathy, Ralph David, 41
Abjection, 181
Activism, 19, 188, 218–19
Acuna, Jason, *alias* Wee Man, 119
Ad hominem, 76, 202, 217–19
Adorno, Theodor, 197–98
Aesthetics, 177, 198
Affect. *See* theories of humor.
African American identity, 7, 15, 104–5, 115, 148, 159
Ahmed, Ahmed, 69, 166,
Ahmed, Sarah, 22
Alexander, James W., 146
Ali G., 149
See also Baron Cohen, Sacha,
Allen, Donna, 212
Allen, O. Wesley, Jr., 38, 48, 136
Allen, Ronald, 38
Ambiguity, 24–25, 112, 113, 133, 211
American Express, 23
Amsterdam, Morey, 84
Anagnorisis, 129, 186
   See also catharsis
Anger, 7, 18, 69, 135–37, 187, 197
Ansari, Aziz, 149–54
Apartheid, 90–91, 185, 204
Arab identity, 33, 104, 184
Aristophanes, 63, 199
Aristotle, 25, 29, 43, 55, 63, 112, 123, 129–32, 186, 194, 217
Asian identity, 149–52, 185–86, 204, 216

Audience, 1–3, 5, 7–8, 11–13, 16, 18, 23, 28, 30–31, 36–48, 61, 75–79, 83–98, 103, 106–8, 112–16, 121–27, 132, 134, 141, 144, 147–51, 154–58, 169, 173–81, 185–88, 195, 199–200, 204–5, 210–12, 214, 216, 219, 225
Auslander, Phillip, 145, 160, 212
Authenticity, 3, 12, 88–89, 115, 138–55, 175, 221

Bailey, E. K., 147
Bakhtin, Mikhail, 29, 68, 151, 196
Baldwin, Lewis, 40–1
Banting, Blayne, 51
Baron Cohen, Sacha, 149
   alias Ali G.
Barr, Rosanne, 88
Barth, Karl, 5, 26, 66, 71, 145, 166–67
Basil of Caesarea, 54, 59
Baym, Geoffrey, 215
Beatty, Paul, 68
Bee, Samantha, 189, 207, 215
Belafonte, Harry, 41
Bell, W. Kamau, 8, 10–11, 206, 215
Benjamin, Walter, 21, 140
Benko, Steven, 1, 108, 152, 199, 212
Bergson, Henri, 29–30, 33, 96–97, 196–97
Berlant, Lauren, 34
Berle, Milton, 95
Berman, Shelley, 89
Bible, 17, 52–54,
   See also, scripture
Binaries, 5, 147, 195

Bits, 2, 38, 43–44, 75, 84, 89–90, 117, 125, 141–43, 157, 209–10
Black identity, 7, 15, 97, 103–5, 139, 149, 153, 159–63, 167, 187, 195, 204
Blair, Hugh, 60
Brecht, Bertolt, 21, 45
Briscoe, Stuart, 61
Broadus, John, 60, 142, 146–47
Brodie, Ian, 28–29, 141, 169
Brooks, Phillips, 57–58
Brothers, Michael, 11
Brown, Roy Chubby, 148
Brown, Sally, 61
Browne, R. E. C., 100
Bruce, Lenny, 5, 9–10, 33, 84–86, 96, 164,
Buffoon, 43, 108, 162
Butler, Judith, 165
Buttrick, David, 26–27, 57, 89

Calhoun, Kendra, 206
Campbell, Charles, 1, 22, 27–28, 33, 68–72, 99, 128, 141, 196
Campbell, Tevin, 173–75
Capitalism, 33, 151
Carnivals/Carnivalesque, the, 68, 196
Carpenter, Faedra Chatard, 206–7
Carpio, Glenda, 38
Carter, Judy, 113, 41
Carter Florence, Anna, 9, 155, 223, 226
Carlin, George, 5, 10–12, 86
Catcalling, 210–11
Catharsis, 24, 45, 113, 117, 123, 129, 135
    See also Anagnorisis
Cedric the Entertainer, 114
Chappelle, Dave, 4, 88, 102–9
Chatoo, Caty Borum, 90, 193, 225
Childers, Jana, 21–22, 167–69
Chitlin Circuit, 84, 120
Cho, Margaret, 10, 33, 88, 140, 178–80
Christ, Jesus, 52, 71, 167, 193
Chrysostom, John, 54
Church
    Black Church, 7, 19, 39, 62, 160, 170–71

Church History, views of humor in, 6, 37, 51–62
    Mainline Church, 141
    Western Church, 62, 164
Cicero, 170, 227
Cilliers, Johan, 22, 27–28, 38, 68
Civil Rights Movement, the, 16–17, 41, 207
C.K., Louis, 10, 88, 140, 149, 154
Clay, Andrew Dice, 203
Clement of Alexandria, 53
Cohen, Ted, 29, 35–36, 94–97, 205
Colbert, Stephen, 201, 215
Colleary, Susanne, 115
Colonialism, 17, 23, 77, 216
Colonization, 77–78
Color-blindness, 195
Cole, Nat King, 17
Comedy
    Alternative Comedy, 3, 88–89
    Audience Impact, 46, 86, 204, 219
    Definition of, 28–29, 31, 171
    Observational Comedy, 15, 43, 88, 133
    The Comical, 4–5, 14, 22, 25, 29–34, 40, 61–2, 65, 74, 78, 82, 90–91, 97, 128, 153, 193, 197–99, 204, 212–13, 225–27
Comedy Central, 10, 12, 90, 103, 117, 198, 204, 214
Comiletical Framework, 24
Commonality, 15
Community, 30, 35, 37–38, 75, 83, 107–12, 228, 228
Cone, James, 166–67
Conservatism, 39, 196
Cooke, Sam, 17
Copeland, Jennifer, 36–37, 176–77
Cosby, Bill, 15, 78, 86, 88, 134, 130, 149
COVID-19, 70, 216
Craddock, Fred, 11, 40, 54, 72, 99, 114–15, 127, 142–43, 164, 201
Crawford, Evans, 24
Critchley, Simon, 31, 65–66, 112, 225
Critique, 5, 30, 32–33, 76, 102–4
Cross, David, 88
Crossover Performer, 15, 86, 156

Courage, 56
Cox, James, 61
Cultural intelligence, 38–39

Dabney, Robert L., 146
Dagnes, Alison, 39–40
Dance, Daryl Cumber, 7
Dangerous Preaching, 16, 124, 190–95
Daube, Michael, 85
Davies, Christie, 198
Davis, H. Grady, 3, 28, 81, 100
Davisson, Amber, 219
Day, Amber, 188
DeGeneres, Ellen, 116, 149–52,
    229–30
Democracy/democratic society, 32,
    39, 75, 80, 90, 196, 218, 227
Dessau, Bruce, 9
de Waal, Frans, 68, 228
Difference, 15, 37–38, 75, 83, 129,
    166, 187, 195, 203
Disability, 45
Disposition, 23–25, 29, 35, 55, 58,
    95, 227
Dissonance, 18, 34, 63, 118, 198
Djalili, Omid, 149
Donovan, Mackenzie, 219
Double, Oliver, 89, 95
Drakeford, John, 60–61
Dreams, 8–9
Duker, Sophie, 19

Eagleton, Terry, 31, 44, 136
Early Church Fathers, 52–54, 59, 217
Eco, Umberto, 157
Edwards, Jonathan, 6
Ellis, Iain, 5, 37
Eloquence, 161, 227
Emotion, 31–32, 37, 43, 46–47,
    66–70, 97–99, 116–17, 123, 136,
    151, 170–71, 197, 221
Empire, 27
    See also Imperialism.
Ephrem the Syrian, 53
Epistemology, 27, 150, 160, 178
Eschatology, 52–53
Ethics, 107–8, 124
Eutrapelia, 55
Exegesis, 17, 75

Extemporaneous Speech, 12, 142
    See also Manuscript.

Failure, 25–26, 122–25
Faith, 1, 27, 35, 39, 50–58, 66, 71, 128,
    157, 167, 171, 190, 194, 228
FCC (Federal Communications Com-
    mission), 219–20
Feldman, Lauren, 90, 193, 225
Ferreday, Debra, 158
Feuerbach, Ludwig, 5
Finney, Charles G., 57, 145, 183
Folly, 22, 55, 226
    Folly of the Cross, 22, 27, 68
Foolishness, 22–23, 27, 39
Fools, 22–23, 27–28, 28, 68
    Holy Fool, 27
Form (rhetorical), 43–44, 61, 65,
    81–101, 110–11
Forms of Laughter, 71–72
Foucault, Michel, 22
Fox, Julia, 215
Fox, Kate, 198–99
Foxx, Redd, 86
Foy, Jennifer, 179
Freud, Sigmund, 8–9, 30, 47, 67–72,
    92–94, 97
Fry Brown, Teresa, 3–4, 11, 43, 171
Function, 11, 22, 47, 56, 62–63, 67,
    71, 107, 112, 167, 188, 188–202,
    217–21, 225
FX (Fox eXtended), 8
LGBTQIA identity, 80, 107, 132–33,
    139, 157, 160, 165, 180, 206, 217

Gadsby, Hannah, 10, 33, 131–37
Garber, Megan, 199
Gardner, John, 118
Garofalo, Janeane, 88
Gervais, Ricky, 116–17, 148
Gilbert, Joanne, 177
Gilbert, Kenyatta, 39
Gilbert, Sophie, 48
Gillota, David, 2, 103, 106, 109
Givens, Adele, 114
Glaser, Nikki, 178–81
Glason, Billy, 84
Goldberg, Whoopie, 203

Gospel, 1, 17, 26–28, 53, 58, 71, 75,
    81–82, 108, 128–29, 136, 141,
    143–44, 146, 162–66, 169, 182,
    195–96
Greece, 30, 170, 205
    Ancient Greece, 29–30, 53, 63,
        170–71, 205
    Greek language, 30, 112, 205
    Greek philosophy, 53
    Hellenistic culture, 53
Gregory, Dick, 12, 14–20, 41, 84,
    86–87, 103, 161, 206
Griffin, Kathy, 88, 178

Haggins, Bambi, 102, 107, 156
Hall, Prathia, 172
Halliwell, Stephen, 53
Harris, James, 200
Hart, Kevin, 138–39, 165, 172
Harvey, Steve, 114
Hayes, Laura, 114
HBO (Home Box Office), 1, 2, 7, 12,
    46, 83, 106, 125, 151, 175, 198,
    214, 218, 226
Hearlson, Adam, 65, 108, 201
Heller, Agnes, 62
Hennefeld, Maggie, 218
Heterosexuality, 87
Hilkert, Mary Catherine, 82
Hitchens, Christopher, 178
Hitler, Adolf, 76–77, 95
Hobbes, Thomas, 65, 194, 227
Hokenson, Jan Walsh, 31
Holm, Nicholas, 32–36, 79, 107, 198,
    202, 218–19
Hooke, Ruthanna, 128, 138, 169,
    182–83
hooks, bell, 203, 209
Hoy, David Couzens, 200
Hughley, D. L., 114
Hulu, 173, 175
Humitas, 198–99
Humor
    Charged Humor, 32–33, 37, 74–75,
        96, 153
    Four Cardinal Humors, 29
    Humid, connection with, 29
    Humorletical,   7, 24

Progressive Humor, 11, 33, 153,
    206, 216
Risky Humor, 33
The Humorous, 5, 14, 25, 31,
    34–35, 38, 82, 128, 198, 201, 212,
    225, 228
    See also theories of humor.
Hutcheson, Francis, 50
Huizinga, John, 56, 212
Hyers, M. Conrad, 21, 58, 193, 227
Hyperbole, 11

Ideology, 83, 98, 107, 132, 215
Imagination, moral. See Moral
    imagination.
Imperialism, 216
    See also Empire.
Improvisation/improvisational, 3, 147
Injustice, 15, 33, 28, 73, 91, 102–3,
    124, 137, 168, 184, 188–91, 198,
    203–4, 221
Intersectionality, 38, 89, 133, 157–60,
    162, 166–72, 187, 201, 204, 208,
    216
Intimacy, 29, 35, 85, 132, 141–46, 155,
    175, 183, 188, 221
Irony, 11, 43, 53, 116, 144, 153,
    156–63, 218
Israel, Jeffrey, 203
Izzard, Eddie, 3, 88
Jacobson, Howard, 196
Jim Crow, 15–17
Jenner, Kaitlin, 105
Jesus Christ. See Christ, Jesus.
Johnson, Elizabeth A., 167
Johnson, Kimberly P., 79, 137
Jokes/joking
    Conditional Joke, 94, 97
    Conditional Affective, 94
    Conditional Hermetic, 94, 97
    Hermetic Joke, 94–95, 97, 205
    Pure Joke, 94
    Joke Telling, 140
Jones, Eleanor, 152, 199
Jones, Leslie, 173–76
Judaism/Jewishness, 29, 68, 85, 95–98,
    149, 167
Justice, 13–20, 22, 33, 38, 41, 44, 75,
    127, 147, 193–98, 201, 214, 220

Kant, Immanuel, 62, 65, 97, 197
Kearney, Richard, 113
Kennel, S. A. H., 142
Key, Keegan–Michael, 121
Kierkegaard, Søren, 65
Kim-Cragg, HyeRan, 39, 139, 168, 172
Kimmel, Jimmy, 201
King, Martin Luther, Jr., 16, 40
King, Stephen, 119
Klinenberg, Eric, 153
Knight, Carolyn Ann, 143
Kondabolu, Hari, 10, 73–80, 103
Krause, Adam, 39–40
Krefting, Rebecca, 10, 30, 32, 74–75, 134, 136, 180, 185
Kreischner, Bert, 118
Kumar, Nish, 10
Kundera, Milan, 51
Kwok, Pui-lan, 139, 172

Language, 81–101
    plain speech, 78
LaRue, Cleophus, 147, 238
Laughter, 1–3, 5–7, 9, 11, 13–14, 21–23, 26–27, 31–33, 35, 38, 40–41, 47–48, 50–55, 59–64, 66–71, 75–76, 83, 94–97, 100, 107–8, 112, 132–34, 137, 158, 161, 169, 176, 179, 187–88, 194–202, 212–13, 217–18, 220, 224–25, 227–28
Lee, Stewart, 3, 10, 88
Leimbach, Joselyn, 150–51
Levinas, Emmanuel, 108
Liberalism, 39–40
Liberation, 20, 167
Limon, John, 33, 181
Lischer, Richard, 41
LL Cool J, 173–74
Lockyer, Sharon, 149
Long, Thomas G., 53, 66, 71, 100, 108, 111, 128
Lorenz, Konrad, 36
Lowry, Eugene, 24, 112–13
Luna Lounge, 88
Lundblad, Barbara, 19

Mabley, Jackie "Moms," 33, 84, 87, 113, 156, 178
Mac, Bernie, 114
MacIntyre, Alasdair, 110–11
Madison, James, 84
Maisel, Remy, 38, 188
Manuscript, 142–47, 220
    See also extemporaneous speech.
Marginalization, 15, 153, 165, 168, 172, 188
Mark Twain Prize, 102
Maron, Marc, 88, 143–45, 201
Martin, Mae, 10
Martin, Steve, 198
McCarthy, Sean, 209, 212
McClennen, Sophia, 38, 188, 218
McCluhan, Marshall, 99
McClure, John, 6, 82–83, 108, 127–28, 139
McCord, James, 228
McCray, Donyelle, 81, 166, 190
McCullough, Amy, 177
McGraw, James R., 17
McIntyre, Anthony, 99
McPherson, James Alan, 87
Mendhurst, Andy, 37–38
Metanoia, 5, 23, 32, 83, 186, 217, 225
Metaphysics, 24–27, 40, 50–52
#MeToo movement, 106, 131, 153–54, 208
Michelson, Bruce, 83
Miller, Joe, 84
Mills, Charles, 209
Mimesis, 43, 112–13
Minhaj, Hasan, 33, 70, 184–91
Minstrelsy, 15, 78, 106, 185, 206
Mintz, Lawrence, 28, 165, 180
Mitchell, Henry, 61
Mitchell-Kernan, Claudia, 15
Mizejewski, Linda, 96, 140, 151–52, 177
Mo'Nique, 114
Morality, 140, 199
    Moral Imagination, 16, 124–17, 192
Morgan, Danielle Fuentes, 38
Morreall, John, 10, 35–36, 53, 62, 68–69, 197
Morrison, Toni, 128

Moss, Otis, III, 163
Murphy, Eddie, 203
Murray, Logan, 11, 83–84
Myers, Jacob D., 50, 139, 143
Myth/*Mythos*, 112, 156, 157, 188

Nachman, Gerald, 18, 89
Nagel, Thomas, 84
Nanjiani, Kumail, 121–22
Narrative, 11, 24, 45, 77, 87, 90–91,
    108, 110–30, 141, 150, 156, 159,
    176, 194, 186–90, 201–4
    Elements of Effective Narration
      Characterization, 121–22
      Description, 119–20
      Emplotment, 117–19
      Theme, 122–24
    Narrative–Inductive Method, 24,
      127–28
NFL (National Football League), 207
Nesteroff, Kliph, 84–86
Netflix, 1, 12, 83, 98, 106, 116, 125,
    131, 134–35, 143, 153–54, 173,
    184, 191, 198, 219, 226
Net Neutrality, 219–20
    See also FCC.
Neoliberalism, 16, 151, 156
Ngai, Sianne, 34
Niebuhr, Reinhold, 35, 58
Nietzsche, Friedrich, 5, 55
Noah, Trevor, 90–91, 189, 204–15
Norton, Jim, 88

Oates, Joyce Carol, 122
Obeidallah, Dean, 33
O'Brian, Conan, 180
O'Grady, Paul, 148
    alias Savage, Lily.
Oliver, John, 76, 189, 199, 207,
    214–22
Oppression. *See* systematic
    oppression.
Oration, 171, 189, 194, 215
Orben, Robert, 84
Origen, 59
Oring, Elliott, 107
Orwell, George, 192
Oswalt, Patton, 88, 201

Parody, 11, 76–77, 124, 217
Pascoe, Sara, 10
Pastoral, the, 4
Patterson, A. Louis, 147
Paul (Apostle), 22, 55
Pence, Charlotte, 217
Pence, Mike, 217
Performance, 2–3, 12, 15, 19, 21–22,
    29–31, 86–87, 96, 109, 115, 135–
    36, 139, 141, 144–45, 148–49,
    155–75, 177–78, 181–82, 204,
    208
Personhood, 58, 115, 139, 148, 168,
    182
    See also Selfhood.
Peterson, Russell, 217–18
Plato, 25, 43, 53, 54, 63, 132, 199–200,
    217
Playfulness, 23, 55–57, 71, 103, 212
Plot, 24, 112–22, 186
    Episodic Plot, 65, 112
    See also Narrative Emplotment.
Polarization, 14–39, 106, 177
Politics/Political Ideology, 107, 132, ,
    134, 153, 157, 160–62, 192–213,
    214–19
    Identity Politics, 103–5
    Party Politics, 5, 134
    Potent Politics, 201–2
    Puny Politics, 201–2
Porter, Ebenezer, 59
Powery, Luke, 17, 61, 68
Praxis, 6, 28, 39, 65, 139, 168, 212
Prayer, 6, 35, 201, 227
Priestly, the, 4, 20, 39, 108, 193
Prince, 174–76
Proclamation, 3–6, 17, 26, 41, 81, 111,
    162, 164, 166–68, 182
Profane, the, 192–93, 199
Profanity, 85, 96, 193, 203
Profluence, 118–19
Prophetic, the, 22, 39, 108, 136, 223
Pryor, Richard, 4, 12, 33, 38, 86–89,
    103, 112, 124–25, 140, 203, 206
Pseudo–satire. *See* Satire.
Punchline, 18,
Puritanism, 54
Purple/Purple Zones, 13–15

Purvis-Smith, Virginia, 177

Queerness/ Queer Identity, 87,
    157–60, 178–79
Quick, Sophie, 13
Quintilian, 59, 170

Racialization, 38, 186–8
Racism, 10, 11, 14, 17–19, 74–76,
    91–92, 103–4, 129, 161, 178,
    185–87, 195, 203–8
Rancière, Jacques, 197
Rape. See Sexual Violence.
Reason, 16, 22, 32–34, 56, 60, 79–80,
    142, 198
Resistance, 16, 19, 44, 145, 188–90,
    199–204, 213
Rhetoric, 5, 11, 15, 26–31, 41, 46–62,
    76–78, 96, 105, 124, 131–33,
    141–46, 148, 157–72, 175, 177,
    188, 198, 209, 212, 217–27
    Rhetorical Strategy, 11, 26–27,
    60–61, 76, 124, 143, 188, 219–20
Rice, Charles, 181
Ricoeur, Paul, 117, 127
Risk, 6–16, 33–34, 48, 74, 103, 109,
    157–58, 169, 179, 190–96, 199,
    224–28
Rivera, Joshua, 189
Rivers, Joan, 148
Reed, Jennifer, 87
Rock, Chris, 4, 7–12, 31–34, 112,
    125–27, 156, 203
Rogan, Joe, 118
Rossing, Johnathan P., 14, 18–19, 92,
    188–89
Russell, Nipsey, 15, 84

Sahl, Mort, 84–86, 140
Sampson, Melva, 137
Sancken, Joni, 137
Sarcasm, 11, 26, 53, 75, 78, 153–57,
    204
Satire, 11, 15, 17, 20, 31, 38–40, 59,
    74–77, 86, 147–50, 188–97,
    204–8, 217–18
    Pseudo-Satire, 217–18
    Satiractivism, 188, 218
Savage, Lily, 148

See also O'Grady, Paul.
Schade, Leah, 13–15, 224
Schleiermacher, Friedrich, 114
Schmit, Clayton, 21–22
Schultz, Thomas, 64
Schumer, Amy, 10, 106, 199
Scott, Manuel, 146
Seales, Amanda, 13, 192, 204–12
Segregation, 16–17, 86, 207
Seinfeld, Jerry, 12, 23, 78, 88, 95, 110,
    113
Selfhood, 9, 38, 111, 115, 134, 163
    See also Personhood.
Selim, Yasser Fouad, 70, 166
Sense of Humor, 4, 8, 24, 40, 53, 57,
    58, 90, 214, 228
Seriousness, 18, 21–25, 41, 51, 59, 60,
    31, 124–27, 198, 212, 214–21,
    227–28
Sexual Violence, 97, 159, 208
Shaftesbury, Lord, 161–62
Shedd, William, G. T., 146
Shlesinger, Iliza, 113
Shore, Mary Hinkle, 56
Sierra, Sylvia, 8, 203–4
Sigmon, Casey, 139
Simmons, Martha, 95
Silverman, Sarah, 10, 88, 96–99, 113,
    165
Sloss, Daniel, 10, 42–49
Smith, J. Alfred, 147
Socrates, 63
Solidarity, 33, 94, 153, 175, 187–88,
    209, 228
Sommore, 114
Soteriology, 51
    Conversion, 26
    Salvation, 37, 51
    Soul–Winning, 25
Sparks, Susan, 23, 56–57, 142, 169
Spencer, Herbert, 67
Spotlight, 16, 138–39, 176
Spurgeon, Charles, 25–26
Stage, 1, 9–10, 13, 17, 22–23, 37, 74,
    79, 84–89, 97, 103, 109, 116,
    133–42, 154–56, 165, 173–79,
    181, 189, 200, 212

Status Quo, 22, 24, 27, 31–32, 38–39, 107, 151, 168, 195, 200, 206
Stereotypes, 13, 32–34, 68, 96–97, 106, 116, 127, 149, 159, 166, 175, 178–91, 186–87, 203–6
Stewart, Jon, 90–91, 204, 214
Stories, 24, 31, 44, 110–30, 134, 137, 130, 175, 187, 190, 207, 215–18
Subconscious/Unconscious, 8–9, 49, 69, 154, 167, 179, 187, 194
Subversion, 34, 77, 108, 157, 177, 170, 199, 218
Success, 5, 8, 10, 14–18, 25–26, 32, 33, 62, 94–95, 112, 117–19, 125, 146, 156, 197
Sykes, Wanda, 4, 33, 156–63
Sypher, Wylie, 194
Systemic Oppression, 15, 38, 91, 97, 103, 124, 129, 159, 168, 188–89, 208, 211

Taylor, Gardner, 3, 147
Technology, 139, 152, 190
    Technoculture, 153
Tenacious D, 88
Theories of Humor/Theories of Laughter, 9, 29, 62–71, 75, 92, 124, 132, 161, 201, 217
    Affect, 62, 29, 70, 75
    Superiority, 62–66, 75, 124, 132, 201
    Incongruity, 63–71, 78, 83, 91, 98, 103, 121, 124, 152, 197, 202, 217
    Relief, 62, 66–71, 161, 212
    Play, 29, 55–58, 62, 68
Thomas, Frank, ix–x, 13, 15–16, 47, 61–62
Thurman, Howard, 35, 50
Tiernan, Tommy, 115
Tolerance, 32, 39
Tomlin, Lily, 87, 178
Tragedy, 48, 63–65, 111, 119, 164, 199
Transformation, 11, 19, 32, 64, 97, 111, 197
    Transformational Preaching, 11, 19, 32
Trivigno, Franco, 64, 199
Trolling, 147, 219–21

Truth, 13, 22, 26, 32, 34, 39, 44, 57–58, 69, 89, 107, 132–33, 136, 150, 162, 166, 183, 199, 208, 211, 223
Tubbs Tisdale, Leonora, 20, 39
Tucker, Terrence, 15–16, 34, 38, 104, 160–61, 203
Turner, William, J., 95–96
Twiss, Jill, 217

Unconscious, 8–9, 49, 69, 167, 179, 187, 194

Vaudeville, 15, 84
Verfremdungseffekt, 45
Violence, 1, 17–18, 34, 47, 90–91, 97–98, 104, 153, 158–59, 187, 191, 208, 216, 221
Vice, 53
Virtue, 36, 43, 53–55, 111, 127, 200, 228
Voelz, Richard, 39, 79, 199

Wagner, Jane, 87
Waisanen, Don, 218
Walaskay, Maxine, 177
Walker-Barnes, Chanequa, 129–30, 195
Ward, Richard, 147
Watson, Mark, 10
Watkins, Mel, 12, 15, 19–20, 33
Webb, Joseph, 51–52, 56, 226
Weber, Brenda, 150–51
Wee Man. *See* Acuna, Jason.
Wesley, John, 6
Western Thought/Ideology, 21, 30, 63, 75
White, E. B., 29
White Supremacy, 8, 23, 38, 87, 104–5, 126, 129, 140, 150, 184, 195
Whiteness/White Identity, 86, 98, 126, 142, 168–69, 189, 207, 211
Wilhelm, Kaiser, 95
Wilkens, Steve, 53
Willett, Cynthia, 33, 69–70, 134, 157, 159
Willett, Julie, 33, 69–70, 134, 159
Williams, Brad, 118–19

Williams, Robin, 4
Wilson, Bobby, 34
Wilson, Paul Scott, 37, 49
Winters, Jonathan, 84
Wisdom, 22–23, 28, 77, 108, 143–45,
    159–63, 210
Wittgenstein, Ludwig, 35
Witz, 67, 92–93, 97
    Gedankenwitz, 92, 97
    Klangwitz, 92–94
Wood, Katelyn Hall, 157, 160, 208

Wood, Roy, Jr., 120–23
Wymer, Andrew, 78–79, 168

Yang, Sunggu, 224
Young, Andrew, 41
Youssef, Ramy, 175–76

Zaid, Maysoon, 166
Zoglin, Richard, 86–87
Zupančič, Alenka, 195, 202

Printed in Great Britain
by Amazon

11858445R00161